HEALTH CARE PRACTI(
AN ONTARIO CASE STU

Patricia O'Reilly

This study offers the first comprehensive analysis of the emergence of health care practitioners in Ontario. Patricia O'Reilly considers the whole range of Western health professionals, from psychologists to podiatrists, examining their roles and relationships in economic, political, judicial, educational, and personal contexts. *Health Care Practitioners* takes as its focus the development of a new regulatory model, the Ontario Regulated Health Professions Act of 1991, and the extensive review of health practitioners that preceded it, namely, the Health Professions Legislation Review of 1983–9. This policy process, which highlighted the relationships that practitioners hold with each other, with the state, and with the public, is placed in both ideational and institutional contexts. O'Reilly contrasts health-sector principles of self-governance, rationality, science, and technology with ideational principles of democracy, free-market enterprise, fairness, and justice. She looks at the emergence of various categories of practitioners, showing how legislative forces have worked to include, exclude, or marginalize them. Her narrative follows the evolution of the professions as a whole from a position of control and hierarchy to one of greater public accountability.

PATRICIA O'REILLY is Assistant Professor, Department of Politics and School of Public Administration, Ryerson Polytechnic University.

PATRICIA O'REILLY

HEALTH CARE PRACTITIONERS

An Ontario Case Study in Policy Making

UNIVERSITY OF TORONTO PRESS
Toronto Buffalo London

© University of Toronto Press Incorporated 2000
Toronto Buffalo London

Printed in Canada

ISBN 0-8020-4420-4 (cloth)
ISBN 0-8020-8224-6 (paper)

∞

Printed on acid-free paper

Canadian Cataloguing in Publication Data

O'Reilly, Patricia Louise, 1954–
   Health care practitioners : an Ontario case study in policy making

   Includes bibliographical references and index.
   ISBN 0-8020-4420-4 (bound)   ISBN 0-8020-8224-6 (pbk.)

   1. Medical personnel – Ontario.   2. Medical policy – Ontario.
   3. Medical laws and legislation – Ontario.   I. Title.

RA399.C3073 1999   331.7′6161069′09713   C99-932446-2

This book has been published with the help of a grant from the Humanities and Social Sciences Federation of Canada, using funds provided by the Social Sciences and Humanities Research Council of Canada.

The University of Toronto Press acknowledges the financial assistance to its publishing program of the Canada Council for the Arts and the Ontario Arts Council.

University of Toronto Press acknowledges the financial support for its publishing activities of the Government of Canada through the Book Publishing Industry Development Program (BPIDP).

Canadä

*For my beloved
lost brother Jim*

Contents

ACKNOWLEDGMENTS ix
ABBREVIATIONS xi

1 Introduction 3

2 Historical Patterns of Ontario's Health Professions Legislation: The Embedded, Marginalized, and Excluded 15

3 Benefits and Burdens of the New Regulatory Blueprint 37

4 The 1960s and 1970s: The Institutionalization of Delivery and Funding 53

5 Overview of the Legislation Review Process in the 1980s of the Ontario Health Professions 70

6 Expertise Turf Wars 81

7 Continuity and Realignment of the Positions of Connection 141

8 The Regulated Health Professions Act of 1991 172

9 Conclusions from the Story 201

NOTES 243
GLOSSARY 345

viii Contents

APPENDICES

1 Exposure, Documents, and Interviews 351
2 Funding 354
3 Health Professions Legislative Review Words 356
4 The Nine Criteria for Self-regulation 359
5 Events Key in the Health Professions Legislative Review 361
6 The 22 Topics 363
7 The Nine Criteria Not Met 366
8 The New Professional Scopes of Practice 368
9 Licensed, Controlled, and Authorized Acts 371

Acknowledgments

First and foremost, I would like to thank my companion, Gordon McRae, for his unfailing support: intellectual, emotional, and financial. Special thanks is also due two of my teachers, Carolyn Hughes Tuohy and Ronald Manzer, whose academic work and teaching skills proved immensely important in terms of the intellectual foundation of my work, as well as the necessary but tricky guidance towards a balance between that which presented itself to me and that which I could feasibly and sensibly discuss. The ability to rein in a student's enthusiastic analysis without choking out the spirit and creativity of that enthusiasm must surely be the mark of an excellent teacher. Thanks also to Richard Simeon, Grace Skogstad, and Evert Lindquist who took the time to make valuable comments and corrections to the manuscript, and to Erik Denison and Flannery Fielding for assistance in the final hour check with the practitioner groups for newly settled issues and new developments. I also appreciated the comments and suggestions of my anonymous readers and the encouragement and quality work from the University of Toronto Press team. Thanks especially to Virgil Duff for his intelligence and wit, not to mention the free drinks and the pleasure of the company of his Bloomsbury group at The Artful Dodger; Siobhan McMenemy and Anne Forte for their editorial efficiency and support; Kate Baltais for a superb job of copy-editing; and Barbara Sale Schon for an excellent job on a difficult index. I am grateful as well to the people at the Ontario Ministry of Health who allowed me the close access to the legislative process and the Health Professions Legislation Review public files requisite to the interpretive intent of my project, especially Mr Alan Burrows. Lastly, I wish to thank the Social Sciences and Humanities Research Council of Canada and the University of Toronto for financial support during the doctorate which produced the foundations of this work; my colleagues at Ryerson Polytechnic University for their moral support, as well as the hallway jokes; and both the Chair of Ryerson's Politics Department, Carla Cassidy, and the Dean of Arts, Errol Aspevig, for allowing me the luxury of returning to my manuscript during the busy days of a new job.

Abbreviations

AHAD	Association of Hearing Aid Dispensers
AHAP	Association of Hearing Aid Practitioners
AOM	Association of Ontario Midwives
ARDT	Association of Registered Dental Technicians
BDC	Board of Directors of Chiropractic
BDDT	Board of Directors of Drugless Therapy
BDM	Board of Directors of Masseurs
BDO	Board of Directors of Osteopathy
BDP	Board of Directors of Physiotherapy
BOD	Board of Ophthalmic Dispensers
BRC	Board of Regents of Chiropody
BRT	Board of Radiation Technicians
CADT	Canadian Association of Occupational Therapists
CCA	Canadian Chiropractic Association
CCO	Chiropractic College of Ontario (now College of Chiropractors of Ontario)
CCSW	College of Certified Social Workers
CDA	Canadian Dental Association
CDT	College of Dental Technologists
CHA	Committee on the Healing Arts (Ontario)
CHS	Canadian Hearing Society
CMA	Canadian Medical Association
CMCC	Canadian Memorial Chiropractic College
CMLT	College of Medical Laboratory Technologists
CMO	College of Midwives of Ontario
CNA	Canadian Nurses Association
CNO	College of Nurses of Ontario

xii Abbreviations

COO	College of Optometrists of Ontario
CPA	Canadian Physiotherapy Association
CPhO	College of Pharmacists of Ontario
CPO	College of Pharmacists of Ontario
CPSO	College of Physicians and Surgeons of Ontario
CSLT	Canadian Society of Laboratory Technologists
DAC	Denturist Association of Canada
DAO	Denturist Association of Ontario
DC	Doctor of Chiropractic
DOp	Doctor of Optometry
DOs	Doctor of Osteopathy
DPA	Drugless Practitioners Act (Ontario)
GBDT	Governing Board of Denture Therapists
GBDTc	Governing Board of Dental Technicians
GP	General (Medical) Practitioner
HDA	Health Disciplines Act (Ontario)
HPLR	Health Professions Legislation Review (Ontario)
HPRAC	Health Professions Regulatory Advisory Council
MC	Midwives Coalition
MD	Medical Doctor
MLT	Medical Laboratory Technologist
MOH	Ministry of Health
MRT	Medical Radiation Technologist
MTF	Midwifery Task Force
ND	Naturopathic 'Doctor'
NPAO	Nurse Practitioners Association of Ontario
OACCPP	Ontario Association of Consultants, Counsellors, Psychometrists, and Psychotherapists
OADO	Ontario Association of Dispensing Opticians
OAH	Ontario Associations of Homeopaths
OAM	Ontario Association of Midwives
OAMRT	Ontario Association of Medical Radiation Technologists
OANaD	Ontario Association of Naturopathic Doctors
OAO	Ontario Association of Optometrists
OARM	Ontario Association of Radiological Managers
OARNA	Ontario Association of Registered Nursing Assistants
OBEP	Ontario Board of Examiners in Psychology
OCA	Ontario Chiropractic Association
OCFP	Ontario College of Family Physicians

Abbreviations xiii

OCLA	Ontario Contact Lens Association
OCOT	Ontario College of Occupational Therapists
OCPh	Ontario College of Pharmacists
ODA	Ontario Dental Association
ODHA	Ontario Dental Hygienists Association
ODtA	Ontario Dietetic Association
ODNAA	Ontario Dental Nurses and Assistants Association
OHA	Ontario Hospital Association
OHIP	Ontario Health Insurance Plan
OHoA	Ontario Homeopathic Association
OMA	Ontario Medical Association
OMTA	Ontario Massage Therapy Association
ONA	Ontario Nurses Association
ONaA	Ontario Naturopathic Association
ONMA	Ontario Nurse–Midwives Association
OOpA	Ontario Opticians Association
OOsA	Ontario Osteopathic Association
OPA	Ontario Physiotherapy Association
OPhA	Ontario Pharmacists Association
OPoA	Ontario Podiatry Association
OPsA	Ontario Psychiatric Association
OPyA	Ontario Psychological Association
OSC	Ontario Society of Chiropodists
OSCC	Ontario Society of Clinical Chemists
OSCH	Ontario Society of Clinical Hypnosis
OSHA	Ontario Speech and Hearing Association
OSLA	Ontario Association of Speech–Language Pathologists and Audiologists
OSMT	Ontario Society of Medical Technologists
OSOT	Ontario Society of Occupational Therapists
OSRT	Ontario Society of Radiological Technologists
PN	Practical Nurse
POC	Professional Organizations Committee
PRA	Patient's Rights Association
RCDSO	Royal College of Dental Surgeons of Ontario
RCHS	Royal Commission on Health Services
RHPA	Regulated Health Professions Act, 1991, S.O.
RMT	Registered Massage Therapist
RN	Registered Nurse

RNA	Registered Nurses Assistant
RNAA	Registered Nursing Assistants Association
RNAO	Registered Nurses Association of Ontario
RTSO	Respiratory Technology/Therapy Society of Ontario
SSRMO	Society of Registered and Remedial Masseurs of Ontario
TMC	Toronto Midwives Collective

HEALTH CARE PRACTITIONERS:
AN ONTARIO CASE STUDY IN POLICY MAKING

1

Introduction

Health care systems throughout the Western world are receiving unprecedented attention to detail. Without such detail – with an incomplete picture – decision makers are unlikely to respond wisely in the current climate of economic restraint. In health care and all policy sectors, the policy makers and stakeholders need as complete a story of reality as possible. The more complete the story, the more likely it is that the designs and solutions arrived at will have the effect sought. One of the most important sets of actors in the contemporary health care story is its practitioners. Their roles and relationships help determine the success or failure of today's health care restructuring projects throughout Canada and the industrialized world. But we know little of the story of who they all are, what they all do, and what their relationships are to one another, the state, and the public. It is this story that I wish to tell here.

Ontario recently redesigned its health practitioner regulatory legislation with the Regulated Health Professions Act of 1991. A lengthy review of the previous legislation, as well as of the complex roles and interrelationships of all of the province's health practitioners, preceded the decisions taken, that was called the Health Professions Legislation Review. International investigation at the time of the review, which began in the 1980s, showed Ontario to be taking the lead by carrying out such an extensive overhaul of its legislation. It is important, therefore, to our general understanding of health care policy to study the documents and legislation produced during this policy project, bearing in mind that health practitioners throughout the Western world have come from similar origins and have developed in much the same manner to those in Ontario. The Regulated Health Professions Act of Ontario is in its infancy, but there is much to be learned from the process itself which gave voice to the approximately seventy-five self-proclaimed health practitioners who wished to participate. This study makes use of those documented 'voices,' as well as historical sources and recent practitioner interviews, as a means of providing a big story or 'grand narrative' of the historical and contemporary development of the health practitioners and the roles they are playing, wish to play, and are either likely or unlikely to play in a restructured health care system.

This is also a political story about the public organization of a sector. The story necessarily was and still is played out in the context of that public organization. The degree or extent of public organization of sectors such as health care is strongly linked to our society's interpretation of the acceptable limits of public involvement or, put another way, the preferred balance of the public and the private. The form that organization takes is also strongly linked to the mode or form of organization which dominates all of a society's public and often private organizations. Weber and social commentators after him point to the pervasiveness in contemporary society of the bureaucratic mode of organization with its elevation of the standards of rationality, specialization, and hierarchy – however interpreted at the time. The public organization of health practices has proven no exception.

Chapter 2 begins the story with the history of prevailing attitudes which accompanied the embedment of particular patterns and tensions in the early organization of Ontario's and, indeed, Canada's health practitioners – embedding, marginalizing, and excluding particular practitioners and their approaches to health care. Here we see how the health care subsystem, like all such subsystems, came up with its own translation of the ideas which were driving change in the larger system in which it lived. Particularly, ideas about appropriate degrees of public organization or 'state interference' and ideas about what form that organization ought to take. It is important to the understanding of contemporary health care to look at this process of translation or interpretation of both the practice and regulation of its professional services as integral to the change which has occurred since then, as well as that which will most likely occur in the future.

Chapter 3 takes a closer look at the new privileges, obligations, and commitments which accompanied this early organization. As the health care subsystem took on the privileges of governance it shifted into a milieu of ideas which had come to dominate the major public spheres of governance, that is, the economic, the political, and the judicial. The distribution of benefits and burdens in these larger spheres would increasingly sit as a standard for that of the self-governing health care sector. Also accompanying the public regulation of Ontario's health practitioners were shifts in both the manifest and latent resources or positions of authority and connection[1] for the health provider groups, the state, and the public. These positions set up tensions which would mould relations in the sector, thereafter.

Chapter 4 looks at the shifts which took place in Ontario's organized health sector in the 1960s and 1970s when the delivery and funding of health care were brought under the umbrella of public organization. The institutionalized patterns of the 1960s and 1970s again repositioned key actors with regard to their power or influence over important decisions being made in the sector, their authority over each other, and their history of inter-and intra-group connections of support, neutrality, or antagonism. With these institutional changes the practitioner groups, the state, and the public all found themselves repositioned in relation both to each other and to the ideational climate of the health sector and its societal environment. That larger environment itself was undergoing shifts in its ideational commitments; the struggle between the embedded ideas of the past and the challenges or alternatives of the 1960s was reflected in the health policy reports of the time. Chapter 4 looks at this struggle between the old and the new and the pressures it began to exert on the health sector's embedded privileges, obligations, and commitments.

Chapter 5 introduces the policy review process: the Ontario Health Professions Legislation Review of 1983–89, which led up to the 1991 Regulated Health Professions Act of Ontario. The decision to open up the sector to investigation provided the space for a fresh round of interaction between the embedded ideas and those that were alternative or propositional. Ideas already dominant in the sector would find reinforcement from internal participants whom they favoured, while alternative ideas could be brought in from either the margins of the sector or its external milieu. Chapter 5 also introduces the ideas in good repute within the Ontario Ministry of Health and the Health Professions Legislation Review in the 1980s.

Chapter 6 focuses on the health practitioners' fight to control the translation or interpretation of health care rationality and expertise to be contained in the forthcoming professional legislation. Here groups struggled to put forth their preferred roles and relationships in the wording of their 'scopes of practice' and 'authorized acts.' Those interpretations which won out would become embedded in the new legislation, so the practitioners all fought to maintain old embedded interpretations, strengthen marginalized interpretations, or introduce new propositions into the organizational blueprints under consideration by the policy designers and decision makers.

Chapter 7 looks at the realignments and continuities of the political resources of connection among the practitioners, the state, and the public which accompanied this interpretive politics and the positions of authority which won out in the struggle. Connections of animosity, friendship, and neutrality were held up, developed anew, or even reversed as lines were drawn over one's place in the new designs. Chapter 7 also points out some of the implications of these realignments and continuities for future relationships within the sector.

Chapter 8 looks at the outcome of the policy process which resulted in the Ontario Regulated Health Professions Act of 1991, particularly with regard to its mandate and its new relationship to the broader economic, political, and judicial principles and blueprints surrounding it. Here we see the benefits and burdens of professional self-governance which have now been embedded in the regulatory mechanisms of Ontario's health professionalism. Chapter 9 draws conclusions from this story of embedment, marginalization, and exclusion, positing that where we might go from here depends greatly on the continuation or disruption of the interpretive dynamic which has played such an important role in deciding who will set and who will uphold today's standards of good health care and professional governance.

Overall, my purpose here is simply to tell a good story about our body of health practitioners and their relationship to their environment over time, one from which to draw understanding and, thus, help direct our policy choices. Some of my readers will wish to move on to the story itself, beginning in Chapter 2, and some of you, those interested in policy methodology, will have noticed the language used above and will have questions about the nature of the telling. For you, I offer the following.

Methodological Introduction

In saying I wish to 'tell a story' I am, of course, signalling my discomfort with the positivist approach to policy analysis, whereby the study of human organization is treated as a science with discernible laws and therefore hypotheses and theses rather than stories. In social analysis I am a causal atheist. We cannot know causality in political analysis because we cannot capture and reproduce social reality, or as Heraclitus put it, we cannot step in the same river twice. Despite our claims to be political scientists, we have never been, nor will we ever be scientists because we can never know its degree of objectivity, which as Hubbard points out, 'hinges entirely on reproducibility.'[2] So the question remains, how close to causality can I come – assuming I do not have the Godlike power of the economist who can hold 'all other things equal.' Without being able to control or ignore externalities, one thing we can do is observe. What form this observation takes or ought to take is a matter of contention.

Positivists observe. But in doing so their intent is to postulate laws and invent models or make use of those previously invented in order to provide the key to their study and hopefully other studies. The more ambitious postulate laws of change which might give us the predictive power we require in order to prescribe better policies for the future. Many, however, make use of grand theories of change in the manner of Lockwood, who uses Hegelian and Marxist theories of change to describe recurring patterns of social change, which others such as Offe can then use to both describe and prescribe political action.[3] No causal atheist could feel comfortable with this psuedo-scientific approach to social analysis. Not because the attempt to come as close to causation as possible, which is all many positivists are actually doing, is a bad pursuit per se, but because our arrogance in assuming our ability to be scientists or pseudo-scientists starts us off at a point of departure which chokes off too much story contained in the lived experience of those who we are observing and, ultimately, judging. The problem with preconceived frameworks is that they encourage the observer to look *for* something and thus often see it, leaving other things unseen. It is also difficult for the reader or another analyst to make use of the work in an alternative manner if she or he is not convinced of the value of that which the original analyst superimposed onto the story. That is, it is difficult to 'unread' a story told through a thesis – like trying to remember the words to a song while another song is playing.

The post-positivist alternative must be an approach that begins with an admission of its own ignorance of causation and is willing to accept the discomfort of unexplainable complexity. There is considerable debate over just how to draw analysis and conclusion from the complexity of lived experience once one has admitted to the impossibility of the objective, scientific methodology; but it is clear one must place oneself in the position of interpreter – one who attempts to give explanation or translation without causation, with only constitution.[4] This will necessarily be subjective, but there are ways of limiting one's subjectivity. Chief among them is the process of hermeneutics whereby one places oneself in the position of the other in order to recover her or his story.[5] Here one moves into the place of real lived experience and begins to 'get a reading on things,' without first imagining a framework with which to direct one's study.

I use the common term 'get a reading' deliberately because it implies attention to words and their implications. But we 'read' a situation in which we are immersed using various means. Like an employee who enters a new work environment, we ask, What is the story here? and we attempt to answer that by careful attention to the language and ideas of the location; but we also make note of positions of power, or politics, and relationships of friendship or animosity. That is, we observe the ideational and the institutional in interrelationship (to which I will return). Even while we observe institutionalized positions and relationships, however, that observation, that reading of context and content, is an ideational activity, for it is only through ideas that we translate or interpret what we see. It is not the size of the boss's office per se which gives us a clue to our relationship to her, but rather the interpretation of power that office size holds for us – as the interpretation of power the word 'boss' holds for us, or the interpretation you might have put on my usage of 'her' in this sentence. So, we need to think about both *what* the observer observes, and *how* the observer observes.

The 'how' of hermeneutical immersion is one of story gathering (not telling) via the context as it presents itself at the time. It seeks to know better through better exposure. What one finds upon immersion in lived experience, however, is not one story but many stories: in this case, for example, each of the health practitioner groups has its own story as a historical group engaged in contemporary politics. One must therefore listen to each of these stories and either attempt to tell each in turn or attempt to tell a larger story which combines as many of them as possible. I have attempted to do the latter, while retaining as much of the former as possible.[6] First, I exposed myself to as many of the practitioner group stories as possible by moving into the policy-making process itself; reading extensively on the history of the practitioner groups (which was often produced by the groups themselves or by academics sympathetic to their experiences); reading all of the practitioner groups' submissions to the policy review process in which they themselves gave voice to their roles and relationships in the health sector; and following this with interviews of representatives of both the governing bodies and associations of all of the newly regulated professionals as well as some of the excluded practitioner groups – particularly those who almost made it in (see Appendix 1).[7]

To tell any reality-based story entails what Goodman referred to as 'decomposition and composition.'[8] First you take it apart, and then you put it back together. If one is attempting to coordinate a number of stories into one larger one, this requires a resorting and development of new frames based on one's reading of the whole.[9] This secondary step, which moves beyond simple observation, necessarily entails a certain amount of judgment and scepticism – as in Gibbons's 'hermeneutics of suspicion' or 'depth hermeneutics.'[10] As Paris and Reynolds point out, the practical reasoning of the actors being observed will have incoherence, inconsistencies, and contradictions, and the analyst has to decide how much is too much.[11] Particularly, when one is listening to *political* stories, that is, stories told to policy designers or political analysts, there is a need to watch for the strategic presentation of the speaker. Interest groups in particular learn to present their comments in a rather complimentary and politically strategic light.[12] Political talk is not casual talk. Any restructuring process throws the everyday interpretations of a sector into confusion because of potential realignments, so the policy actors, particularly the recipients of said policy, begin to actively engage in a deliberately interpretive process. That is to say, as a political-story teller, I am interested in more than just the various actors' interpretations of their life story; I am interested in the process by which they engage in the politics of interpretation, by which they fight to embed their preferred interpretations and override those of others. That politics of interpretation is documented in this story. It is also judged – not objectively, but hopefully hermeneutically.

Although the grand-story teller cannot provide 'proof' of good judgment in her or his story and in the development of its interpretive frame, nevertheless standards might still be applied during the process as a guard against relativism. Aside from the honest attempt at hermeneutical immersion as a starting point, which seeks to suspend judgment until the resorting process, in the gathering of stories one ought to look for balance from the following: (a) history, to better understand the current situation and its development of various interpretations over time; (b) a comparison of words or claims with deeds, especially with regard to espoused principles; (c) non-contradiction, as we will see in judgments which were made during this policy story about the claims of various groups about themselves and others; (d) data or studies which support – especially generally unaccepted – interpretations by specific groups, as we will see in cases like midwifery and chiropractic; and (e) holism, for the broader the set of stories included in the telling – of health care groups and other actors – the more likely the accuracy of the larger story being told, or the less likely the 'untruth' of partiality. Lastly, a hermeneutics of replacement might be engaged in whereby the larger story is read by its subjects for their recognition,[13] or non-recognition, and revision of the story via collective interpretation and critique such that there is a growth of the story over time – with the original one still standing as one subjective interpretation in one place and at one time.

The whole storytelling process of immersion and decomposition followed by composition and telling, and later retelling, will necessarily impose a greater simplicity than exists in reality, but it also attempts to retain as much complexity as possible. Which elements of complexity are retained in one's resorting, development of a frame or judgment in composition is the subject of considerable questioning in social studies.[14] In fiction there is the luxury of drawing understanding from something as brief and local as a dropped piece of string,[15] but a political story, unlike a fictional one, must be true to the whole context of real social experience. It must be set within its lived context of multiplicity and change. But to draw understanding from the political also necessitates consideration of political power, especially when engaging in interpretive analysis. Political power is central to the interpretive process as it is experienced within the political story. As one political-story teller, Heilbrun, notes, 'The true representation of power is not of a big man beating a small man or a woman. Power is the ability to take one's place in whatever discourse is essential to action and the right to have one's part matter. This is true in the Pentagon, in marriage, in friendship, and in politics.'[16] Perhaps *what* the observer observes in a political story ought to be the ideational and the institutional meeting as a site of power for future struggles for both continuity and change.

The Ideational and the Institutional

[A troubled community leader asks Jacob the baker to answer the two questions which he, the leader, is being asked in a repetitive dream.]
'The first question ... is "What supports the walls of a city?"'
'That is easy,' says Jacob. 'Fear supports the walls of a city.'
'But what supports the fear?' asked the man, 'For that is the second question.'
'The walls.' answered Jacob.
                              Noah Ben Shea, *Jacob the Baker* (Random House Audio Books, Canada)

There is an ongoing dispute between the academic camps of political studies which focus on either institutionalist and structuralist studies or cultural and ideational studies,[17] though increasingly both camps have found it necessary to forage in the other for help with explanations which have eventually become so strained as to require the view from the opposite site.[18] Institutionalist analysts, although still lending primacy to the institutional, have moved to incorporate both elements of social interaction into their analyses; but just how to do so is still rather problematic.[19] Giving voice to the importance of the other kind of analysis, while using only bits and pieces of its analytical technique, tends to imply there are two viewpoints which offer equally valid ways of looking at the picture. This is misleading, however, because these are essential elements, not viewpoints; the picture contains both. Both the ideational and the structural components of the whole exist in relationship to each other within that whole. Both our way of thinking and our way of organizing are intertwined, indeed without the ideational there would be no structural. Every political structure or institution we could possibly name grew out of ideas and continues to be influenced by the constant pressure of further ideational forces. But, while the ideational both penetrates and sits apart from the structural, the opposite is not true. The structural never sits – it cannot sit – apart from the ideas which are either embedded in it or pressing up against it.

Introduction   11

One way of thinking about this might be contained in a scene I watched one Christmas where two of my nieces were playing the game 'Snakes and Ladders' – all the while pleading with the rest of us to join in. The players with their own ideational strategies and the board (a new version of 'Snakes and Ladders' where the pieces, or structure, can be moved about) were both undergoing change. As new players were coaxed in, they brought new ideas with them, but these ideas were limited by those which had already been designed into the organization of the game itself both by its original inventor and by the players who had been at work at it that evening. As time went on, many, but not all, of the non-embedded ideas or creations invented by each player became embedded, as each in turn moved to institutionalize them by redesigning the board. On and on it went with constant interplay between the ideational and the structural.

As ideas push up against our human constructs, some become embedded or structured into our organized life, some are marginalized, and some excluded. The embedded ideas, that is, the given or constitutive ideas – those which are structured into the system – give us 'What is.' But structured or embedded components, while giving a great deal of direction to our lives, do not control us entirely. People like to think of themselves, and act, as agents of their own destiny. 'What is' is always surrounded by 'What might be.' The propositional, then, constitutes a pool of possibilities and pressures. An institution is both what it is (the structured) and what people are trying to make it into (via human ideas). But it is not, I would argue, the institutions per se which bring about change, it is the shifting emphasis of internal and external ideas which provide the impetus for change. An institution is the product, at any given time, of continuous struggle between its embedded ideas and the propositional ideas contained in it and in its societal milieu. It exists as a focal point in a sea of alternatives.

Methodological consideration of either the role of ideas or the role of institutions has proven difficult, so it is even more difficult to make use of both of them together. I have attempted to do the latter in a manner in which the two might be seen in relationship to each other, and this has resulted in a somewhat different orientation to ideas and institutions. First, it seems to me, ideas are used too narrowly in most political analysis. There is a tendency to think of ideas as principles (or values) only. Writers in this area tend to be the moralists of the field, and other analysts admire their work. I think this is mostly because the work is morally concerned (and tells an intelligent story) rather than because it *demands* attention to the role of ideas. Just as in our larger society we tend to bracket off the moral as the realm of religion and philosophy and let it speak *at* society, in our political analysis we tend to think of the writers of principle as speaking *at* the rest of us – and we ought to listen even if we do not. I would argue we need to broaden our conception of the ideational to move beyond this bracketing off of ideas from mainstream political analysis. Even the authors who provide convincing evidence of the role of principles (or ideology) in politics often end with a reference to pragmatism rather than principle.[20] Why is this? I think it is the 'other ideational' they are seeing. For this I have used a distinction within ideas of both principles and blueprints.

Principles are just as we refer to them in common parlance, that is, as our foundational or substantive ideas, values, or beliefs; principles are conceptualizations of what we believe to be good (as in the Aristotelian good). Blueprints are our ideas (or plans) of how to organize our lives in a positive way; they therefore contain (often only implicitly) not only statements of principle, but also non-principled goals to be sought after and a means to their attainment. Some blueprints flow directly from the principles we deliberately or overtly set out as guides to our societal actions and relationships, but we have not as a society chosen to construct an organized society based fundamentally on principles. We sometimes organize our lives according to our desires, fears, ambitions, and so on. We sometimes argue, therefore, from original positions taken, not from principles, but from some favoured blueprint which grew out of these other objectives. If we broaden our conception of the ideational to include both principles and blueprints, we can no longer choose to leave the role of ideas to our morally concerned colleagues. Ideas become a necessary element of good political analysis because even those political actions void of principle cannot exist without some form of ideational blueprint. Without the thought and plan for action there would be no organization of society, much less public policy.

I am, of course, experimenting here, and as it turns out, my original intention to carry this distinction between principles and blueprints through the text of my story was hampered by the complexity of the story itself. The distinction grew heavy with so many stories within my story. So, as you will see here, I have simply used the distinction throughout the text where it appeared appropriate. It needs more work – on a smaller story. I will return to the question of its potential in the conclusion.

Regarding institutions, where my approach differs from that of the new institutionalists is related mostly to our different points of origin. Institutionalists tend to look out from the institutions (standing at the window) and set them in the world. They ask what has shaped and continues to shape the institutions (power, ideas, interests, say), but they are really more interested in what the institutions are shaping (things such as power, relationships, or pol-

Introduction   13

icy), that is, the role of institutions in politics. Here the institutions and the people who control them are the prime movers, the prime instruments of change, and/or the prime target for reform. Other factors, including ideas, might also be weighed to determine their role, but they tend to be brought in secondarily. This can, of course, be reversed by other analysts, such that the role of ideas becomes the primary focus – with the analyst floating over the institutions looking down through a film of ideas. A deterministic ideational approach would see ideas as prime movers and look for causation and a prioritization of ideas. An interpretive ideational approach, however, does not even ask for the prime movers – because that can never be known. Although it sees ideas, that is, their interplay as integral to the political story, it looks for the coexistence of both ideas and institutions in real life and sees the ideational as constitutive. Rather than causality, it looks for joint presence – like a couple who, although we do not know their exact relationship, did arrive at the party together and leave together.

To think of this metaphorically, one might say political analysis can be presented to others as either a picture or a story. Those interested primarily in institutions and structures tend to present, even draw, a picture that shows the things (institutions and people) and factors (relationships, ideas) at work; they present us pictures. Those primarily interested in ideas present a story. Stories cannot be contained in pictures, because 'a picture can't say ain't.'[21] A picture cannot present us with its own negation.[22] Only an idea can present its own negation. A picture might tell us enough to read off the current state of relations, but it tells us little of the potential overthrow or restructuring of those relations, because the source of that negation of the here-and-now lies in the ideational realm – where there is a story of the interplay of the embedded and the propositional which accompanies change. The story, like a good film, tells us not only what is, but also what might be. And when it tries to convey or tell the 'what is,' it has to do so by way of development of the interplay between the ideational and institutional over time. It has to tell a broader, richer story – one which provides possibilities or hints of change, such as the fall of the Berlin wall, or globalization, *before* they occur. The propositional may be embodied in one of the components of a picture, such as an interest group, but if we look only to the group, the proposition dies when the group dies or moves on. To look to the idea itself is to keep it alive despite its disembodiment, to know it sits in the 'library of ideas' which can come to direct our future.[23] The ideational tells us more. It also encourages us to ask, as we would in a good film, how people's interpretations of ideas end up situating them in relation to others; how ideas get played out, bringing some people to the forefront of the picture, pushing some to the background, and leaving others out of the picture all together – to be seen by the storytellers not the photographers. But not to romanticize the ideational; alone it is a frightening thing for any analyst. The institutional provides a necessary contextual grounding of the ubiquitous and sometimes ephemeral nature of the ideational.

Attention to contextualized ideas encourages attention to signs of inclusion and exclusion. Set within the context of history and ideational victory, the words used in policy making take on meaning laced with power or authority and legitimacy. Just as the phrase 'the eldest son' has long told the listener more than facts of gender and birth location, so too does the phrase 'scientific practitioner' or 'alternative practitioner' tell us more than mere description of that practitioner's work. They all carry connotations of historical benefits and burdens attached to institutionalized positions and relationships. Sometimes these benefits and burdens are more concretely manifest (in the eldest son's inheritance of the family business, for example), and sometimes they are more latent (in the disinheritance of the other siblings, or in the son's implicit accountability to the family patriarch, for example), but they are generally understood by those involved. The privilege of presence in decision-making forums may be implicit for some but in need of justification for others. This decision-making positioning makes important one's relationship to the other actors and to the state – as the 'policy community' literature points out[24] – but it also sets those actors and the state within an ideational milieu the importance of which I hope to here demonstrate. We will see how both embedded ideas and propositional or alternative ideas have played an important role in the shaping of contemporary health professionalism. Ideational investments and divestments taken from either its own particular history or its broader milieu have not only helped realign the institutionalized benefits and burdens of the sector over time, but they have also set up patterns of commitment which will continue to influence any change or restructuring that we might see in the future.

Thus an interpretive ideational analysis necessarily becomes an interpretive ideational–institutional analysis where attention to the history of interpretive struggles over ideas and the power linked to those ideas forces us to see an evolutionary process where policies, such as those of institutionalized professionalism can be seen and interpreted as an emergent product.[25] Where ideas and institutions coexist in a complex and changing world with each propping up the other – like fear and the walls of a city.

2

Historical Patterns of Ontario's Health Professions Legislation: The Embedded, Marginalized, and Excluded

To understand today's political struggles in health care we must begin with its history of embedment and divestment. The European precursors to our present-day health care organizations embedded health care practices with the ideas of a highly controlled, hierarchical society.[1] As time went by, the embedded world of the medical practitioner of the Middle Ages underwent the pressures of the alternative ideas of the modern liberal, democratic organization of society. The political role of the church was superseded by an enlarged role for the state which carried a new balance between the private actions of citizens, such as running a health care business, and the public pursuit of a civilized society. In the Western world, at least, the latter pursuit has been dominantly interpreted, under the ubiquitous heading of 'progress,' as the attainment of both knowledge and economic wealth. One greatly admired body of knowledge throughout the world has been that of science. The claim to scientific expertise was used with effect, first by the medical practitioners and then by other health practitioners, to argue for a more protectionist role for the state than is commonly upheld in modern Western society.[2]

The Early Legislation

In the territories which would later form parts of Canada, only the elite of seventeenth-century society made use of official medicine, which was, in any case, merely 'an array of squabbling practitioners of diverse stripes.'[3] British-governed Quebec passed an act in 1788, which elevated a new group of practitioners above the fray, allowing the British-educated, 'scientific' practitioners to set and pass more demanding licensing requirements.[4] The economic liberal ideal of unhampered private enterprise, however, continued to leave the nineteenth-century 'Canadian' state a reluctant participant in the setting up of entrepreneurial monopoly.[5] Considerations, such as the paucity of available practitioners, as well as the questionable authenticity of the acclaimed scientific standards, weighed against the granting of licensed monopolies.[6] In the end, though, the protectionist arguments were backed by liberal claims to appropriation rights and private property which linked particular practitioners to the new sciences and technologies.[7] Scientific practitioners, once having successfully presented themselves as the rightful owners of the scientific expertise of a progressive society, could then link that expertise to humanitarian concerns for the general welfare of the populace – one of the few routes to an override of the restriction against state intervention. During the mid-nineteenth century, the state set up a blueprint for professional licensing[8] which embodied regulatory mechanisms which still, to this day, allow the health professions to select and govern their own members as well as prosecute those outside the profession who attempt to work within the exclusive clinical territory of the profession.[9]

It was not only the medical practitioners, however, who succeeded in presenting themselves as the bearers of scientific expertise in warrant of regulatory protection. There were also various alternative health practitioners competing with the new medical scientists in Europe and North America in the nineteenth century. What the alternative practitioners shared was a disaffection with the common medical practices of the day, especially the notorious blood letting and purgings favoured by the eighteenth- to twentieth-century physicians. The reality of the early scientific expertise in healing, on which the original professional legislation was based, was considerably weaker than many contemporary readers might think. Health providers of the time practised their learned healing arts with widely varying degrees of sophistication. In fact, all of the early healing was based primarily on empiricism or random experiment and observation, rather than scientific method.[10] The scientific application of facts generated in the laboratory was sparse, even into the twentieth century.[11] Any healing practitioner utilizing only the science-based diagnoses and treatments of the day would have had a considerable amount of leisure time.[12]

Although the medical men continued to argue their own superior status as scientifically based practitioners, making much of the distinction between themselves and the 'wicked pretenders' and 'quacks,'[13] practitioners who represented a scientific alternative to medicine, the homeopaths and eclectics particularly,[14] succeeded in winning legislative protection for their brand of health care, in 1859 and 1861 respectively. The opposition from the medical practitioners was hindered by the legislators' reluctance to grant business monopolies in health care. There was also some reason to believe that medicine's claims to scientific superiority might be somewhat contaminated by entrepreneurial intent.[15]

The threat that the alternative practitioners presented to medicine soon began to diffuse somewhat by the development of internal disagreements within homeopathy.[16] These divisions, which were imported into Canada from the United States, weakened the group's political response to the opposition of the medical profession in both countries. Only during times of intense threats did they display much semblance of unity.[17] The homeopaths' influence had also been weakened, numerically and theoretically, by its earlier split into the 'pure' and the 'eclectic.' The pure practitioners attempted to stay as close to the early teachings of the discipline as possible, while the eclectics began to mix homeopathic care and other milder forms of care with some of the more effective and less heroic treatment regimes of the medical practitioners.[18]

By 1869 the Ontario medical profession had succeeded in uniting the separate medical, homeopathic, and eclectic regulating boards under one Medical Council with representation of all three on the governing body.[19] Originally there was considerable opposition within the medical profession to such a plan, because it implied a certain amount of acceptance of 'two bastard branches of medicine.'[20] However, most opponents were brought around to accepting the move when the advantages were pointed out. Not only would this eliminate all other alternative practitioners other than the homeopaths and eclectics, such as the botanic healers and midwives, but it would also provide the means of limiting the total supply of health practitioners in the province, as well as eventually eliminating the homeopaths and eclectics through entrance examinations set by the medically dominated examining board, the Medical Council. So successful were the medical men[21] in achieving all three of these ends that they caused an unwanted reversal of this legislation by yet another Medical Act in 1874; at this time changes were incorporated such that homeopathic and eclectic students 'were excused from writing certain licensing examinations which were replaced by others more suited to their [own] theories.'[22] This gave the homeopaths some breathing space, but it was too little, too late, for the eclectics who by this time had given in to the dominance of the orthodox medical profession and joined their ranks.[23]

It seems likely that the demise of the eclectics was inevitable, given the untenable position they found themselves in. Their eclecticism had been born of indecision as to which type of scientific health care was most effective: the heroic techniques of the medical practitioners or the more conservative techniques of the homeopathic practitioners and others who professed faith in the body's ability to heal itself if interfered with only very minimally. Most eclectic practitioners would eventually have to make a choice for one or the other, since the scientific climate that followed this period would force a clear distinction between the two brands of science.[24] The question of the compatibility between the two has returned to us today in the form of a debate about excessive technological utilization versus preventive and less-invasive health care, but at the end of the nineteenth century you were either committed to the heroic possibilities of the new sciences and their technologies, or you were cautious of them, not both. In an 1872 decision based on the argument that 'there was not enough difference [between eclecticism and medicine] to warrant the perpetuation of a [non-medical, scientific] sect,' the two eclectic council members merged the group with the medical profession.[25]

Eventually, the homeopaths too would fall under the shadow of the medical profession, partly because of the internal divisions among its practitioners and the failure to set up an educational institution in Canada,[26] but probably more importantly because their brand of science was never able to prove itself in the academic scientific arena. We have seen how the promulgation of scientific medicine as theory preceded its general therapeutic effectiveness. In the beginning all of the new 'scientific' practitioners, homeopaths and eclectics included, could make use of the rhetoric and excitement surrounding the new sciences,[27] but as time went by, evidence of these claims to the therapeutic benefits of the sciences had to be forthcoming. While the medical profession went on to back its claims with few but dramatic cases of medical discoveries, such as antiseptic preparations for surgery, diagnostic radiation, and penicillin,[28] the homeopaths did not.

The Rise of the Specialists

At the same time as the state was helping to legitimize the new scientific rationalism, it was also lending legitimacy to the bureaucratic elements of specialization and hierarchy. The practitioners we have seen thus far being granted the earliest self-regulatory legislation were whole body practitioners who purported to treat the whole person of whatever ailments might afflict her or him, rather than the specialists who purported only enough knowledge to treat specific body parts and functions or malfunctions. Two specialist provider groups had also entered the North American health care market in the late nineteenth century, the dentists and the pharmacists, representing not so much alternative scientific practices, since they both utilized the same general body of knowledge as that utilized by the medical profession, but rather, alternative forms of organization of scientific health care. They were the precursors to the present-day highly specialized division of labour within the increasingly complex realm of scientific and technological application.

Surgery and dentistry had grown up out of the trades of barbery or butchery – where one learned to handle a knife. Some of these men went on to become health practitioners, generally after a stint at a battle-front, but they were the low men on the medical totem pole. The general surgeon's position improved in the broader medical profession as the latter's art increasingly moved towards invasive treatments, but the dentists sought autonomy. According to one historian, 'Many so-called dentists [of the mid-nineteenth century] were scarcely entitled to the name'; itinerant dentists were sometimes quick to leave town.[29] Understandably, these 'scientists,' like the medical 'scientists,' were reluctant to leave their source of employment, or its educational institutions, to the vagaries of the market.[30] Despite some opposition from dentists who 'did not want the government interfering in their affairs,' a small group of dentists pressed for their own body of self-governing legislation.[31] With the help of the same pro-science, pro-public welfare arguments used during this time by the scientific medical practitioners to help override the free market liberal orientation of the time, the dentists' self-proposed legislation passed, with some minor amendments, in March 1868.[32] A self-regulating monopoly had been won. The protection the dentists had sought and won from the state moved them into the elite club of health practitioners who could now practise their profession with considerably less risk of market failure.[33]

Another specialist group hoping to gain that same advantage was pharmacy. It represented an interesting, and to this day, contentious, addition to the major divisions which developed among the health care providers, in that it combines both a professional career and a merchant career. The Ontario Pharmacy Act of 1871, which legislated the first registration and licensing of Ontario pharmacists, allowed pharmacists control over the compounding and selling of poisonous substances.[34] This element of the pharmacist's work, for which a certain level of skill was required, constituted only a small dimension of the occupation, however; the bulk of a pharmacist's income (about 95 per cent) came not from the sale of poisonous concoctions but from patented and usually prepackaged drugs and medicines (about 65 per cent) as well as 'toilet and fancy articles and sundries.'[35] This merchant orientation has always shaped the dynamics of the pharmacy profession. The state had been reluctant enough to grant monopoly powers to the practitioners who sold their clinical services to the public; the licensed protection of a merchant monopoly was even more contentious, especially with the public press 'screaming "closed corporations."'[36] But the fear of potential criminal abuse of poisonous substances; the inaccessibility, expense, and 'visible horrors that attended the "heroic" techniques' of the medical doctors; the hearty sale of sugar water concoctions; and the ease of obtaining a patent for potentially dangerous medicines with 'secret curative properties' helped sway the legislators in the pharmacists' favour.[37] The business of pharmacy was considerably helped by its link of the entrepreneurial to the scientific – much as it is today, with the same types of arguments and actors still being drawn into the debate over pharmacy's professional boundaries.

Although the specialty of pharmacy did succeed in winning legislation similar to that of the specialty of dentistry, it did not succeed in gaining the same sort of autonomy from medicine as dentistry did. Despite pharmacy's appearance of professionalism, the medical profession controlled the medicinal prescription – leaving pharmacy in a marginal role in the health care sector. It did not have enough authority to control its key scope-of-practice territory. Physicians not only controlled the utilization of the pharmacist's chemicals and compounds, but they themselves were also free to engage in the production and distribution of pharmaceuticals without the assistance of a pharmacist. The new legislation had given pharmacists the illusion of professional autonomy, but the reality of their marginalized position would continue to affect their professional and political authority.

Another marginalized group of health care practitioners were nurses, whose assistant role to the medical profession left them relatively low on the status hierarchy. It was not until the early twentieth century that nurses began to push for professional status, but their success was limited.[38] Even as late as 1951, when nurses gained some measure of self-regulation with the passage of the Nurses Registration Act, exclusive licensure was still denied them.[39] Probably the best indication of the inability of nurses to break away from the control of the medical profession lies in the fact that they were unable to maintain the fundamental and highly symbolic right to control their own members' education. In a sector where legitimacy rests so heavily on its claim to clinical expertise, to be denied control over that expertise is to be denied the hallmark of professionalism. Nurses were not given this sort of control.[40]

In a prolonged attempt to raise the status and functions of nursing, splits developed within the group. The 'traditionalists' continued to equate the functions of nursing with those of motherhood and the role of the 'physician's handmaiden.'[41] Meanwhile many mid-twentieth century middle-class nurses began to advocate a more autonomous professional emphasis on the body of knowledge on which their standing rested. This push for advancing the credentials of a particular provider group in order to elevate it to the level of a profession has become a common pattern in the story of twentieth-century health care, as it had been for the very first professional groups. Provider groups that found themselves in a subordinate position in the health care system often began to demand more and more education with higher and higher entrance and examination standards for their would-be members. This, in turn, fostered another common pattern in twentieth-century health care, that is, a hierarchically based gradation of clinical specialization within an already specialized segment of health care. As each subgroup within a group such as nursing moved up, another tended to move into the place it had vacated. As the rising status of the registered nurses, for example, left them reluctant to 'do the dirty work'[42] of nursing, others come forth to perform the necessary tasks. So the assistants to the medical doctors began to require their own assistants. Even these assistants, the nurse's assistants, referred to today as practical nurses,[43] now require the assistance of an orderly to whom they might assign unwanted tasks. All of this has set up a pattern of increased striation in health care.

Developing Patterns of Health Care Practice

These early successes and failures[44] of the health practitioners set up patterns which would continue to influence policy making in the sector to the present day. The eighteenth- and nineteenth-century Canadian market had produced four types of practitioners: whole body practitioners, specialists, merchants, and assistants. Contained within these market-based divisions were further divisions based on the type of knowledge (scientific or empiric) as well as the degree of application of that knowledge (heroic or conservative). As the scientific paradigm began to take shape in the late nineteenth century, the groups that had represented alternatives *within* that scientific paradigm (homeopaths and eclectics) were at first accepted and then slowly marginalized, while the groups that represented alternatives *to* that science (as we will see, Thomsonians, Grahamians, Christian Scientists, native healers, midwives, botanics, and potion salesmen, for example) were excluded. As set out in Table 2.1, those market-based categories which remained embedded in the professional health care subsystem at the turn of the twentieth century were whole body, heroic scientists (medicine); specialist scientists (dentists); merchant scientists (pharmacists); and assistants to scientists (nurses).

Further developments in the organization of health care in Ontario in the early to mid-twentieth century extended these patterns as well as expanding the categories within which the practitioners might be placed. The early practitioners were joined by both more practitioners and more attempts at mobility throughout the range of health care practices. New specialists continued to develop in the sector. As the medical profession itself became more and more divided into specialties,[45] so too, did the practices of those outside the parameters of established medicine. Specialists developed to service particular ana-

22 Health Care Practitioners

TABLE 2.1. Practitioner group positions of the 1800s

	Embedded	Marginalized	Excluded
Whole body	Medicine Homeopathy Electicism		Thomsonian healing Grahamian healing etc
Specialist	Dentistry Surgery		Midwifery
Merchant		Pharmacy	Botanic healing Potion sales
Assistant		Nursing	

tomical body parts or physiological functions which had either previously been the exclusive domain of the medical profession (for example, eye specialists, ear and speech specialists, feet specialists, and brain specialists) or had been ignored by the medical profession (for example, nutritional specialists, and body movement or ergonomic specialists). There might also be a number of specialists within these 'body part' or 'body function' specializations creating still further striation.[46] Some of these new specialists saw their role as dependent on or complementary to medicine or dentistry, while others wanted independence from the dominant professions.[47] As these divisions grew, so too did tensions. Lower members of the hierarchical ladder fought for upward mobility, while those on the top fought to stay there.

Among the new practitioners of the twentieth century there developed two new categories: the technologists who could run the new instruments of medical technology and a group of healers who used special techniques such as spinal manipulation, muscle massage, and mental counselling, rather than pharmaceutical medicines or technological instrumentation. Most of these practitioners specialized in particular technologies or techniques, but a few, like the earlier homeopathic and eclectic healers, saw themselves as whole body or complete care practitioners. With one exception (optometry),[48] all of these new technology and technique specialists would become either marginalized as semi-professionals in the sector or excluded from it altogether.

Marginalized Specialist Practitioners: The Drugless Practitioners Act

The Ontario legislation which clearly demarcated the semi-professional from the professional, as well as the heroic therapeutic application of scientific knowledge from the conservative therapeutic application of empirically based knowledge, came about in 1925.[49] This legislation was the Drugless Practitioners Act, and it included the osteopaths, naturopaths, chiropractors, masseurs, and chiropodists; physiotherapists were added later.[50] These practitioners were not, as the name implies, all 'drugless' practitioners, nor were they all working outside of the medical science paradigm; they were all, however, of insufficient stature in the early twentieth century to win their own legislated acts.[51]

The naturopaths, osteopaths, and chiropractors considered themselves to be whole body practitioners capable of treating all or most of a patient's symptoms. Naturopathy, an offshoot of the European Hydrotherapy – Nature Cure health movement, came to North America at the turn of the nineteenth century.[52] According to one report, there were few naturopaths in Canada prior to the First World War, and their numbers remained small in the 1920s and 1930s.[53] Naturopathy's basic therapeutic claim rested on the idea that the human body was capable of restoring itself to health and homeostasis if the ingredients natural to it (namely, good food, water, and air) could be maintained at the same time as all harmful ingredients (toxins) were removed. It was, therefore, essential to the practice that it remain 'pure' or uncontaminated by the ideas and treatments, especially pharmaceuticals and surgical techniques, being developed by the medical profession. Distinctions between practitioners have developed from various interpretations of 'natural' and from various choices of stimulative treatments, such as hydrotherapy, electrotherapy, acupuncture, muscular–skeletal manipulation, and, today, homeopathic remedies. A few minor medical techniques did seep into the practice of naturopathy,[54] but it remained essentially non-medical, conservative, and empiric.

Both osteopathy and chiropractic were founded in the United States in the late nineteenth century.[55] Disaffected with the inefficacy of orthodox medicine, their founders had become interested in techniques which hypothesized a need to loosen trapped body fluid, especially that of the spine.[56] Both the osteopaths and the chiropractors were weakened, as had been the homeopaths before them, by the tendency of their membership to split into two factions: one purist and the other eclectic (the distinction being referred to within osteopathy as regular osteopathy versus broad osteopathy, and within chiropractic as straight chiropractic versus mixed chiropractic). The distinction was really one between the anti-medical practitioners who preferred to remain true to their founders' reluctance to tamper too much with the body, and those willing to pick up some of the interventions, albeit the less heroic ones, of the medical profession. American osteopathy, moving more and more towards broad osteopathy, managed to portray itself as a parallel profession to the medical profession, encompassing a complete system of medicine and surgery – which has been licensed in all fifty states.[57] Canadian osteopathy, more in keeping with its British counterparts, came to be seen more as a complementary specialty to medicine.

Ironically, neither the strategy of remaining distinct from the medical profession nor the strategy of assimilation proved very successful in the long run. To distinguish oneself from the dominant ideational force within any policy sector is to risk subordination, or even elimination, within that sphere. Ontario's osteopaths have continued to diminish in numbers until the present day.[58] But the same can be true for those who associate too closely with the techniques of the dominant group in any sector in that they can end up becoming indistinguishable from that group, thus serving little purpose. The American osteopaths, although maintaining much higher numbers than in Canada, have become essentially assimilated into the medical profession there, in the sense that there is less and less practical distinction between the two.[59]

The chiropractors in both the United States and Canada, in contrast, have suffered neither fate. 'Although faced with continuous opposition from organized medicine, [they] have not only survived for [over one hundred] years but have prospered, as measured by such indices as numbers, income, legal and political status, and public acceptance.'[60] Although the Ontario chiropractors were marginalized within the DPA, they eventually succeeded with a most effective political lobby in gaining access to the coveted medical insurance coverage of the Ontario Health Insurance Plan.[61] Their success, however, came at the price of settling for a limited scope of specialized practice. In the end, of the whole body practitioners competing with the medical practitioners, the naturopaths and osteopaths were able to gain only a very limited degree of legitimacy as whole body practitioners, while the chiropractors were forced to specialize.

Furthermore, the alternative practitioners, the homeopaths, eclectics, naturopaths, osteopaths, and chiropractors, had failed to provide proof of the scientific theories or claims on which their diagnostic and therapeutic techniques were based,[62] while the medical profession, backed by the work of an increasing number of state and philanthropically funded scientists, had developed a growing base of scientifically proven knowledge. No longer could these alternative practitioners represent themselves as alternative within science. Regardless of how they saw themselves,[63] they now clearly represented alternative-to-science practitioners.

The massage practitioners[64] constituted another group of conservative, empiric, practitioners who had been placed in the less-than-prestigious Drugless Practitioners Act. An amendment to that act restricted their practise to prescription from a physician, osteopath, chiropractor, or naturopath.[65] By the mid-twentieth century, three types of massage work had developed: that 'conducted in recreation clubs, steam baths, private practices, and so on ... undertaken primarily to increase muscle and skin tone and not for therapeutic purposes; ... another used by sports trainers which might include limited therapeutic assessment and treatment; ... [and a third] remedial or therapeutic massage, which was given on the prescription of a physician as part of a rehabilitation program.'[66] The first was associated with prostitution, so the other two types of therapists aligned themselves with the medical profession in order to disassociate themselves from their more dubious cousins.[67]

Two other types of therapy, physiotherapy and occupational therapy, developed out of the need to physically and mentally rehabilitate returning war veterans. Physiotherapy specialized in physical function or body movement, while occupational therapy attempted to restore both mental and physical function through the use of 'activities of work, re-education, recreation, interpersonal relationships, activities of daily living, and self-help devices.'[68] Both occupations were taught, often jointly, within a faculty of medicine, and as such, were obviously influenced by the medical mode of thought. Although the occupational therapists set up their own association and university training course prior to the enacting of the Drugless Practitioners Act,[69] they were not included in either the 1925 legislation or the 1944 amendments. Physiotherapists, included in the 1944 amendments, were placed under the supervision of a physician or one of the 'major' drugless therapists in the institutions in which many of them were employed. Before controls were placed on physiotherapists, private entrepreneurial practices had also developed. For a while the entrepreneurial physiotherapists held their ground and even made a major gain in the early 1960s when their private practices were categorized as 'facilities' under the Hospital Act with the government sharing in their cost; however, these agreements were frozen in 1964.[70] Within physiotherapy, there had developed a division between those who were content with their dependency on the medical profession and on the institutional facility managers where they were employed (mostly in hospitals and chronic care facilities) and those who still fought to practise independently.

One type of new practitioner which met with a higher degree of success than the other 'drugless' practitioners was the chiropodist. Like most alternative health care practices, chiropody covered an aspect of care generally neglected or underserviced by the physicians and surgeons. It specialized in treatment of the foot, including minor surgical interventions where necessary. One branch of chiropody, the American-trained branch, succeeded in obtaining a separate Chiropody Act in Ontario, in 1944, despite opposition from the medical profession, as well as a lack of support from the British-trained chiropodists who tend to view their role as supplementary to medicine.[71] Although the act itself was not very different from the Drugless Practitioners Act, regulatory revisions made by the chiropody profession in the 1950s elevated the educational requirements to such a level as to 'virtually exclude British chiropodists from practising in Ontario.'[72] Having raised their entry standards, however, the American-trained chiropodists (podiatrists)[73] subsequently failed to win legal allowance for the expanded scope of practice those standards encouraged, thus leaving little incentive for those trained in the United States (where they are allowed to practise within this expansive educational scope) to migrate to Canada. American-style chiropodists/podiatrists had succeeded in elevating themselves right out of the regulated market.

Other specialist groups, such as the dieticians and the psychologists, were granted limited recognition via registration in the mid-century Ontario health care legislation.[74] In dietetics new practitioners moved in to fill a space largely neglected by the medical profession, but it is also an area of practice, like that of massage therapy, which elicits little animosity from the elite providers. In the past it has tended to stay well within the range of acceptable medical theory. Over time, conflicts have arisen between the mainstream, university educated dieticians and their alternative health care competitors or 'nutrition specialists' working outside the medical paradigm.

Psychologists, who had a separate Psychologists Registration Act (1960), worked essentially within the scientific paradigm in the sense that they made use of methodologies such as statistics. They specialized in human behaviour, rather than the functioning of molecular or physiological systems. Through a host of tests processed through statistical analysis, psychologists, each acting as both scientist and applied practitioner, attempted to develop pictures and hypotheses of both normal and abnormal human behaviour in the context of contemporary society. They were not so much anti-medical science, rather, they perceived themselves as providing a balance to the 'disease model of mental health' with the '[previously] neglected ... focus of the psychological and social aspects of patient care.'[75] In this sense they represented, and continue to represent, an alternative within science.

Specialization within Specialization

During the twentieth century the division of services to particular body parts or body functions continued. Care of the teeth, which had already developed into the specialized area of dental care, was joined by specialized care of the

Historical Patterns of Ontario's Health Professions Legislation 27

eyes and ears. Within each of these fields of care, further specialization also began to develop with the twentieth-century rise of technologies and therapeutic treatments, resulting in an internal division of clinical and entrepreneurial territory composed of (a) an elite medical or dental practitioner, (b) an independent technologist–merchant of goods and/or services, (c) either a dependent technologist and/or a dependent technique specialist, and (d) an assistant.

Medical doctors (general practitioners or specialists) and dentists were joined first by the new technologist/entrepreneurs. In vision care, as instruments for assessing magnification or refraction became available on the market, new operators set up business. Like the early nineteenth-century health practitioner groups, the first eye care practitioners possessed varied levels of expertise and intent. Retail stores (mostly pharmacies), wanting to profit from the sale of eye glasses, were using either the eye-testing equipment or the standard eye chart which had then been developed to sell spectacles directly to consumers. Itinerant competitors had also sprung up in the form of travelling salesmen.[76] Technological specialists,[77] who called themselves optometrists and opticians (the latter were also referred to as ophthalmic dispensers),[78] had also set up their own businesses, and it was they who succeeded, in 1931, in obtaining dominance in this portion of health care.[79] Despite anti-monopoly opposition,[80] market monopoly or oligopoly was being handed over to the new scientific specialists who were managing to take control over the technical instrumentation being developed.

During this time a new distinction, which was to become important to future health care practice and politics, was developing between the technologists who would go on to operate as independent merchants and the technologists who would become dependent on the medical or dental professions in much the same manner as pharmacists had. For example, the optometrists practised independently, diagnosing the need for, fitting, and selling of spectacles or lenses to their customers, while the opticians fit and sold the new eye care technology to customers only when provided with a prescription from them by a physician.[81] The optometrists also represented a new category of merchant; one where the practitioner provided both merchandise (as had pharmacy) and a clinical service (as had medicine and dentistry). Optometrists would begin to elevate their educational and training standards to distance themselves from the lesser-educated opticians by upgrading their service functions, but it was the merchant function which seemed to provide the strongest impetus for the push to achieve self-regulatory status. Those practitioners of this type of specialized care with little or no merchandise from which to profit, the auditory and speech–language specialists,[82] made little effort to be included in the early to mid-twentieth century legislation.[83]

28   Health Care Practitioners

In a similar story to that of vision care, technical developments in dental care led to a struggle for control over new dental appliances, such as crowns, bridges, and dentures. One branch of technologists, the denturists, or dental therapists as they were also called, fought successfully for independence from the dentists, while the other, now referred to as dental technologists or dental technicians, continued to work under the prescription and/or supervision of the dentists. The dentists had effectively blocked early attempts at independence on the part of the denturists, but an agreement in 1945 led to a separate act being created for them. The self-regulation granted therein was rather limited, however.[84]

Like the opticians and pharmacists, denturists are a predominantly commercial group with an obvious interest in getting professional status as an assurance of economic monopoly, and their policy-development input really comes primarily from their economic position. In 1971 the denturists organized the Ontario Denturists Association to fight for the right to operate independent businesses which would sell complete dentures to the public in the same manner as other denturists were then doing in a few other Canadian provinces.[85] This would, of course, if it were to succeed, result in lost revenues for the dentists, who, like the medical profession, fought long and hard to push their competitors out of practice.[86] In the end, the denturists won legislation which would allow them to practise without dental supervision in clinics which would sell complete dentures directly to the public.[87] Quite simply, they were able to provide cheaper dentures at a time when the public was calling for government assistance with dental expenses[88] – the dentists having failed to come through on a promise to do the same.[89] Interestingly, this group, like the new eye care entrepreneurial group, was, despite its own oligopolistic intent, bringing competitive market forces back into the health care system.

Like dentistry, medicine had also developed its dependent technologist groups. As new developments in the sciences became increasingly translated, in the twentieth century, into new instrumentations of technology, the institutions of organized medicine, especially the hospitals, began to staff their laboratories with technical workers. These technology groups, like the others we have seen, soon began to ask for legislation similar to that of other educated professionals. By 1963, the radiation technologists had won a separate act which allowed them to operate in a manner similar to that of the selfgoverning professions, although with less internal control than the elite professions.[90] The medical laboratory technologists had argued for similar legislation, but failed to attain it; instead they were placed under the control of a more generalized laboratory legislation.[91] As time has gone on, more and more technologies, and therefore technologists, technicians, and tech-

Historical Patterns of Ontario's Health Professions Legislation 29

nical assistants, have developed, with a resultant increase of pressure on the outdated legislation to expand to meet the changing nature of its subject.

The other two dependent groups which developed in these specialized areas of care were the technique specialists and the assistants. No dependent technique specialists developed in vision care;[92] however, the field of dental care developed the speciality of dental hygiene. Dental hygienists have been to dentistry what registered nurses have been to medicine.[93] They are trained to perform minor functions which would otherwise be performed by the dentists. Like the medical nurses, they have become increasingly well educated and resentful of their subordinate position to the dominant professionals under whom they work. In the past, the dentists successfully fought to maintain this patron–client relationship with 'their' hygienists.[94] The dental hygienists, like the nurses, have slowly raised the academic standards, that is, entry, education, and training standards, of their occupation in an attempt to gain legitimacy. This 'credentialist' move has increasingly distanced them from the less educated dental assistants who have expanded to fill the space they have vacated.

As the specialized practitioners, in general, increasingly won control over the rights to practise their particular techniques or technologies, their educational requirements increased in complexity and duration, usually with accompanying expectations of both higher levels of pay and exemption from the more menial tasks which had often been expected of them. This, accompanied by the fact that elite practitioners were losing ground financially to some of these new practitioners, led the elite practitioners to attempt to circumvent the need for the independent specialists by encouraging the development of more assistant groups whose 'surplus value' would go to their medical or dental employer.[95] As newer practitioners, such as chiropractors and optometrists, have raised their professional standing, they too have developed assistants.

The Excluded

The earliest excluded practitioners were the empirics who advocated an alternative to the scientific rationalism which had gained acceptance in the eighteenth- and nineteenth-century organization of health practices. Early alternative whole body practitioners, such as the Thomsonian[96] and Grahamian[97] healers, rejected the 'heroic techniques'[98] of the medical practitioners. The Grahamians (or Hygienics) steered away from the use of any medicines, rejecting even the botanics in use at the time. Both the Hygienics and Thomsonian movements, and other similar systems of care, such as that of the much older native practices, as well as the religious healers who had also developed, such as the Christian Scientists,[99] failed to sustain their mass popularity in North America, although they remained important to small or scattered populations of patients. Various reasons are put forth for this,[100] but one of the most likely is that these alternative forms of care failed to keep pace with the late nineteenth- and early twentieth-century push for scientific and technologically based answers to society's problems. As we have seen, those practitioners who could sell themselves as alternative within science rather than alternative to science were able to gain legislative sanction in North America in the mid-nineteenth century. The early merchants, such as the botanic healers and potion salesmen failed to win state support, despite strong public support,[101] predominantly because of their close association with both trade and empiricism.

The early midwifery specialists were also much less inclined to invasive or heroic practices than the medical men, so they tended to do much less harm than their medical counterparts.[102] They continue to practise successfully to the present day in many Western countries. However, the North American medical profession did succeed in excluding midwifery from the nineteenth-century practitioner legislation; under the 1875 Medical Act, against a tide of public support for midwifery, the midwives were legally prevented from charging fees for their services.[103] In effect, professional male birth attendants were to be paid, while the non-professional female birth attendants were to work voluntarily. During the twentieth century a relatively small number of midwives continued to practise outside the institutions of health care. They tended to be located in areas such as the far north where they would pose no threat to the area's medical practitioners.

The story of the take-over of North American birth assistance by the medical profession from the hands of its traditional experts, the midwives, provides ample evidence of the use and abuse of the societal power positions granted by a history of hierarchy and prejudice. Everywhere in the historical documentation of this transition of power is to be found evidence of the use by the medical profession of the gender, class, and race prejudices of the day to destroy the traditional practice of midwifery – along with any other challengers to the medical monopoly.[104] The same sexist and racist biases which helped to eliminate the competition of the midwives was also used to keep women and racial minorities out of the medical profession itself.[105] Heagerty refers to the Toronto school of medicine for women, opening in 1906, 'at a time when there was no provision in Canada for such study upon the part of women, but a resolute opposition to their appearance at the bedside of the sick.'[106] Women were apparently 'better suited' to the subservience of nursing than the autonomy of 'doctoring.'[107]

Likewise the common racial prejudices of the day were reflected in the professions. Just as the anti-American sentiments of colonial Canadians were used by the medical practitioners to discredit the American-trained homeopaths and eclectics,[108] so too were the common prejudices of the time employed to discredit those of lower racial status than the dominant Anglo-Saxon race.[109] Issues related to race have been little studied with regard to the Canadian health care system, but when they have been studied, here and in other countries, evidence suggests the embedment of dominant social hierarchies in the sector.[110] Calliste notes that Canadian-born women of colour were not admitted to Canadian nursing schools prior to the mid-1900s.[111] Brown documents the drive in the United States at the turn of the twentieth century to shut down black medical colleges, leaving only enough open to graduate sufficient numbers of black medical doctors to treat 'their own kind' in the inner cities where the elite medical practitioners were often reluctant to practise.[112] The report which had come out of that drive, and which was to wield considerable weight in all of North America, also resulted in the shutting down of the American women's medical colleges as well as almost all of the colleges with tuition fees manageable for the working class.[113] In colonial 'Canada,' with the victory of the English-speaking citizens, French-speaking citizens were discriminated against – a discrimination which would typically mark all sectors of social organization. As Kett points out, 'With McGill [one of the leading Canadian medical schools] under English domination [in the mid-nineteenth century], French-speaking students in Montreal had little opportunity to obtain medical instruction.'[114]

Class prejudice left its imprint directly on the organization of health care. In the regulatory legislation I have been reviewing here, this could be seen at the most simple level; those who attended the elite of society got the legislation they pushed for, and those who did not, did not.[115] The medical profession itself viewed its newly acquired nineteenth-century legislation as 'class legislation'; complaining openly, as was the common practice of the elite of the day, against the 'obnoxious opposition' of the working class, either in the form of political opposition or entrepreneurial competition.[116] Lenoir notes this trend in his discussion of the class domination (first the bourgeoisie and then the middle class) of the foundation of all Western medical expertise[117] – an expertise which, as we have seen, was to ensure the status elevation of the profession well beyond the days when professionals openly complained against the impropriety of social egalitarianism.[118]

Some people, of course, found themselves discriminated against at more than one level. For example, the nineteenth-century medical licensing board's requisite of Latin for admission to medical schools kept out not only the uneducated classes often of low status racial groups, such as the Irish or French, but

32 Health Care Practitioners

also kept out females of any class, since girls 'were routinely discouraged' from studying Latin as well as 'receiving less rigorous and less scientific training at every educational level.'[119]

These patterns of inequality were carried on into the mid- to late twentieth century. For example, there were no predominantly female provider groups among the elite practitioners, and both predominantly female provider groups in the Drugless Practitioners Act, the massage practitioners and the physiotherapists, had been placed under a 'minor' delegation within this legislation, while their male counterparts had been granted the 'major' supervisory position over them.[120] Similarly, female nurses never reached the same level as their male professional counterparts in the professional legislation under which they were regulated.[121] And nurses who were also women of colour could expect difficulties of both access and equality of treatment within the profession of nursing throughout the twentieth century.[122] North American female midwives continued to be labelled as incompetent despite evidence suggesting the superior results of twentieth-century midwifery practices over those of the medical practitioners in terms of both mortality and morbidity.[123] Immigrants to Canada – especially those of colour – continue to experience discrimination as both health care practitioners and health care patients.[124] General ideas about people's proper place in the social environment, which set up particular positions of sex, class, and race in our major institutions,[125] encouraged replication of those positions in the health care work environment. For all the talk of the objectivity of science, the subjective minds of its purveyors was readily apparent.[126]

Conclusion

By the late twentieth century, patterns of inclusion, marginalization, and exclusion had been embedded in the health care sector.[127] Early acceptance, in the nineteenth century, of Western principles and their accompanying blueprints had lent itself to acceptance of a particular degree and mode of organization of health services. The degree of state-backed organization of the health sector reflected the political and economic ideas in good repute at the time. The liberal–democratic principle of public welfare and its concomitant blueprint of minimalist state interference for the enhancement of that welfare were reflected in the allowance of regulated health professionalism per se. Likewise, the liberal–capitalist free market blueprint of reluctance to interfere in the market was reflected in the high degree of autonomy and trust awarded those self-governing health professionals. The state was willing to back up the requests of (certain) practitioner groups for monopolistic-type regulation of the sector, but it was an arm's-length regulation allowing as much entrepreneurial and clinical freedom as possible within the professions themselves.

We also saw how a particular mode of organization, one based on scientific, bureaucratic rationalism, became embedded in the early institutions of health care professionalism. Ideas of formal (objective, universal) rationality, specialized expertise, and hierarchy formed the nucleus of the dominant mode around which any organization of the sector revolved. By the mid-nineteenth century, the independent, heroic, scientific practitioners had won the professional monopolies they fought for, while the independent, conservative, empiric practitioners and the dependent science-based practitioners were either marginalized within or excluded from those same monopoly privileges. Divisions between the whole body, specialist, merchant, and assistant health practitioners were also given institutional sanction along society's lines of gender, class, and race hierarchy.

Challenges to this embedment came from both within and without. By the early to mid-twentieth century, new whole body practitioners and new technology and technique specialists sought access to, and mobility within, the Ontario institutions of health care. Alternative whole body practitioners, such as the naturopaths, osteopaths, and chiropractors, sought equal status with medicine but, failing to come up with scientific proof of their contributions, were either confined to a limited role within the organizations of health care or excluded from that organization. Some of the new technologists, the optometrists and denturists, won limited independent merchant power, while the early scientific merchants of pharmacy sought to sell both their merchandise and their services, and the early empirical merchants of natural drugs continued to trade outside the organized subsystem of health care. Alternative technique specialists, such as the midwives and massage therapists, continued to practise their own brand of health care.

In general, by the late twentieth century, prior to a major review of the health practitioners in Ontario, the status of autonomous professional was still limited to heroic, scientific practitioners (one whole body group, medicine, and two merchant–service specialists – dentistry and optometry).[128] Those practitioners accepted into the system as *dependent* merchant, technique, or technology specialists were applying the scientific doctrine which formed the basis of medical science, or, in the case of massage therapists, were practising non-competitive work which they were willing to have supervised by medical referral. The *independent* merchant–service or technique specialists[129] worked mainly outside the dominant institutions of health care often fending off considerable pressure from the elite practitioners for their elimination, especially where they represented an entrepreneurial threat to them, as did, for example, the chiropractors, midwives, denturists, and opticians.

The excluded practitioners consisted of a collection of historically excluded independent technique specialists, such as occupational therapists, speech-language pathologists, and social workers, and independent merchant–service specialists, such as audiologists and botanic healers; new (even more specialized) merchants, such as contact lens and hearing aid dispensers; and new independent technology specialists and assistant groups that had either failed to win any self-regulatory legislation, for example, medical laboratory technologists, or had never attempted to gain any such autonomy, for example, medical, dental, and nursing assistant groups.

Tensions associated with this organization had also been embedded there. Splits between the pure and the mixed forms of practice continued to divide practitioners within their otherwise similar practice areas. One's position of complement rather than alternate to medicine, or dependence on rather than independence from medicine, would continue to be a considerable source of tension and, in some cases, direct conflict. The ever-increasing specialization of the health sector continued to lead to disputes over practitioner autonomy as well as ownership of the parts of the process, particularly in areas where services and merchandise could be split into diagnosis, prescription, fitting or making, and selling, that is, where service crossed over into merchandise. The regulatory divisions between professionals, semi-professionals, and non-professionals continued to act as both a source of empowerment for some and discontent for others – leading to strategies, such as credentialism, to elevate the status and authority of the provider group. As various groups, such as registered nurses, succeeded in this objective, it opened the process for the creation of yet another provider group to perform the functions thus vacated; therefore creating another potential source of tension between specialties. These tensions, accompanied and exacerbated by social tensions associated with embedded gender, class, and race prejudices, would be played out over and over in the struggle to gain acceptance for the underlying ideas and structures in which each health practitioner group had long invested.

Overall, the sector's ideational interpretation of the principle of 'good health care' was translated into both a medical blueprint and an alternative blueprint, but it was the former which won control of the sector. Those practitioners who threatened either the medical definition of health care or the entrepreneurial gains of the elite practitioner groups, or both, had been either contained and limited in their health care practice, or excluded from the institutions which legitimated and funded the established provider groups. Good

Historical Patterns of Ontario's Health Professions Legislation 35

TABLE 2.2. Practitioner group positions up to the 1990s

	Embedded (professional)	Marginalized (semi-professional)	Excluded[a] (non-professional)
Whole body (independent)	Medicine	Naturopathy Osteopathy	Homeopathy
Merchant–service specialist (independent)	Dentistry Optometry	Denturism Podiatry	Audiology Botanic healing Potion sales
.... (dependent)	....	.... Pharmacy Chiropody Opticianry	.... Contact lens dispensing Hearing aid dispensing
Technique specialist (independent)		Chiropractic Psychology Dietetics	Speech–language pathology Occupational therapy Social work Midwifery
.... (dependent)	....	.... Physiotherapy Massage therapy	....
Technology specialist (dependent)		Dental technology Radiological technology	Medical technology Respiratory technology
Assistant		Registered nursing Dental hygiene Nurse assistance	Medical assistance Dental assistance

[a]This is only a partial list of the excluded (see Chapter 5 for more).

health care continued to be defined as heroic medical care practised either by the medical profession itself or by the rising number of specialists who studied from the same scientific texts as did the medical profession.[130] These were the rational practitioners, while the rest were, by definition, irrational.

Rationality, however, is a tricky business. It needs to be kept in mind, both for historical record and for the understanding of today's health care issues, that unproven ideas are not necessarily erroneous ideas. Questions never asked are questions never answered. It could be that we do not yet have the basic knowledge with which to understand the curative nature of minute doses of medicines or the relationship of a correctly aligned spine to the workings of our internal organs and systems – as the homeopaths and chiropractors, respectively, have long professed. The alternative practitioners did not have their own laboratories in which to prove (or disprove and move on from) their hypotheses.[131] Funds which were provided for the investigation of medicine were not provided for others. The medical profession has had a vested interest in pressing for its preferred questions, those that fit into its already developed paradigm of the workings of the human body. Even today, it is not as open to ideas as the scientific ideal would dictate. Good science is driven by curiosity; all alternative hypotheses remain open until proven false. Good science looks for the 'top quark' or 'neutrino' and celebrates the discovery even if it might turn the foundation of contemporary science on its head.

3

Benefits and Burdens of the New Regulatory Blueprint

The nineteenth- and twentieth-century reorganization of the health practitioners provided a new regulatory blueprint of monopolistic licensure for some, less-protectionist certification and/or registration for others, and exclusion for the rest. This blueprint, once institutionally adopted, reshaped the distribution of benefits and burdens within the health sector, particularly for the provider groups, the state, and the public.

Part I: Economic, Political, and Judicial Benefits and Burdens of Self- and Other-Regulation

What the elite health care professionals won with their gaining of licensure for their profession was, first and foremost, the right to restrict the practice of their own members as well as any intruders on their self-defined practice territory.[1] This monopolistic privilege was granted via the mechanism of professional self-regulation, or self-government. A professional governing body or college was empowered to set and enforce entry, educational, training, and practice standards for all members and would-be members of that profession, as well as to discipline both its own members and any external intruders on its professional scope of practice.[2]

The health care market had become a state-protected market, so the benefits and burdens of its participants had been shifted into the public sphere of governance where the rights and obligations are rather more demanding than those of the private sphere of the free market,[3] since the state is itself constrained by the principles and blueprints adhered to in a liberal democratic society. Those constraints are based in large part on the contemporary democratic blueprint of public participation and consent, set within a representative, responsible, and accountable governing system.[4]

The Ontario health practitioner legislation of the nineteenth to mid-twentieth centuries showed not so much the participation and consent of the public, but rather that of an elite fraction of that public as it had come to be organized into effective interest groups. Similarly, we have seen how the beneficiaries of professional privileges represented those most benefited in the broader social milieu. Responsible governance, on the other hand, was a key concept in the setting up of the early patterns of professionalism. Self-regulatory status set the professionals apart in a type of subgoverning system. Mechanisms of accountability were put in place to help ensure the quality of that governance; in practice, however, all of the early measures taken in Ontario to ensure public accountability were weak at best.[5] Not until the mid-twentieth century, for example, did professional incompetence become cause for disciplinary action.[6] Despite mechanisms for external review, the regulated practitioners were left essentially to their own devices.[7] In fact, the governing college was as much, or more, a union for the protection of the professional members themselves, as it was a protector of the public interest.[8] Given the standards of governance set in the broader political milieu, it is interesting that nothing was embedded into the mechanisms of professional self-governance which replicated some of the most important mechanisms of public accountability believed necessary to the good governance of the larger system – to which it is ultimately accountable.[9] That raises the question: On what foundation did this autonomy rest? This was to become the focus of much of the contemporary debate about organized health care.

With the granting of self-governance to health professional groups, legal procedural rights and obligations normally reserved for the judicial arm of the state's legal authority were passed over to the professional governing body. That body was now obliged to challenge,[10] or given the privilege of challenging, the right of a professional member or non-professional member to practise within the scope of the licensed profession. The medical acts of the late nineteenth century set up mechanisms to prosecute practitioners who were practising medicine without a licence.[11] However, effective prosecution was hindered because there was no precise legal definition of what constituted medical practice, often making it difficult to obtain a conviction.[12] This problem was to remain until the development of the legislation of the 1990s; as new practitioners appeared over the years, the medical profession often claimed they were 'practising medicine,' although most of these practitioners were using techniques neither taught nor used by the medical profession.[13]

The legislation of the late nineteenth century mandated the appointment, by the profession's council, of a disciplinary committee which could prosecute a member of the profession on the grounds that he had engaged in 'infamous or disgraceful conduct in a professional respect,' the penalty for which was expulsion from the profession.[14] The accused were given checks against abuse of the process similar to those used in the Canadian judicial system, for example, peer assessment, offence and prosecution location consistency, written records, notice of hearing and charges, defendant counsel, oath taking, evidence calling, examination and cross-examination of evidence, and the right to appeal decisions in the provincial courts.[15] In 1896 the process was expanded to include a complaints committee 'to advise the Prosecutor whether to proceed in doubtful cases.'[16] The disciplinary committee, the complaints committee, and the mechanisms of redress for the accused have remained important mechanisms of prosecution and protection within the profession to this day.

Like the broader judicial system, this legal subsystem of professional self-governance tended to favour the rights of the accused over the victims. Patients were given few rights or privileges in these procedures. This was to become one of the points of contention in the 1960s debates about professional authority. Since the colleges 'were disposed to be lenient' towards their own members,[17] and patients had no legal recourse for appeal of decisions made within the relatively closed system of professional self-governance, critical appeals for the opening up of the system to more scrutiny would be put forth.

Part II: Shifting Positions of Authority and Connection

The process of institutionalization necessarily produces particular patterns of relationship between the key actors involved in that process. The Ontario health practitioner legislation of the nineteenth and twentieth centuries contained, within it, benefits and burdens of investment or divestment of political resources of position. These I have categorized as gains or losses of authority or connection. What I would like to emphasize here are the shifting relationships among the health practitioner groups, the state, and the public which resulted in either beneficial or detrimental shifts in the positions each held with regard to one another.

Positions of Authority

We have seen the history of the granting of health practitioner regulation to many of those who pressed the Ontario state for it. The relationship this new legislation produced between these health practitioner groups and the state, as well as between the state and the practitioner groups left outside the legislation, sits on a continuum ranging from autonomy to exclusion, as in Fig-

Figure 3.1. Positions of authority.

---
authority ------ delegated authority / agency / proxy ------ exclusion

                   more authority ------ less authority
                   (weak agency)   (strong agency)

---

ure 3.1. We have seen how the early practitioners who convinced state officials of their scientific expertise were given professional status which allowed them considerable autonomy from the state, while the practitioners who failed to convince the policy makers of their need for professional or semi-professional recognition took on a position of exclusion.[18]

Within this differentiation between autonomy and exclusion, there also lies a mid-point which has taken on more and more importance in contemporary health care relations of authority. Between the two poles of autonomy and exclusion is a point of delegated authority or proxy: what Tuohy and Wolfson referred to as an agency relationship.[19] The exact legal definition of agency is debated by legal practitioners and scholars but it is generally accepted that, 'agency is the relationship that exists between two persons when one, called the agent, is considered in law to represent the other, called the principal ... A person is an agent only in so far as his acts can result in some alteration of the (legal) situation of the one for whom he acts or purports to act.'[20] In health care, without state regulation of the health practitioners, the relationship is a private entrepreneurial relationship where the principal is the patient seeking care and the agent is the health practitioner who agrees to act on the behalf of that patient (who needs an agent because of his or her lack of health care knowledge). Under public regulation of the health practitioners, however, the state is also acting on behalf of the patient ensuring responsibility and accountability of the practitioners (who might abuse their agency relationship with the patient because of the latter's ignorance of health care knowledge). When the health practitioners won the regulation they sought in the nineteenth and twentieth centuries, then, under their own design of professional self-governance they placed themselves in a position whereby they were not the only representatives or agents looking out for the interests of the patient. Under public regulation, a patient has double-agents, the health practitioner and the state, and this is further confused by the fact that under professional self-regulation, the health practitioners also act as agents of the patients/public *through* the state, that is, the state delegates its own governing authority (under which its agency authority for the patients/public rested) to the governing body of the health practitioner groups. Now, for example, an individual doctor is acting as an agent of her or his patient in the doctor's practice or clinic at the same time as that same doctor's professional governing body (or College) is acting as an agent (in proxy for the state) for the same patient. In reality, until quite recently, the regulated health practitioners were allowed considerable autonomy in interpreting their proxy relationship for the state, and it tended to be interpreted in terms of competency of clinical practice with regard to individual patients. That is, public accountability measures were sparse, so the new professionals acted only weakly as agents of the public through their delegated state authority. Today (as we shall see later) there has been a shift in this triangular relationship of representation and authority between the practitioners, the state, and the patients.

Self-governance of the professionals and semi-professionals also helped reshape the dynamics of authority both within the regulated practitioner groups themselves and between the regulated and unregulated health practitioner groups. The site of authority within the newly regulated groups began to be shared by the two organized bodies which grew up in response to, or were set up by, the early legislation; the voluntary association of the profession which acted as a lobby group to fight for, retain, and expand the legislation, and the governing body which was created as a result of the legislation.[21] What has perhaps been most interesting about the relationship between these two main bodies of the regulated practitioners has been the *small* amount of friction which has existed in the relations between them. They ought to be natural opponents – the governing body, or college, being a regulatory arm of the state meant to serve the interests of the public, and the association being a type of union meant to serve the interests of the practitioners – but there has been enough shared purpose exhibited between the two over the years to call into question the ability of these self-regulating practitioner groups to self-regulate. The fundamental question of professional commitment to the public would become central to the health policy debates of the 1980s and 1990s.

Authority relationships between practitioner groups became institutionalized as well. Some groups were given authority over others, for example, the prescription authority of the medical profession over the pharmacy profession, the supervisory authority of medical and dental doctors over nurses and dental hygienists, or the delegation authority of medical and dental practitioners over their respective technical workers, as well as the same for registered nurses over nursing assistants and hospital aids. These hierarchical lines of authority served, at least in principle, the bureaucratic requirement of accountability and efficiency, but there was a price to be paid for this hierarchy. The supervised often began to resent the supervisors and call into question the basis of their authority. As we shall see in our discussion of the latest round of health practitioner regulatory legislation in the 1980s and 1990s, this question of the justification for control of one group over another was to remain central to health policy debates.

The control of both the health practitioners and the state over the public was also affected by the legislative changes developed up to the mid-twentieth century. Prior to the regulation of the practitioners, the public were no more than consumers of health care services, that is, individual patients in a personal relationship with individual practitioners. With the shift into the public realm brought about by the professional and semi-professional regulatory legislation, however, the public takes on a democratic or political significance which goes beyond the private market relations of consumers and providers. As we shall see in discussion of more contemporary health care dynamics, with this shift tension over who best represented whom, and whose authority overrode that of another, was now embedded in the state–public–practitioner relationships. This tension was further exacerbated by a push in the 1970s for patient's rights which was backed by philosophical arguments against paternalism, judicial arguments in favour of individual autonomy, political arguments for egalitarianism, and economic arguments of free market rationality. As we shall see, these critical pressures would take on further importance as the relationships of the sector were opened for scrutiny by the review and modification of the legislation for the health professions that took place in the 1980s and 1990s.

Positions of Connection

In any political process, as in everyday life, some people are more connected than others. Who you know matters. Patterns of connection influence the way participants are likely to treat and respond to each other within their structured environment as well as the benefits of power one might or might not enjoy. The recipient of friendly or even indifferent gestures from other actors in the system will likely fare differently than the recipient of hostile or paternal gestures – particularly if those gestures are coming from the more influential actors. We have seen how the Ontario practitioner legislation embedded a hierarchy consisting of a small number of licensed, independent professionals, a marginalized group of either non-licensed or dependent semi-professionals, and a collection of non-professional workers. This legislation had also legally empowered the regulated groups to protect their clinical scope of practice from intrusion by other unlicensed, unregistered, or uncertified practitioners. This positioning contained within it a set of power relations which would influence the relationships already found among the community of actors –

TABLE 3.1. Positions of connection

	Supportive	Non-supportive	Antagonistic
Among equals	Friends	Strangers or acquaintances	Enemies (fair fight)
Among unequals	Patron–client	Strangers or acquaintances	Enemies (David and Goliath)

some more equal than others. I have categorized the positions of connection held by the various health practitioners in Table 3.1.

During the territorial battles leading up to the granting of the medical practitioners' professional legislation, medicine had clearly positioned itself as the enemy of all other practitioners who held alternative views to its own. Both alternative-to-science groups, such as midwives, botanics, and natural healers, and alternative-within-science groups, such as homeopaths and eclectics, were the targets of a constant barrage of accusations of quackery from the regular medical practitioners.[22] This medical opposition was also backed in North America by the financial interests who benefited from the utilization of medicines or drugs; pharmaceutical profits would be slim indeed under the homeopathic formulas.[23] We have seen how North American midwives, in particular, were targeted as enemies of the medical profession, a position which nearly resulted in their extinction.[24]

Even the health providers whose practice utilized the same body of science, and therefore sat within the same knowledge paradigm as that of the medical profession, such as the pharmacists, were subject to the less than friendly attempts by the medical profession to block their independence.[25] The medical doctors' right to practise pharmacy as well as their prescription control over the pharmacists placed them in a patron–client relationship with pharmacy. This, of course, placed the pharmacists in an unequal and vulnerable position. The patron can choose to provide quiet client-driven support, or he can choose to be domineering. Only dentists, whose work was seen as an unattractive subspecialty of medicine, went unhindered by the medical practitioners. But the dentists themselves would, as we have seen, take on the same sort of patron–client position towards other dental care groups as had the medical profession towards its own.[26] Those who did succeed in leaving the fold, the denturists especially, would take on the position of enemy to the elite professions.

These original positions of connection were only overruled by governing officials where the enemies of the elite practitioners of medicine and dentistry were seen as equally scientific and therefore equally capable of curing diseases and disorders. Where the practitioner group under attack by the established practitioners professed a philosophical alternative to science (as had the natural healers and midwives), or where the practitioner group worked under a patron–client-like relationship with the medical or dental profession (as had the nurses and denturists), the elite profession's arguments for their competitors exclusion from protective or independent legislation prevailed. The attitudes of all of the elite professions towards others were made all the more important by the fact that these elite groups had the authority to put their attitudes into action by prosecuting all practitioners out of favour with them. The nineteenth-century legislation, in sanctioning specific means of marginalization and exclusion via licensure and the granting of policing and judicial-like functions to the five original provider groups, also sanctioned a hierarchical set of attitudes and patterns of connection.

In the early part of the twentieth century, the North American medical profession convinced the president of the Carnegie Foundation to survey and assess the institutions of medical education in both the United States and Canada, a survey which included the countries' homeopathic training schools. The ensuing report, the Flexner Report, taken up by legislatures across the United States and Canada, is credited by historians with wiping out almost all but the most elite science-based educational centres in both countries.[27] So the remaining 'knaves and fools'[28] of North American health care who did not fit the medical blueprint were pushed either out of practice or into a lower status body of legislation which clearly demarcated them from the medical practitioners. They were also pushed into relationships of animosity, patronage, or neutrality.

Connections between the medical or dental profession and the new specialists who trained in the same basic life sciences as they did ranged from the cooperation and support of friends, the ambivalence of casual acquaintances, the domination and deference of patronage, and the hostility of enemies. Dependent groups of both the new techniques and new technologies, such as physiotherapists, dieticians, dental hygienists, and medical or dental technologists, were treated with favour as long as they remained content in their dependency. But any attempt on the part of the dependent to gain some measure of independence resulted in the same sort of hostility experienced by the independent alternative practitioners, such as the chiropractors and naturopaths.

The modern-day eclectics, the osteopaths, who at least favoured some of the new scientific techniques and therapies, fared no better in their relations with the elite of health care. From the onset, the Ontario medical profession fought against the osteopathic intruders – mainly by way of accusations of 'dogmatism and cultism.'[29] Nowhere is there any sign that they actually tested the osteopaths' scientific hypotheses. Even when the College of Physicians and Surgeons of Ontario did do an adequate study of the American training facilities in 1964,[30] its negative conclusions were highly suspect given (a) those same institutions had met the standards which had been laid out by the Flexner Report and which were modelled after Johns Hopkins – one of the most elite orthodox medical training schools in the country, and (b) American osteopaths were at that time sitting and passing the same qualifying examinations that all medical students sat at the end of their training.[31] Just as the nineteenth-century eclectics had failed to find a middle ground between the heroic, scientific medicine and the conservative, empirical health care of its day, the eclectics of the twentieth century, the osteopaths, would fail to find favour with either side of its dichotomous nature. In the long run, thanks to their inclusion in the Drugless Practitioners Act, osteopaths never really presented much of a threat to the Ontario medical profession. Their placement alongside the other drugless practitioners ensured that they would remain outside the circle of power. They would fail to befriend either the medical profession or the alternative practitioners; but, as we shall see, the importance of the ambivalent position they hold within health care would be brought to the fore once again in the late twentieth century, at a time when heroic medicine and alternative medicine are, at least at the fringes, looking for their 'complementarity.'

Non-Elite Connections

While each group's position with regard to the dominant professions of medicine and dentistry was of considerable importance to its well-being, other relationships also played an important role for some groups, particularly those groups which were legally connected through the Drugless Practitioners Act. We have seen, for example, how a hierarchy of practitioners was set up in the DPA amendments of 1944 when the physiotherapists and massage therapists were placed under the supervision of the osteopaths, chiropractors, and naturopaths or drugless therapists. Relationships here also contained their share of strain. Although the medical profession has often been accused of unfair behaviour with regard to its treatment of any practitioners who threatened its clinical and entrepreneurial territory, this is not to say other practitioners, given the rewards of power, would have been any less likely than the medical profession to resort to its tactics. Evidence from the United States suggests that osteopaths, once in a position to do so, fought just as hard and dirty against the chiropractors as did their powerful medical enemies against them.[32] The chiropractors have done the same to a lesser degree to the physiotherapists and the naturopaths, once they themselves attained some of the fruits of privilege.

The naturopaths and chiropractors shared the closest relationship of the DPA groups. Many practitioners were cross-registered under both categories.[33] The cross-over of practice territory has had both advantages and disadvantages of efficiency,[34] but more importantly the chiropractors, who had at one point benefited from the dual label,[35] began to become nervous about their association with naturopathy. As the chiropractors turned more and more towards a designation of themselves as alternative *scientists* to the medical profession, the naturopathic label became a liability. During the fight for inclusion in the medicare funding programs, the Ontario Chiropractic Association chose to disassociate itself from its naturopathic cousins.[36]

In its relationships with other health practitioners, chiropractic has been both the target and the instrument of hostility. While the medical profession has always been quick to object to the chiropractor's strengthened position, likewise the chiropractors have been less than generous with similar wishes from other health providers who might, in turn, threaten their clinical territory. Chiropractors have fiercely opposed any advancement of the physiotherapists' autonomy – afraid they will move into chiropractic territory, especially that of spinal manipulation.[37] From the physiotherapists' perspective, the enemy chiropractors were fought off partly with the help of the physiotherapists' medical friends.[38] The problem with this, however, was that their medical friends liked them just the way they were. As long as they were content to remain under the control of medicine or chiropractic, the physiotherapists had friends, but as they have moved, more recently, to gain autonomy, they have become rather less likeable.

The chain of command and differences of approach to therapeutic treatments have also affected the lower levels of the hierarchy. Physiotherapists themselves often 'regard masseurs with disfavour,' even though they themselves are trained to do some massage.[39] The masseurs, or massage therapists, have never been educated in the life sciences in the manner in which the physiotherapists are educated, so they have been positioned in the physiotherapists' eyes as unequal strangers. Even where semi-professionals or non-professionals have shared an approach to health care, however, relations have not always been friendly. For example, registered nurses opposed the attempts of the nurses' assistants to elevate their status in much the same way as the medical profession opposed the same for them.[40] The same estranged relationships have, therefore, developed at the bottom of the hierarchy as at the top.

It should be noted here that at least some of the opposition of the science-oriented practitioners towards the empirics has been based on legitimate concerns for public safety. The healing arts, being also the healing businesses,[41] have, of course, attracted their share of charlatans – in every practitioner category. Concerns about quackery are justifiable. It should also be noted that, once the elite professions had been granted licensure for their practices, they were under legal obligation to pursue and prosecute those practising from outside the licensed scope-of-practice territory. Blame for the overly generous boundaries that these licensed professions were given should rest with the lawmakers rather than the professionals given such free reign. Having said this, however, one cannot read through the comments made by the elite professionals over time and fail to get a sense, as Hamowy did,[42] that entrepreneurial concerns played a large part in the vigour with which particularly competitive practitioners were pursued. One contradiction stands out both historically and today: if it were really the quality of patient care which concerned the professionals in their drive to keep quacks out of the health care sector, why have they been so lax in pursuing the uncovering and prosecution of their own members who prove to be less than competent?[43] The medical and dental professions may well have been committed to the pursuit of high quality scientific health care, but it was a rather outward-looking gaze they cast about for violators. Nor can their inability to take to heart the best of the scientific agenda – its open-minded curiosity – be explained away as good intention. We cannot know exactly what the mixture of beneficence and greed was, but we have every reason to believe that the latter was at least as prevalent as the former.

Positions of Connection for the Public

As we saw with regard to the early divisions of health practice which had grown up in the free market of health care, the public was willing to support a broad variety of practitioners. However, as the range of available practitioners became more and more limited with the increasing organization of the sector, the public came increasingly under the patron–client control of the dominant practitioners. The public also became more divided into what I refer to as, (a) the patient, (b) patients, and (c) the public. The individual patient held her or his primary relationship with the health practitioner, and as the latter became more and more likely to be a science-based, medical expert, this relationship became increasingly based on a paternalism between unequal participants. The individual recipient of health care (the patient) also existed as both part of a body of patients, or aggregate of individuals (patients), and a collective or community of long-term health care recipients (the public).

With the nineteenth- and twentieth-century shifts in benefits and burdens connected with the broader economic, political, and judicial blueprints which were increasingly exerting pressure on the health care subsystem (more on this in the next chapter) came potential shifts in the relationships held with the patient, the patients, and the public. The judicial blueprint would tend to emphasize the individual patient; but this, as we saw earlier, was frequently offset by the judicial emphasis on the individual professional. In the fight between individual rights, the professional had clearly proven to have the better connections. The economic free market blueprint would tend towards concern for the aggregate of consumers of health care services, that is, the patients; however, as we saw earlier, those services were increasingly being given monopoly protection which again favoured (in economic terms) the professionals over the patients. The political blueprints would tend to emphasize the interests of the public as a community or collective, but, as we have seen, the state proxy which stands as the safeguard of the public interest had been little enforced and so, once again, the professionals had proven to be better connected than their public counterparts.

Conclusion

In Chapter 2 we saw the institutionalization of principles and blueprints which reflected both the broader social climate of ideas and the more particular interpretations adopted in the health sector. Various actors took on various significance in the sector with regard to its developing paradigms of knowledge and governance. Chapter 3 takes a closer look at the redistribution of benefits and burdens which accompanied the sector's public institutionalization.

The grant to professional self-regulation which had been bestowed on the health professionals brought professional benefits, such as economic monopoly, political self-governance, and judicial process. The price for these benefits was the burden placed on the new representatives of public sovereignty by the rule of law. Our favoured political blueprints of public participation and consent set within a representative, responsible, and accountable governing system, which set the moral standard of governance in the nation, necessarily stood as the template for self-governance; but it was a template at odds with the elite privileges already embedded into the organizations of health care. Public participation was predominantly elite interest group participation, and the consent sought was predominantly the consent of the medical or dental profession. Similarly, the more powerful professions represented the most socially privileged. Responsible governance was to be ensured by a professional governing body or college, but this body was more a political lobby group or union for the profession than a disinterested body of governance. Its record as a disciplinary body for all practitioner groups was entirely suspect.

This desk copy is sent to you with the compliments of

University of Toronto Press

Health Care Practitioners in Canada: An
Ontario Case Study in Policy Making

TITLE

Patricia O'Reilly

AUTHOR

CLOTH: 0-8020-4420-4 $60.00

PAPER: 0-8020-8224-6 $24.95

If you choose to adopt this book as a course text, please contact your local University bookstore. If you have any questions regarding University of Toronto Press books, contact the marketing department at (416) 978-2239.

OUTSIDE OF CANADA DOLLAR PRICES ARE IN US DOLLARS

UNIVERSITY OF TORONTO PRESS - HEAD OFFICE:
10 St Mary Street, Suite 700, Toronto, ON, M4Y 2W8   Fax: (416) 978-4738

**CANADIAN, US, AUSTRALIAN,
and R.O.W. (excluding Europe) ORDERS can be sent to:**
University of Toronto Press, 5201 Dufferin Street, North York, ON, M3H 5T8
Tel: 800-565-9523 / (416) 667-7791 / Fax: 800-221-9985 / (416) 667-7832

US ORDERS can be sent to:
University of Toronto Press, 2250 Military Rd, Tonawanda, NY 14150
Tel: (716) 693-2768 / Fax (716) 692-7479

EUROPEAN ORDERS can be sent to:
Marston Book Services, PO Box 269, Abingdon, Oxon, OX14 4SD
Tel: (01235) 465500 / Fax: (01235) 465555

Accountability measures, too, were weak at best, and those that were adopted were little enforced by the ultimate authority, the state. That is, public accountability while there in ideational blueprint, in written legislative form, showed few signs of actualization. Overall, there were few de facto checks and balances on the powers of professional governance.

Judicial obligations also accompanied the privilege of judicial process which had been designated to self-governing professionals, but these too had a distinct air of favouritism to them. While the rights of the accused professional were upheld, those of the wronged recipients of care were given little concern. Competence of practice was not even considered grounds for prosecution until the mid-twentieth century and even then, critics point out, the odds were greatly against the patients. The fair treatment sought through the judicial processes was interpreted in the health care subsystem, as it was in our larger societal system, according to material principles, such as effort, contribution, merit, need, and private ownership. Such principles had gained particular interpretations in Canadian health care over the years to the advantage of medically led heroic, scientific (high technology, heavy pharmaceutical) care provided at the most authoritative and lucrative levels by (establishment male) professionals. Those whose contribution failed to fit the dominant paradigm of good health care as interpreted by the judicial-like bodies within these professional subgovernments were ruled incompetent, and gone after by those with the licence to do so.

Further investigation here of the more latent positions of influence and power, that is, the positioning of actors regarding potential influence in both their everyday relationships to one another and their ongoing relationships to the public and the state (and therefore, public policy) has also provided a better understanding of the embedment, marginalization, and exclusion of its actors along with the tensions inherent to this positioning.

During the eighteenth to mid-twentieth centuries in Ontario, the licensed medical and medical-like professionals saw a shift from their old guild-based position of relative autonomy from the state to a more contemporary position of weakly enforced agency for the state. The non-medical semi-professionals moved from a position of exclusion to one which legally constituted a stronger agency than its medical and medical-like counterparts, but in practice operated under the same sort of weak agency relationship as those tied to the medical paradigm. The non-medical, non-professionals or excluded practitioners were legally positioned outside the organized health care sector, but those who managed to survive often held a limited degree of freedom from interference as long as they did not elicit too high a degree of animosity from their state-connected competitors.

Internal practitioner group authority began to become divided between the group's mandatory governing body (college or board of directors) and its voluntary association. The state's legal relationship was with the former, while its political relationship was with the latter. In practice, the two roles were often confused by both the practitioners and the state officials. Positions of authority between practitioner groups had been given legal sanction through the judicial powers of licensure, certification, and registration, and this allowed some practitioners to curtail the activities of others. The same could be done through the powers of prescription, supervision, and delegation allotted to particular practitioner groups.

Positions of authority over the public were confused by the jockeying between the professionals and the state, both of whom considered themselves to be serving the interests of the recipients of health care. These 'consumers' of health services were being represented at three levels: that of the individual patient, that of the aggregate of patients, and that of the community or the public. Furthermore, while the state and the professionals each continued to argue for their agency positions with regard to these patients or public, they themselves had begun to argue for more autonomy, backed by philosophical arguments of anti-paternalism which held a certain ring for the society of the day.

Supportive, neutral, or antagonistic positions of connection between health care practitioner groups grew out of the redistribution of benefits and burdens of the eighteenth- to mid-twentieth-centuries' organization of the sector. The antagonism of the medical profession towards its early alternative-within-science competitors (homeopaths and eclectics) and its early alternative-to-science competitors (midwives and botanics) began a long history of antagonism towards any practitioners utilizing theories of healing that were not of medical making. Likewise, dentistry defined all clinical and entrepreneurial competitors as enemies and fought hard to have them excluded, or at least contained. By the mid-twentieth century, with the help of the state sanctioning of medically defined scientific health care, the two dominant professions maintained (a) insider relationships ranging from cooperation to hostile patronage with the other practitioner groups who operated within the organized institutions of health care, such as nurses, pharmacists, physiotherapists, dieticians, medical technologists, dental hygienists, dental technologists, and assistants; (b) outsider relationships of either ambivalence, for example, with the masseurs, or hostility with the alternative conservative empirics, such as the naturopaths and chiropractors, the alternative scientists (the psychologists), and the competitive merchants (the denturists); and (c) an insider–outsider relationship of distance with the eclectic or moderate practitioners wishing to combine various techniques of the two poles of contemporary health care, the medical heroic and the conservative empiric.

Neutral positions of connection were encouraged between the institutionalized practitioners and the excluded practitioners; they existed in different worlds. Non-supportive or antagonistic positions of connection among the marginalized practitioners were reinforced by their containment in the less than prestigious drugless practitioner legislation that was developed in the mid-twentieth century. The independent-minded practitioners, such as the chiropractors and chiropodists, sought to distance themselves from their less scientific companions in order to be accepted into the medically based institutions of health care and health funding. The push for legitimation also split off the dependent-minded practitioners, such as the physiotherapists, from the non-university educated practitioners of their field, the masseurs, as well as splitting the latter group into unfriendly camps, the legitimate therapeutic massage therapists and the suspect masseurs. As it had for nursing, credentialism made old enemies into friends and old friends into enemies.

Positions of connection for the recipients of health care had strongly favoured the professional's interpretation of the relationship to the patient despite judicial, economic, and political arguments in favour of the autonomy of the individual patient, the free choice of the aggregate of patients, and the collective interests of the public. It was the health care professionals' position as agent for or patron to the patient which prevailed in the organizations of health care in the mid-twentieth century.

The embedment of both the more manifest economic, political, and judicial benefits and the more latent positions of power or authority among the key actors of the sector set up tensions which would be carried directly into the Ontario policy review of the 1980s. The economic monopolies afforded some practitioner groups would continue to be a source of ongoing turf wars among the practitioner groups as well as a target for critique by advocates of the free market blueprint. The handing over of governance to the professions – problematic in its own right – would present problems similar to those which could be found in the larger system of governance in which the health subsystem sat, such as the difficulty of ensuring accountability. The judicial processes of a self-regulated subsystem, likewise were problematic both as a reproduction of a larger system and as a 'neutral' body run by those with a vested interest in non-neutrality towards both rival practitioner groups and dissatisfied patients.

Tensions surrounding the new positions of authority and connection within the sector, predictably, would be based on resentment over clinical controls which placed one practitioner group in a position of power over another, as well as the history of animosity which would inevitably build up in a system designed around the legal control of professional groups over the clinical and entrepreneurial practices of semi-professional groups and non-professional groups. This would result in considerable pressure for change to the principles and blueprints of the sector. There was also significant pressure for change coming from outside the health care sector, as we shall see in Chapters 4 and 5.

4

The 1960s and 1970s: The Institutionalization of Delivery and Funding

While the organization of the health care providers was continuing in the mid-twentieth century, the organization of both the delivery and funding of health care[1] was also being influenced by the patterns which had dominated that earlier organization. This new organization would both exacerbate the public–private tension and continue to invest in the scientific–bureaucratic rationalism along with its specialization and hierarchy. As the welfare state developed, public funding programs were put in place for hospitals and medical services.[2] The combination of public funding and private decision making, which was adopted in the 1960s and 1970s, left a somewhat precarious balance which would influence policy making in the sector to the present day.[3] With the availability of public funds, health services in Ontario were provided by institutional bureaucracies, such as those of hospital and nursing home care, as well as being linked to a complex series of federal, provincial, and local bureaucracies.[4] The former included a varied mix of professional, semi-professional, and non-professional health care workers.[5]

As the health sector was expanding, so too was the scientific–bureaucratic mode of rationalism being enhanced. As health care became more scientific, the hospital, which had originally been set up for humanitarian reasons, 'developed into a centre of scientific medicine and a focal point of medical education and research.'[6] Modern rationalism, embodied as it was in the science-based care givers, elevated the medical practitioners to the pinnacle of the organization. But, ironically, it also provided justification for the rise of a group which could offset the power of the medical profession; the bureaucratic element of contemporary organization called for a cadre of administrators to run the complex operations of that organization. While the medical staff of the hospitals or the individual medical practitioners still enjoyed a fair degree of control over the decisions made within their domains, a potential source of balance to their power was now embedded in their organizations.

The institutionalization of health care delivery and funding also reinforced the specialization and hierarchy we saw embedded in the health provider legislation. The specialization of health care tasks was exacerbated by the large bureaucratic organization of the hospital system, while the public funding system helped stamp the visible hierarchies of both the hospital and the private domain. The state welfare blueprint superimposed on the health care subsystem was one of basically unrestricted state payment (via the Ontario Health Insurance Plan) for the particular sanctioned services of the medical profession,[7] restricted state payment (via OHIP and hospital salaries) for the marginalized semi-professionals,[8] and non-payment for all services provided by those non-professionals not employed by the health care institutions (see Appendix 2). In this way the new institutions radically strengthened the distinction between the included and the excluded by drawing a line between what would be paid for and what would not. When a few of the non-elite practitioner groups, such as the chiropractors, managed to win the fight for inclusion into the provincial public funding program in the 1970s and 1980s, they did not just gain enhanced income security, they gained public legitimacy.[9]

Hierarchical ordering by race, gender, and class was just as pervasive within the new institutions, especially hospitals, as it was in other areas of society.[10] The hospital setting also reinforced positions of authority and connection already embedded in the health sector. While a hospital legally placed the overall responsibility of the running of its organization in the hands of its board of trustees (composed of members of the community in which the hospital is located), the medical staff have long acted as the gatekeepers of the hospital beds. As one commentator put it, '[As the hospital became] the centre of scientific medicine ... there inevitably ensued a period of medical paternalism and of domination by doctors.'[11] A key element 'through all the various institutions of the [medical] profession and at all stages of the medical career ... [was that of] medical "sponsorship."'[12] In the hospital this placed a high degree of control over which practitioners would be allocated hospital staff appointments, internships, and hospital privileges. In this way the hospital setting reinforced the internal group hierarchies of the health providers.

Nursing and other assistant groups were also affected by the rapid expansion of institutionalized health care. Large numbers of trained nursing staff were required, so the hospitals developed programs of learning linked to institutional care.[13] This resulted in the development of various specialty divisions within and under nursing. There are now specific grades of nurses and nurse-type assistants performing a graduated series of tasks.[14] Likewise, the laboratory needs of the hospital resulted in the development of laboratory employees, such as the clinical chemists, technologists, technicians with less education than a technologist, and assistants with less education still. Dissent has arisen between and within these professional, semi-professional, and non-professional work groups, with the result that relations have sometimes become strained. The more highly trained workers, for example, resent having to perform housekeeping and unpleasant tasks that they believe more suitable for their lesser educated or uneducated associates. Everyone seems to want to keep their subordinates subordinate. In this sense the organization of health care delivery has exacerbated the tensions resulting from the hierarchical specialization which had already been embedded in the health sector.

The institutionalization of the delivery and funding of health care also marked a shift from the work relations of the past. One of the main problems for nursing unity, for example, has been a split between the ideal of professional status for which some nurses are striving, mostly the educated elite, and the reality which many rank-and-file nurses face each work day,[15] a reality which has led them to fight the labourer's fight instead of the professional's fight.[16] Likewise, the medical profession and the hospital technologists have had to face this tension between a professional image and unionlike concerns. The introduction of public health care funding in the province of Saskatchewan in 1962, for example, resulted in a bitter strike by the medical profession there, and similar action has been taken in other provinces more recently.[17] Such action presents a particularly strong dilemma for a group, such as the medical profession, which as a whole has long held itself up as more than a run-of-the-mill, or rank-and-file, labour group.

With the introduction of public funding the positioning of the medical profession, *vis-à-vis* the state took on a new dynamic. We have seen how the development of the nineteenth-century regulatory legislation had positioned the elite professions as agents of the state; however, this relationship was a static one. Measures of accountability had been designed into the original legislation, but there was little or no ongoing interference by the state.[18] Now with the introduction of medicare, ongoing interaction had to be set up between the state and its funding recipients, mainly the medical profession. As these interactions, mostly over fees,[19] became increasingly common, the practitioners began to build up a set of decision-making relationships with the state, based on their respective positions of authority within the sector. The spectrum of possible decision-making relationships is shown in Figure 4.1.

At one end of the spectrum, the practitioner group is left essentially autonomous, that is, it has the say in decision making. The less autonomous position of negotiation implies exchange and argument between strong players, such as

56   Health Care Practitioners

Figure 4.1. Positions of authority and 'say.'

---
autonomy ------ delegated authority / agency ------ exclusion

　　say ----- negotiation ----- consultation ----- audience

---

a powerful interest group and the state, which is meant to come up with a decision on issues or policy – which has not therefore been predetermined. Consultation implies an engagement or dialogue of a less powerful group with the state which includes the possibility of opening up the issue or policy objective to new directions other than those originally mandated. Audience implies the granting by the state of a conversational forum in which a weak group may comment on an issue or policy which has already been more or less decided on prior to the forum.[20] Lastly, the state actors may decide to take total control over policy making, to the virtual exclusion of other interested participants, even if this pre-empts the everyday authority of certain groups. State funding of the health sector shifted the more powerful practitioners from a position of autonomy to a position of negotiation, and the less powerful practitioners from a position of exclusion to one of consultation or audience.[21]

Most of the positions of authority and connection seen in Chapter 3 were reinforced by the institutionalization of health care delivery and funding. Only those practitioners whose health care philosophy was compatible with that of medicine's (such as that of the few dentists in the hospital),[22] or whose hierarchical position was subordinate to that of the medical profession while still serving the latter's needs (such as nurses, physiotherapists, and diagnostic or laboratory technologists), or whose relationship of connection with the medical profession as a whole was friendly, or at least neutral (such as audiologists, chiropodists, and psychologists) would be allowed to work in the hospitals or institutional 'homes.' The empirics (such as the midwives and naturopaths) were, of course, kept out. (See Appendix 2 for a more complete list of who was in and who was out.)

The individual patient's relationship to the health practitioners was only beginning to take on a new perspective. Mediated by the new institutional developments, it began to take on a distance previously foreign to the patient–practitioner relationship. A patient entering hospital, for example, would now come into contact with a host of experts – breaking down the intimacy more common to the private form of care, as well as the old patterns of authority common to the traditional relationship. Patients (as an aggregate) were beginning to take on new meaning as the delivery and funding of health care necessarily repositioned them as an economic unit of concern. Likewise, the public (as a community in long-term relationship to health care) was undoubtedly being brought to the fore with the introduction of public funding to the sector. The payers were now the public represented by the state. Shifts in any one level of the patient–public position might well result in shifts to another level. For example, the tighter the structures of control over the aggregate body of patients, such as through mandatory patient referrals and a limited number of practitioners for whom OHIP was available, the less choice or authority either the individual patient or the public had. As we shall see, however, the role of the public as a long-term collective was soon to be enhanced.

Ideational Shifts

The institutionalization of a large portion of health care services through the development and funding of hospital care and its key participants, thus, helped both to reinforce traditional patterns and to create new ones. Old patterns of medical dominance continued, carrying with them the ideological imperatives we have seen develop through the nineteenth and twentieth centuries; but the shift in the health sector blueprint to public funding also, in a sense, reset the immediate ideational climate of the sector. Now, rather than being another economic market sector with social side-effects, health policy became a social policy sector with economic side-effects. With this shift came a certain disjunction between the ideas which had been embedded in the earlier regulation of the health practitioners and those that were developing both within the sector and within the society of the 1960s and 1970s.

The newly embedded welfare or social ideas now sat alongside not only the ideas and products of the old, but also the alternative ideas of the newer-still. As the people and processes of the Ontario health care sector entered the 1960s, they entered a period of intense ideational struggle between the traditional and the propositional. The blueprints of progress, for example, which were once defined almost exclusively as economic accumulation and scientific and technological development, were by the mid-twentieth century being tempered by the idea of a progressive or civilized society in which the state ought to take a more active role in helping ensure the provision of the basic needs of its citizenry. This shift of orientation would result in the questioning of many related ideas. Our society's foundational tenets were being scrutinized, and this force of change would come to affect all policy sectors in the Western world.

The general ideational orientations coming from the broader societal context in which the health care system was situated were tapped into and enhanced by the ideas and recommendations of the official reports produced in Ontario during the 1960s and early 1970s – particularly, the McRuer Report (1968), the *Report of the Committee on the Healing Arts* (1970), and the *Report of the Professional Organizations Committee* (1980).[23] Although the health policy literature commonly suggests the Ontario reports of the 1960s and 1970s were put to little use,[24] I would argue that these reports have played a significant role through their influence on the ideational climate surrounding later legislation. Their impact can best be seen by observation of their ideational orientations: they provide a record of the key propositions of the time – propositions which will continue to pressure, and often enter, the established institutions of health care.

Just as the degree of state intervention into society was undergoing a realignment, the embedded modes of organization were also being called into question by the 1960s.[25] Political philosopher Sheldon Wolin, for example, pointed to the inherent characteristics of power and control contained within the order and efficiency of bureaucratic organization.[26] Commentaries on the Ontario health care system showed signs of a challenge to this bureaucratic order. In his Committee on the Healing Arts volume on the medical profession, produced in the late 1960s,[27] Grove pointed to the dehumanizing effects of an increasingly bureaucratized form of health care. He commented on the hospital environment as follows:

> The hospital is fast becoming a centre for the delivery of health care ... But the hospital is a curious kind of bureaucracy, with overlapping hierarchies: the medical staff, with its own organization; the nursing staff, and the paramedical and ancillary staff with theirs; and the lay administration, also increasingly professionalized. Managerially hospitals are out of date, for they still run largely on the basis of an outmoded paternalism of the medical profession. This is a universal fact, one which is leading some critics of contemporary hospital management to put forward new ideas, centring essentially on the notion of the hospital as an 'arena' of medical care. In this 'arena' there would be a highly pluralistic 'negotiated order' [rather than a superior–subordinate structure] of professional people working together – not 'under' but 'around' the pivotal position of a hospital manager or chief executive.[28]

The authors of the Committee on the Healing Arts Report went so far as to recommend a breakdown of some of the established bureaucratic organizations of institutionalized health care. While the idea of joint educational facilities to foster 'better understanding between the different professions,' along with 'multi-disciplinary health clinics' where various establishment and non-establishment health care workers could work together, may not seem terribly radical today, in its own day it was positively startling.[29] The committee's report reflected a critical openness to the shifting ideas of its own societal milieu; but it was an openness ahead of its time – at least in relation to the slow-moving nature of the bureaucracy. Most of the report's recommendations failed to appear in the ensuing legislation.[30]

The spirit of the 1960s and 1970s also contained within it a respect for the ethical and spiritual dimensions of human nature, which showed up in the form of a revival of alternative health care, especially in the United States, and therefore, indirectly for Canada.[31] Although this revival of low-intervention, low-drug, low-technology care tended to be restricted to small populations, it helped keep alive various alternative practitioners, such as midwives, who were, consequently, still around to be organized into interest groups to push for inclusion in the 1980s' and 1990s' health care legislation in Ontario.

More specifically, these social challenges to bureaucratic organization called into question the dominant bureaucratic blueprints of formal–objective rationality, specialization, and hierarchy. The stranglehold of the 'science-as-reason' assumption of the nineteenth and early twentieth centuries was beginning to be challenged in the 1960s, and this was reflected in the reports of the Committee on the Healing Arts.[32] Grove's criticism of the medical profession's attack on naturopathy reflected a more open approach to the utilization of scientific rationality. He argued,

> It is surely going too far [for the doctors] to refer to the naturopaths' concept of treatment 'by the use of nature's agencies, therapeutics, processes and products' as 'meaningless jargon.' It is true that the modern GP is more likely to pump us full of antibiotics than to prescribe sunshine and exercise; but have they so soon forgotten the Mediterranean cruise and the advice to 'take the cure' that their forefathers prescribed, often with good results? In fact, it is hard for the layman to accept the doctors' contention that naturopathy is 'scientifically meaningless.' If a doctrine attempts to stress the benefits of nutrition and vitamins but fails to use the right medical jargon, does this make it unscientific? It may well be that it is, but the doctors will have to make a stronger case than mere abuse.[33]

Grove also pointed to the increasingly dehumanizing nature of institutionalized health care where specialists divided the person into various body parts.[34]

Alternative ideas about people's proper place that once only occupied the realm of critique – that once sat as mere proposition – began to become embedded in the larger society. As the political and judicial spheres increasingly embraced ideas about egalitarianism and civil rights, for example, the stark contrast to the non-egalitarian, prejudiced ideas embedded in the health care organizations became more and more evident. The reports of the McRuer Commission and the Committee on the Healing Arts, like other 1960s' challenges, questioned hierarchical assumptions which had previously gone unchallenged by establishment commentators.[35] For example, conventional attitudes about the participation of women and minority racial and ethnic groups in work positions of affluence and authority were questioned.[36] Later, at the end of the 1970s, the Professional Organizations Committee implicitly reinforced similar concerns about the entrenched bureaucratic characteristics with its emphasis on the importance of including *all* interests, that is, those of the para-professionals or ancillary health care workers and the public, as well as the usual elite interests, in any assessment of contemporary professional organizations. Thus, the broader societal shifts with regard to our foundational economic, political, and judicial principles and blueprints inevitably found their way into the health care system.

The Economic, Political, and Judicial Critiques

Many analysts have made reference to the pervasiveness of our contemporary market system into all aspects of our lives,[37] and nowhere is this better illustrated than in health care where market-type efficiency is being increasingly argued for, and applied to, life itself. Free market or free enterprise pressures continue to play an important role in the health care debates. We have seen how the freedom and welfare dichotomy was embedded in a private practice / public payment system of delivery and funding and how pressure continued for both more freedom and more welfare.

The call to freedom took the form, especially in the 1970s, of arguments against professional monopoly or oligopoly. Arguments and rhetoric against state intervention by both the excluded practitioner groups and contemporary free market economists became common during the 1970s.[38] Practitioner groups already well positioned within the protective wall of professionalism argued for post-monopoly entrepreneurial freedom. The economic analysts tended to argue for an opening up of the system to provide more balance between the powerful monopolists or oligopolists, such as the medical and dental professions, and the weaker entrepreneurs or innovators, such as the new low-technology practitioner groups or the non-professional medical suppliers of, for example, eye or ear care products. The self-regulation granted to professionals was argued by some economists to be excessively costly and inefficient, as well as stymying innovation; counter-arguments claimed that self-regulation was a necessary evil given the knowledge gap between the professional and her or his client; but still others argued it provided little protection for the clients.[39]

Conversely, welfare arguments began to pressure all societal organizations in the post-1960s' era. Privileges, such as those which had been granted to the scientific practitioners as an appropriation and property gain of science as product, were increasingly being brought under scrutiny. As other interest groups, environmentalists especially, gained acceptance for arguments based on common ownership or stewardship of public goods, they helped create an ideational climate conducive to a shift away from state support of private ownership of public resources – including the products of science and education. They also, in doing so, helped bring about a shift in authority. As Tuohy predicted in the mid-1970s, 'In the final stages of this [shift from ownership to stewardship] governments must come to treat professional technologies as public property and must assume authority over the management of that property.'[40]

The principle of egalitarianism, which featured so prominently in the 1960s, can be seen running through the reports and legislation on health care in the 1960s and 1970s. The McRuer Report emphasized the legal civil rights orientations of its day, while the Committee on the Healing Arts and the Professional Organizations Committee both recommended a more balanced consideration of all 'vulnerable interests' – including the non-elite.[41] The Medical Insurance Act of 1966 embedded this egalitarian emphasis in the form of the federal government's emphasis on universality, comprehensiveness, and accessibility, that is, on equal access to good health care services regardless of income, need, or location. As the efficacy and fairness of democratic blueprints of responsible, participatory, consensual, representative, accountable government were emphasized in the 1960s' critique, the self-governance of the professions was also held up to criticism. The Committee on the Healing Arts Report criticized the 'inadequate or even merely nominal supervision over and responsibility for the [existing] legislation ... by government' and called for the coordination of all health professions.[42] That is, the provincial government was found lacking in the fulfilment of its agency responsibility to the public. Its obligation to ensure mechanisms of control over the authority it had abrogated to the health practitioners was not being met. The important role of the state in maintaining a new balance of the freedom–welfare dichotomy – one in keeping with the broader societal shifts in the preferred balance of these two principles – was emphasized by the CHA critique. Like other policy or institutional analysts in other fields at the time, the CHA drew on liberal market arguments for individual rights and economic efficiencies at the same time as it called for government responsibility towards social needs.[43] The

Professional Organizations Committee, while more oriented towards free market arguments than the CHA, also agreed with the need, in the case of health care, to balance rights to freedom with welfare concerns.[44]

The contemporary political orientation towards increased levels of public participation and consent was also reflected in the health care story. Individual and group public consultation took on increased importance in health policy formation. The interest group consultation undertaken by the CHA showed the importance it placed on public participation. It solicited 99 briefs, received 199 completed questionnaires, held 106 hearings, and arranged 47 meetings of interested parties.[45] Likewise, the POC made a concerted effort to consult, share research, and release documentation of the orientation of its work 'prior to a major set of public meetings.'[46] Despite efforts to include the unorganized public, however, it has been primarily the organized practitioner groups who have shown interest in participation.[47] Public input has been predominantly left to the mechanisms of representation.

Representation of the public on professional councils and committees was argued for and won in the 1960s and 1970s, but as we saw earlier, the question of who best represents the public is a difficult one. The health practitioners view themselves as the representatives or agents of their patients; the state views itself as the representative or agent of the public; and now the patients and members of the public themselves were demanding to place their own representatives on the governing structures of the professions. Questions about fair representation of the public remain problematic to the health sector, just as they are throughout all of our policy sectors.[48]

The 1960s' orientation towards enhanced democratic scrutiny of the governing elite also showed up in a renewed emphasis on public accountability in the health sector. All three of the reports focused on here emphasized the importance of mechanisms of accountability meant to ensure the protection of the public interest. They sought to push administrative accountability towards a broader political accountability.[49] The political orientation of the 1960s towards the public interest was to become very influential and very controversial for all contemporary policy debates. Both the McRuer and the CHA reports emphasized the public interest as the litmus test of the granting of self-regulation. That is, the relevant question with relation to self-government was not what it could do for the profession, but rather: 'Is self-government necessary for the protection of the public?'[50] This same public interest orientation showed up in the discussion paper solicited by the minister of health as a follow-up to the CHA Report.[51] It could also be seen in the POC Report which, a decade later, wrestled with the difficulty this logic had presented for professionals and governments alike.[52] As we shall see, this public interest orientation was strongly present in the policy process which resulted in the Regulated Health Professions Act of 1991.[53]

Had the self-governing system of the professions really been a governing system in the full sense of the word, with democratic elections, its own ministerial responsibility, and so on, it might have been able to argue its case for serving the public interest. But, as we have seen, it was a system designed to govern a select group of health care interests only. In a liberal democratic society, the state is the lone governing entity invested with the mandate to serve the public, and as such the historical handing over of its governing function to particular interest groups now necessitated that it either (a) ignore its responsibilities to the public and refuse to interfere with the professions; (b) take back the governance of the professions; or (c) leave the system of self-regulation intact but move to ensure more public accountability from the professions. It chose the last.

Critics of the health care sector and its professions called for a tightening of the mechanisms of public accountability. Expressing concern for the lack of overall coordination and control of the health care institutions and professionals, the CHA Report had called for more government participation and planning to coordinate and integrate services and professional groups; as well as more direct public participation in the 'formulation of general regulatory policy.'[54] The McRuer Report had called for governmental review and approval of professional regulations, as well as the introduction of public ('lay') representatives on professional governing bodies.[55] The POC emphasized the three-way relationship between the right to self-governance as conferred by legislative sanction of self-regulation; the corresponding duty of the protection of the public interest; and the control mechanism needed to ensure the fulfilment of that duty, that is, formal accountability.[56] Working papers produced for the POC went further in making recommendations for external review agencies to assess or promulgate and interpret professional regulations and rulings.[57] The POC staff study rejected these suggestions, but did suggest mechanisms to take professional issues to the 'broad representative political arena,' that is, the cabinet and legislative committees. These recommendations were not included in the final report.[58]

The 1960s' and 1970s' critiques of professionalism also emphasized the need for a tightening and enhancement of administrative accountability in the professional self-regulatory institutions. As we saw in Chapter 3, some measures had already been taken in the health care professional legislation towards ensuring accountability, but they were weakly designed and rarely enforced. Until the 1960s and 1970s Western states demanded little in the way of accountability from their professionals – preferring to place their faith in the professionals themselves. But with the 1960s' waning of faith in the governing elite, came a similar scepticism towards the professional elite. Consumer scepticism about the objectivity of the professional governing bodies, and anti-elitist concerns for public access to professional careers, helped create a critical climate surrounding the professions.[59]

The CHA recommended 'constant public scrutiny' of the 'dangerous' and 'monopolistic powers of the professional governing bodies.'[60] The McRuer Report argued for a strengthening of due process assurances necessary to individual civil rights, but its main focus, in typical judicial fashion, centred on the professionals who were called before the governing body tribunals rather than the patients or victims who had initiated charges – except where the complainant was an aspiring professional.[61] The CHA, however, did extend its concern to the public complainants, as did the POC, which repeatedly emphasized the need to take all 'vulnerable interests' into account.[62]

The institutionalization of health care delivery and funding, in itself, led to an enhancement of the administrative aspects of health care. The overriding federal imperative of public administration standards contained in the Canada Health Act[63] ensured a certain amount of political accountability by the provincial health care institutions and actors to the federal government. More particularly,[64] the administrative logic of health care institutionalization resulted in the introduction of accountability mechanisms within the hospitals, such as (limited) checks on overservicing and underservicing via quality controls for medical practitioners (with clinical discretion largely preserved), as well as record-keeping and auditing standards. In addition there was growing concern for responsibility to efficiency and effectiveness in terms of cost management. For example, while the private entrepreneurial area outside the hospital was initially left relatively unchecked, quality and cost control mechanisms were now being introduced into both the public and the private spheres of health care – for the latter, via, for example, private fee-for-service price and volume controls. More and more, as the state has had to restructure the health care system to adjust to cost constraints, financial accountability has become a necessity.[65] The POC academic staff (Trebilcock, Tuohy, and Wolfson) brought this concern to the fore, and the POC Report itself argued 'policy choices should "above all" be infused with a sense of priority in the expenditure of regulatory resources.'[66] Likewise the CHA Report had referred to the need for 'economy and efficiency' – especially with regard to the use of personnel such as 'paramedicals and allied health personnel.'[67] It was not financial accountability, however, that would become the focus of the 1974 Health Disciplines Act which followed soon after the POC Report.

The 1974 Health Disciplines Act

The mechanisms of administrative and political accountability were targeted for improvement in the Health Disciplines Act of 1974. Measures to enhance the due process aspect of administrative accountability were mandated. 'Clear and consistent structures and processes for professional tribunals' were set up for the five professions included in the act: medicine, dentistry, pharmacy, optometry, and nursing.[68] Three committees to deal with registration, complaints, and discipline were made obligatory for each professional college or governing body, and avenues of appeal to the courts were established for the defendants and the college – but not the complainants.[69]

The heightened political accountability which had been called for in the reports of the 1960s and 1970s was introduced in the form of ministerial and lieutenant governor in council empowerment to review, approve, initiate, and make regulations to the act.[70] These were given legislative form in the HDA provisions for public representatives on the governing body council of the colleges and the college committees. It also set up a Health Disciplines Board composed of lay members with a mandate to hear appeals of complaints committee decisions sought by a defendant or complainant, or appeals of registration committee decisions sought by applicants. It could enforce its decision – pending appeal to the courts, in the case of the registration committee, by either the complainant or the committee.[71] Tuohy has argued that the public need for the political resources of information and access was not well enough met by either of these measures, suggesting the need for an external advisory body, further representation of affected interests on professional governing councils and committees, and the release of detailed annual reports from professional bodies – possibly presented to a standing committee of the legislature.[72] As we shall see, all of these recommendations were incorporated in the 1991 Regulated Health Professions Act.

Financial accountability measures were not introduced in the Health Disciplines Act of 1974, except perhaps indirectly in the sense that the new mechanisms of governmental input could potentially take on a fiscal concern. It was not until the cost constraint pressures of the 1980s and 1990s that financial accountability was seriously, although somewhat covertly, introduced via the back door of quality control. By the late 1990s there would no longer be much need for *justification* of strengthened measures of financial accountability.

The Health Disciplines Act did little to reshape the tangled configurations of health provider interests. Despite continuous pressure from disaffected provider groups and strong recommendations from the CHA in 1970 to realign the positions of the provider groups, the only change to the nineteenth-century configuration of regulatory legislation and interest groups (see Table 2.1) was the inclusion of optometry as a licensed, self-regulating profession.[73] The Health Disciplines Act reinforced the mid-twentieth-century patterns set up during the organization of the health sector. In doing so, it solidified the medical profession's position as the judge of good health care – marginalizing and excluding the alternative judgments of others. But it also committed the medical profession to a narrow interpretation of health and medicine, at the same time as it committed the doctrine of scientific health care to a narrow group of practitioners. It locked medicine and the medical-like specialists into an exaggerated self-esteem antithetical to the open growth and development of alternative approaches to health care; and it locked applied medical science or research into a limited and limiting paradigm where the requisite openness of scientific inquiry was impaired. In the same manner, it locked the marginalized and excluded practitioner groups into overly defensive positions with regard to their ideational base, again limiting the growth of the base itself. Likewise, the idea of moderation which formed the basis of eclecticism, and its attempt to find the best of both extremes, was pushed out by both the self-esteem of the elite and the defensiveness of the aspiring elite. Eclecticism had found a home only with practitioners who failed to gain a foot-hold in either the establishment or the surviving alternative fields of health care, and the new legislation of 1974 did nothing to change this.

Despite these weaknesses, the Health Disciplines Act signalled a changing ideational climate. The public accountability measures which were put in place were – however weakly effectual in practice[74] – significant in terms of the changing attitude towards self-governance. No longer would the governing bodies of the health professions be assumed to be acting in the best interests of the public that they were licensed to serve; no longer would they be automatically trusted. This shift in the relationship between the professions, the state, and the public would come to play a significant role in the next round of professional policy debates in the 1980s.

Conclusion

The 1960s' and 1970s' institutionalization of Ontario's delivery and funding of organized health care modified the health sector's blueprint in a manner which further embedded the existing tensions around governance and rationalism. Public funding, in general, came to reflect the bivalent pull of all contemporary liberal, democratic governments over the freedom–welfare dichotomy. Public payment was accompanied by private decision making in an organized health sector which was bound to expand in a less than coordinated manner. The scientific, bureaucratic rationalism embedded in the earlier provider legislation was reinforced in the 1960s and 1970s. Hospitals became centres of scientific medical treatment, education, and research. Heroic health care and specialization increased as old hierarchies among the health practitioners were reinforced inside the rapidly developing health care institutions, especially those of the public reimbursement system, or OHIP. Existing positions of authority and connection were reinforced and exacerbated, particularly with regard to the medical profession's role as gatekeeper of the sector. Old patterns of race, gender, and class discrimination were also stamped into the new organizations as they developed.

At the same time as the embedding of scientific, bureaucratic rationalism favoured the dominant profession of medicine, it also encouraged the rise of a group which could, and would, come to challenge that dominance. The bureaucratic managers inside both the therapeutic treatment centres and the policy-making centres of health care would be forced to move, within a few decades, to offset the open-ended and costly entrepreneurial and clinical discretion of the institutions' gatekeepers. Accompanying this pressure would come responding pressures within the practitioner groups, such as that towards a realistic labour or union orientation to issues rather than the behaviour traditionally associated with the ideal of the gentleman professional. A new history of strategies and expectations began to grow up around the shifting patterns of relationships accompanying these mid-century developments. Public funding brought on episodic encounters between the state and the medical profession which necessitated closer contact than earlier regulatory relationship had entailed. The relationships between the public, the practitioners, and the state were also being affected by the increasing distance between the patient and the practitioner in the institutionalized settings of health care delivery, as well as by the need to view the recipients of health care as both aggregate patients in economic terms and a collective public in long-term relationship with a sector which was now both publicly regulated and publicly funded.

Other challenges or alternatives to the newly embedded ideas and people of mid-twentieth-century health care in Ontario existed in its external milieu. The 1960s' ideational struggle between embedded and alternative visions of society began to show up in the critical health policy reviews of the 1960s and 1970s. Reports by the Committee on the Healing Arts, the McRuer Commission, and the Professional Organizations Committee criticized health policy legislation for being out of step with the principles and blueprints which were beginning to force change in the larger political, judicial, and economic institutions. As the degree of state intervention in the broader public organizations of society increased, it allowed for similar arguments for enhanced state participation in the coordination, accountability, and fairness of the health sector organizations. Likewise, the embedded scientific, bureaucratic mode of rational organization of health care was held up for scrutiny by the 1960s' critique of its foundational elements.

Pressure from the ideational milieu surrounding the health care subsystem was being brought to bear on the privileges, obligations, and commitments we saw captured in the institutions of health care by the mid-twentieth century. The external economic influences supported a free market, anti-monopoly stance which would encourage the breakdown of some of the licensed monopolies of health care practitioners, at the same time as public welfare arguments favoured a shift away from the traditional support of property to a stewardship which would encourage more state control and management of the public property of science and technology. Broad political–judicial arguments in favour of increased measures to ensure fairness and a higher degree of egalitarianism were also encouraged by the health policy reviewers – ideas which were being translated into a broader acceptance of all interests in the health field, including those of the weaker participants, such as the public and the marginalized or excluded provider groups.

As our broader liberal democratic blueprint of public participation and consent set within a representative, responsible, and accountable governing structure was being scrutinized and reshaped by the 1960s' critique, this blueprint, when held up against the mechanisms of self-governance practised by the professionals, showed up a large number of flaws in that self-governance. Many of the checks and balances developed for the broader system of public governance were recommended for enhancement in the health professional system of governance, especially those related to accountability. The health professions legislation which was developed in the heat of these critiques, the Health Disciplines Act of 1974, fell short of expectations. New accountability measures were designed in the HDA in the form mostly of administrative and judicial due process accountability measures. Political accountability was enhanced somewhat, but less than that recommended; financial accountability was virtually ignored. Recommendations for coordination of the subsystem overall, particularly those which might have eased the high degree of tension among the health practitioner groups, were also ignored. Overall, the change the mid-1970s' legislation brought to the everyday practices within the structures of health care was minimal. The importance of that legislation rests mainly in the ideational shifts it initiated.

Even those ideas of the 1960s and 1970s that were not realized in the 1974 legislation still existed as forces for change. All of them put pressure on the health care sector to create new space to accommodate them. They were now available to be called up to play a role in shifting the foundational principles and blueprints which had historically been embedded in the health care institutions and relationships. Whether or not they had been realized in legislation, they represented the most influential alternatives of the day, and as such, played the important role of raising both official consciousness and general expectations. Only the idea of (a limited) public accountability was picked up and embedded in the new health legislation of the mid-1970s. The other ideas of the 1960s and 1970s would remain in the realm of the propositional. Suggestions for structural change coming out of these reports recommended a broader acceptance of alternative forms of health care, for example, multidisciplinary health clinics. These alternatives did not disappear; they waited in the library of ideas,[75] thus providing a pool of propositional ideas with which to challenge the organizations of health care. By the 1980s the climate within the Ministry of Health had shifted sufficiently, partly as a result of the thinking contained in the Committee on the Healing Arts Report and partly for reasons of its own, to allow for the initiation of another legislation review which would in the end come to echo much of the spirit of the 1960s.

5

Overview of the Legislation Review Process in the 1980s[1] of the Ontario Health Professions

Proposed restructuring of the Ontario health professions legislation in the 1980s, which began with the Health Professions Legislation Review in 1983 and culminated in the Regulated Health Professions Act of 1991, came as a result of the ad hoc relations which had developed over time in the sector. Interest group pressures on the Ministry of Health had reached inordinate proportions by the early 1980s.[2] In November 1982 Health Minister Grossman announced a review of the regulatory legislation governing Ontario's health professions. It was decided that the task would best be done by a review team external to the ministry.[3] The review was to be headed up by Alan Schwartz, a Toronto lawyer who had on occasion acted as a policy adviser to Health Minister Grossman. The consulting work required to assist Schwartz was put up for tender and the Canada Consulting Group won the bid.[4]

Although much was made of the external, that is, objective nature of the review, it would be misleading to accept the inference that the review process was done without ministry direction. The consultant tender processes are, of course, biased towards the ministry's favoured principles and blueprints. The ministry, after all, *picks* the consulting group it judges best for the job – what sounds good to their ears is probably already ringing there. Not only did the ministry set the agenda,[5] which included suggesting the new structure the proposed legislation was to take, it also kept a close eye on the developments as they occurred. During the entire review there was input from the Ministry of Health, that is, the review was done 'externally' as claimed, but there was a well-used back door to the review offices.[6] One of the academic advisers to the project commented, 'When we first met with Schwartz, he saw his job in very political terms – in relation to Grossman's need to have the group conflicts and demands on him mediated.'[7] Both the political and the bureaucratic arms of governance were influential in the policy process which led up to the Regulated Health Professions Act of 1991.

The Health Professions Legislation Review ('the review' or HPLR) was to report directly to the minister, and its final report was to be presented in the form of draft legislation, therefore taking the form and characteristics of a legal document rather than a policy review. Referring to the recommendations of the 1969–70 reports of the Ontario Committee on the Healing Arts, the original guidelines pointed out the need for a review and rewriting of existing legislation in order to 'cull out the anachronisms' and give the ministry the authority to 'keep a watchful eye on the legislation and behaviour of the professions in the future.'[8]

Health ministry officials expressed concern about the quality and cost-effectiveness of existing services, undue proliferation of new health care occupations, and unwarranted upgrading of the qualifications of any discipline, all of which had also concerned the Committee on the Healing Arts. It was believed a restructuring of the legislation was necessary in light of the 'perceived status hierarchy' which had inhibited reform attempts made within the existing Health Disciplines Act. A new legislative blueprint was suggested by the ministry, whereby one umbrella act would regulate all of the health professions jointly; it would be accompanied by a series of individual acts for each profession which would cover details such as the profession's scope of practice and regulation-making powers.

The impetus for the review, as the HPLR team saw it, came from health care professionals and would-be professionals, hospital administrators and other employer groups, Ministry of Health bureaucrats, government officials, and the public. The existing system was generally thought to be uncoordinated and statutorily outdated, too restrictive for efficient utilization of health care providers (meaning, at least partly, too restrictive to allow for the utilization of cheaper, but still safe, health care providers than those currently providing services), unfairly exclusive in the definition of what constituted medical professionalism, and, finally, too closed, unresponsive, and unaccountable to the public, especially in relation to complaint investigation and discipline processes.[9]

The stated purpose or terms of reference (April 1983) of the Health Professions Legislation Review was to make recommendations in the form of draft legislation, which would:

1. Determine which currently regulated health professions should continue to be regulated;

2. Determine which currently unregulated professions should be regulated;
3. Update the procedures in the Health Disciplines Act, primarily to fine-tune procedures introduced in 1974;
4. Incorporate any substantive reforms or additions considered appropriate;
5. Extend the structural and procedural reforms introduced by the Health Disciplines Act to all other health professions to be regulated;
6. Develop a new structure for all the legislation governing the health professions; and
7. Settle outstanding issues in several professions.[10]

The consultants emphasized the need to follow up the recommendations of earlier reports, especially the 1980 *Report of the Professional Organizations Committee*. The review team suggested the establishment of a 'council of wise advisers,' the core of which would be composed of three academics (Carolyn Tuohy, Michael Trebilcock, and Stefan Dupré), all of whom had participated in the creation of that report.[11] This advisory group was set up, but it met only infrequently with the HPLR team. According to one of the advisers, 'It was a very limited relationship. [However], we did insist there had to be some framework brought to bear on the process. So we argued for the ideas put forth in the *Report of the Professional Organizations Committee*. We said, "Here is a debate; here are the contenders; and here are the principles around which we feel this debate ought to revolve – or rather, which are relevant to this particular debate."'[12] The orientation and recommendations of the POC have been discussed in the preceding chapter. The basic thrust was one of anti-trust or pro-competition and therefore deregulation or minimal regulation.[13] At the time of the HPLR in the early 1980s this orientation was still dominant. The ideational climate of the review was, in the words of one of the review team members, one of 'pro-competition, pro-freedom-of-choice, and suspicion of government regulation.'[14]

Other assumptions of the review process were set out in the report (see Appendix 3).[15] In tones reminiscent of the McRuer Committee on the Healing Arts, and Professional Organizations Committee reports which had gone before it, the HPLR report commented on these basic principles: 'The important principle underlying each of the criteria [used "to analyze the merits of the health practitioners' requests made for self-regulation"][16] is that the sole purpose of professional regulation is to advance and protect the public interest. The public is the intended beneficiary of regulation, not the members of the professions. Thus the purpose of granting self-regulation to a profession is not to enhance its status or to increase the earning power of its members by giving the profession a monopoly over the delivery of health services. Indeed, although these are common results of traditional regulatory models, they are undesirable results, and the model of regulation we recommend aims to minimize them.'[17] (See Appendix 4.) This claim to the primacy of the principle of public interest as justification for professional self-regulation was to be qualified, however. The review team members, presumably with ministry agreement, had also accepted the assumptions of the POC Report that self-regulation could not be attained without the 'relative satisfaction' and 'cooperation' of the self-regulators.[18] In among the constant references to the public interest were fewer, but nevertheless pronounced, references – including the title of the report itself – conveying the review's commitment to balancing the public interest with the interests of the professionals.

The HPLR team initiated its formal process (see Appendix 5) by publishing '22 Topics,' in September 1983, which were meant to set the agenda for the review. These and all other documents related to the review process were open to public scrutiny. The '22 Topics' (see Appendix 6)[19] were accompanied by a letter explaining the purpose of the review to be, among other things already mentioned above, the recommendation for revisions to existing health professional statutes which 'may appear desirable in the public interest.'[20] More than 200 groups and individuals had identified themselves to the review team as having an interest in the review, and they were contacted by the review team for their input with regard to the '22 Topics.' These and subsequent responses were referred to by the review team and later official participants, as 'the submissions.'

The Health Professions Legislation Review encompassed an impressive array of practitioner interests and constituted a very great effort of communication. A large number of interest groups and stakeholders – approximately seventy-five of which belonged to self-defined health practitioner groups[21] – were involved in a process that was surprisingly open to dialogue both among the participants and between the participants and the HPLR team. Health care providers, for example, were forced, most of them for the first time, to describe themselves and their contribution to health care. Then amidst workshops, meetings, and consultation sessions, these provider groups were asked to comment on each others' written submissions – opening up a dialogue between often antagonistic groups which, as many of them later commented, had never before been countenanced, much less recorded. In this particular policy process, the entry stage of the process eliminated no one from the upcoming policy race; all interested parties were allowed to participate.

Of the more than 200 groups and individuals who had originally expressed interest in participating in the review process, 120 submitted formal written responses to the HPLR team's '22 Topics,' indicating the interest of approximately seventy-five health provider groups in gaining professional self-regulatory status.[22] Among these[23] were the following provider groups:

Aestheticians
Ambulance care providers (or casualty care personnel)
Art therapists
Athletic therapists
Audiologists
Bioenergetic analysts
Biomedical engineers
Biological photographers
Botanic medicine practitioners
Child care workers
Chinese medicine practitioners
Chiropodists
Chiropractors
Christian scientists
Clinical hypnotists
Clinical chemists
Colon therapists
Consultants, counsellors, psychometrists, and psychotherapists
Contact lens fitters
Dance movement therapists
Dental technicians
Dental hygienists
Dental nurses
Dental nursing assistants
Dentists
Denturists or denture therapists
Diagnostic medical sonographers
Dieticians
Electroencephalogram (EEG) technologists
Electrologists
Esthetics and cosmetology practitioners
Food service supervisors
Health record administrators
Hearing aid dispensers
Herbal therapists
Holistic medical doctors
Kinesiologists

Marriage and family therapists
Massage therapists
Medical hydrotherapists
Medical laboratory technologists
Medical radiological technicians
Medical physicists
Medicine (i.e., physicians and surgeons)
Midwives
Natural scientists
Natural hygienists
Natural healers
Naturopaths
Nutritional consultants
Occupational therapists
Ophthalmic assistants
Opticians or ophthalmic dispensers
Optometrists
Oriental therapists
Orthopticians
Osteopaths
Pastoral counsellors
Pedorthists
Pharmacists
Physiotherapists
Podiatrists
Practical nurses
Prostheticists and orthotists
Psychoanalytic psychotherapists for children
Psychologists
Psychometrists
Public health inspectors
Pulmonary and cardiovascular technologists
Radiological technicians
Reflexologists and deep muscle therapists (Alzner school)
Registered nurses
Remedial gymnasts
Respiratory technologists
Self-healing therapists
Sexologists
Shiatsu therapists

76 Health Care Practitioners

Social workers
Speech–language pathologists
Straight chiropractors
Therapeutic recreation therapists
Vascular technologists

Since it had been decided that the HPLR process was to remain open to scrutiny, each respondent received copies of all other respondents' submissions, and all interested parties (health provider groups and others) were 'encouraged ... [to continue as] active participants.'[24] The review team then undertook the difficult task of organizing and questioning the submissions of the aspiring provider groups. Not surprisingly, they found many claims to good intentions, especially the provider groups' claims of 'service of the public interest.' They treated these claims with scepticism, forcing the participants to 'explain more fully or re-examine their opinions, to reconcile elements of their point of view that seemed contradictory, and to address the often differing opinions of other related groups.'[25] Analysis of the initial submissions was thorough, and consultation was not taken lightly. As a result of the serious attitude adopted by the HPLR team, in their own words, 'The currently regulated professions realized that they would not be allowed to rely on their current status to avoid difficult issues, and the new professions realized that they would be taken seriously provided they gave serious consideration to the issues.'[26]

The participants were expected to respond in a second submission to the comments and questions raised by the HPLR team with regard to their initial submissions. This they did, for the most part, with considerably more care than they had taken in their initial submissions. This process was repeated, with up to eight submissions from some groups. In early 1985 the review team put forth their 'Nine Criteria for Self-Regulation' which were to be used to determine who should be given professional status under the reformed regulatory system. The nine criteria were (see Appendix 4):

1. Relevance of the proposed self-regulating group to the Ministry of Health
2. Risk of harm to the public
3. Sufficiency of supervision
4. Alternative regulatory mechanisms
5. Body of knowledge
6. Education requirements for entry to practice
7. Ability to favour the public interest
8. Likelihood of compliance
9. Sufficiency of membership size and willingness to contribute

Leaving aside the administrative question of which ministry should regulate which professional groups, the most significant information being sought with regard to the nine criteria was that related to two aspects of self-regulation: necessity and feasibility. Is it necessary for the prevention of public harm to have a practitioner group regulated, and is it possible for that group to ensure the mechanisms for, and compliance with, the standards being designed for self-regulation of the health professionals?

Upon further questioning of their suitability for self-regulation using the nine criteria (see Appendix 7 for the successes and failures in meeting these criteria), by April of 1986 a list of thirty-nine professional contenders was shortened still further to twenty-four. The thirty-nine potential self-regulating professions, with the twenty-four winners indicated in bold, were:

Athletic therapy
Audiology
Biological photography
Chiropody
Chiropractic
Clinical hypnosis
Clinical chemistry
Dental hygiene
Dental technicianry
Dentistry
Denture therapy
Diagnostic medical sonography
Dietetics
Health record administration
Hearing aid dispensing
Marriage and family therapy
Massage therapy
Medical laboratory technology
Medical physics
Medical radiological technicians
Medicine (i.e., physicians and surgeons)
Midwifery
Naturopathy
Nursing assistance
Nursing
Occupational therapy
Opticianry or ophthalmic dispensing
Optometry

78   Health Care Practitioners

Osteopathy[27]
Pharmacy
Physiotherapy
Podiatry
Psychology
Psychometry
Pulmonary and cardiovascular technology
Respiratory technology
Shiatsu therapy
Speech–Language pathology
Vascular technology

   While this elimination process was going on, the HPLR team had begun the process of designing profession-specific legislation, as well as an omnibus statute which was to cover all the health professions.[28] Preceded and accompanied by information and discussion workshops for the provider groups, in the fall of 1986, the review team offered a 'topics paper' on 'Legal and Procedural Issues Associated with the Self-regulation of Health Professions,' to the, by then, twenty-four that were to be recommended for self-regulation. Its focus was on general principles. These principles were not up for debate. Participants 'not well acquainted with self-regulation,' and some very well acquainted with their own versions, were educated on these basic principles.[29] From this 'a public interest framework' was established.[30] Also during that same summer, a 'Scope of Practice Workshop' had been held in order that each provider group could present its own version of its scope of practice. The results were circulated for comment by all other participants.

   By October of 1986 the HPLR's first set of 'Legal and Procedural Proposals' (the 'green book') was circulated for comment by the provider groups. By December of 1987 the review's initial scope-of-practice statements for each provider group and lists of proposed licensed acts (health care or medical procedures) were also made public. In the summer of 1988 the review's revised 'Legal and Procedural Proposals' (the 'red books') including the proposed individual professional acts and initial proposals concerning professional title usage were circulated for comment by the provider groups. By the end of 1988 the HPLR team had produced its report and the health professions legislation recommendations were tabled in the Ontario Legislature by the minister of health in January of 1989.[31] The report was presented in the form of draft legislation, almost all of which has now been enacted into legal statute in the Regulated Health Professions Act of 1991.

1980s' Ontario Health Professions Legislation Review 79

The Ministry of Health's Professional Relations Branch (PRB) was given the task of following up on the HPLR recommendations. This branch was intended to

1. Create a forum for discussion and debate about issues of concern to the professional and non-professional provider groups;
2. Act as a liaison between the health providers and the minister of health as well as between government ministries on issues related to the health professions;
3. Administer regulatory matters, including the processing of existing regulations; and
4. Provide direction to, and administration of, the functions of the Health Boards Secretariat (under which the review and appeals processes are regulated).[32]

The creation of this branch had signalled the clear intent of the minister to move towards a much more systemic method of dealing with the time-consuming effort of engaging in interest group pluralism.

When the HPLR report was handed over to the Professional Relations Branch, it was clear that the task of administering its implementation and revisions would subsume most of the other, albeit complementary, functions of the branch. It was also clear that its mandate was not to start at square one with the proposed professional legislation. The review had been put into draft legislation for a reason: there was a strong emphasis on producing legislative change rather than having yet another ministry department shelve yet another expensive report. One of the later personnel additions to the HPLR team, Linda Bohnen, was hired at the Professional Relations Branch to work on the proposed legislation, providing continuity between the external review process and the ministry policy process.[33] Both she and the branch director, Alan Burrows, engaged in extensive consultation with the practitioner groups which had been recommended for regulation under the new act, as well as with the practitioner groups which had not. They also coordinated meetings between these groups and the minister of health, as well as responding to public inquiries and complaints about the proposed legislation and, later, the enacted legislation.[34] Over the course of the whole project all three of the major political parties of the province were in power.[35] However, partisan politics did not appear to have much effect on the overall direction of the new policy. Unlike many such reports, the Health Professions Legislation Review report had a very strong determining role in the final legislation, regardless of the partisan swing.

During both the legislation design and formal drafting processes, intense debate took place over the rightful practitioner positioning which would ensue from the new legislation. We turn now to those debates to better understand the ideational dynamic between the old embedded policy and its potential restructuring, and thus to better understand its outcome.

6

Expertise Turf Wars

The restructuring process initiated by the Health Professions Legislation Review called into question the privileges, obligations, and investments contained in the existing legislation, with its history of favouring some practitioners and marginalizing or excluding others. We have seen the patterns this historical process embedded as it continued to organize the health sector in keeping with the sometimes static, sometimes shifting, principles and blueprints of the larger societal milieu in which the sector lay. Two aspects of organization on which I have concentrated, the degree of organization and the mode of organization, played important roles in shaping these patterns. They were central to the disagreements and debates which surfaced during this restructuring process.

Questions about the degree or extent of organization of the health sector focused on the acceptable balance of 'the public and private' or 'the role of the state.' An interpretation of that balance had been set in the late nineteenth and early to mid-twentieth centuries. Within the health sector, the blueprint which lay at the heart of this interpretation was that of professional governance, or self-regulation backed by state protection of the professional privileges and obligations concomitant to that delegated governance. This, then, could be expected to play a central role in the inevitable power struggles stimulated by the new policy process.

Also, like other organizations of the nineteenth and twentieth centuries, the health sector embodied characteristics which were marked by rationalist, specialized, hierarchical modes of organization. Disputes related to the rationalism and specialization of health care took the form predominantly of questions about the constitution and rigour of the knowledge or expertise required for health practices. The bureaucratic blueprint also carried with it a hierarchy of practitioners which either embodied the new rationality, sat as alternative to it, or attempted an eclecticism which drew from both. This, in turn, embedded positions of authority and connection among the actors engaged in the health sector. Chapters 6 and 7 will look at the struggles of the health provider groups to maximize their benefits and minimize their burdens under the redefinition of health care's blueprints of governance and rationality, as well as the related positions of authority and connection among them and between them and the state and the public.

Practitioner Stories

As the practitioner groups entered the policy review process of the 1980s, they each carried with them their own set of interpretations of their role or purpose in health care per se; their role and purpose in the organized health sector; and their relationships (in actuality and preference) with other practitioners of the sector, the state, and their patients or clients. With the opening of the institutionalized sector to restructuring, each practitioner group was given the opportunity to present these interpretations to the policy makers. Through their written and oral communications they did so. This chapter presents those interpretations as they were presented with regard to the key subject of rationality or expertise. It also documents the successes and failures of the newly regulated practitioners in embedding their preferred interpretations into the new legislation of the 1990s. As a whole, it also, of course, represents my interpretation of their interpretations, since I am present as political-story teller.

'We Fight and Fight for a Word on a Page'[1]

As we saw in the historical development of the health practitioners of Ontario and North America, the market had produced a variety of health practitioners of whom, (a) some were given full state protection which translated into a virtual monopoly of their self-defined service-territory; (b) a few were given reluctant state protection for their merchant monopolies provided there was a requisite degree of scientific expertise needed to produce and assess that merchandise; (c) some were given limited state protection from the attempts of the elite practitioners to put them out of business; (d) some had been placed under the direction of either the medical or dental practitioners; and (e) some had been left to fend for themselves in a hostile climate. The 1980s' review of the health professions legislation signalled the willingness of the state to disrupt the old patterns. New blueprints began to emerge – with the potential to shift the positions of the health providers and redefine old privileges and obligations, perhaps, even the nature of health care expertise itself.

One favoured blueprint which had originated in the Ministry of Health[2] for restructuring the professional legislation during the 1980s would exchange the various categories of legislation for an omnibus act which would lay out terms and conditions for all regulated health practitioners.[3] Thus, with the professionals 'bound by almost identical legal and procedural provisions,' the public would have the 'same rights and remedies in relation to them all.'[4] Separate profession-specific, or clustered profession-specific, acts were recommended for each profession to accompany this omnibus act. The content of the scope of practice or area of expected practice for each professional group would be laid out in a new scope-of-practice model. First was the scope-of-practice statement which would describe, but not license, the profession's scope of practice by providing information about 'what the profession does, the methods it uses, and the purpose for which it does [these things].'[5] Along with protecting the public by the provision of clear, useful information, this description would help prevent the 'undesirable effects' of professional 'monopoly' in that the professionals themselves would no longer hold exclusive licensure over their practice territory.[6] Second was the innovative idea of licensing, not the health professionals themselves as had previously been the case, but rather, particular procedures or acts deemed harmful. These licensed acts, later referred to as controlled acts and authorized acts, could then be legally performed only by qualified health professionals specifically authorized to perform them by their own professional statute. In this way a kind of balance would be struck between the old monopoly of practice of the elite professionals and the more flexible and cost-efficient utilization of alternative providers, or between protecting the public and the 'public's ... freedom to choose.'[7] Third was the harm clause, also referred to as the basket clause, safety-net clause, or Section 27.04. This clause would make it 'an offence to treat, offer to treat, or advise in respect to any human health condition in circumstances in which the treatment, offer of treatment, or advice [or any omission of them] might result in harm.'[8] Professionals acting within their legislatively defined scope of practice were not to be subject to this limitation; it was meant as an added guard against the 'unqualified, incompetent and unfit,' or 'quackery.'[9]

Practitioner Expertise

The potential opening of the hierarchical positions of health professionalism which was brought on by the policy review of the early 1980s was, of course, accompanied by intense debate over the nature of professional or non-professional functions. The licensed procedures allotted any practitioner group would depend heavily on that group's claim to expertise. Practitioners from the whole body, merchant–service specialist, technique specialist, technology specialist, and assistant health practice categories[10] advanced arguments regarding their scope and breadth of health care expertise and the appropriate recognition they believed this ought to garner.

The fight over the details of both the licensed or controlled acts and the scope-of-practice statements was long and hard. Practitioner groups fought back and forth on detail after detail of the wording of both the scope statements and the controlled acts. No other health policy designers in Canada had attempted the daunting task of sifting through the minutely detailed claims by the various groups regarding their areas of expertise – a task which continued relentlessly on through the Health Professions Legislation Review process, the Ministry of Health Professional Relations Branch work on the legislation, (to a much lesser extent) the committee stage of the legislative process, and even beyond the royal assent and proclamation of the legislation itself with the development of regulations to the legislation and the avenue for further change opened by the setting up of the ongoing Health Professions Regulatory Advisory Council as well as the enhanced ministerial input mandated by the new legislation. It was a tedious and difficult process, but the HRLP team took a no-nonsense approach from the start. Time and again they demanded clarification and proof of any and all claims made by the practitioners about either their own members or other practitioners. No loose rhetoric was tolerated. For example, led by the medical and dental professions, the professionals regulated by the 1974 Health Disciplines Act (medicine, dentistry, pharmacy, optometry, and nursing) collectively argued against restructuring the regulatory model, primarily by self-asserting claims, the gist of which were: we have had these privileges for a long time; we have served the public of Ontario well; so, in the interest of public benefit we ought to keep those privileges.[11] But, to its credit, the review team scrutinized all such 'We are good because we say we are good' assertions.[12] It continued to defend the proposed restructuring of the licensing design. In the end, despite the opposition of the most powerful interest groups in the sector, the review's major recommendations did end up in the Regulated Health Professions Act of 1991.[13] Each regulated profession is now guided by its own scope-of-practice statement (see Appendix 8), and all regulated practitioners are restricted by a set of controlled or authorized acts specific to the profession to which she or he belongs (see Appendix 9, plus the individual professional acts). Given the history of contention over these boundaries of practice, this alone constituted a major accomplishment.

In the way of power politics, however, concessions had to be made along the way. The elite opposition to the new design of the regulatory legislation played a strong role in the review's relenting to the pressure to design a harm or basket clause to limit unqualified practice. The clause was very controversial. Because of its perceived potential to unduly restrict unregulated practitioners, it resulted in an intense lobby effort, and successive ministers disagreed on what to do about it. In the end a so-called basket clause was put in, but it had been modified such that only 'serious physical harm,' rather than any harm (including less serious physical harm or even mental harm), was subject to violation of the act.[14]

The expertise issue which caused the greatest contention and on which considerable energy was spent towards resolution, was the question of whether or not specific professions would be allowed to refer to their practice as involving the diagnosis of diseases and disorders. Under the old legislation, medical physicians and dentists were the only practitioners allowed to diagnose. The maintenance of this monopoly of practice would have inhibited opening the system to other care providers, many of whom claimed they too could communicate a diagnosis to the patient.[15] The crux of the battle was the use of the diagnosis function as a gatekeeping mechanism. Those who could diagnose would be those professionals who would see a patient first and then, only if that professional deemed it necessary, refer her or him on to a particular specialist. Needless to say, all practitioner groups fighting for independence of practice wanted to be allowed to diagnose, and both practitioner groups previously privileged with the diagnostic scope of practice – medicine and dentistry – wanted to keep that privilege limited to themselves.[16]

Interestingly enough, the elite medical and dental 'scientists' could produce no proof of their long-standing assertion of their singular success in undifferentiated diagnosis. In fact, there was evidence to suggest otherwise. Practitioners, both within the medical profession and outside it, who focus on particular parts of the body, appear to be capable of recognizing the symptoms they are specifically trained to treat, as well as referring patients on to other practitioners for those symptoms falling outside their range of expertise.[17] Chiropractors, for example, have a higher success rate than general or family medical practitioners at recognizing and treating specific back and neck problems;[18] here it is the all-round educated medical practitioners who have traditionally failed to refer their patients on to the most appropriate specialized care providers, rather than the other way around.[19] The denturists make a point worth investigating; they claim a practitioner does not need to diagnose in order to refer, she or he need only be able to recognize abnormalities. If this is true, it argues against the necessary linkage of the diagnostic function with the gatekeeper role – at least in some cases. Having said this, however, there remains the problem which the medical profession rightly points to, of the whole body practitioners such as the naturopaths whose diagnostic claims are often based on unverifiable physiological hypotheses. Ought they be allowed to communicate a diagnosis based on these hypotheses if their patients are taking these diagnoses as truth – preventing them in some cases from obtaining treatments based on verifiable scientific treatments? Today's family physicians also claim that the large number of uncoordinated health practitioners now available to the patient leads to fragmentation of care because there is no knowledgeable gatekeeper keeping an eye on the bigger picture.[20]

In the 1991 RHPA only five provider groups were allowed the privilege of diagnosis: medicine, dentistry, optometry, chiropractic, and psychology.[21] But the HPLR team, in what appeared to be a rather clever effort to allow the outsiders in while still appeasing the more powerful groups, exchanged the word 'diagnosis' for 'assessment'[22] for the RHPA groups which did not win diagnosis. This word would then serve the same general purpose as had diagnosis. The winners in this word-play, predominantly non-elite practitioners, however, did not trust the intentions of the policy designers and makers who wished to utilize assessment in the draft legislation. Their distrust was encouraged by their legal counsel, and so they continued their fight for diagnosis.[23] They knew there was power in the word 'diagnosis' and the new word 'assessment' was, as yet, untested. They lost this fight, however. For the time being, they have had to settle for assessment and hope it will really come to mean diagnosis.

Whole Body Practitioners

Medicine

We have seen how the state-protected blueprint for progress via scientific and technological development favoured the use of so called scientific medicine over empirically based health care; heroic medicine over low intervention health care; complex specialized care provision over a more general holistic approach; escalating pharmaceutical and surgical treatment regimes over milder, or so-called natural treatments; and the relatively unquestioned utilization of technological diagnostic and treatment measures over a more careful approach to the use of medical technology. The health care blueprint for progress thus embedded the dominance of the medical profession, as well as its pharmaceutical, surgical, and technological approaches to care. This blueprint had provided the basis for medicine's hegemony in the health care sector as well as the grounds for the marginalization or exclusion of other practitioners.

With the opening of the question of professional expertise brought on by the 1983 review, the medical profession (particularly the GPs) had to fight to protect its sphere of expertise if it was to protect its practice turf from the invasion of competitive practitioners and hold fast to its own commitment to the superiority of the medical sciences. State sanction of its monopoly rights had been heavily premised on that expertise. The ideational slant of the Health Professions Legislation Review, openly professing itself as 'pro-competitive and pro-freedom of [consumer] choice,' threatened to be more demanding of the medical profession in its proof of the validity of that hegemony than any other external scrutiny had been.[24] Furthermore, the governments to whom that report would be handed had a stronger reason to diminish that hegemony than any other state actors had in the history of Canadian health regulatory policy. Health care had become a costly and conflict-ridden business for the state. If the cost-containment arguments of the resource managers and the cheaper health providers were being listened to by the distributors of the public purse, then medical professionals (particularly the GPs) were facing stronger competition than they had for some time.

There were other signals of changing attitudes that threatened the hegemony of the medical profession (and dental profession in its particular sphere). Health care's institutionalized hierarchies which had been out of step with the egalitarian rhetoric of the McRuer, Committee on the Healing Arts, and Professional Organizations Committee reports, but which had survived these earlier assessments, were once again being battered by talk of egalitarianism, anti-monopoly, and broad-based participation.[25] Signals coming out of the Ministry of Health were indicating a shift in attitude. In 1982 and 1983, just as the HPLR process was beginning, Health Minister Grossman, was making references to the medical profession's need to compromise and end the old rivalries within health care, as well as engage in 'intense dialogue' with the public[26] – all unfamiliar words for the reigning medical and dental directors of their particular health spheres.

The talk about 'getting along' sent a signal to the dominant groups that they were going to have to be less antagonistic to their new health provider neighbours, while at the same time signalling to the grab-bag of previously marginalized or excluded providers that their day may have come. The new technique and technology specialists, in particular, had been gaining ground for some time, and they had the important argument of cost containment on their side since few of them earned incomes comparable to the elite practitioners. Although the HPLR designers of the new regulatory legislation were adamant in their assertions that this process was not being directed by the cost-control talk growing louder and louder each day in the Ministry of Health, the mandate of the review had included scrutiny of the efficient use of resources.[27] The broader climate was, if not very visibly, nevertheless inevitably, present in the gaze of the upper-level ministry personnel who kept an eye on the HPLR process. For the elite practitioner groups, who themselves were certainly aware of this major concern,[28] cost control meant lost control.

The move to open up the licensing monopolies of the elite professions represented a threat to the hegemony of the medical definition of rational health care in that it would allow any and all practitioners to present their case for whatever procedures they wished to perform. As one member of the review put it, 'The new scope-of-practice model ... [was] more egalitarian.'[29] Not surprisingly, the elite professionals who had long monopolized their preferred scopes of practice were not happy with this proposal, while the non-elite practitioners who had long wanted to break up that monopoly were. Both medicine's governing body (the College of Physicians and Surgeons of Ontario) and its professional association (the Ontario Medical Association) protested the new design proposed for the legislation. They wished to retain the old licensing system – of licensed professionals rather than licensed procedures. They argued that the definitions of these controlled acts were bound to stir up controversy and would leave the practice of medicine open to non-medical practitioners – which, of course, was true, but which was also fully expected by those in charge of the policy process. Voicing concerns for the quality of health, the medical profession continued to fight (with others) against the new legislative design.[30]

Other Whole Body Practitioners: Naturopaths, Osteopaths, and Homeopaths[31]

Although medicine had been able to dominate modern health care, it had not been able to eliminate alternative health providers, some of whom also saw themselves as whole body, primary contact practitioners. As they entered the HPLR/RHPA policy process, the naturopaths, or drugless therapists as they were inaccurately called in previous Ontario legislation, still saw themselves as alternative scientists to the medical profession. In their submissions to the review, both the naturopaths' governing board and their association argued that naturopathy constitutes an alternative form of medicine. They referred to themselves as 'doctors' and 'physicians' engaged in 'medical care.' They argued for use of those titles, as well as for 'primary contact' (with patients) and 'diagnosis' (without mandatory 'referral'), as well as public insurance

(OHIP) coverage, hospital privileges, access to clinic laboratory tests, legal status as medical practitioners (that is, medical signature on legal documents), and the right to engage in 'the full range of obstetrics and gynaecology.'[32]

This amazing 'wish list' of the naturopaths stems, I assume, from their long history of considering themselves (like the osteopaths, eclectics, homeopaths, and to some extent the chiropractors) as equally valid alternatives to the conventional medical profession. What is amazing is not that they might have held on to such a hope for so many years, but rather that they might think to convince the HPLR team and the ministry officials of this claim. It had never served to impress officials in the past,[33] and the likelihood of it doing so during this process was very low. They claimed, for example, that their students were trained in the basic sciences, but when questioned about the credentials of their practitioners, they had to admit not one practising naturopath had the basic science training to which they had alluded in their early submissions.[34] This in itself would not necessarily have excluded the naturopaths from the final list of regulated professional groups – others were given the chance to upgrade their standards prior to admission to the new act – but the naturopaths were ultimately unable to convince the policy designers that their system of health care rested on any discernible body of knowledge.[35] Nor was their case helped by the perception that their governing body was in disarray and had not disciplined a single member of the profession in sixty years.

In April 1986 Health Minister Murray Elston announced that naturopathy would be deregulated because it was 'based on a philosophy of natural healing that makes it extremely difficult to define standards of practice.'[36] The naturopaths then turned, as they had in the past, to the political realm, and by September of 1987 they had elicited a statement from Premier David Peterson indicating that he would take a second look at his government's intentions to deregulate naturopathy.[37] They also launched a letter-writing campaign from their patients. This got the attention of the minister's office – as similar campaigns had in the past. By the time of the introduction of the bills to the House in June 1990, Liberal Minister Elinor Caplan announced that there would be further debate over the issue of naturopathy regulation, to be carried out by the interim Health Professions Regulatory Advisory Council – with naturopathy's regulation under the Drugless Practitioners Act to continue in the meantime.

Throughout this debate officials replied to the naturopaths' and their patients' concerns that the occupation of naturopathy would not be destroyed by its failed bid for inclusion in the new health professions legislation, and that naturopaths would still be able to work as unregulated practitioners, much the same as would other unregulated practitioners, such as acupuncturists, shiatsu therapists, marriage and family therapists, social workers, psychoanalysts, and so on. The catch, however, was that these same officials could make little or no guarantee of the range of services these unregulated practitioners would be allowed to provide. The new legislation would regulate particular health care procedures and any practitioner group which was not granted the controlled acts granted to another profession would be unable to make use of these procedures in its practice.[38] According to the president of the Ontario Naturopathic Association, eight of the thirteen controlled acts granted to the RHPA professionals 'apply in some form to the practice of naturopathy ... and are required for us in order to be trained sufficiently to be responsible naturopathic practitioners.'[39] Despite all the disclaimers from the minister's office, the new legislation would prohibit non-regulated practitioners from performing some, or perhaps many, of their previous functions.[40] This was as clear to the naturopaths as it was to other health practitioners who did not make it into the new legislation, so, many of them continued to fight to get in. At one point, in what seemed to be a political decision, it appeared that the naturopaths would be given inclusion in the RHPA by the New Democratic government, but the government was defeated in an election before any such change was made.[41] The next governing party, the Conservatives, asked the Health Professions Regulatory Advisory Council for a report on this issue and public consultation meetings were held in 1995.[42] However, by mid-1999 neither the ensuing HPRAC report to the minister nor the government's decision on the issue had been made public. Their association, the Ontario Association of Naturopathic Doctors (which continues to use the RHPA protected title 'doctor,' although it does not have the authority to do so) planned to 'file an access to information request for the [HPRAC] report' as well as start up another letter-writing campaign (by the practitioners and their patients/clients) to the minister and members of parliament, and lobby the provincial Liberal government to get the issue included in their next election campaign.[43] They have been told that the naturopathic report from HPRAC may be sent back to HPRAC for 'possible further review of some aspects of the proposal to regulate naturopaths under the RHPA.'[44] The naturopaths have found the delays frustrating. They have put considerable effort into this process despite limited resources (their lawyer is volunteering the time), and they think the two-year span between the submission of the HPRAC report and any word back to them, unnecessarily long.[45] For their part, the government has pointed out 'the question of the regulation of naturopathy with its broad scope of practice is very complex, and its implications are potentially far reaching.'[46] This is quite true; we have seen how important the issue of primary contact (without referral) has been to the history of turf wars among the practitioners. Any ministry officials versed in the health sector would be wary of this step and all it would

Expertise Turf Wars 91

entail and imply – particularly at a time of institutional and community restructuring within the sector as a whole.

Like the naturopaths, the other whole body practitioners, the osteopaths and homeopaths, entered the 1980s' policy process weakly positioned. The osteopaths reported only thirty-two aging members practising in Ontario in the early 1980s. They had failed either to carve out a specific field of practice beyond that of the medical profession or, alternatively, to join them as another medical specialty.[47] While their counterparts in the United States predominantly did the latter,[48] Ontario osteopaths continued to argue that they constituted the best of both medical and chiropractic-like expertise: 'By combining our unique osteopathic principles and practices with traditional diagnostic and therapeutic procedures such as drugs and surgery, we are trained to practise a comprehensive and balanced system of health care.'[49] As we have seen, however, eclecticism does not seem to pay off in the business of health care. Although the osteopaths were originally included in the medicine act of 1991,[50] the medical profession argued against this inclusion,[51] and somewhere on the road to proclamation the osteopaths were moved back to the old system of regulation by the Board of Directors of Osteopathy under the authority of the Drugless Practitioners Act.[52]

Today, in Ontario, after having been limited in their functions by the small scope of practice allowed them under the Drugless Practitioners Act, those practitioners trained only in (American) osteopathy specialize in manipulative and adjustment functions. A Canadian training centre for osteopathy, the Canadian College of Osteopathy, started in 1992 by a European-trained osteopath from France, Philippe Druelle, trains practitioners of other disciplines, such as physiotherapists, occupational therapists, nurses, or medical doctors, in a five-year (part-time) program for osteopathic manual therapy.[53] A working group including students and graduates of the CCO set up a 'Transitional Council for the College of Osteopathic Manual Practitioners of Ontario' in 1998–9 to educate the public on what they do and to prepare to apply for inclusion in the RHPA. One member (who is also a trained medical doctor) suggests that while the graduates of the CCO are well trained in manual knowledge, 'They need to have more knowledge in disease processes in order to recognize medical problems that require assistance and treatment by a physician.'[54] She also comments, 'The public needs to know the difference between an osteopathic manual practitioner [trained in a centre such as the CCO] and the short [weekend] program ... [they] need to know the difference between who can play a little tune on the piano and who is a concert pianist.'[55] Compared with the strength and organization of osteopathy at the time of the HPLR, there appears to be a revival of this practitioner group. It will be interesting to see what success these contemporary eclectics will have in their attempt to combine the two old factions of health care.

Homeopathy has not fared well in Ontario, although it is commonly practised in the United States and Britain, as well as other parts of the world. Despite its inclusion in the early legislation of the 1800s, by the time of the report of the Committee on the Healing Arts, in 1970, there were only six aging homeopathic physicians practising in Ontario. There had been no additions to their numbers in the previous decade.[56] The homeopaths argued during the review for professional status in the new regulatory legislation, but they failed to make even the short-list of thirty-nine. They continue to argue their suitability for inclusion, but the health minister has, as yet, not initiated a review of their case to the advisory council (HPRAC).

Homeopaths may be experiencing a small revival in Ontario. They have set up a new association, the Ontario Homeopathic Association,[57] and have started educational courses in Toronto leading to what they refer to as 'certification of homeopathic practitioner.' Their president estimates the numbers in Ontario to now be 'a couple of thousand,' of whom, 'a couple of dozen are qualified homeopaths' who have certification from other countries which the Ontario association considers acceptable.[58] There also appears to be a number of so-called alternative practitioners, for example, naturopaths, kinesiologists, and Chinese medicine practitioners, who use homeopathic treatments.

It is impossible to say to what extent these alternative practitioners might prosper – especially as whole body practitioners. They are still the empirics going up against the scientists. So far they have had little success in entering the established system of health professionalism. Despite their enthusiasm to join that system,[59] they are being forced to act as limited specialists practising outside the official circle of health care professionals. The future success of these alternative whole body practitioners is anyone's guess, but it is more than likely that any success on their part will be closely linked to the overall success of (and public pressure for) the new form of 'complementary health care' (to which I shall return).

The Merchant–Service Specialists

The merchant–service specialists entered Ontario's 1980s' policy review with the tensions associated with the double identity we saw earlier, that is, based on both their merchant and their service roles. Just what it means to be a 'professional merchant group' has never been very clear. Some (for example, dentists, optometrists, and audiologists) are able to sell both their services and their merchandise, while others (for example, pharmacists and denturists)

Expertise Turf Wars 93

have tended to roll their service fees into the price of the merchandise they are providing. All fought during the 1980s' policy review to retain as much control as possible over both aspects of their work.

Pharmacy

Pharmacists have long fought the battles of a group closely associated with trade. Because they do not charge independently for any health care service, they tend to protect their merchant function, while at the same time trying to expand its scope. In addition, we now see the pharmacists attempting to further safeguard themselves by promoting the services that their customers receive with the purchase of pharmaceutical goods. The emphasis of the pharmacy profession during the 1940s and 1950s was 'to improve pharmacy by improving education,'[60] but today we see a more political organization which is using the public media to create a new image for the pharmacist. This image is one of a knowledgeable and reliable professional, a pharmaceutical expert who has an independent role to play in the health care system. Whether or not this attempt to raise the legitimacy of the profession can overcome the diminution of the pharmacist's status to that of a physician's 'pill counter' remains to be seen.

In their HPLR submissions, the pharmacists' governing body (Ontario College of Pharmacists) and their provincial association (Ontario Pharmacists Association) argued to retain and expand both their merchant and service functions in several ways. They attempted to expand their present virtual monopoly[61] over the custody, compounding, and dispensing of drugs, by arguing for a legal requirement that all hospitals place these functions under the 'direction' of a licensed pharmacist.[62] The association used an anti-monopoly / fair trade argument here, suggesting that the hospitals had an unfair competitive advantage.[63] This was, however, more than an economic matter for the pharmacists. It was also a matter of professional expertise. If hospital pharmacies do not need professional pharmacists to operate successfully, why then do other pharmacies need them? Obviously this has never been a very comfortable situation for the pharmacists. In the end, they failed to gain ground on this dispute. Ontario pharmacy personnel 'referring to themselves as pharmacists' must be RHPA-regulated pharmacists, that is, accredited by the pharmacists' college under title protection, but hospital pharmacies are exempt from this regulation.[64]

Another issue of importance to the profession was that of the pharmacists' corporate ownership of pharmacies. Previous legislation[65] had required that the majority of owners of a pharmacy corporation be pharmacists. While the

Committee of the Healing Arts had sat on the fence for this one, HPLR had argued that this requirement unnecessarily restricted free trade and encouraged a monopoly of ownership of pharmacies. It recommended that the majority of the corporation's directors be pharmacists.[66] The Ontario College of Pharmacists opposed the removal of the original requirement arguing it would create pressure on pharmacists to favour business decisions over professional decisions, as well as provide opportunities for illegal drug trafficking and money laundering. The issue was dealt with in the Drug and Pharmacies Regulation Act which requires that pharmacists hold both a majority of directorships and a majority of (each class of) shares of a pharmacy.[67] The pharmacists lost some control here.

The pharmacists moved to retain their merchant territory in other ways as well. They were concerned to maintain their practices of fitting and selling prosthetic and orthotic devices (over the objections of the Ontario Association of Prosthetists and Orthotists), fitting and dispensing hearing aids, performing diagnostic tests, such as the pregnancy test, and selling of personal health monitoring devices, such as blood glucose monitors.[68] Interestingly enough, pharmacists were allowed to continue these practices even though they fell under other practitioners' or merchants' areas of greater specialty, and despite all the official talk about demonstrable knowledge in relation to a group's scope of practice.[69]

Perhaps the most interesting of the pharmacy group's attempts to maintain and expand its expertise territory is related to its attempt to carve out a 'consultant role ... involving an increased emphasis on patient counselling.'[70] One sees signs of this new role in advertisements and fact-sheets from the large drugstore and pharmaceutical companies,[71] but whether or not the public will increase their reliance on this service remains uncertain. In 1983 pharmacists were commenting on what they perceived as the unenthusiastic attitude of the patient towards this consultant role, but by the late 1990s advertising dollars continued to be spent and the OCPh had developed standards of practice related to the documentation of this pharmacist/patient dialogue.[72] Problems related to this counselling function have arisen regarding professional liability, education overkill, and friction with individual medical practitioners.[73] The medical governing body (CPSO) has come out in support of the pharmacists on this issue, but where individual opposition has occurred the pharmacists' college responds, interestingly, that their new scope-of-practice statement includes this mandate.[74]

Another aspect of the consultation role for the pharmacists which might prove of importance in the future is providing advice to funding agencies on the cost–benefit ratio of drug utilization. As drug utilization rates and prices rise, there is increasing pressure from both public and private payers to examine the possible overuse of pharmaceuticals. Both the pharmacists' governing college and professional association became involved in such projects in the 1990s.[75] If the pharmacists do succeed in enhancing their consultation role with both their clients and third-party payers, they will have managed to carve out a stronger service role with which they might maintain their professional status.

Several of the issues raised during the review with regard to the elevation of the pharmacists' public image as health experts or consultants were related to the expansion of the pharmacists' turf into that of the other practitioners and dispensers of medicines. The HPLR's proposed scope of practice and controlled acts for the pharmacists had limited their functions 'upon the order [or prescription] of a practitioner legally qualified to prescribe drugs.'[76] but the pharmacists succeeded in having this phrase deleted from both their scope statement and their controlled act limitation.[77] This victory was relatively minor in one sense, since the pharmacist is still not free to *prescribe* pharmaceuticals, but it did signal greater recognition of the pharmacists' expertise in that it can be interpreted as recognizing their role in making professional judgment calls about their clients' medication regimes.[78] The necessity for such a check implies, of course, that physicians are doing a less than competent job of either or both prescribing medications and communicating with their patients about their prescriptions – otherwise there would be no need for the pharmacist's check on the 'judicious use of medication.'[79]

Pharmacists also fought for more control over non-prescription drugs. They argued against the sale of non-prescription patent medicines, such as cold and flu products, in grocery stores or corner stores, and they were successful in averting this entrepreneurial invasion.[80] They also requested designation of a distinguishable area of the pharmacy for visual control of non-prescription drugs by the pharmacists. They argued that this would encourage the public to seek professional advice from the pharmacists in the adjacent dispensary. This issue remained not settled by mid-1999 because of pending legislative changes to classifications and controls over food and drugs, but the pharmacists were still arguing at this time that these products ought 'to be within ten metres of the dispensary.'[81]

Pharmacists argued for a new classification of 'Schedule C products,' such as anti-fungal drugs, which would not require prescription but which would require that they be sold only by a pharmacist (or intern or registered pharmacy student under the supervision of a pharmacist). There have been some interesting developments along this line in the United States. For example, legislation was passed in Florida in 1985 allowing pharmacists there to prescribe certain kinds of medicine. A three-way classification of drugs was set up: prescription medicines, over-the-counter products, and a new classification of drugs for which pharmacists were given the authority to write prescriptions directly to the public, for example, 'anti-histamines, decongestants, lice medication, mild antibiotics, and fluoride treatments.'[82] The legislation had been fiercely resisted by the American medical profession but they failed to stop it, although they had succeeded in doing so in other states which had considered adopting similar legislation.[83] American pharmacists considered this an important victory. A professor of pharmacy at the University of Florida commented, 'This is the first piece of legislation to grant greater independence and authority to pharmacists to prescribe medicine. Other health professionals said it couldn't be done; physicians would never let us get away with it. Pharmacists look at this as a professional and moral victory.'[84]

Ontario did develop a list, called Schedule C, of drugs which must only be sold in a pharmacy. It also decided that the sale of a drug listed in Schedule C must be made by the pharmacist, pharmacy intern, or pharmacy student under supervision by a pharmacist although no prescription is required.'[85] Pending legislation, according to the Ontario College of Pharmacists, will (loosely) only require that 'if the product requires supervision, it will be on a Schedule Two (the new name for Schedule C) which means it will be kept behind the pharmacy ... If the products are up front, it is up to the patient to ask the pharmacist, or for the pharmacist to be pro-active and ... approach them.'[86]

During the HPLR policy process, the Ontario Pharmacists Association also asked for a small extension of the pharmacist's privileges which, while minor in nature, had major symbolic weight. They asked that a regulation be written 'permitting the pharmacist to provide a limited quantity of certain prescribed drugs to a patient with whom the pharmacist maintains a patient-medication profile until he or she is able to obtain further authority from a prescriber.'[87] This was hardly a radical request, given the pharmacists' expertise with drugs and the fact that the legislation controlling pharmacy already refers to the 'professional judgement' of the pharmacist, but it was not included in the new Pharmacy Act.[88] It does symbolize a willingness by the Ontario pharmacists, however, to challenge the medical control of drug prescriptions – if only at the margins. These prescriptions have long been the key to much of medicine's domination of health care in general, but particularly with regard to the limiting of the pharmacist's role.

Even if Ontario pharmacists do manage to increase their professional service functions, their primary role is still that of the merchant, which in itself may cause trouble for them. The market forces surrounding them may prove to be more dangerous than the administrative and political officials. In their submissions to the HPLR, pharmacists made frequent reference to their place in the community, but this romantic picture may represent reality less and less. Increasingly, pharmacists have moved away from, or been pushed from, the role of small community merchant to that of one actor among many in the large corporations which are coming to dominate the pharmacy market. As one official put it, 'In behind the Ontario Pharmacy Association, is Shoppers Drug Mart.'[89] Not only will corporate managers infringe on professional autonomy, as the American medical profession has increasingly come to realize,[90] but they also like to direct all market decisions. This may mean pharmacists will come to have diminished autonomy, or worse still, be circumvented. The pharmacists' organizations have also fought the development of the mail order pharmacy in Canada.[91] In the competition war between the large drugstores and the mail order companies, one of the bargaining chips appears to be the pharmacist's dispensing fee.[92] The pharmacists, like all small merchants, will find it hard to compete among the 'big guys,'[93] but worse still, there is now a move to by-pass the pharmacist altogether by using medical doctors; the physicians in Ontario, and many other jurisdictions, can legally dispense drugs to their patients, although they do not often do so.[94]

Overall, the dual nature of the pharmacy profession has provided for an interesting story. As a merchant group, the pharmacists did well to win professional status. I would argue, however, that they have not done very well as a professional group. The key indicator for professional status is clinical or service autonomy,[95] that is, control over the expertise of one's field, and the pharmacists have never had this. From the start, they were placed under the virtual control of the medical profession's power of drug prescription. Without the authorization of another profession, pharmacists could not even provide services to the public based on their knowledge of pharmaceuticals, much less their merchandise of compounds of those pharmaceuticals. Their professional status has largely been symbolic in nature – there simply because the existing legislation said it was. This symbolic appearance has taken them a long way,[96] but appearances can only go so far: policy decision makers are becoming increasingly uncomfortable with the professional–profit link.[97] The more the government emphasizes the handing over of its governing role to professional agents, the more it starts to sound wrong to have professional groups whose main purpose is the selling of health care products for profit. If the pharmacists can present themselves as health service providers in the drug consulting role, or even win a bit of movement into the prescription domain of the medical profession, they may succeed in making the ministry officials and politicians a little more comfortable.

There is also some indication in the late 1990s that the pharmacists can enhance their consultative role through their relationship with the government itself. Recent initiatives such as a joint government–professional committee set up to investigate, among other things, 'the appropriate use of prescription drugs and medications' throughout the health care sector point to a new partnership between the government and pharmacists. As the Ontario Pharmacy Association sees it, 'The initiatives that will come from this partnership will look to save millions of dollars and improve the health and quality of ... [the] people of Ontario.'[98] There would, of course, also be some interesting developments if the recently proposed national, publicly funded 'pharmacare' program[99] was to come to fruition.

Dentistry

Historically, dentists started out as providers of a health service, but today's dentists profit both from the sale of their services and from the sale of merchandise related to their area of expertise (dentures and other dental appliances). This latter development places the dentists in conflict with the other entrepreneurs in dental care, particularly the denturists. The service function of dentists has also been eroded by their own preventive programs as well as by other practitioners who have moved in as their service assistants, particularly the dental hygienists. Unlike that of the medical profession, dentistry's hegemony of expertise has been seriously threatened. Even though they positioned themselves at a greater distance from the state than medicine, mainly by avoiding state funding of their services, they have slowly been losing control over their work. The same market spirit which had led them to fight any potential universal 'denticare' program has crept up behind them; other entrepreneurs have been moving into their practice territory. Dentists entered the HPLR/RHPA policy process angry because their traditional position of strength as members of an established elite professional group was eroding.

Aside from the issue of control over the governance of the profession (discussed later) the main issues of concern for the dentists during the HPLR were related to their diminishing hegemony of service expertise (discussed in the dental hygienist, technologist, and assistant sections below) and their battle to control the merchant portion of the business of dental care. However, arguing for a monopoly of merchant expertise had never proven very successful, as we saw in the case of pharmacy. Combining elements of both merchant and service types of expertise, the dentists argued that as the only dental care providers trained in the comprehensive diagnostic skills necessary for first contact with the patient, they ought to be the only entry point for dental patients, thus, placing all other dental care workers either in the employ of dentists, or able

Expertise Turf Wars   99

only to sell their products directly to dentists – a recommendation which would require the denturists to relinquish their legislatively sanctioned independence.[100]

The fight between the dentists and the denturists[101] is notorious for its animosity. During the review both accused each other of gross entrepreneurial interest, which of course is not far from the truth. The problem is not so much entrepreneurial greed, since our contemporary society appears to admire this characteristic, but more that both groups want the profits from the same market. Having lost the fight with the denturists for the provision of full dentures to the public, dentists had been trying to hold on to at least part of the market by retaining control over the provision of partial dental appliances. At the same time, the denturists had for some time been illegally producing and selling partial dentures. The dentists' college pointed out that this continuing work with partial dentures was a good indication of what they considered the less than excellent record of the denturists' governing board. The denturists' governing body, the Governing Board of Denture Therapists, disputed the accusation altogether.[102]

The denturists' strongest counter-arguments to the broad range of claims made by dentists were aimed at the 'first contact / diagnosis' function, which dentists claim to be necessarily held by dentists, and dentist only, for reasons of safety. The Denturist Association of Canada pointed out that there were no data to support the dentists' claim that good dental care requires that the gate-keepers of the system be dentists.[103] The Ontario governing board argued that denturists do not need to diagnose, they only need to 'recognize oral abnormalities' in order to refer their clients for treatment by a dentist, and for this they are well trained.[104] Likewise the Denturist Association of Ontario, making use of a 1981 report headed by Bernard Dickens, which had come out in their favour,[105] reminded the review team that, 'based on the evidence before him ... Dickens worked from the entirely reasonable assumption that given adequate training, denture therapists [or denturists] would be able to distinguish between a healthy and an unhealthy mouth.'[106] Lastly, the denturists' federal association pointed to evidence suggesting that dental consumers across Canada appear to be satisfied with the products obtained from their denturists.[107]

In the end, the denturists not only fended off the attempt of the dentists to deprive them of their legal standing as autonomous practitioners providing full dentures, but they also won the 'partial [dentures] fight.'[108] It must have been a very sweet victory.[109] It was certainly a politically astute campaign. The denturists used all the right words in their submissions – the governing body's second submission in June 1984 is a particularly good example of their political cunning. Here they say such things as,

> It is only when the Royal College of Dental Surgeons demonstrates its aim *to eradicate or to dominate* that the Governing Board of Denture Therapists disagrees. Surely there is room for the *particular expertise* of both groups of practitioners [dentists and denturists]. Given the *freedom to choose*, the patient is best assured of a prosthesis which is personally fabricated and fitted and at a price *which is affordable.* He *may choose* to go to the dentist and to pay more or he *may choose* the specialized personal contact with the Denture Therapist [denturist] who is able to offer a prothesis at least as good as that provided by the dentist at the *lower cost. Choice* is the key to the broader issue *if the public is truly to be served*.[110]

Aside from the sexist language, this quote shows a high degree of awareness of the concerns of the policy formulators. Other astute words and phrases were used: 'the *subservience* of all other dental health workers ... [in] the dentists' ... [proposed] *monopolistic* arrangement'; 'the desire of the dentists ... to be *beyond the scrutiny and control* ... of the public'; and 'the dental profession's ... position ... runs counter to the *tide of liberalization* which is running in our society today.'[111] (For the correspondence of this language with that of the HPLR Report, see Appendix 3.)

Eye, Ear, and Speech Merchant–Specialists

The eye, ear, and speech specialists had also developed along both merchant and service categories – some independent of the dominant profession and some dependent, as discussed in Chapter 2.[112] Although medical professionals were allowed to practise in these areas, optometrists, opticians, audiologists, and speech–language pathologists[113] eventually grew to dominate the health practice in their respective fields. Medical specialists such as the ophthalmologists in eye care and the otolaryngologists in speech function, tend to concentrate on disease pathologies – much like what we saw in childbirth with the 'crisis' concentration of the obstetricians as compared with the 'normal' concentration of the midwives.

In the eye care field, two new provider groups had developed simultaneously, the optometrists and the opticians (or ophthalmic dispensers, as they were also called).[114] The optometrists developed into the more highly (university) educated specialists, while the opticians remained as a less educated merchant group. Unlike dentistry where the non-elite service specialists, the dental hygienists, remained out of the merchant business, the optometrists crossed over into merchant territory. They provide a diagnostic and treatment service as well as a dispensing service. This has resulted in considerable tension between them and their rival merchant group, the opticians. Today the specialization has gone even further, with the development of another merchant group, the contact lens dispensers.

In the communication function groups, the university educated specialists parallel to the optometrists are the audiologists and the speech–language pathologists. Audiologists specialize in hearing function, while speech–language pathologists specialize in speech and language function.[115] The two have worked closely from the beginning and appear to maintain friendly relations, notably because they have no reason to fight over the provision of the same health care merchandise. The speech–language pathologists, having no mass merchandise to dispense, such as eye glasses or hearing aids, have not been affected by the merchant aspects of their profession; they remain as service providers. The audiologists, as dispensers of hearing aids, do have a rival merchant group, the hearing aid dispensers.

The main tensions over expertise for the eye care and ear–speech care groups came from the coupling of the service function with the merchant function, the prescription function with a dispensing function, and the professional function with the ownership of the facilities providing these professional functions. As in the dentistry debates, questions were asked about the legitimacy of allowing those who profit from health products, such as eye glasses and hearing aids, to also act as the professional judges of the need for such appliances. This is, of course, also the same sort of question which arises out of the private practice / public payment circumstances of the medical profession – they themselves being the so-called objective judges of whether or not the services from which they profit are clinically necessary or appropriate. Analysts, officials, and politicians, alike, are uncomfortable with the potential for abuse created by this overlap in the service–merchant or service–entrepreneurial functions.[116]

Optometrists and audiologists fought to keep both their prescription function and their dispensing function, as well as win the coveted diagnosis wording.[117] The prescription function had been wrestled from the grip of the elite professionals, and the dispensing function was now under attack from practitioners who, much like they themselves had done, kept creeping up behind them in pursuit of a share of the market. These merchant competitors wanting to sell (mostly) eye glasses, contact lenses, and hearing aids, called on the ideational force of the free market; in response, the service voice of the service–merchant groups called on welfare arguments of public interest. When the Regulated Health Professions Act was passed, optometrists won both prescription and dispensing rights, as well as the privilege of diagnosis and the use of the title 'doctor.'[118] Audiologists, although they did win an authorized act allowing for the prescription of hearing aids, failed to win authorized acts for dispensing hearing aids or diagnosis, as well as failing to win the title 'doctor.'[119] There were no good reasons given for this discrepancy.

Generally, medical opposition to the development of these eye and ear–speech practitioner groups was mild, or at least appeared to be in comparison with that of the dentists towards similar practitioners. Perhaps what is more significant is that these new groups represent more of a medical specialty than they do an alternative to medicine. Unlike the chiropractors (discussed shortly), they have always been educated within the scientific medical paradigm. In a sense, they are like the dentists; they just came later. Since no powerful and highly lucrative medical specialty, like that which overcame the midwives, grew up in the areas of eye and ear–speech care prior to or along with their development, these new practitioners, while not having an easy time getting established, had a better chance than those practitioners who were 'beyond the pale.' Iridologists, for example, who are the alternative practitioners or quacks of eye care,[120] did not stand a chance of getting into this new legislation. Those who did get in were not 'out there' in terms of their credentials. In fact, in an interesting turn of the table, optometrists, audiologists, and speech–language pathologists were part of a new breed of practitioners who dared to question the credentials of the medical profession – especially those of the general or family medical practitioners.[121] The optometrists' association even went so far as to propose that 'ophthalmologists be required to refer to optometrists those problems lying within the scope of optometry and outside of ophthalmology's usual area of practice.'[122] Here the non-medical service group was recommending that the medical specialists refer patients to them. The ophthalmologists responded with the medical profession's standard 'we treat the whole body' response – again, no specifics provided.[123]

Eye, ear, and speech service and service–merchant practitioners were themselves the target of accusations of both under- and overeducation. The Association of Hearing Aid Dispensers, for example, argued that audiologists are both overeducated to test hearing and undereducated in hearing aid selection.[124] Optometrists and opticians also had to defend their credentials in the opposite direction to that which is generally implied by the term. That is, they had to argue that they were not overly educated, in order to protect their turf from less highly trained assistants. An industry lobby group, Vision Care Council of Canada, argued that many of the optometrist's or optician's tasks are routine and could easily be performed by less highly trained (but optometrist-supervised, optician-supervised, or physician-supervised) assistants[125] – a common enough accusation throughout this policy process.

As with the dental business entrepreneurs and pharmacists, there was some concern expressed about the professional–corporate tension for the opticians (or ophthalmic dispensers), the contact lens dispensers, and the hearing aid dispensers. Should they be given professional status, their professional loyalties could be divided. As we saw for pharmacy, behind the dispensing groups sit the corporations. As an academic analyst, Boase pointed out, 'The Ontario Contact Lens Association, the Board of Ophthalmic Dispensers, and the Canadian Guild of Dispensing Opticians accuse one another of "large company connections," "Imperial Optical Influence," and "good political connections."'[126] There is some evidence to suggest the truth of this: the Board of Ophthalmic Dispensers, in response to the questioning of the HPLR team, provided the information that 'more than 90% of the executive of the Ontario Association of Dispensing Opticians are employed by the Imperial Optical Company, in their executive staff.' They went on to estimate that 50 to 70 per cent of the opticians in the province were employed by 'Imperial.'[127] The optometrists' association also expressed concerns about corporate influence, but the opticians' association denied allegations of undue influence.[128]

The corporate interests formed their own lobby group late in the process (the Vision Care Council of Canada) to press for the same sorts of things that the large health institutions pressed for in this process, that is, more labour (or health) categories with cheaper labour personnel allowed to perform the tasks of the lower levels. The dispensing groups and their corporate allies argued for a breaking down of the eye care processes.[129] The distinction commonly used was one of prescription–fitting–dispensing. With this distinction the dispensing group (opticians) could argue that the service specialists (the optometrists or physicians) were the specialists in the prescription function, while they specialized in the functions of both fitting–adjusting–assessing, and dispensing–supplying–providing – thus, taking over aspects of the process in much the same way as the pharmacist takes over the process after the physician prescribes a drug.[130] The new Opticians Act does recognize the above distinction allowing for the optician to 'provide, fit, and adjust' subnormal vision devices, contact lenses, or eye glasses under the 'prescription' of an optometrist or physician, although it does not allow them to take over the process in the manner of a pharmacist, since it also allows optometrists and physicians to 'dispense.'[131]

While the opticians (or ophthalmic dispensers) were arguing for their share of the process with an eye to the optometrists' bid for the same, others were eyeing their territory. Aside from the ongoing problem of mail order dispensers from outside the province,[132] a new group of dispensers had grown up to service the contact lens market. These contact lens dispensers attempted to win professional status under the Regulated Health Professions Act, despite strong opposition from the formal opticianry group, but they failed.[133] Today this is the more confusing because many contact lens dispensers are trained as, and also work as, opticians.[134]

The same had happened to the new dispensing group in hearing care; the hearing aid dispensers applied for self-regulatory status, but did not get it. The decision makers seemed reluctant to grant any (predominantly) merchant group self-regulatory status, and none of the *new* merchant groups got into the RHPA (see Table 6.1). Of the old practitioner groups, opticians, already having been given regulatory status (along with the optometrists, in 1919), would have had to have had this status removed from them to be excluded from the new legislation; and the other similarly placed group, the pharmacists, had enough status to be untouchable with regard to deregulation despite their lack of real power.

Merchant–Service Specialists of the Feet: Chiropodists and Podiatrists

The foot specialists who grew up outside the medical profession were divided into an independent group who refused to associate with the medical profession, considering themselves an alternative to it (the podiatrists trained in the United States) and a more dependent group who saw their work as complementary to that of the medical profession (the chiropodists trained mostly in Britain). The podiatrists had spearheaded the fight in Ontario for a more independent profession, which had resulted in considerable gains for both branches of the profession by the time they entered the HPLR process (see Chapter 2). Under a 'Chiropody Act,' they had managed to break away from the less than prestigious drugless practitioners legislation and go on to win some gains in their scope of practice, as well as the privilege of billing OHIP for reimbursement of their services.[135]

Despite all this, while the chiropodists came out of the HPLR/RHPA process ahead, the podiatrists[136] came out decidedly on the losing side. The chiropodists had argued for a broad range of scope and controlled acts, including diagnosis.[137] They were given 'assessment,' rather than diagnosis, but they were also given a broader range of activities than their previous legislation had allowed (minor surgery and injections to the foot, as well as limited drug prescription).[138] During and after considerable debate over the exact scope of practice which ought to be allowed the podiatrists,[139] it was decided that they would be placed in the chiropody legislation with the stipulation that no new

Table 6.1. Practitioner group positions after the Regulated Health Professions Act of 1991

	Embedded (professional)		Excluded (non-professional)
	More than Equal	Equal	
Whole body (independent)	Medicine		Naturopathy Osteopathy Homeopathy
Merchant-service specialist (independent)	Dentistry Optometry	Denturism Audiology Chiropody	Podiatry Botanic healing
....	....	....	....
(dependent)		Pharmacy Opticianry	Contact lens disp. Hearing aid dispensers
Technique specialist (independent)	Chiropractic Psychology Midwifery	Speech-language pathology Occupational therapy Physiotherapy Massage therapy Dietetics	Social work Marriage/family therapy Psychometry Athletic therapy Clinical hypnosis Shiatsu therapy Clinical chemistry
....	....	....	....
(dependent)	Nurse practitioner (extended class)	Dental hygiene Registered nursing	Health records Medical photography
Technology specialist (dependent)		Dental technology Medical radiation technologist Medical lab technologist Respiratory therapist	Sonographic technology Vascular technology Pulmonary/cardiovascular technology
Assistant		Practical nursing	Medical assistance Dental assistance

registrants would be accepted after a specific date 31 July 1993.[140] Any podiatrists wishing to register after the inception of the new legislation would have to do so as chiropodists – with the latter's limited scope. So the podiatrists have essentially been phased out.[141]

The reasons for this decision are not all that clear. The usual 'failure to meet the 9 Criteria' answers were given (see Appendix 7), but there were others who did not quite make the grade who eventually got in. It could not have helped that there was no educational facility in Canada, but it is also quite likely that the podiatrists' aspirations as an alternative to medicine, unlike the complementary role of their cousins the chiropodists, played some role here.[142] Like the alternative practitioners we saw at the beginning of this chapter, those who directly challenged the medical monopoly were less likely to succeed than those who sought to complement it. The podiatrists' billing of OHIP was another likely factor; some immediate cost reductions would ensue with their demise – although there is also a case to be made for their cost savings over the long run (see below).

One thing that seemed unusual in all this was the reaction of the podiatrists' association. One might expect (especially having read the angry and bitter retorts from many of the losers in this process) that the podiatrists' association would have responded similarly; however, their voice was a subdued one. Despite having made a good case for the cost savings associated with the practice of podiatry compared with that of the orthopedic surgeons,[143] they seemed not to bother to argue much over the ultimate decision. The tone of the later submissions is polite, with no objections being voiced to their rejection. However, this acquiescence may have occurred because the practising podiatrists, of which the association was entirely composed, were themselves being grandfathered into the system. It was the future podiatrists who had lost out.[144]

Another new group of merchants in this area of health care, the pedorthists who fit and sell corrective footwear out of independent shops, and the morticians who had been placed under earlier registration legislation, as well as the botanics and contemporary potion salespersons, were unsuccessful in winning inclusion in the Regulated Health Professions Act of 1991. Unless they had managed to enter the regulation system in the late 1800s or early 1900s, in keeping with a long history of state concern for the creation of health care merchant monopolies, those who appeared to be no more than the providers of specialized merchandise were kept out of the regulated arena.

The Technique Specialists

The rise of the technique and technology specialists in the twentieth century had brought new competitors to the battle over health care goods and services.

Expertise Turf Wars 107

Some of these practitioners, such as the chiropractors, had gained considerable strength by the early 1980s, but most had remained either in marginalized positions of dependency on the medical and dental elite or in positions of exclusion or obscurity (see Table 2.2). All moved to better their positions via the new professional regulatory legislation.

Neuro–muscular–skeletal Specialists: Chiropractors, Physiotherapists, and Massage Therapists

Chiropractors entered the HPLR/RHPA policy process from a position of strength. Despite considerable opposition from the medical profession, they had managed not just to survive as some of the other outsiders had, but to prosper. Their practices were flourishing, and they had gained enough political say to join the small club of practitioners allowed public reimbursement (by OHIP) for their services, although on a more limited basis than medicine. In their HPLR submissions, both their governing body and their association pressed for that which they had not managed to win in the twentieth century in Ontario.[145]

The major issues of concern for chiropractors were primary patient contact, diagnosis, manipulation, and ancillary procedures, such as 'exercise therapy, light therapy, thermotherapy, hydrotherapy, electrotherapy, mechanotherapy, and nutritional counselling.'[146] They were granted primary patient contact, that is, their patients are not obliged to first get a referral from another health practitioner for a chiropractic visit. Like other non-elite practitioners, chiropractors fought long and hard against some of the preferred wording of the review, especially that of assessment of patient disorders rather than diagnosis.[147] Chiropractors were allowed to both 'assess' and 'diagnose.'[148] So they were the only non-elite group[149] to be allowed, however ambiguously, into the 'diagnosis club.'

Chiropractors also came out on the winning side with regard to other concerns. For example, spinal manipulation or adjustment was allowed them in their authorized acts,[150] and while the ancillary procedures to which they referred as important to their practice were not specifically mentioned in their scope, or given them in their authorized acts, these procedures were not prohibited from use by anyone, so chiropractors are still free to practise them. As well, two other clinical activities (related to the extremities and anal verge) for which chiropractors fought in the later stages of the HPLR policy process were eventually granted to them, despite opposition from the medical profession.[151]

Another contentious clinical procedure issue which did not get entirely settled during this policy process related to chiropractic ordering of x-rays and the ordering and performing of laboratory tests.[152] The chiropractic governing body argued that, although these functions ought in principle to be controlled acts, in practice, the issues, especially the x-ray issue, were too complex for the HPLR team to settle without great difficulty.[153] Both areas had a history of contention; both crossed into medical territory. The Committee on the Healing Arts had recommended 'hospitals be required to release x-ray films to chiropractors upon the request of the patient' – a move the medical profession had long opposed – but the review team and the MOH Professional Relations Branch officials recommended that these issues be dealt with by other legislation, rather than the RHPA.[154] Today, chiropractors are allowed to order and perform x-rays, but are not allowed to order or perform laboratory tests, although they are still fighting this latter decision which appears to be based more on cost than on clinical issues.[155]

Other issues related to the breaking up of the old order of health expertise were brought forward by the chiropractors with regard to professional status. Most Ontario chiropractors had, for some time, been referring to themselves as 'doctors of chiropractic' although their training did not confer this degree and the Health Disciplines Act had restricted its use of the title 'doctor' to physicians, dentists, and optometrists.[156] Chiropractors wanted the 'doctor' title to be officially allowed them by the new legislation.[157] Although the Committee on the Healing Arts had been opposed to the extension of the title to other practitioner groups, surprisingly, the medical profession (or other holders) were not hostile to the idea.[158] The review, in keeping with its generally egalitarian thrust, recommended that chiropractors be allowed use of the title 'doctor,' and this was confirmed under the new act.[159] Similarly, the status of the educational program and facilities of chiropractic was brought up. The Canadian Memorial Chiropractic College argued for an educational licence and permission to confer a university degree – a move that they had been pursuing for some time.[160] A similar move by the optometrists had preceded their success in gaining inclusion into the exclusive club of the 1974 Health Disciplines Act. This time, however, the review team felt that the issue was beyond their mandate, and so it was left for further debate among the appropriate authorities. As of mid-1999, university affiliation was in progress and expected to come to fruition.[161]

All in all, the majority chiropractors[162] came out on the winning side, having gained many of their key objectives at least partially. They fared less well in their attempts to limit or control the clinical territory of their rival practitioners (as will be discussed in Chapter 7). Today they have a lot going for them. A 1993 report commissioned by the Ontario Ministry of Health, coupled with similar studies coming out of the United States, provided the kind of information needed to convince ministry officials of the effectiveness and safety of chiropractic care, as well as its dramatic cost savings.[163] The Ontario study by Manga, Angus, Papadopoulos, and Swan also pointed out 'the untested, questionable or harmful nature of many current medical therapies' for the treatment of low-back pain.'[164] A second study by Manga and Angus in 1998 has further argued the advantages of economic efficiency and patient equity with enhanced utilization of chiropractic treatment (and enhanced access via greater coverage under OHIP).[165] The tables have been turned. The evidence indicates that the experts here are the chiropractors, while the medical practitioners have turned out to be the quacks.

Physiotherapists

Another neuro–muscular–skeletal function group, the physiotherapists, entered the 1980s' professional policy restructuring process weakly positioned. They had been classified as minor practitioners in the Drugless Practitioners Act and, despite their efforts, had failed to better their subordinate position;[166] their work still had to be prescribed by a medical doctor. Their main objective, therefore, was to gain independence from this assistant role to medicine.[167] They did win primary contact with patients, except in some practices covered by other legislation.[168] This was no small victory, since primary contact was such a sacred issue for the medical profession and since it has allowed physiotherapists to practise independently, although many continue to work dependently in the major health care facilities. Today, the hundreds of new independent clinics or offices are not automatically covered by third-party funding (via OHIP and the Work Place Safety and Insurance Board):[169] licensed, registered clinics can bill for third-party reimbursement (of partial payments only, for OHIP, similar to those of chiropractic) only with a referral from a physician. Those few remaining clinics still operating under the old agreements referred to in Chapter 2 can still bill OHIP directly without physician referral. Patients can also choose to use the services of any physiotherapist privately, paying directly.[170]

Physiotherapists were not happy that they had been granted 'assessment' of patients' conditions rather than 'diagnosis.'[171] They pointed out the gender bias contained in the new hierarchy of practitioners who were now authorized to make a diagnosis,[172] but the anti-hierarchical principles of the HPLR team, the Ministry of Health Professional Relations Branch officials, or the politicians involved in the process, failed to materialize in this case.[173]

Physiotherapists were allowed two controlled acts that they wanted, spinal manipulation and tracheal suction; but they failed to win approval for several others for which they also fought.[174] As a result they argued that they had been left worse off by the new legislation than they had been with the old.[175] They also argued that the leaving of so many of their procedures to the public domain necessitated a better guard against abuse by would-be physiotherapists who tend to claim they are doing 'physical therapy.' They were given the restricted use of the titles 'physical therapist' and 'physiotherapist.'[176] They left the HPLR/RHPA process rather disaffected. They did gain considerable independence, but the physiotherapists' association continues to call for 'direct access extended into third party payment agreements administered by companies and governments,'[177] that is, physiotherapists still want independence from the medical profession.

Massage Therapists

The massage therapists entered this policy process in, technically, much the same position as the physiotherapists: both had been relegated to a minor position in the drugless practitioners legislation, and both had had little success up until the 1980s in swaying policy decisions in their favour. The massage therapists, however, were further disadvantaged by their lack of a close educational association with the medical profession, although some medical doctors were referring patients to massage therapists for treatment, at the time.[178] The lack of documented medical research on massage therapy, such as that which has been produced for physiotherapy, called the massage practitioners' expertise into question and put them in danger of being placed in the to-be-excluded category of health practitioners. At one point, they, like the naturopaths, were slated for exclusion from the new legislation by the HPLR, but unlike the naturopaths, they managed to convince the review team that their practices presented enough potential harm to the public to warrant their regulation under the RHPA.[179]

Unlike the physiotherapists, massage therapists practised independently of the medical profession. The latter profession had little or no input into the actual training or procedures used by the massage therapists. One gets the sense that massage therapy is considered by the elite professions to be a fairly harmless activity. This worked to the massage therapists' advantage in the sense that they had little practitioner opposition to their request for self-regulation, but it also worked to their disadvantage in terms of being taken seriously. The HPLR's body-of-knowledge criterion was only weakly met by the massage therapists and could, therefore, have potentially cost the group their entry into professional status.

To strengthen their chances in the HPLR and RHPA processes the massage therapists emphasized the distinction between themselves and the untrained or very weakly trained practitioners of massage – particularly those associated with 'body-rub parlours' or prostitution houses.[180] The point here was not to stop less trained practitioners from providing relaxation massage; rather their objection was to the claim by others to be performing therapeutic massage.[181] Only massage therapists, they argued, are trained in both the medical sciences and the therapeutic treatment of physical dysfunction and pain related to the soft tissue and joints.[182] In the new act they were given protection for the title 'massage therapist' to distinguish them from non-therapeutic/relaxation masseurs, although they were not given the term 'therapeutic' either here or in their scope of practice or authorized acts.[183] They remained concerned about this omission.[184]

Unlike all other health practitioners who were arguing for independent practice of their trade, that is, without mandatory referral or supervision by other health practitioners,[185] the massage therapists did not, originally, ask to be allowed to diagnose their patients' health problems. In their early submissions they even went out of their way to acknowledge this as medical territory.[186] Somewhere in the process of policy learning, however, they were convinced – probably by consulting lawyers, as many other groups were – to change their scope request to include 'diagnosis.'[187] They did not get it, and by 1997 they had relaxed their concern for this word – although I was told that 'if their controlled acts were to be opened again, they would still want it.'[188]

Despite the HPLR's early recommendation that the massage therapists be excluded from the new legislation, they ended up winning on almost all of the big issues: they got in, they got independent practice, they got a protected title, and they got a loosely enough defined scope of practice to allow them to function at a level suited to their intentions.[189] They did not get any authorized acts, nor did they get some of the particulars they wanted included in their scope of practice,[190] but since many of the things omitted there were not considered harmful enough for restricted practice in general, they are still at liberty to perform these functions.[191] All in all, this quiet little group did surprisingly well.

Technique Specialists of Speech–Language

Another therapeutic practitioner group, the speech–language pathologists, won self-regulatory status for the first time. They, like all of the new service groups, had to worry about potential encroachment of their expertise turf from both above and below. Their association argued that speech–language pathologists ought not to be supervised by, for example, a physician or a medical specialist, such as an otolaryngologist, given the 'unique, specialized [and "comprehensive"] body of knowledge in which they trained'; although they ought to supervise those who 'lacked the academic and clinical expertise needed to practice reliably and competently and so to provide optimum service to the public.'[192]

Like all such middle-positioned practitioners, the speech–language pathologists wanted 'their' procedures authorized to them and only them; however, they did not succeed in thus protecting their self-defined expertise turf. Towards the end of the review, the speech–language pathologists renewed their efforts in this direction. Psychologists had been given diagnostic powers which could, theoretically, be used to prevent the speech–language pathologists from labelling speech disorders.[193] To protect an element of their practice which they considered essential, the speech–language pathologists argued, with the support of the psychologists, that they too ought to be given the diagnosis, or even, assessment, of speech disorders as an authorized act.[194] They were not successful in changing the legislation but they, like others, still hope to impress the decision makers with their concerns over this issue.[195] By winning exclusive title for the terms 'speech–language pathologists' and 'speech therapists,'[196] they did at least succeed in limiting unregulated practitioners from presenting themselves to patients as speech–language pathologists.

Technique Specialists of Mental and Social Health: Occupational Therapists and Psychologists

Of the three postwar rehabilitation groups (physiotherapists, psychologists, and occupational therapists) only occupational therapists entered the 1980s' policy process without prior regulating legislation.[197] Occupational therapists argued for inclusion in the proposed legislation. Aside from typical concerns about credentials,[198] their main thrust was a request for sixteen authorized acts which, in a diminution process common to the dynamics of the review, was later pared down to four, but ended up at zero.[199] The HPLR assessment concluded that occupational therapy was not invasive enough under the 'bodily harm' criterion to warrant regulatory control of any of its procedures, or the granting of the diagnosis function.[200] This bodily harm criterion presented a problem for several practitioner groups throughout the HPLR process, the legislation-making process, and the ongoing requests to the advisory council (HPRAC). The practitioners associated with mental functions, however, had to face a particular problem related to the issue of harm. There was a clear tendency among the policy reviewers and designers to view the body as nonmental. Not surprisingly, those practitioners who dealt with mental function disagreed with, and were probably a bit insulted by, this assumption; but the reason it took on considerable importance was that it threatened to exclude these practitioners from the new legislation. In keeping with the express emphasis on the public interest, the defining characteristic of that legislation was to be the need for regulation based on the potential for harm to the public. If mental interference was, by definition, not harmful, the practitioners of mental health were logically excluded from that regulation. Politically it was obvious that the more powerful mental practitioners, the psychiatrists, would not be threatened by this. Psychologists also were unlikely to be left out of the new legislation, since they had been previously regulated and since they hold university doctorates; but the occupational therapists, social workers, marriage and family therapists, plus a whole host of mental counsellors, such as pastoral counsellors, were in danger of being excluded.

Psychologists, as predicted, fared better than occupational therapists, winning a scope and authorized act containing the diagnosis function, as well as the title 'doctor.'[201] One interesting aspect of the practice of psychology which led to debate is its combination of scientific research and therapeutic treatment. Psychologists argued that their work is unique in the contribution it makes to our scientific understanding of mental health; they pressed the HPLR team and later the minister and Professional Relations Branch officials to recommend legislation designed to recognize the research orientation of the profession, giving them jurisdiction over that research as well as protection for their psychological test interpretations.[202] Like the nurses, the psychologists failed to convince policy makers to broaden the scope of their new act to include research. They also failed to protect their practice of test interpretations. They continued to argue for the latter.[203]

Other expertise issues which arose during the policy process were similar to those we have seen for many other practitioner groups. The medical specialists in the field of mental health care, psychiatrists, argued against the advisability of allowing non-physicians to have primary contact with the patients of this health care area, on the grounds that organic disorders would be misinterpreted as psychological or psychotic disorders by the psychologist who is not trained to identify and/or diagnose them. Psychologists countered with the argument that physicians would similarly miss psychological disorders, not being adequately trained to identify and/or diagnose them.[204] In the end, psychologists were granted the right to practise independently of the medical profession, although they continue to refer any organic assessments and drug treatments to their medical counterparts.[205] This could see further development, however, because there is a growing movement in the United States to have psychologists trained and licensed in 'psychopharmacology' – a designation which would include the prescription of drugs. In an interesting reflection of the profession's concern for its 'medicalization,' the Ontario psychology profession is divided on the benefits of such a move.[206]

Disagreement between psychologists and less educated practitioners in the field took the form of an attempt by the psychologists, whose previous legislation carried the requirement of a PhD for registration, to exclude non-PhD practitioners, both those with a Master's of Arts degree in psychology and those with alternative education, training, and experience in counselling, for example, psychometrists, psychotherapists, pastoral counsellors, and so on.[207] The issue was left unresolved until 1994 when it was decided that practitioners with a Master's in psychology would be regulated under the Psychology Act. In a related victory, psychologists won title protection to distinguish themselves from the alternative practitioners of mental health; the term 'psychologist' is reserved exclusively for PhD psychologists, while the term 'psychological associate' is reserved exclusively for the Master's of psychology practitioners.[208] Both are still concerned, however, that the practice of psychotherapy is not protected in Ontario, that is, it rests in the public domain.[209]

Social workers had been excluded early on in the HPLR process with a rather odd decision that their case would be best dealt with under another government ministry, the Ministry of Community and Social Services. The reasons given for this were always rather vague,[210] and it seemed peculiar since that ministry did not regulate any other professions and did not have the mechanisms to do so.[211] The social workers continued to pressure for inclusion in the Regulated Health Professions Act, while government officials continued to argue that social workers did not fit there. The Ministry of Community and Social Services did develop regulatory legislation in 1998–9 which now regulates both university graduate 'social workers' and community college graduate 'social service workers' under terms and conditions similar to those of the RHPA.[212]

Psychometrists and the marriage and family therapists did not make it into the new legislation, although they had been on the 'almost-made-it' list of thirty-nine (see Appendix 7 for their weaknesses in terms of the HPLR's 'nine criteria'). With this exclusion, their main concern was whether or not they would be able to continue to practise, or to practise independently.[213] As we saw earlier, if some groups were allowed authorized acts for, in this case, anything resembling mental counselling, this would exclude all non-licensed practitioners whether regulated or not from performing the same, or potentially even similar, procedures. They were told this was not the intent of the designers of the legislation or of the minister and that because they could still assess their patients's conditions – assessment of mental health not being a controlled act – they could continue on as before.[214] They, and their lawyers, were not convinced; they would prefer the security of inclusion in the Regulated Health Professions Act.

Technique Specialists of Birth: Midwives

Midwives entered this policy process in a very weak position. Midwifery had been devastated in North America, as we have seen, but it was never quite wiped out.[215] In the past several decades there has been a small but important resurgence in the demand for midwifery assistance in Canada, attributed primarily to the contemporary women's and consumers' movements, both of which were disaffected with the medical approach to childbirth.[216] It was no longer just a fringe or lunatic group who wanted a different, more humane type of childbirth program. It was the educated and the influential who started to pressure the established definitions of good maternity care, substituting their own rational assessments for those of the medical experts. In their submissions to the review, the midwives' organizations emphasized this public support. A provincial organization called the Midwifery Task Force (not to be confused with the 1987 government sponsored Task Force on Midwifery in Ontario) had been set up expressly to create pressure for independent legislation for midwives. It was composed of both consumers and professionals. Other childbirth organizations and organized women's groups were also exerting pressure for change.[217]

The midwives' submissions to HPLR were persuasively constructed. First they spoke in a united voice. The Ontario Association of Midwives submitted jointly with the Nurse Midwives Association of Ontario, despite some friction between the nurses and the midwives (some of whom are nurse–midwives and some lay midwives). The Midwives Coalition argued clearly and succinctly for the regulation and professional autonomy of midwifery. Their most powerful tool was probably the comparative analyses and statistics they used to show up the oddity of the Canadian / North American case. It is difficult for others to argue that midwives are incompetent quacks when they are used extensively throughout the world – particularly when the developed countries with the highest rate of utilization of midwifery have the lowest mortality and morbidity rates for both mother and child.[218] It is also difficult to argue the incompetence of the contemporary North American midwives when studies in the United States show that midwives 'achieved a better perinatal and maternal outcome,' in circumstances in which they attend large numbers of births without any medical assistance, some in the exact same circumstances as the medical profession.[219] These are glaring facts, and the Midwifery Coalition made certain that the HPLR team was exposed to them. They rebutted the experts with alternative expertise.

Midwives also made certain that some of the normal North American confusions or prejudices about midwifery were cleared up in the minds of the review team. For example, they pointed out that midwives do not want to 'take over' childbirth. Their primary role has always been that of assistant to the mother in the normal process of birth, not in abnormal or high-risk situations which they see as belonging to the expertise of the medical profession.[220] The Midwifery Coalition also argued that, besides being the 'safest form of maternity care' for normal births, they provide a much more 'continuous, personalized, and preventive care' than does the North American institutionalized version of childbirth.[221]

Like others, midwives were accused by the elite profession, on whose turf they tread, of being incompetent to distinguish the normal from the abnormal – thus the need for the medical (or dental) gatekeepers of the system. This accusation reflected the ignorance of the 'scientific' professionals of the existing, readily available, scientific studies (mentioned above and in Chapter 2) which had already proven the midwives not only capable of referral of high-risk maternity cases, but also of superior overall care, even without the help of the medical profession.[222] Midwives, however, dared, as did similar specialist groups (denturists, dental hygienists, chiropractors, audiologists, speech–language pathologists, psychologists, and nurses) to question the qualifications of the elite professionals to do the work on which they, the technique specialists, focused.[223] Health care expertise is now being challenged on its own grounds.

Other aspects of the midwives' submissions to the review showed considerable political sophistication. In keeping with the ideational climate of the review or the ministry, they used words such as 'consumer demand,' 'informed [patient] choices,' 'public input,' and 'Native family ... fragmentation.'[224] They also suggested the targeting and training of lower-class and immigrant women in midwifery, in particular, Native women in their own communities,[225] and they promised both quality and cost efficiency, arguing that 'routine and unnecessary obstetrical interference [is] dangerous ... [and] extremely costly.'[226]

During the HPLR process the decision was made to treat midwifery as a special case. Based on the nine criteria for self-regulation alone (see Appendices 4 and 7), their request for professional self-regulation would have had to have been denied. One member of the HPLR team suggested that midwives were in a unique legal position because of the danger of their being prosecuted for criminal negligence in the event of a death during delivery, and, therefore, they needed more than just the time to upgrade in order to meet the terms of the nine criteria.[227] But it seems likely that there were other factors, such as the gender composition and public support of midwifery, involved in the decision to include midwives in the new legislation; others who had reason to be included were not given the same advantages.

The most important advantage for midwives came with the setting up of a special task force to look into their situation and needs for future integration into the health care system.[228] Task forces are expensive; this was no small concession to midwives, and they benefited greatly from it. Two issues of concern for midwives related to their new affiliation with hospitals. One of them, which is probably the most contentious issue regarding midwifery, concerns the choice by the mother to give birth at home. Obviously, as long as midwives were kept out of the institutional maternity care system, they could only deliver babies outside those institutions, but once they were included in the official health care system, they would have to be allowed to use those institutions. Given the midwives' long-standing criticism of medical paternalism and its abuse of drugs and technology during medically assisted births inside those institutions, they were now placed in a somewhat awkward position with regard to both birth location and the use of drugs commonly administered in the hospital. To offset these concerns, the midwives emphasized the importance of the mother's/patient's informed choice – which would include the choice of birth attendant, technology, and location. They fought hard to have home-birth sanctioned by the Midwifery Task Force, but it recommended only Ministry of Health-approved health facilities, including out-of-hospital community clinics, as possible locations for midwifery practice, with more study of the issue of home-birth.[229] During the development of the regulations to the legislation, however, home-births and a limited range of authorized acts for (injection, inhalation, and prescription) of drugs were included.[230] Today's midwives offer women a choice of hospital or home birth: 'The midwives' role of providing care for women who want to give birth at home is not a choice that is accepted by the [official] medical profession ... But within the system, it is accepted on a practical level that midwives attend homebirths and the obstetric and nursing staff that work in the hospitals ... support midwives to do that ... by providing support if it doesn't work out at home and midwives have to move in to the hospital with their clients ... it is a back-up system.'[231]

One interesting aspect of the midwifery story concerns the midwives' relationship to scientific health care. The original decision to apply for admission to the new regulatory legislation was not made lightly; there was considerable concern among practising midwives in the province about going in with the establishment. Midwives had spent many years working outside the established medical and legal systems, and any potential alliances there brought concerns about the midwife's relationship with her patient or client group.[232] Although the assumptions of the HPLR team clearly associated regulation with the public interest, the midwives' experience had taught them that it was the unregulated provider groups who were most responsive to the demands of their clients. Given that midwives assumed these clients were capable of good decisions based on informed consent,[233] it followed that those clients ought to be in control of their health assistants, rather than the other way around. As one midwife put it, 'Even though pregnancy is normal, it is also stressful, and people need guidance; but with the medical model, they take the ball and run with it.'[234] Midwives involved in the review process were afraid of being forced, in becoming accountable to the state, to diminish their level of accountability to, and concern for, the birthing mothers; this resulted in 'a very highly emotional internal debate about "selling out."'[235] When, in the midwifery philosophy, 'maintaining responsiveness to patient's choices ... is one of your strongest guarantees against the negative things of institutionalization,' anything that threatens that long-held guarantee is likely to be approached with some fear.[236] At the time of the health practitioners legislation review in the early 1980s, midwives, or at least the majority of them, encouraged by the initial response of the review team,[237] chose to enter 'the system.' By the late 1990s, an influential midwife who had lived through the whole process and was now continuing to design the parameters of the midwifery profession commented, 'The integration of midwives in Ontario has been remarkably successful on a number of counts, all of the midwives in Ontario have received hospital privileges which I think is something quite noteworthy given that we were outsiders to the system, we weren't always accepted and there still is some resistance ... One of the things I [also] think was very important about the way in which we legislated midwifery is that we did keep homebirth as a fundamental part of the system, and we established ourselves as autonomous primary care providers. Those two things I think are incredibly valuable in what I would call resisting the dangers of legislation.'[238]

Midwives were helped in their pursuits by good timing. Their introduction into the hospitals in Ontario corresponded with the early stages of hospital restructuring in the province, and 'people saw that cooperating with the midwives might get them political points ... Midwifery was popular ... [It was] seen as progressive and community oriented.'[239] A good indication of their acceptance into the establishment was their involvement in the restructuring decisions, for example, in one Toronto hospital amalgamation project, midwives were represented on all of the committees party to these decisions.[240] They will likely continue to be looked upon favourably with hospital management, given the fact that the women they assist 'spend a minimal amount of time in the hospital ... and rarely use the post-partum floor – freeing it up for the women who really need' these expensive resources.[241]

Overall, midwives not only found themselves in favourable circumstances during this policy-making process, but they were also astute enough to present themselves well. This might explain why, despite their lack of pressure group characteristics, and their inability to measure up to the exacting nine criteria set by the HPLR, they still came out as big winners. Interest group theory has often claimed that the most effective interest groups have the right resources. If they are highly organized, headed by strong leadership, cohesive but large in number, wealthy, status-bearing, well connected, and so on, they are more likely to succeed. Midwives fit almost none of these criteria, and yet they were probably the single most effective interest group of the whole process.[242] A non-integrated, uninfluential, weakly financed handful of women succeeded where much more powerful groups failed.[243]

More Technique Specialists: Dieticians, Nurses, and Dental Hygienists

Three other technique specialist groups applying for self-regulatory status had become closely associated with the institutions and practices of medical and dental care. Dieticians were involved in nutrition, mostly in hospital, long-term care, and psychiatric institutions. Nurses and dental hygienists were associated with a service which placed them as both specialized practitioners in their own sphere of work and assistants to the medical and dental professionals. These positions, of course, would mould the debates over expertise which surfaced during the HPLR.

Dieticians entered the 1980s' policy process hoping to move beyond their registered (but not licensed) status to that of a full professional group. Their area of expertise, long ignored by medicine, formed only a very minor part of the medical profession's concerns at the time of the review, so dieticians were in little danger of opposition from that quarter. They did, however, represent a potential threat to unregulated health care groups and merchants; this was clear in the debates surrounding their requests to the review for self-regulatory status.

Originally, the dieticians' association requested a scope of practice, controlled acts, and title protection, which would 'exclude non-licensed persons from practising dietetics and nutrition.'[244] It was soon made apparent to them, however, that this expansive monopoly would not be given them, so they adjusted their requests to include exclusive rights to the more limited area of 'therapeutic nutritional care ... and counselling.'[245] In the end, they were given a limited scope (without either the term 'therapeutic' or 'counselling'), no authorized acts, and title protection for 'dietician' rather than their favoured 'nutritionist.'[246]

The dieticians' failure to win control over the title 'nutritionist' for which they continue to argue,[247] was partly related to the HPLR and Ministry of Health commitment to the idea that only harmful health procedures ought to be controlled or regulated, leaving all other procedures open for public or entrepreneurial use. But it was also related to the fact that the unregulated groups and commercial enterprises, such as health food store owners, lobbied hard to prevent professional monopolies in their areas of interest.[248] Because the term 'nutritionist' was not reserved for dieticians, other practitioners of nutrition, such as the naturopaths and kinesiologists, as well as a host of health food entrepreneurs, are free to continue their 'nutritional consultations' or 'nutritional counselling.' Surprisingly, dieticians also failed to win their bid for control (along with MDs) over the prescription of 'therapeutic diets,' but this was probably because of the limitations and cost increases this would have placed on smaller health care institutions and home care programs. As with the nursing groups, some of the seemingly odd HPLR decisions were made to protect Ministry of Health programs which have traditionally made use of a cheaper, less-qualified labour force.

Overall, dieticians ended up better positioned than they had been. They are now members of the professional community. They were not able to gain control over the practice territory that they considered their own, but this was a common failure for those groups crossing into the merchant area (unless they had managed to win their gains years ago). Diet plans, including hefty-priced diet powders and packaged meals, are now big business, and officials are not very comfortable with granting professional monopolies in such markets.

Nurses

Nurses entered the latest regulatory policy debate in Ontario caught between the desire of some of their members to act as independent service providers and the desire of others to maintain the role of assistant to the medical profession. They were also caught between the work positions of professionals and labourers. Their semi-professional status with professional aspirations, coupled with the reality of non-autonomous work conditions under institutional managers or medical practitioners, left many rank-and-file nurses more concerned with labour negotiations over wages and work conditions than with legalistic arguments over the compositions of professional committees. So while the nursing elite was pushing to raise the official scope of practice or educational credentials of nurses in general, many of the beneficiaries of such reform were asking questions such as, 'How many jobs will this legislation protect?' or 'Will it give us more say with hospital management?'[249] That is, their concerns centred less on expertise than on labour conditions, and they quite rightly perceived the policy review as being relatively unconcerned with the latter.

Four official nursing groups presented submissions to the Health Professions Legislation Review: the governing body for all nurses, the College of Nurses of Ontario; the professional association for registered nurses, the Registered Nurses Association of Ontario; the professional association for nurse assistants, the Ontario Association of Registered Nurses' Assistants; and the nurses' union, the Ontario Nurses Association.[250] The college appears to have gone to great lengths to solicit the participation of all of its members;[251] however, one segment of nursing, the nurse assistants (now called registered practical nurses) would argue that their so-called participation was no more than mere audience. They wanted one thing – independence from the registered nurses – but the college argued against this, and the practical nurses lost.

The submissions made by the College of Nurses primarily reflect their concerns about nursing independence, scope of practice, and credentials. They argued that registered nurses ought to be allowed 'primary contact' with patients independent of referral from medical professionals; a range of both independent and interdependent functions; an expanded scope of practice which would include the function of diagnosis as well as 'management, research, and education'; title protection for 'nurse' including jurisdiction to charge 'non-members' using that title; and nursing specialty credentials.[252]

The submissions from both the Registered Nurses Association of Ontario and the Ontario Nurses Association echoed many of the concerns of the governing body. One significant difference between the RNAO and the college was the former's insistence on a minimum requirement of a university baccalaureate for all registered nurses by the year 2000; the college did not back up the RNAO on this.[253] The ONA disagreed with the college over some aspects of their recommendations as well. For example, it back-tracked on its tacit support of the college's bid to keep the nursing assistants within the domain of the college.[254] The ONA also supported its graduate nurses who were arguing with the college over conditions of their inclusion in the new legislation.[255] As well, the ONA argued in support of nurses concerned about such issues as entry and re-entry educational requirements, disciplinary hearings, complaint protection, inter-jurisdictional mobility, potential conflict for nurses between the desires of their employers and the standards expected of them by their governing college, and so on.[256]

Overall, in the new legislation, registered nurses gained some limited auton-

122   Health Care Practitioners

omy from the medical profession to perform specific procedures which used to be designated strictly medical and which the nurses had long been performing anyway.[257] The HPLR had recommended that all of the nurses' proposed authorized acts be made contingent on order or authorization by another health professional.[258] The nurses argued against this, and the new Nursing Act allowed for the development of a regulation which, when written, laid out the terms under which an RN may independently 'initiate' or 'order' (to an RPN, for example) a procedure.[259] This, then, has given registered nurses a degree of independence that they did not formerly have. Nurses, both RNs and RNAs or practical nurses, also won their claim for protection of the title 'nurse.' Previously it had only been the term 'registered nurse' which had been protected by title, so any care provider could legally call herself or himself a nurse. For reasons of both status and job security, trained nurses had long resented this. They also argued that it was potentially dangerous. They did succeed in getting this changed in the new Nursing Act.[260] They did not succeed in getting the diagnosis or 'management, research, and education' functions added to their scope-of-practice statement. Like many others, nurses had to settle for assessing patients' conditions.[261]

The broad range of activities which nurses had wanted was resisted partly because other groups might ask for the same, necessitating the rewriting of all of the scopes of practice which had already consumed considerable time. One of the biggest issues was that of the university degree requirement for entry to registered nursing practice, long sought by the Registered Nurses Association. Only about 10 per cent of the registered nurses in Ontario had a Bachelor of Science or higher degree at the time of the review, and Ministry of Health and Ministry of Colleges and Universities officials were concerned about the ramifications of imposing a degree requirement.[262] The official government position mentioned four primary concerns, related to the quality, supply, and cost of nursing care, as well as accessibility to the profession.[263] They did not support the request for extension of the educational requirements of registered nurses. Later in the legislative process, Minister Caplan expressed particular concern about the problem of restricting accessibility to the profession, arguing that the BSc requirement would discriminate against ethnic minority and low income students. Interestingly, here was a case where a racial–women's issue / class–women's issue argument was used against one of the female practitioner groups. At this time, the entry to practice standards for registered nurses still allows entry to those holding an (educational) college diploma. The Registered Nurses Association has seen this as an indication of the low status in which nursing care is held, and on the access issue, they pointed out, 'When other professions have wanted to upgrade their education requirements, you [did not] hear these same type of [arguments] ... It's like people expect the nurses to be scientifically capable, but all they think the nurses need is a little education based just on caring, and they don't need actual degrees. This is probably because nursing care is invisible while medical care is very visible and apparent. People don't see all the activity behind the scenes; they don't see why we are called the glue that holds the system together.'[264] By December 1999 the College of Nurses of Ontario had 'identified new entry to practice standards for registered nurses ... [which] will include the requirement, beginning in January 2005, of a baccalaureate in nursing as the minimum education for Ontario applicants for initial registration as a registered nurse.'[265] Assuming the proposed regulation for the baccalaureate requirement receives ministerial approval and therefore the educational requirements to practice are finally elevated, there is still, however, the problem of the gap between the rigour of the university educated nurses' training and the reality once they start to practise. As one BSc nurse put it, 'We learned so much and we used so little. I was totally unprepared for the conformity. The structure was extremely rigid. There was no room to challenge the system. There was so little care, compared to the rules and note-taking. It was very disappointing ... not at all what I expected. By a year and a half, I thought, I can't keep going on with this; mobility didn't matter, it was the same in all the types of jobs within nursing. I quit.'[266] So the push to elevate nurses' credentials might not have the effect its proponents hope for, even if it were realized. While the better educated nurse is 'feeling very frustrated' about her job conditions,[267] her less educated, less socially advantaged counterpart may well 'be happy just to have a job.'[268]

Nurses also argued that they ought to be allowed to delegate their newly authorized acts to care givers who often take their place in out-of-hospital settings, particularly the personal care attendants who tend incapacitated patients at home. This was the sort of difficult problem the HPLR team, and the officials who followed them, occasionally had to deal with in the conflict of common sense over regulatory consistency. On the one hand, it made no sense to cripple the existing system of home care or utilization of cheaper aides in health care institutions, such as old age homes. On the other hand, the need for regulation of any health care procedures which could potentially cause harm to patients if performed inadequately was the very basis on which the concept of regulatory control rested. In the end, these issues were kept as quiet as possible, mostly being shoved off to the regulation-setting process following the more dramatic enactment of the individual acts. There the common-sense (economical) path was most likely to be followed. So far there had been 'no major change' in the 'delegating/teaching/assigning/supervising,' issue, except for an 'increased responsibility of the [nursing] associations and college to educate their members on proper protocol for delegating and assigning and education on the difference between delegating and supervision.'[269]

At the more theoretical level, questions remain about the ability of registered nurses to carve out their desired independent practice.[270] Nurses specialize in the techniques of patient care,[271] but, as we saw in the quote above, 'care' is generally not considered to be intellectual or scientific territory, it is usually thought of as innate (a mother's care), or learned by association (a woman's world or women's issues), or purview of a private organization (such as the church or a philanthropic organization),[272] rather than an area requisite of expertise. It remains to be seen whether or not nurses can turn care into a science,[273] particularly since the patients themselves may not want their care to undergo any such reinterpretation.[274] Likewise, the nurses' emphasis on the holistic and preventive aspects to their definition of health care[275] is yet to be taken seriously by policy makers. It remains to be seen whether or not this latter claim will come to bear any real weight in the system, and even if it does, one also sees signs of the medical profession moving to claim the new holistic, preventive territory for itself.[276]

Even in the turbulent 1980s and 1990s, while Ministry of Health rhetoric referred to 'enhancing the role of the nurse,' nurses themselves complained about their lack of input into important restructuring decisions.[277] In 1989 the Ontario Public Hospitals Act was amended to require greater (staff and management) nursing participation on public hospital committees; and from 1994 to 1998 the Ontario government set up a Nursing Effectiveness, Utilization, and Outcomes Research Unit, a Joint Provincial Nursing Committee, and a Nursing Task Force, all with strong nursing participation meant to 'help government develop policy.'[278] Initiatives such as these are encouraging, but as one college member put it, 'Our influence depends on the [whims of the] government.'[279] It also depends, in these days of hospital downsizing and sectoral restructuring, on economics. One of the main concerns of the professional association continues to be the casual employment of transient nurses and the effects this is having on continuity of care: 'there is a barrier to caring because there is no attachment to the patients and nurses become frustrated with having to work in different environments each day ... Many are leaving. Those that are staying are becoming more militant.'[280]

Nurse Practitioners

One interesting development in health care is that of the increased utilization of nurse practitioners. These primary care nurses had mostly functioned to service remote areas where doctors could not be encouraged to locate, working in what has been referred to as a nursing-station system linked to medical advisers through radio and telephone communication. The system appears to have worked well, too well for the critics of independent nursing care.

The distinction between the nurse and the medical practitioner has always rested in the nurse's lack of authority to diagnose or recommend treatment. In theory, working under the supervision of a doctor, the nurse provides secondary management of the patient.[281] The medical doctor provides primary contact diagnosis – a function necessary, supposedly, to the sifting of patients into risk categories. In reality, however, extended care nurse practitioners, like a whole host of now-legitimate practitioners, such as optometrists, audiologists, chiropodists, denturists, dental hygienists, and midwives who were once considered incapable of recognizing the symptoms of disease and disorder, have shown themselves to be more capable than their medical detractors claim.[282]

Despite evidence that the utilization of nurse practitioners could help reduce costs, while still maintaining high-quality care, their acceptance has been slow.[283] In a report released at the time the HPLR began its investigations, the 1983 *Medical Manpower for Ontario Task Force Report*, the authors acknowledged and then quickly dismissed important studies which indicated possibilities for more efficient utilization of health care personnel.[284] By the 1990s, however, other considerations besides 'attitudinal barriers to widespread substitution for the role of the physician'[285] were being taken into account in the revamping of the health care system. Practical political and economic blueprints for change were helping reset priorities in favour of cheaper alternatives to the present system. In February 1994 Minister Grier announced her intention to begin training nurse practitioners as primary care providers.[286] There was no official mention at that time of the nurse practitioners displacing general practitioners – although the medical doctors themselves were mentioning it.[287] The medical detractors argued not against resultant higher levels of patient mortality and morbidity, for which there was little or no evidence; rather they pointed to (debatable) effects, such as increased cost and practitioner burn-out in isolated communities.[288]

Today, nurse practitioners have won a professional independence long sought by the leadership of the nursing profession. Backed by a positive assessment from HPRAC,[289] the nurses' college developed regulations to the 1991 Nursing Act which allow 'extended class' nurse practitioners to function more independently than the 'general class' nurse, that is, as 'primary care givers' with a specific set of authorized acts – which include the coveted diagnosis.[290] The term 'nurse practitioner,' is not a protected title, so any registered nurse can legally use it (under medical directive or advanced medical protocol from a doctor). The college was not interested in fighting this,[291] their intent here was to ensure the 'RN, NP (EC)' is qualified as a registered nurse and nurse practitioner of the extended class (which includes quality assurance review).[292] Nurse practitioners, in general, have tended to work in community health care settings rather than in the institutional health care settings where the RN predominantly practises. The amendments to the legislation only cover nurse practitioners in primary care, not acute care. 'The acute care nurse practitioners have faced some opposition to regulation in hospital settings because of the Public Hospitals Act which restricts their scope of practice ... And most hospitals are managed by an advisory board which is run by physicians ... who are uncomfortable with 'regulating' the nurse practitioners.'[293] As the shift towards community-based care is stepped up, nurse practitioners, now called RN(EC), may come to play a more and more important role.[294] It will be interesting to see how well they fare in the near future.

Dental Hygienists

Another group of practitioners who cross over into both the technique–specialist and assistant categories are dental hygienists. They too have been striving for more independence. Although both the McRuer Commission and Committee on the Healing Arts had recommended independent governance for dental hygienists, they remained within the jurisdiction of the Royal College of Dental Surgeons, with observer status only.[295] While the RCDSO argued in its HPLR submission for continuance of the status quo, the Ontario Dental Hygienists Association argued for the professional autonomy that they claimed had been promised them at the time of the passage of the Health Disciplines Act.[296] They spoke of the 'unfair and undemocratic' nature of the 'legislative and judicial powers ... of the dental profession allowing it to regulate the affairs of others ... who have no part in formulating the rules by which they are governed ... [in] an inequitable ... indefensible ... system.'[297] The HPLR team did recommend that the dental hygienists be given self-governing professional status, and by March of 1987 the government had agreed. The dentists were not pleased.[298]

Unlike dentists, dental hygienists had little to lose in this policy process, and much to gain. As one hygienist said of the new legislation 'How can it hurt, it can only be good?'[299] Their political strategy was astute, with their association leaders proving to be good lobbyists.[300] It was clear that the old paternal relationship was now threatened by the regulatory independence of the new dental hygiene college; but the degree of independence that the hygienists could now attain would depend on how Section 5, subsection 1 of

Expertise Turf Wars 127

the new act was interpreted.[301] The key question was, could dental hygienists implement the procedures 'ordered' by a dentist without that dentist being present? This distinction would be crucial for both dentists and dental hygienists because it would determine whether or not hygienists could perform their range of authorized acts outside the dentist's office, or 'off-site'[302] with 'self-initiation.'[303] With the more liberal interpretation, the dentist's order would act more as a prescription – in which case, from the dentist's perspective, it would not have much teeth to it.[304] For the prescriber, the dentist, to lose the direct supervision of the hygienists' work would, of course, be to lose a cut of the profits they generated from within the dentist's office complex.

The interpretation of the wording of the new legislation is still being fought over; it has constituted a tough battle for dental hygienists. From the beginning of this legislative process the hygienists presented a strong case for independent or self-initiated practice. They spoke of the 'inherent conflict of interest' for the dental profession between its 'economic interests' and 'its responsibility to ... the public.'[305] Their submissions were well written and well argued; for example, they astutely argued that the dentist's interpretation of how things ought to be in the dental care field would limit the provision of cheap dental care services in institutions, such as nursing homes and prisons (later adding schools and the home).[306] Their association also made good use of data on dental hygienists' capabilities. They also pointed to their successful utilization in other jurisdictions, including their work under prescriptionlike 'direction' in British Columbia and 'supervision à distance' in Quebec.[307] They pointed out studies which suggested the dental hygienist's ability to assess abnormal dental conditions for which dentists wanted to maintain primary contact.[308] Despite all this, however, the issue of self-initiation (or primary contact) for dental hygiene remained unsolved well after proclamation. The issue was referred to the Health Professions Regulatory Advisory Council which reported to the health minister in May 1996.[309] HPRAC came out in favour of an amendment to the Dental Hygiene Act 'to allow dental hygienists to perform their authorized acts of scaling teeth and root planing including (incidental) curetting of surrounding tissue without an order, subject to appropriate restrictions in regulations and standards ... established through consultation with other health professionals, particularly dentists and physicians.'[310] The advisory council saw this recommendation of 'limited self-initiation of these controlled acts ... for any patient, including new patients ... as fulfilling the public interest principles of access, equality, accountability and quality of care, while not constituting an increased risk of harm.'[311] The minister of health decided not to act on HPRAC's recommendations and met with the dental hygienists in October 1996 (after he had met with the dentists) and asked them to go back and work things out with the dentists.[312] This a bit like asking a small Canadian company which is economically involved with Cuba to go work things out with U.S. Senator Helms. As the College of Dental Hygienists said in a public letter to the minister, 'The effect of this is to ensure that the Royal College of Dental Surgeons of Ontario continues to manage the delivery of dental hygienists' services in Ontario.'[313] As of mid-1999 there were some dental hygienists who had opened their own clinics and were performing non-controlled acts, such as polishing and whitening, but the dentist's college had introduced an amendment to the RHPA to make even acts in the public domain regulated acts. They had also developed a regulation on how to give and receive an order, which had been countered by a regulation from the dental hygienists' college on receiving an order.'[314] (See also the section on Assistants below.)

The question arises, if dental hygienists are not capable of 'cleaning people's teeth (or even 'whitening' teeth) while at the same time recognizing signs of abnormality, why are they considered professionals? The government decisions also raise questions of financial accountability, particularly because there are considerable public funds going to civil service and institutional dental plans. It is particularly interesting that a minister of a budget-slashing Conservative government, such as the late 1990s' Harris government, would rule against a relatively easy case (with HPRAC backing) for reducing costs within the system.

The Technology Specialists

Dental and Medical Technologists[315]

The technologist groups were relatively quiet during the HPLR, although they, like almost all health care providers of any stripe, did ask for professional status. Dental technologists entered the HPLR process without much to lose: the nature of their work (supplying dental appliances as ordered by a dentist) had always left them vulnerable to the elite provider group. Their past regulatory legislation left them with little professional autonomy. They had little influence in policy, in fact, state officials had helped maintain the dependent relationship they had long held with the dentists.[316]

Amid references to their good relations with the dental profession, the Governing Board of Dental Technicians,[317] with whom the Association of Registered Dental Technicians were in general agreement,[318] asked that the dental technologists be placed under regulatory control because of 'the technical and material nature of the health services [they] provide, ... the complex set of working relationships [in their] profession, [and among] other health service professions and [non-registered] dental laboratory technicians, ... the rapidly advancing technology of the profession, ... and the serious long-term consequences for the patient of inadequate or incompetent, unregulated practice of dental technology.'[319] They did succeed in gaining professional status in the new legislation.[320]

One issue of concern to both the dental technologists and ministry officials was related to the business aspect of their occupation. They were concerned about the ownership and/or licensing of dental laboratories. Previous legislation had required majority ownership of a dental laboratory by a registered dental technician, but a commercial dental laboratory lobby group had argued that there was a potential conflict for the technical staff / owner between her or his professional and business interests.[321] Despite giving a nod to the validity of this point, the Governing Board of Dental Technicians argued that the former statutes ought to be maintained and that registered or licensed dental technologists 'should be in control of the technical operations of a dental laboratory at all times.'[322] Interestingly enough, they did back down on the ownership issue when the commercial lobby group continued to press its objection, backed by, surprisingly enough, the Association of Registered Dental Technicians.[323]

The dental technologists' governing board and the association continued to press for the licensing of dental laboratories. They were concerned that 'anybody could open up a dental laboratory and operate without an RDT [registered dental technologist/technician].'[324] The decision was made, however, that all Ontario dental technology laboratories had to be 'supervised' by an RDT or a dentist – with all the incumbent debate over interpretation of the word 'supervision.'[325] Like other technical or technique–service provider groups, dental technologists were, and still are, concerned about being replaced by cheaper, non-registered technicians or assistants with less formal education, or sometimes only in-lab training. Like nurses, dental technologists want to maintain their supervisory position over these laboratory assistants.[326] More recent concerns centre on the lack of consistent training standards for these assistants and their use or misuse by dentists.[327]

Late in the process, the dental technologists, their expectations raised by seeing what other groups had gained, argued for major changes, such as an expanded scope, some authorized acts, and a better guarantee on their oligopoly of dental appliances.[328] They were not successful in these attempts,[329] but they have realized a considerable degree of legal control over the regulation of their own profession with their inclusion in the new legislation.

The three medical technical groups which made it into the new legislation,

130   Health Care Practitioners

medical radiation technologists, respiratory technologists (or therapists as they now prefer to be called), and medical laboratory technologists, also argued over the content of their scope-of-practice statements[330] and the controlled acts allowed them.[331] As we saw earlier, the radiation technologists and medical laboratory technologists had been regulated by prior statute, but the respiratory therapists had not.

There were several medical technology groups who made it through the first cut, but failed to make it into the new legislation (see the list of thirty-nine potential self-regulating professions in Chapter 5). The cardiovascular technologists applied for inclusion in the new legislation, but they failed to meet the HPLR's nine criteria. They were quite unhappy with this decision and will likely continue to argue for inclusion in the RHPA.[332] Technologists using diagnostic medical-imaging energy forms other than ionizing radiation, such as ultra sound waves or nuclear magnetic resonance, also wanted self-regulatory status, but they failed to achieve this because the HPLR team felt that they did not sufficiently satisfy the nine criteria. Despite considerable controversy and lack of support from the HPLR,[333] by the time the legislation reached royal asssent a phrase had been added to the radiation technologists' scope leaving room for their use of these 'other forms of energy.'[334] A later regulation (107/96) categorized these energy forms as electricity, electromagnetism, and sound waves.[335]

The difficulties over territory and the level of risk associated with tasks performed by the various technological groups is exacerbated by the rapidly changing nature of the new technologies employed. The emergence of these groups has been sporadic, as has been the development of related legislation. It seemed obvious to these practitioners that new legislation ought to include mechanisms or wording to deal with the changing nature of their expertise. The medical laboratory technologists, for example, commented,

> The word 'technology' is almost synonymous with progress and change ... It is possible that disputes may arise with other health professions mainly in regard to scope of practice. As new technologies emerge it may not be immediately obvious which profession should assume responsibility. An example of this lies in the new instruments that have the ability to monitor a patient's metabolic status by non-invasive techniques. It may seem logical to assume that such an instrument would be regarded as imaging and therefore the responsibility of one of the imaging technologies, either radiography, nuclear medicine or ultrasound; however, monitoring of metabolic status has previously been assigned to the laboratory.[336]

Surprisingly, the medical technology groups' many references to this need to pay particular attention to the changing nature of technology did not seem to be taken very seriously by the HPLR team. The proposed legislation they drafted, on the whole, made little provision for this fundamental problem. It was only at the ministry level as the fine-tuning was going on in the Professional Relations Branch that these concerns were addressed to a limited degree and some revision made to the legislation. However, problems continue to develop as the technological field becomes more and more complex.

The medical radiation technologists, for example, dealt in the past only with ionizing radiation and this activity was, and continues to be, regulated under the (1990 revised statutes) of the Healing Arts Radiation Protection Act.[337] Today's medical radiation technologists, however, are increasingly cross-trained in the use of electromagnetism (for magnetic resonance imaging, or MRI) and sound waves (for diagnostic ultrasound and lithotripsy) – thus the late addition to their scope of practice mentioned earlier. These later technological developments have been regulated by various means, for example, the majority of Ontario hospitals and the CPSO use the American system of registry and examination for diagnostic medical sonographers, since there is no Canadian registry, so the MRTs doing (endovaginal and endorectal) diagnostic medical sonography need to comply with the American standards. To confuse things further, the medical exemption to the ordering of the regulated forms of energy allows them to order, for example, an MRI or ultrasound from anyone regardless of their degree of training. This, then, can be used to circumvent the regulated group of practitioners, such as medical radiation technologists, leaving the latter powerless to deal with complaints about these unregulated practitioners,[338] and so on.[339] This hodge-podge of legislation was supposed to have been simplified by the new legislation, but the RHPA did little towards this end.

Respiratory therapists have had similar problems; for example, when a respiratory therapist has had additional training in a specialized area, such as echocardiography, this raises regulatory questions. Is she or he a respiratory therapist or an echocardiographer? What regulation is applicable? These problems continue to develop as the health sector and its technologies continue to develop. The recent rise of the nurse practitioners, for example, raised questions about the possibility of their taking and/or reading x-rays, as well as their giving orders to a respiratory therapist. The new legislation does not answer all of these questions, and they are unlikely to go away.[340]

Another tension over expertise turf in the technology field which was brought to the fore by the review was related to the credential issue which we have seen surface as an issue for other practitioner groups. The voluntary association of medical laboratory technologists, the Ontario Society of Medical

Technologists, for example, fought for more control over the educational requirements of their members. Their educational requirements were previously not defined in the Laboratory and Specimen Collection Centre Licensing Act which applies to all clinical laboratories in Ontario. Ministry of Health proficiency tests measured the performance of the laboratory, not the competence of the technicians and technologists working there. The new legislation, therefore, needed to set up better educational requirements and eligibility criteria for registration – as was the standard for the other professional groups – so arguments ensued as to what those standards should be. The OSMT took the position that all registrants should have passed the Canadian Society of Laboratory Technologists' certification examination before being allowed to register under the new act.[341] For this they were accused of making a power grab, since their members are the ones trained to pass these exams; official insiders claimed that 'OSMT wanted control [of the laboratory].'[342]

This was an interesting expertise issue because it represented both a long-standing bottom-up dispute and a long-standing top-down dispute. The bottom-up component of the issue came out of a history of tension between the medical laboratory technologists and their more highly educated bosses, the clinical chemists and sometimes MDs. The former is a predominantly female group, while the latter are predominantly male. So this was a hierarchical issue with both gender and educational connotations.[343] Clinical chemists represent a group who are neither technologists nor traditional health professionals, but who have a background in clinical chemistry, biomedical engineering, and/or biomedical physics[344] and have chosen to work in the health field. They all applied to HPLR for self-regulatory professional status, and the clinical chemists and biomedical physicists made it onto the short-list of thirty-nine. Failing to meet the nine Criteria, however, they did not make it into the RHPA.[345] The clinical chemists had suggested the alternative of affiliation with the College of Physicians and Surgeons, but the CPSO was not in favour of this suggestion. The clinical chemists then pressed for their second best alternative, a 'College of Health Care Scientists or Allied Health Care Specialists of similar academic background.'[346] This too was turned down, so they continued to press the advisory council (HPRAC) for inclusion, fearing that they might be squeezed out of existence without the same type of regulation granted their co-workers, the medical laboratory technologists.

During this dispute, the medical laboratory technologists did not hesitate to make some rather inflammatory suggestions: first, that laboratory scientists be included in the legislation governing the medical laboratory technologists, and second, that the headship of the laboratory be shared by a medical or scientist director and a technical director, with the latter coming from the proposed

College of Medical Laboratory Technologists.[347] This would not only elevate the authority position of the technologist in the laboratory, but it could also, according to the clinical chemists, eliminate them, unless they chose to study for and write the CSLT certification exams required by the college for membership. I suspect the claim by the clinical chemists to the threat of their extinction, should this recommendation be implemented, was exaggerated for rhetorical purposes; surely if they were capable of supervising the laboratory, they could also pass the CSLT exam without a great deal of effort. The real issue, it would appear, was more one of pride and anger.[348]

For their part, medical laboratory technologists realized during the review process, that they would do well to soften their opposition to the applied scientists. By the later submissions they were saying, 'Other laboratory specialists who should not be denied the right to practice are clinical chemists and microbiologists.'[349] The 'med lab techs,' however, are probably right to argue that the scientists and medical professionals are overqualified[350] and therefore unnecessarily expensive personnel to be utilized in the running of a medical laboratory, especially since the tests done there are already ordered by a physician or dentist. This is a common, and likely quite justified, complaint throughout the health care system. If the less educated professionals are capable of doing the everyday work, they are likely, after years of experience and perhaps a few courses, quite capable of also managing that work. That they are not now doing so may well be more a reflection of the traditional superior–subordinate gender relations[351] in our society than any common-sense calculation on the part of the higher officials who set up or condone these hierarchical relations. The HPLR team did not recommend changing the management structure of the laboratory – it is unlikely that they would have seen this issue as within their purview.

Another interesting component to the credential issue is the same one we saw earlier for nurses: while the medical laboratory technologists do not want to be directly supervised by those higher up the status hierarchy, they themselves argued to directly supervise those below them, the laboratory assistants.[352] Those assistants are, at the same time, claiming, as the registered practical nurses claim of the registered nurses and the registered nurses claim of the medical doctors, that the technologists are overtrained for some of the tasks they are performing.[353] As the OSMT recognized, 'The role of the medical laboratory assistant has evolved within the past decade, and is expected to continue to evolve in the upcoming years. As the operation of instrumentation becomes simplified and salaries increase, it becomes cost effective to hire medical laboratory assistants for many of the tasks previously performed by technologists. The role of the technologist is evolving similarly and the scope of practice has expanded to include the overall administration of the laboratory in many instances. The definition of these roles and the scope of practice of various members of the profession may need to be re-defined from time to time.'[354] Like nurses, medical laboratory (and other) technologists will not likely be able to argue that they ought to be given elevated status and functions, while at the same time retaining all of the work they might wish to do, especially when others can make the same claims to the overqualification of their training as they themselves are making with regard to those above them. Issues of expertise territory and delegation of duties continue today, as they will inevitably do so in the future.[355]

The Assistants

The assistant groups are on the lowest rung of the expertise hierarchy. Historically they have been defined by the fact that they do not have a distinct body of knowledge, having been trained only in the most basic of the foundational principles of the groups they are meant to assist, if that. To put it simply, they have grown up to provide manual not mental labour, making them, as many of their supervisory groups claimed, an 'extra pair of hands.' The pattern has developed such that the more education and/or entrepreneurial success the practitioner groups have acquired, the more likely they have been to require assistants. This has been true for the medical and dental professions as well as the later merchant–service, technique, and technologist groups we have seen develop.

The gist of the HPLR/RHPA issues of expertise with regard to the assistant groups lies in the goal to either limit or expand their allowable areas of responsibility. Those employers who profited from the 'surplus value' of their assistants fought to expand both their scope of practice and their ability to work semi-independently. Those who were threatened, either in terms of expertise or entrepreneurial profit, by the competition of assistants, sought to limit both the scope and independence of these assistants. For example, dentists and medical specialists, such as ophthalmologists, wanted to expand the duties of their assistants as well as the 'delegation' of responsibilities allowed them, both of which translate into the ability of the elite professionals to bypass the increasingly expensive services and merchandise of the mid-level specialists, as well as providing some protection against their walking off with large chunks of the services and merchandise from which the elite practitioners had long profited. Ophthalmologists, like dentists, had moved to train their own assistants (orthoptists)[356] rather than work with the alternative practitioners who had grown up in the field.[357] In an attempt to resist this potential bypassing of some of their services, the optometrists' association and governing body argued to have orthoptists included under both the medical and the optometry legislation, thus ensuring that orthoptists would remain as assistants of both of the dominant professions of eye care.[358] This, however, was resisted by both the ophthalmologists and the orthoptists themselves – a resistance which succeeded.[359]

Provided they were happy to remain as assistants (as the nurses would tell you) the assistant groups, then, had the backing of the elite professional groups when their concerns were brought up during the HPLR. We have seen the dentists' reaction to any loss of their merchandise profit and potential loss of service profit from any other dental practitioners. The dentists' reaction to such loss or threat of loss consisted of pressure to limit the denturists' range of merchandise and dental hygienists' authorized acts (and thus potential independence), coupled with an attempt to expand the duties of dental assistants who were willing to remain under the control of the elite profession.[360] In the past, dental assistants had not worked inside the patient's mouth; that had been the dividing line between them and dental hygienists. But during the HPLR, with the backing of their employers (dentists),[361] dental assistants requested that they be allowed to do some minor intra-oral procedures, as an extra pair of hands for the dentist – like a surgical nurse.[362] Originally dental hygienists had agreed to some of this expansion of the assistants' scope, but they later argued in their brief to the review that the assistants' association had exaggerated the extent of their agreement.[363] The issue reflects an interesting ambivalence: dental hygienists, like registered nurses, want, on the one hand, to have someone there to do the work they do not want to do themselves; on the other hand, they have to be careful that these people do not end up displacing them. Even the elite practitioners are struggling with this delicate balance.

Ironically, the moment *any* group moves up the hierarchy of duties, it too has to have its lower level support group. Dental nurses and assistants themselves argued for an upper and lower level assistant. The level I certified dental assistant would continue on with the old scope of practice, while a new level II certified dental assistant would be given an expanded scope which included intra-oral duties.[364] To justify this, the dentists' association argued that there was a shortage of dental hygienists. Ministry officials did not concede this point, however; and there was no evidence produced to substantiate it.[365] The Ministry of Health did not approve the level II assistant at this time, nor did they grant separate regulatory status to the dental assistants. However, as of mid-1999, the dental college was in the process of introducing a level II dental assistant (to replace the old preventive dental assistant) in the province as well as changes to the legislation which would allow the dental assistants

'10 or 12 duties ... (to expand their scope of practice) so there will be a fair bit of extra assistance available to dentists for things that have only been available to hygienists ... Our legislation, once we have the regulations, will allow a dentist to delegate some of their own controlled acts to properly qualified people.'[366] So the dentists appear to have won in their fight to use dental assistants to replace much of the dental hygienists' work.

The assistant-like groups which have developed some sort of niche in the technique specialist category of health care, for example, nurses, dental hygienists, and physiotherapists, were given professional status in the Regulated Health Professions Act. The physiotherapists' work does not now require the prescription, order, supervision, or delegation of a medical doctor, so they are now positioned as independent technique specialists. Dental hygienists, however, have not yet won enough autonomy through key controlled acts or freedom from direct supervision to be considered independent. They might best be seen as dependent technique specialists. Likewise, registered nurses, although they are now licensed to perform some independent duties in their own technique specialty, still rest within the category of dependent technique specialists in that they also function on the order of other professionals. At the same time, the new extended class nurse practitioners have moved to the independent technique specialist category – in that, as we have seen, they have specific independent functions related to primary care.

The nursing group formerly referred to as registered nurses' assistants provides an interesting example of a group struggling to move out of the assistant category. Historically this has been an assistant-to-an-assistant group, not a position one might expect to hold professional status. However, they did manage to win inclusion as a professional group in the RHPA – nor would they appreciate being referred to as an assistant group, much less an assistant-to-an-assistant group. Now called registered practical nurses[367] they, like the RNs before them, were/are hoping to be viewed as having their own specialty (fitting a category I would refer to as technique specialists) and thus their own separate profession. They fought hard for this during the review, and they had influential allies: both the McRuer Report and a staff member of the Committee on the Healing Arts had supported their earlier push for more independence.[368] But they also encountered strong opposition from the registered nurses organizations, including the nursing governing college (CNO) which was supposed to represent the RNAs as well as the RNs.[369]

The nursing assistants were not granted a separate act: they were included with the RNs in the 1991 Nursing Act, as 'registered practical nurses.' When it first became clear to them that they were not likely to get autonomy from the RNs, they continued their arguments for a separate college within the joint

Expertise Turf Wars 137

profession,[370] or failing that, at least equal representation on the joint college council and its committees and staff.[371] During the development of the 1991 RHPA, they were unsuccessful in both of these requests – although they did succeed in increasing the level of representation on the joint nursing bodies.[372] After the enactment of the RHPA, the registered practical nurses continued to pressure for a separate governing college and the issue was referred to the advisory council (HPRAC). They recommended, however, that the RPNs not be granted a separate college – mostly on the grounds that the two bodies of nursing were not distinct enough to warrant their regulatory separation.[373] Other considerations were also taken into account at this time.[374] Although the RPNs had hoped to press for a separate college during the five-year RHPA review, by mid-1999, a representative said the issue was on the back-burner, and there was not much political will left for the fight. She also said the college council had passed a resolution on parity of RN and RPN representation on the college council and staff, in 1998, but a 1999 council presidential election in which an experienced RPN lost to an inexperienced RN by two votes had left the RPNs very disappointed and disaffected.[375]

Despite all this, registered practical nurses did make impressive strides, and they may find themselves in a better bargaining position in the near future. They have one major factor working in their favour, that is, their affordability. As money gets tighter, institutional managers have greater incentive to utilize the cheapest labour available for the work they require. The Ontario Hospital Association backed the RNAs' request for an expanded scope of practice, although, notably, they did not support any move away from the employer–employee control mechanisms, such as those that professional autonomy might bring.[376] It is in the hospital managers' interests to be able to have the cheaper practical nurses performing as many skilled tasks as possible. 'More and more hospital administrators [seeing] the value of utilizing RPNs' are encouraging their expansion into areas, such as dialysis care, which used to fall within the purview of the RN.[377] In fact, an RPN official claims 'the roles are now very blurred between us and the RNs. The RPNs [training] program today is close to the RN's program ten years ago.'[378] However, as the RPNs move to elevate their standards of practice, with the wage raise expectations this tends to foster, the institutional managers begin to look elsewhere.

Although practical nurses appeared to be less credentialist than registered nurses in the 1980s,[379] they did argue during the HPLR process for the updating of their nursing skills.[380] As one nursing assistant told me, they are no more favourably inclined than registered nurses are towards 'being stuck with all the dirty work.'[381] However, the need for a level of work which does not require a great deal of schooling is likely to continue, and to be accommodated by those who can afford neither the time nor the expense to attain the increasing educational standards. There were also a number of categories of less formally trained assistant groups, such as the orderlies and health care aides, or 'generics' (as the non-regulated workers are now called), to whose defence the Ontario Hospital Association also sprang.[382] They too are being used to replace their more educated, more expensive cousins.[383] It seems, as the ladder of expertise extends upward, it simply acquires another bottom rung.

The registered practical nurses association, the RPNAO, has expressed concerns about the implications of the increased utilization of non-regulated practitioners in institutional settings. They have 'asked the government to [develop] policy and set limits to the amount of unregulated workers being used.' They argue, 'The government also must monitor the staffing mixes and who is ultimately responsible for the unregulated worker as this has never been addressed. It is not clear who is responsible, both groups of nurses can delegate to the untrained workers. There is a growing concern that no one is responsible or accountable – is a RPN going to be held accountable for their delegation? The college has put out a guide book on delegation to help us with this, but it is still legislatively and legally unclear.'[384] Despite the exhaustive work of the past fifteen years, there remain many complex issues to be sorted out within this legislation.

Conclusion

The expertise turf wars waged between the health practitioners engaged in the Health Professions Legislation Review and the Regulated Health Professions Act (1991) policy processes were played out over the new scope-of-practice definitions and controlled acts which were to be allowed the newly regulated professions – and which were, therefore, to be disallowed the excluded practitioners. The dominant professions of medicine and dentistry fought to maintain their hegemony of diagnosis or primary contact with patients to ensure their positions as gatekeepers of the sector. In this, they were only partially successful, and so the door has been opened, if only a crack, for the possibility of a less restricted definition of health care expertise. But it would likely still be a scientific interpretation of expertise which would prevail. The conservative empirics who professed to be whole body practitioners met with little success. Neither the osteopaths, nor the homeopaths, nor the naturopaths have as yet been allowed into the new legislation, and the chiropractors were forced to back off their claims to whole body expertise and act only as limited practitioners of a specialized type of care, in order to join the designated professionals of health care. There is little indication to this point that medicine has much competition in whole body practice. Having said this, however, the facts may only speak for themselves. Few health policy analysts would have predicted the strength of today's midwives. There is considerable restructuring of health care in today's climate of downsizing, and where there is systemic change there is always the possibility of particular change. Some of these alternative practitioners may find themselves in the right place, at the right time.

The merchant–service specialists struggled to overcome the reluctance of the policy designers to grant a professional monopoly to the merchants of health care. They emphasized the professional service aspects of their occupation at the same time as they sought to expand their merchant territory. With the exception of the morticians – rather dubious health professionals – those who had won legislative gains in the past kept them and gained more; and those who had failed to win the earlier privileges also failed here, unless, as had been the case with audiology, they could clearly be presented as the providers of an important health care *service*. The elite of the merchant–service specialists, the dentists and, by 1974, the optometrists, fought to distinguish their skills from those of the newer or other technologists-turned-merchants, the denturists and opticians; while they in turn argued that their expertise was superior to that of the technical assistant groups which were being utilized by that elite to circumvent their work. In the end, what had changed within the merchant–service specialist groups was the elevation to full professional status from semi-professional status for denturists, chiropodists, and opticians, and the elevation from exclusion for audiologists. The latest wave of even further specialized scientific merchant–service (but mostly merchant) practitioners, such as the contact lens or hearing aid dispensers, were not given professional status nor were their empiric counterparts in the drug and potion business, the botanics and 'natural products' merchants.

The biggest change brought about for the practitioner positions was that related to the recognition of the twentieth-century technique specialists, some of whom had remained dependent on the elite practitioners to prescribe or order their services, and some of whom had functioned independently of the mainstream health care practitioners for many years. The *dependent* practitioners argued for more autonomy from their supervisors and most won it – along with full professional status. The most impressive gains here were made by the physiotherapists in their grant of primary contact. Dental hygienists also succeeded in winning a higher degree of professional recognition – although the clinical and entrepreneurial independence now allowed the physiotherapists is still being denied the hygienists. Registered nurses, dieticians, and massage therapists were given professional status, while the more highly educated clinical chemists and medical physicists were not; apparently, one's connection to the educated, scientific community did not pay off here.

Of the *independent* technique specialists, the most impressive gains were those of chiropractic which not only won professional status but also joined the new elite of health professionals, having been given primary contact, diagnosis, and the title 'doctor' – all this for the former quacks of ergonomics. Likewise, psychologists joined the elite. Midwives, too, made impressive gains, moving from a position of excluded empirics to one of independent professionals. Speech–language pathologists and occupational therapists joined the health professionals, while others who had been short-listed – social workers, marriage and family therapists, psychometrists, athletic therapists, clinical hypnotists, shiatsu therapists, clinical chemists, medical physicists, health records administrators, and medical photographers – were left out. In all, given the history of powerful interest group opposition to these technique specialists, they made some very impressive gains. Where they failed in their pursuits – where everyone mostly failed – was in their attempts to maintain as wide a monopoly as possible over their services or goods. The system that was opened up for them was, likewise, opened up for their competitors.

Technologist and assistant practitioners who had not sought to become independent merchants of their technical appliances, or entrepreneurs of their services (that is, who had stayed in a dependent relationship with the group to which they provided goods or assistance, the medical and dental technologists and the medical, dental, and nursing assistants) were given full professional status only if they had already been recognized in previous regulatory legislation. Newcomers attempted to carve out their own territory, but were to remain on the outside. The new 'outside,' however, was not the old 'outside,' that is, it had undergone a reinterpretation. The non-regulated practitioners were repeatedly assured that the state was not out to destroy them, that they were free to go on practising their brand of health care as long as it did not present a danger to the public. And although this assurance was met with scepticism, the general climate of acceptance of the many long-excluded practitioner groups who had been granted professional status, as well as the opportunity to prove the legitimacy of one's group in the future,[385] meant that the outsiders were now facing, if not a supportive state, at least a relatively non-antagonistic state. The relationship shifts brought on by these policy decisions and the interactions between the state and the practitioner groups, and among the practitioner groups, are the subject of Chapter 7.

7

Continuity and Realignment of the Positions of Connection

Earlier we saw the overall patterns of connection which had developed over time among the provider groups. Some were antagonistic, some neutral, and some supportive, thus making up the relationships of enemies, strangers, or friends.[1] As in any policy process involving a large number of affected interests, old friends might be deserted or new enemies made. As designs for the realignment of the historical positions of authority were put forth and accepted during this policy process, the health practitioner groups struggled to adjust to the implications that this realignment would have for those positions of connection which had developed throughout the sector.

State Connections

The new positions developed for the practitioner groups under the Regulated Health Professions Act moved the formerly privileged groups away from the overly friendly, autonomous, relations they had previously enjoyed with the state. The key profession of medicine, for example, was being shifted to a less favourable position *vis-à-vis* the state than that which it had enjoyed for some time. There were signs of a little less trust, a little less cooperation, support, fidelity, and so on.[2] The Ontario Medical Association was still able to negotiate with the state over issues directly affecting it, such as fee-for-service rates, but it suffered losses along with its wins.[3] The medical professions was also moving closer and closer to a position of consultation, even audience in some cases, over decisions which affect the whole of the health care system.[4] For a time after the enactment of the new legislation, the medical representatives appeared to have little voice in the changes happening throughout the sector, but by mid-1998 the Ontario College of Family Physicians commented that it had been 'listened to more in the last six months ... than it had been in the last five years' (although the examples given were in regard to federal rather than provincial consultation).[5] The College of Physicians and Surgeons of Ontario also commented at this time on their good relationship with the Ontario Ministry of Health, saying, 'The Ministry now works with the Colleges as a group – not just the CPSO. They communicate with us; they let us know what they are planning and what they are thinking about doing; and they incorporate our suggestions.' Overall, the old friendly relationship is being replaced by a more neutral one; medicine now knows itself to be under the 'watchful eye'of the public guardians. This new relationship still shows signs of the supportive, amicable relations of the past, but it is now a tempered relationship of support coupled with obligation.

Conversely, many formerly less privileged provider groups have moved away from the overly suspicious relations that they have traditionally held with the state. The technique and technology specialists, for example, have moved more towards a position of consultation – in a shift from the opposite end of the spectrum where they, unlike the elite professionals, had previously been either excluded or allowed little more than mere audience to decision-making processes. Merchant–service groups have shown some shift towards more voice (and therefore more autonomy) for the non-elites of this category who continue to break up the monopoly of dentistry in particular – in keeping with the state's at present strong free market orientation. Pharmacy, which has little market competition, in comparison, may, as we saw earlier, gain the support of the state through its new consultation role with today's policy makers concerned with drug and medication overutilization.

Finally, the non-regulated practitioners who were not included in the RHPA have moved from a decided exclusion from any decision making in the organized health sector to sit somewhere between the position of audience and genuine consultation. There is a sense that they are no longer silenced in a way that outsider groups had previously been silenced, but it is also hard to imagine their concerns carrying any great weight in important decisions being made within the sector. Their shift to the slightly safer, less antagonistic position of strangers to the state may, however, allow them the possibility of entry into the system at some later date. The avenues have now been left open for further attempts on their part to do so.[6]

Group Connections: Internal

The patterns of connection within the practitioner groups were affected by the policy process of the 1980s and 1990s. Distinct roles between the profession's governing body and its voluntary association were both expected and demanded in this legislative process. The agency role of the governing body was kept distinct from the unionlike role of the association; submissions to the Health Professions Legislation Review were solicited from both. Because of the emphasis placed on the issue of professional self-governance during the policy review, there was a certain legitimacy given the voice of the governing body, perhaps over that of the association. The latter had always engaged in a fair bit of rhetoric, and a great deal of that was probably, like that of all union negotiations, often perceived by its recipients as a sort of expected exaggeration – part of the bluff. Such rhetoric did, however, signal a certain degree of incompatibility between the present pragmatic attitude of the policy decision makers inside the state and the traditional role of the health practitioner associations. One effect this sort of incompatibility might spawn is a tendency for the state to turn its ears to the more moderate voice within the professional group, that is, the governing body, or college, thus widening the gap between the group associations and the state, as well as between the two professional organizations.

Another internal tension within medicine, which was heightened during the policy process, was that brought about by the distinction of interests between the leaders of particular specialties in medicine and the leaders of the profession as a whole. Assumedly each of the medical specialist groups would like the full support of both the association (OMA) and the governing body (CPSO) in their objectives. But as the demands from the state continue to pressure the leadership of the profession, that leadership of both the governing body and the association will have to trade off some of its loyalties to, or sympathies with, these internal specialist groups[7] for benefits accrued to the entire profession. Likewise, family physicians sometimes have reason for dispute with the specialists. The Ontario College of Family Physicians is concerned that the reduced role of the family practitioner in areas of care such as obstetrics, and in acute care and home care institutions, is leading to increased fragmentation of patient care as well as inflated costs.[8]

As various professions, such as nursing and the technology specialists, continue to develop internal specialties, this divided loyalty between the whole and the parts, or the parts and the parts, will affect more of the sector's practitioners. Internal tensions within the alternative practitioner groups tend to revolve around the division between the straight old school specialists and the mixed or more eclectic practitioners who have adopted the techniques of other practitioners over time. Here, the policy makers tend to favour the more straightforward specialists, presumably because they are more readily understood and possibly contained.

144 Health Care Practitioners

Group Connections: External

The patterns of connection among the practitioner groups were, of course, affected by the policy process. Some were disrupted, and some were reinforced. These patterns had developed out of a mostly bitter history of clinical and entrepreneurial competition among these groups – the dynamics of which had been laced, as we have seen, with the social prejudices of their day. Not surprisingly, the latest round of professional legislation making saw a revival of much of this history; it also, however, saw, and itself elicited, a considerable amount of compromise and adaptation with regard to these relationships. It is one of the hallmarks of this legislation that its formulators put an exhaustive effort into dealing with this aspect of the health care dynamic – previous legislators, particularly the designers of the 1974 Health Disciplines Act, chose, perhaps forgivably, to side-step this formidable task.

Medical and Other Whole Body Practitioner Connections

In politics and professional monopolies, the connections that count the most are, of course, those held with the most powerful. If you cannot be their friends, you would at least prefer to be strangers on neutral territory, or willing clients of their benevolence, rather than their enemies, or clients to an unwelcome patronage. In its relations with the other health provider groups the medical profession has, as we have seen, traditionally chosen to either patronize, prosecute, or ignore other practitioners. As Grove commented in the late 1960s,

> We tend to find the medical profession acting paternally and sometimes protectively towards the hospital-based occupations of nursing and paramedicine [those under medical supervision]; with disdain towards others, such as optometry; and with positive hostility towards some, such as chiropractic and naturopathy ... In other words, those who practise under some degree of medical paternalism, and economic and social dependency, on the medical profession – are generally exempt from censure ... Those who practise independently of the medical profession, however, are more suspect ... This group is not all of a piece, ... osteopaths are third-rate doctors, but at least they have some medical training. Chiropodists and masseurs often work with, and under doctors. Optometrists are bearable, as long as they stick to their last. Chiropractors ought to work only on prescription from a doctor. Naturopaths are beyond the pale.[9]

The bulk of energy expended by the medical profession on its relationships with other health practitioners had traditionally been reserved, as we have seen, for those who threatened either its valued entrepreneurial territory or the integrity of its clinical expertise.[10] This latest policy event, however, showed signs of change. There was still some opposition from the medical profession to those they consider quacks, such as the naturopaths, but a great deal of the elite profession's historical opposition to other practitioners had subsided, and the overall tone of the medical profession during the policy process was distinctly moderate, particularly that of its governing body, the College of Physicians and Surgeons of Ontario.

The initial submission made by the CPSO to the Health Professions Legislation Review made suggestions for collaborative and independent relationships, which should have appeared to many other provider groups as quite supportive. Even some of the practitioners who perform only 'delegated' tasks, such as the home care helpers, were mentioned as potential independents.[11] The CPSO also spoke of the importance of encouraging communication and improving coordination of all health practitioners – going so far as to make specific recommendations for cross-profession referrals and transfer of patient records.[12] While there were ambiguities here – especially with regard to medicine's gatekeeper role[13] – when the CPSO was pressed for specifics in a second submission to the HPLR, it came up with a list which was somewhat surprising given the history of relationships between medicine and the other practitioners. In the first place, examples for inclusion in the elite position of fully licensed professionals included optometrists, chiropractors, chiropodists and podiatrists, physiotherapists, and psychologists – all former enemies or clients of a paternal relationship with at least one faction of the medical profession. Second, the CPSO developed a classification scheme which would register, for example, cardiology technicians, dental hygienists, nursing assistants, and radiological technologists, and recognize, for example, health record administrators, marriage and family therapists, and social workers.[14] Nowhere in the CPSO submissions was there any sort of diatribe against other practitioners.

In their June 1984 submission[15] the CPSO stated clearly, 'This College does not take the position that any other profession should be regulated in some manner by the CPSO.' (Although it should be kept in mind that they were referring here to regulation specifically. The medical profession might still exert control or influence over other practitioners via, say, referral, prescription, order, supervision, or delegation.) The CPSO also expanded on its previous recommendation for the establishment of a 'Health Professions Advisory Council' which would allow for ongoing input from groups with regard to their preferred scope-of-practice definitions, as well as have the power to review 'the procedures used in the regulatory process by the health professions.' Further, it softened its previous statement in its January 1984 submission about the need for referrals from medicine to other independent practitioners, and ended its submission with statements such as the following: 'The CPSO does not believe the public should be arbitrarily "protected" by legislative provisions which limit access to health providers.' All in all, theirs was a rather generous approach to their former enemies and client practitioners.

This acceptance of, and cooperation with, many of the other practitioner groups in the sector signals an attitudinal shift for the medical profession which, as one leader of the profession put it in the mid-1990s, was 'not possible ten years ago.'[16] We have seen the historical evidence of the medical profession's general animosity to any other practitioner groups who threatened its self-defined clinical or entrepreneurial territory. During the course of this policy process, however, we see a shift away from much of the elitism and paternalism which had marked earlier relations. Some of this new attitude was probably the result of genuine acceptance of other practitioners, at least up to a point,[17] and some probably came from the pressures being exerted on the medical profession by a more demanding body of health consumers and a determined group of bureaucratic officials and policy reviewers. The signals from the state officials were clear: everyone was expected to do their part in relieving the tensions among the practitioner groups. The HPLR team gave equally clear signals of the same commitment. And both, as we have seen, made constant reference to egalitarian principles. Any politically astute group would have to have been uncharacteristically imperceptive to have refused to give in to some of this pressure.

Groups were asked to comment on each other's submissions, with all polemic clearly discouraged, as well as meet face-to-face to discuss their differences with the, once again, clear imperative that they come to agreement. Some of these mandatory sessions among the practitioner groups served little purpose other than to review old grievances, but many resulted in both a better understanding of the other's position on issues, and some sort of agreement over issues of contention. At the same time as the review was progressing, interaction among provider groups was increasing at the community level and this exposure, according to an influential OMA representative, resulted in the development of 'good functional relationships' and 'coalitions with other professionals' which had previously been 'unthinkable' and which had now established a precedent of 'efficiency ... [and] trust.'[18] As of mid-1998, the president of the Ontario College of Family Physicians was speaking very positively about the new roles of midwives and extended class nurse practitioners, as well as the potential for 'close collaborative relationships' and 'cooperation' among various (non-whole body) practitioners – although she did consider 'the family physician as the only one trained to see the whole broad spectrum of health care.'[19]

One relationship that remains less than friendly is that between medicine and the other whole body practitioners. In concrete terms the alternative whole body practitioners, such as the naturopaths, homeopaths, and osteopaths, appear to present little, if any, threat to medicine. However, there is potential here for a more subtle disruption which could set a precedent that the medical profession would not be happy to see. The alternative practitioner challenge strikes at the core practice of medicine's gatekeeper role, namely, that of general diagnosis. Because the alternative whole body practitioners wish to diagnose human diseases and disorders based on an alternative philosophy of health care altogether, they also advocate, or at least infer, a certain degree of circumvention of the medical model of health care. Notably, during the public meetings in 1995 of the Health Professions Regulatory Advisory Council (HPRAC) regarding naturopathy's bid for inclusion in the RHPA, the objections from medicine (CPSO, OMA) rested primarily with the naturopaths' claim to be capable of independent diagnosis with sufficiently broad functions (as controlled acts) to follow through with treatments related to these diagnoses.[20]

Medicine's reaction here was probably tinged with an element of genuine concern for the consumers of health care for what they consider bad or even dangerous medicine, as well as the obligation on the part of the College of Physicians and Surgeons to guard medical practice in the province: keeping in mind these alternative whole body groups have long insisted they are practising medicine and continue to refer to themselves as doctors, despite the title protection in the 1991 RHPA for this designation.[21] As was pointed out earlier, however, little effort has been made to apply medicine's own scientific standards to assess properly the value of the contributions of such alternative practitioners – even in the case where those practitioners also hold a medical licence.[22] Whether or not these alternative practices are doing any harm to the public is a question the medical profession has done little towards answering – despite both its constant assertions of this harm as fact, as well as its considerable influence on the public and private purses of health research.[23]

The eclectic osteopaths, who claim to practise both conservative medicine and alternative health care, were unable to elicit the support of the practitioners of either. They entered the HPLR process still clearly angry at the failure of predecessor state regulators to live up to their 'verbal assurances' during the setting up of the Drugless Practitioners Act in 1925 that osteopathy, as a 'non-drugless, medically trained' practitioner group, would soon thereafter be 'provided' with 'more suitable legislation.'[24] Osteopaths attempted to convince the review members of their distinct approach to health care, making the claim that 'no other physician of the healing arts has the basic understanding of [our] therapeutic approach. The MD knows nothing of manipulative theory or practice, and the chiropractor lacks too much of the totality of medicine to justify his application of the manipulation he espouses.'[25] But this claim elicited little response from the policy designers or the professional groups it targeted – the latter indicating how little power the osteopaths really have. They appear, then, to be rather uninfluential and friendless at this stage. Their small numbers leave them with little bargaining power in times of policy restructuring. Neither were they able to elicit the support they needed from the medical profession; they were at one time slated for joint regulation within the CPSO, but the medical profession succeeded in having this decision reversed.[26] Osteopaths entered the policy process in a weak position, and they left it even weaker.

Naturopaths probably best represent the viewpoint of today's empirics. They seem little inclined to present themselves as scientists despite their polemic use of the term 'medicine.' Gort and Coburn have given evidence indicating that, while naturopaths did attempt to 'give the right answers' in one influential report, their assessment of what it would take to influence the policy development process in their favour tends to be weak at best.[27] Both prior to and during the HPLR process they appeared to have grossly underestimated the importance of the level of scientific and technological training taken as a standard by outside analysts for the assessment of all health practitioners.[28]

During the course of the review process, while other alternative practitioners, such as midwives and chiropractors, in danger of being labelled empirics and left out of the new group of professionals, dug up any scientific data they could find to prove that they had a distinct 'body of knowledge,' naturopaths openly referred to their 'use of instinct.'[29] (A holistic medical doctor once gave me, over the course of a single conversation, more articles on the scientific basis of natural healing – related, for example, to recent studies on stress and diet as determining factors in illness – than naturopaths brought forth over the course of the entire review.)

An earlier national study[30] found naturopaths to be individualistic and apolitical.[31] Although they had a national association by the mid-1960s, few practitioners had bothered to join. The resultant lack of cohesiveness of the group as a whole almost certainly contributed to their poor showing in that study as

Continuity and Realignment of the Positions of Connection   149

well as later in reports on health care practitioners.[32] Naturopaths have not, however, been entirely without political acuity. They have had three political campaigns, all in reaction to negative official comments or recommendations for legislative change, and all involving the targeting of politicians with heavy letter-writing campaigns from supporters of naturopathy. The first came just after the 1964 report by the Royal Commission on Health Services.[33] At that time, naturopaths across Canada began the same kind of sophisticated lobbying campaign for inclusion into the national health insurance plan as had succeeded for chiropractors.[34] Although Ontario naturopaths failed to attain their goal,[35] they did demonstrate their ability to engage in pressure politics. These same tactics were again employed with more success in 1974 when naturopaths managed to avoid deregulation, and in the early 1990s when they managed to stay a second decision to have their practice deregulated.[36] The Regulated Health Professions Act of 1991 had excluded the naturopaths, but a political campaign centred on patient letter writing and directed at a new, more sympathetic NDP government succeeded in staying this decision. While apparently incapable of playing to the pro-science bent of the health bureaucracy decision makers, naturopaths have had much less difficulty playing the politicians – although some of the delay of the response to the HPRAC report on naturopathy's most recent bid for inclusion in the RHPA was suspected to be linked to the fact that the more sympathetic NDP government had been replaced by a less sympathetic Conservative government.

The connections that have counted for naturopaths, then, have been those held with the public consumers of health care,[37] as well as their elected officials. Support from their fellow practitioners was not forthcoming in the HPLR/RHPA process, not even from their long-standing friends, the chiropractors. At the time of the review, over half of registered naturopaths were chiropractors, and a sizeable minority of registered chiropractors were also registered to practise naturopathy. This constituted the largest overlap of membership between any two health professions.[38] The Board of Directors of Chiropractic argued that this overlap should not be allowed; individual membership should be restricted to one college. This issue raised tangential concerns,[39] which if dealt with for naturopaths and chiropractors, would also have had to be dealt with for other overlapping professions. (For example, there is overlap of pharmacists and physicians, nurses and physicians, and nurses and midwives, the latter two of whom also raised this issue.[40]) The decision was left to be made later. As of mid-1999, the chiropractic college was still recognizing dual registration with 'members of other health professions ... and unregulated health professions [*sic*]' and was using a policy guideline to lay out requirements for dual registrants, such as 'inform[ing] the patient that the proposed treatment is outside the scope of practice of chiropractic' ... and in the case of unregulated health practitioners ... 'the registrant shall also inform the patient that the College of Chiropractic may have no jurisdiction over the matter.'[41]

What was perhaps most interesting with regard to this naturopathy–chiropractic relationship was the desertion of the naturopaths by their former friends, the chiropractors. These two groups had always been on the same side of the tracks in relation to the health system hierarchy, but now the chiropractors were dissociating themselves from a group which was not exactly in official favour. The reason given by the Board of Directors of Chiropractic for their recommendation of disassociation with the naturopaths was that joint practice was confusing for patients – they went expecting chiropractic treatment and were given naturopathic treatment – as well as for OHIP and the insurance companies funding chiropractic care but not naturopathic care, and for the board itself, which did not consider itself qualified or willing to develop and regulate standards of practice for naturopathy. The bottom line, however, was that chiropractors deserted their old friends in their time of need.[42] Even after chiropractors had secured their own gains under the RHPA, they continued to argue to restrict the practices and regulation of naturopathy.[43]

The relationship between naturopaths and homeopaths seems to be the least conflict ridden of the naturopaths' relationships with other practitioners. They share an alternative-to-medicine philosophy and appear to make use of each other's diagnostic and treatment modalities – particularly on the part of the naturopaths' in their usage of homeopathic treatments. Homeopaths came out in support of RHPA regulation of naturopathy during the 1995 HPRAC review of the case; however, their purpose in attending these public meetings was clearly as much to argue their own case as that of the naturopaths.[44]

For the naturopaths' part, their attitude towards other health practitioners was somewhat ambiguous. On the one hand, they themselves did not appear to want control over other practitioners since they spoke of overlapping health procedures, such as 'acupuncture, nutrition, x-ray, manipulation, massage, botanicals, physioelectro-therapeutics, counselling and colon therapy, to name but a few,' and they claimed not to want to 'have any authority over practitioners in another profession.'[45] On the other hand, they also suggested 'holistic medical practitioners [MDs] ... would require considerable training in addition to their existing background ... to become adequately trained in naturopathic medicine'[46] and they pointed out their 'concern with those individuals who are not registered with any other board and who are not qualified as a primary contact practitioner.'[47] In other words they wanted more control over unregu-

Continuity and Realignment of the Positions of Connection 151

lated practitioners whom they considered inadequately trained. The sense one gets here is that, given a position of authority themselves, naturopaths would likely act to exclude others who failed to meet the naturopathic standards of practice in much the same manner as the medical profession has acted towards them.

Continuities and Realignments of the Merchant–Service Connections

Dental Connections

Shifts in the power differential within the merchant–service groups, as we have already seen, have been dramatic. Dentistry, of course, had never held anywhere near the power of the medical profession in the health sector as a whole, but it has long been the most influential group within its own specialized field of care. As such, it has also been the group it would be best not to have antagonized, but antagonize them their ancillary groups have done. First one group of technicians, the denturists, managed to enter the dental market providing full dentures legitimately and partial dentures 'under the table.' Then, the dental hygienists began to press for the autonomy in Ontario which some of their colleagues had won in other jurisdictions. Now, with the voice given them by the HPLR, the remaining dental technologists were giving reasons why they too should be self-governing. The only group which still appeared content with its subordinate role under the dental profession was the assistant or nurse group; however, the example of both the registered nurses' relations with the medical profession and the nursing assistants' relations with the registered nurses might give any dominant group reason to worry about this last category of workers as well.

Overall, the submissions of both the dentists' governing body, the Royal College of Dental Surgeons of Ontario, and its voluntary association, the Ontario Dental Association, displayed ample signs of their wish to act as the head of all dental care practice.[48] They also displayed signs of a paternalistic and at times arrogant attitude coupled with a fear for the future.[49] The ODA's position was further clarified by a public letter written at the time of the early stages of the review by the association's president, Ron Bell, for the dental association's publication, the *Ontario Dentist*: 'The point is that we at the ODA do not want to see dentistry being practised by a collection of individuals other than dentists. *We simply cannot allow* our hard-won scope of practice to be chipped away and parcelled out to various groups, even when the cause is as worthy as better care for seniors.'[50] It is interesting to note here how the dentists did not even bother to pretend to be putting their patients first, as so many others were doing when they couched their entrepreneurial interests in the language of 'serving the public interest.'

The dental profession's opposition to its competitors made the opposition of the medical profession to its competitors seem mild indeed. The difference in reaction from the two old elite groups, however, might well be explained by the vastly different positions they each hold in relation to the overall provision of health care. Medicine is so solidly entrenched throughout the whole range of health care practices that it is hard to see it as in any way seriously threatened by other practitioners, many of whom are doing the work the medical professionals do not want to do anyway. Dentists, on the other hand, have a great deal to lose. As one official put it, while thinking of the differences between the behaviour of the medical profession and that of the dental profession throughout the whole process, 'Medicine has so much already, they can afford to be sanguine ... Dentists, on the other hand, carved out a very restricted scope of practice from medicine ... Now their work is disappearing.'[51]

Partly through their own efforts at prevention of dental disease and decay, dentists have found themselves being needed less and less. The development of ancillary dental care groups, that is, the technical or technique service groups (dental technicians, denturists, and dental hygienists) has also meant that many of the dentist's previous tasks can now be performed competently by others. These alternative service providers are not only capable of taking over some of the work of the dentist, but also their services (particularly those of the dental hygienist) help prevent the development of the sorts of diseases and disorders over which the dentists hold a practice monopoly.

The fight between dentists and the denturists was discussed in Chapter 6 with regard to the issue of expertise. Perhaps their positions of connection are best summarized here by the denturists themselves in a comment they made in reaction to the proposal that they be 'clustered' with the dental profession in the new legislation. To this, they responded: 'We start by putting our cards on the table. The Denturist Association of Ontario is unequivocally opposed to any form of clustering with the dental profession – whether by statute or by regulation. There is no middle ground on this issue. That luxury has been denied us by years of deliberate antagonism and wilful obstruction on the part of organized dentistry.'[52] In dental care everyone's cards were on the table. During this policy event, you were either a dentist, a friend of the dentists, or an enemy of the dentists.

In all the vying for position during the course of the review and the later stages of the policy-making process, dentists were their own worst enemy. Despite the obviously egalitarian climate of the HPLR, dentists loudly proclaimed their commitment to hierarchical control. Signs of their arrogance showed up in their newsletters as well. An editorial of the *Ontario Dentist* in 1985 opened with the very succinct statement: 'The Health Disciplines Review Board is currently considering a presentation from the Ontario Dental Hygienists' Association that supports expanded duties, separate collegial status and the first steps towards independent practice. It therefore appears that hygienists and dental assistants have forgotten that *they exist solely to support dentists.*'[53] This statement was then backed up in a follow-up letter by an official of the RCDSO.[54] (The dental hygienists made sure the review team saw this inflammatory exchange).[55] In comparison with the dentists' more-than-obvious bid for control, dental hygienists did not appear to want to control anyone.[56]

There was also considerable evidence that dentists were not just posturing here. The RCDSO did not appear to be able to be trusted to treat hygienists fairly. As the Ontario Dental Hygienists Association pointed out to the review team, despite pressure to do so for over thirty years, the RCDSO had refused to allow for any representation of hygienists in its organization even though the RCDSO was the legal joint-governing body for both dentists and hygienists.[57] In 1980 two hygienists had been allowed to sit on the governing body, but they were there as observers only; they were not given any voice. I was told by one inside RCDSO official that the fact that there were a number of 'very self-serving dentists on Council [during the 1980s] ... was very well-known.'[58]

All in all, dental hygienists looked like moderate, considerate, egalitarian women who had really been treated unfairly – which, of course was not at all far from the truth. Dentists, by comparison did not look quite so good. When it became apparent that 'their' hygienists were going to come out of the process better positioned than they had gone in, dentists stepped up their promotion of the idea of a 'level II' dental assistant with which they could ultimately replace the dental hygienist.[59] From the dentists' perspective, dental hygienists were really supposed to have been a dental assistant (as we saw in the quote above). Dental hygienists had not grown up outside the professional circle, as chiropractors had. They were originally trained in dental faculties of the university system at the request of the dentists themselves,[60] so they were considered the dentists' property, so to speak. With the potential loss of control over that property, dentists moved to replace it.

Throughout the whole policy process dentists remained entirely conservative – never giving in, never bending. Even where a tiny bit of graciousness could have been shown, it was refused.[61] Despite the emphasis, even necessity, of improving relations within the health care field during this policy process, the self-proclaimed leaders of dentistry appeared to make no attempt whatsoever to improve on the notoriously poor relations in the dental sector, in fact quite the opposite.[62] Some of the reaction on the part of dentists stems, assumedly, from their not unreasonable fear that their work is disappearing – manners count for less when you are fighting for your job.[63] It may be, that the recent trend towards dental cosmetics will save the elite profession,[64] and thus, soften some of their antagonism towards their fellow practitioners. Or it may be that dentists will continue to erode the territory of hygienists, at least, with the winning of an expanded scope of practice and delegation of controlled acts for dental assistants, as we saw in Chapter 6.

Pharmacy

In its relationship with other practitioner groups, the connection of importance for pharmacists has always been that with the medical professionals. As we saw earlier, the latter have been less than generous in the past in allowing their fellow practitioners to develop their autonomy. But if medicine was putting up any great fuss over pharmacy's attempts to limit medical control over its professional functions, this would have had to have been going on behind the scenes,[65] for there is not much evidence of any sizeable opposition. The pharmacists' college did admit to possible professional conflict over prescription judgment-calls between the pharmacist and the physician, in which case they argued that the pharmacist would have to go with his or her 'professional judgment.'[66] This is the same answer almost every other provider group gave to this same type of question,[67] but it does not deal with the fundamental conflict, which is the extent to which another practitioner might override the judgment of a physician if that physician should object to her or his interference. The neutral ground between these two groups could become more antagonistic if this issue were to be brought forth by the medical profession. The president of the Ontario College of Family Physicians expressed concern about the potential side-effects of uncoordinated patient care, which might include negative interactions from both mixed pharmaceutical drugs (purchased at separate pharmacies by patients shopping for a best price) and 'herbal and complementary products' being added on to other treatment regimes. The OCFP president says it is the family physician who ends up 'picking up the pieces,' and she recommended a stronger coordinating role for the family physician.[68]

With regard to other practitioner groups, pharmacists have now legally extended their professional scope of practice into the expected territory of other health practitioners, that is, territory for which the others are the best trained specialists in the field. The merchandise of prosthetics and orthotics, hearing aids, and diagnostic and health monitoring instruments are usually sold in pharmacies, so other specialist merchants have reason to fear the aggression of the pharmacy profession on their entrepreneurial territory, especially because these other merchants do not carry the status of being 'professionals.' This, of course, is creating tension between these groups.

The College of Pharmacy also showed interest in another specialized area. They had argued to the review that a check ought to be put on herbalists who were potentially selling drugs.[69] This was not done by the Regulated Health Professions Act, although it might be done in the future under other legislation, particularly that related to the federal food and drugs regulations currently under revision.[70] This is an interesting area where future disputes will likely erupt, because the sale of herbal or 'botanical' or 'natural' products is becoming increasingly lucrative, a fact which has not escaped the notice of the large pharmaceutical companies. If pharmacists were to win control over even part of this market, these companies would stand to gain. Of course, it should also be said that some of these products may indeed prove to be harmful or poisonous substances in which case pharmacists may be within their professional mandate to attempt to control their distribution.

Another group which the pharmacists were keeping an eye on during the HPLR process were chiropodists and podiatrists. In this case another provider group was treading into pharmacy territory. One of the proposed authorized acts for the to-be-regulated profession of chiropody involved the prescription of designated drugs related to the treatment of the foot.[71] The pharmacists' college voiced its concern, not over the prescription authorization, but over the possibility that chiropodists or podiatrists might begin to dispense these drugs – thus cutting into the pharmacists' virtual monopoly over the dispensing of all drugs which carry a dispensing fee.[72] As we saw in Chapter 6, chiropodists won an authorized act for prescribing drugs related to their specific type of care,[73] and although this is a very limited authority, it is the precedent which would, of course, concern pharmacists. This market territory is going to remain, as it has always been, carefully guarded by any who presently hold the balance of power there. Friendships and animosities will be defined on these terms.

For their part, chiropodists had, as we have seen, attached themselves as complements to the medical profession and thus ensured the cooperation of that profession for whom they posed little clinical and/or financial threat; while their American-trained counterparts, the podiatrists, had insisted on the appropriateness of their maintaining medical-like procedures, such as minor surgery.[74] Chiropodists were allowed into the RHPA, and podiatrists were

156   Health Care Practitioners

phased out. Perhaps the fact that the former were friends of the medical profession while the latter were not, is coincidental, perhaps not. The reasons for both groups' final outcome were, of course, related to their success or failure in meeting the 'nine criteria' (see Appendix 7), but since the details of this reasoning were never explained to the public, the final report consisting of draft legislation with a brief introduction,[75] it remains unclear as to exactly why, based on objective criteria, the group complementary to medicine succeeded in getting included in the act, while the less-than-accommodating group did not.

One interesting relationship dynamic within podiatry was that of the less than supportive position that podiatry practitioners took with regard to their colleagues in training. There is little evidence of the podiatrists' support for students of podiatry, who were cut out of the new legislation; while they, the practising podiatrists, were allowed to be grandfathered into the system. This stands in rather sharp contrast to the loyalty the medical profession tends to display to its students.[76]

Practitioners of the merchant–service field specializing in foot care who were 'beyond the pale,' in this case, reflexologists, did not get included in the new legislation. Neither is the profession of chiropody threatened by assistant groups who might take over their work. The purely dispensing footcare merchant group, the pedorthists who fit and sell corrective footwear out of independent shops, did not get included in the new legislation, although they still might represent a future threat to chiropodists. Pedorthists do a substantial amount of business – business that chiropodists, who have no dispensing licence, would presumably not mind profiting from. Because of shared market interests in the fitting and selling of orthotics, there is also a potential for conflict between chiropodists and chiropractors, as well as occupational therapists and nurses specializing in foot care. As with all the health merchants, there is plenty left to fight about.

The merchant–service specialists of eye care and ear–speech care encountered some opposition to their professional advancement from the medical elite, but it was nowhere near as vitriolic as that faced by the merchant–service groups of dentistry. The medical profession had developed its specialties in these areas late in the game, so the new twentieth-century merchant–service practitioners, especially those of eye care, the optometrists and opticians, had an established position by the time that there were any significant number of medical specialists to oppose their advancement. Ophthalmologists[77] did attempt to curb some of the increasing power of optometrists by drawing on the whole body or primary contact and diagnosis arguments of the medical profession. They submitted a lengthy commentary on the optometrists' initial submission to the review. This commentary was meant mostly to persuade the HPLR team of the limits to the optometrist's abilities, and of the suitability and cost effectiveness of the ophthalmic medical health care team consisting of the ophthalmologist (MD) at the top, with a group of support technicians and assistants (orthoptists and ophthalmology assistants) working under supervision. The ophthalmologists' medical association could not have been much more obvious about their belief in the importance of the dominance of the medical role than was stated in the following passage: 'The Ontario Medical Association believes that it is in the public interest to have considerably more emphasis directed to the fact that the whole of medicine is concerned with eye health care – with all its medical as well as its attendant political, social and economic implications. Basically, the whole of eye health care is a medical concern, a medical responsibility, a medical problem, a medical function; and total eye health care properly lives within the scope of practice of medicine.'[78] Despite these unsubstantiated 'arguments,' the indications coming from this policy process suggest that the medical specialists did not carry a great deal of clout in the final policy decisions.[79] Ophthalmologists continue to dominate the areas of pathologies and surgery of the eye, but their greatest competitors, the optometrists, joined the regulated health professions club as 'doctors' who were granted the privilege of diagnosis as well as winning on all of the big issues of concern for their group – including some which clearly tread on old medical territory.[80] By 1999, the optometrists had also succeeded in having the minister of health refer (to HPRAC) their request for an expanded scope of practice.[81]

The opticians' relationship with the ophthalmologists is more friendly than that of the optometrists. There is less conflict over clinical territory. In fact, ophthalmologists sometimes hire opticians to work in conjunction with them.[82] Where the opticians' functions cross over into the optometrists' entrepreneurial territory there is considerably more conflict. One area of contention is that of advertising. Optometrists contend that the College of Opticians ought to be preventing the shady advertising of the big optical companies which employ opticians, but the college replies that it only has jurisdiction over its members per se; it does not 'control corporations.'[83] Another entrepreneurial issue in this field, which dates back to the early 1900s, is the selling of optical appliances by mail order. This practice is not regulated, and if the service is provided outside the province, the provincial governing body has no jurisdiction.

Another potential threat to the merchant–service specialties in general comes from the general medical practitioner or family practitioner. Like dentists, any medical professional, including a GP or FP, is allowed not only to practise in the same areas as these new specialists, but also to sell the merchandise which arises from them. In that sense, they could potentially threaten both the service work and the product profits of these new practitioner groups. The main threat here probably comes more from the medical use of assistant groups, such as the orthoptists of eye care or the physician's assistants who fit hearing aids. So the middle groups, the merchant–service groups, are again watching for encroachment from both the old elite practitioners and the ever-present assistant groups coming up behind them.

Technique Specialists Connections

The Neuro–Muscular–Skeletal Specialists

The new technique specialists had, as we have seen, either attached themselves to the medical or dental professions, or fought to be accepted as professionals in their own right. The dominant practitioners of the neuro–muscular–skeletal (body movement) area, the chiropractors, physiotherapists, and massage practitioners, had a long history of relations both among themselves and between them and the medical profession.

The medical profession had, of course, long antagonized chiropractors by claiming their services were useless (as they have for years, against all forms of health care they themselves long refused to investigate, such as spinal manipulation, acupuncture, colonic irrigation, and so on), but, as we have seen, chiropractors managed to stay around long enough to prove them wrong. The argument between the medical profession and chiropractors during this policy process was not over the question of whether or not chiropractors were quacks, but rather over the territorial intrusion of medicine *into* chiropractic. The historical tendency has long been for medicine to first proclaim invalid any health care procedures not originating from within its own or ancillary practices and sciences, and then later to move to appropriate as their own those practices which have held up over time – preferably taking them away from their original practitioners, as happened in the case of hypnosis.[84] This tendency worried chiropractors, especially after the medical profession indicated its interest in obtaining the inclusion of 'spinal manipulation,' the foundational technique of chiropractic, in its scope-of-practice statement and/or authorized acts. In addition the ancillary groups to medicine who specialized in the neuro–skeletal–muscular area, physiotherapists and massage therapists, were pushing for the same. Chiropractors fought hard against this invasion of their turf.

One influential medical spokesperson indicated to me his opinion that chiropractors were just getting 'hung up' on a technicality with their concern for this 'spinal manipulation' wording. He argued that the phrase was needed by the medical profession simply to acknowledge that orthopedic surgeons commonly made adjustments to the spine in the course of their work.[85] This claim, however, seems weak: during the whole policy process everyone fought and fought over the most exact use of wording; to argue for someone else's 'words' was to hold up a red flag – as this spokesperson well knew, having himself been party to many heated debates over his own profession's 'words.' Even the closely related phrase, 'spinal adjustment' would have carried different connotations, both clinically and legally. This was a clear invasion of turf, and everyone knew it. While the Ontario medical profession had seemed little inclined to practise 'spinal manipulation' up to that point, interest in 'manual medicine' in the United States and Europe, has been steadily rising.[86] Also, recent studies of the efficacy of spinal manipulation, compared with the inefficacy of common medical practices, particularly with regard to lower back pain,[87] could quite conceivably have both the family practitioner and the medical osteospecialists looking at this method of relief for the suffering of the many 'back' patients they have long failed to alleviate.

Chiropractors spent considerable effort to convince the HPLR team that it was inappropriate to allow the medical profession, the physiotherapy profession, or the massage therapy profession to practise spinal manipulation. All three types of practitioners are, according to chiropractic spokespersons and the studies they cite, inadequately trained to engage in the practice of spinal manipulation.[88] All three professions, however, were given either authorized acts, or enough scope, to perform spinal manipulation.[89]

Although chiropractors fought hard to avoid any invasion of their own turf, they were not above making a bid for that of others. They argued against any monopoly of control over the production and dispensing of orthotics by chiropodists and podiatrists, as well as the exclusive provision of non-prescription drugs by pharmacists.[90] Physiotherapists were also targeted for chiropractic control. Chiropractors argued that physiotherapists ought to be placed under indirect supervision of both medicine and chiropractic via patient referrals, that is, they fought the physiotherapists' bid for primary contact with patients.[91] Chiropractors also argued against the physiotherapists' possession of a restricted title, or exclusive use, of the term 'physical therapists.'[92] Physiotherapists did, however, get both primary contact and the restricted title.[93]

For their part, the physiotherapists responded to the chiropractors' recommendations by making use of their advantaged position of having been university trained[94] (something chiropractors had been fighting to be allowed for

160   Health Care Practitioners

some time) as well as their membership on the medical team[95] – the College of Physicians and Surgeons had supported their HPLR bid for independence from medical referral and even recommended their direct billing to OHIP.[96] Although Boase makes reference to an internal document of the OMA which argued against allowing physiotherapists primary contact with patients,[97] the OMA did not seem to translate this into any serious opposition to the physiotherapists' independence during the review process.[98]

Like almost everyone else, physiotherapists did not want any diminution of their own practice territory,[99] but, again like almost everyone else, they were not adverse to the idea of their expanding into that of others.[100] They were, however, much more broad-minded and sympathetic to the traditional outsider practitioners than were many of the other previously regulated health practitioners. They expressed support for independent regulation or joint regulation for (and their own intentions to cooperate with) acupuncturists, shiatsu therapists, occupational therapists, recreational therapists, kinesiologists, and massage therapists.[101] Physiotherapists did not deride their competitors in the way that we have seen several of the other professions do so. Even their association submissions, the more polemic voice of the two contributing professional bodies, did little more than express concern for some of the negative comments made against them by their traditional enemies, the chiropractors. For example, the Ontario Physiotherapy Association simply corrected what they considered to be the chiropractors' mistakes with regard to their comments on physiotherapists, at the same time as they called for peaceful coexistence between the two professions.[102] Given that this is a group which refers to itself as a 'legitimate and integral part of orthodox medicin   the physiotherapists' submissions to the review were impressive in   ort of a broader, more sophisticated holistic definition of health care.

In comparison, chiropractors appear to be moving towards a more insulated, narrow definition of health. We have seen how they failed to support their naturopathic colleagues, and with regard to physiotherapists they still tend to give the impression that physiotherapists have little to offer despite years of working on the same elements of body movement as chiropractors. Although physiotherapists have, for years, trained within the medical model of care which has been so blind to the benefits of chiropractic, this does not mean that they have not developed skills and techniques which could be of value to chiropractors and vice versa. It is unfortunate to see the chiropractic profession acting as narrow-mindedly as the medical profession has for years. They should have learned something from their years on the outside, but it seems to be difficult for some groups to shake the 'enemy' mentality, especially after years of having to fight for their very existence.

A group which did represent a generous attitude in its relationships to other practitioner groups, even those who could potentially threaten its entrepreneurial territory, was that of massage therapy. The submissions made to the HPLR by massage therapists are striking in the sense of fairness they displayed towards other health care practitioners. More than any other group they went out of their way to be fair to the concerns of all other health practitioners, including those they might well have seen as their enemies. Their governing body's recommended scope-of-practice statements for its own profession clearly stated the massage therapist's limitations in relation to other practitioner's territory, for example, that of chiropractic, medicine, and shiatsu.[104] The board also encouraged the inclusion of 'outsider' practitioners who had not previously been granted self-regulation, for example, homeopaths, shiatsu therapists,[105] aestheticians, acupuncturists, reflexologists, athletic trainers, and Chinese massage therapists.[106] But most striking of all was the massage therapists' generous attitude towards other practitioners who have begun to invade the turf commonly attributed to their own profession. Here they suggested that any other practitioners using massage techniques, such as physiotherapists (who could pose a real threat to them), nurses, aestheticians, and reflexologists take courses from a school of massage therapy in order to ensure that they were being trained properly![107] It was not only the governing body which made such suggestions, but the association (usually the voice of anger for a profession) also sounded much the same in their submissions, claiming this overlap of professional services was 'positive ... in order to provide optimum health care,' and that the massage therapists too ought to be learning from, or working closely with, other practitioners, such as chiropractors, homeopaths, and naturopaths:[108] 'Within health-care settings, a multi-actual approach based upon cooperation, rather than establishing authority over health-care workers is not only advisable, but also preferable for the benefit of the patient. Massage therapists have always been ready to consult for the benefit of the patient.'[109] Nor did their willingness to listen to others extend only to health practitioners such as themselves. The association suggested that members of the public ought to help set their *educational curricula*.[110] It is hard to imagine such recommendations coming from most of the other provider groups.

Birth Specialists

The professional status of midwives was not won without opposition from other provider groups. Not surprisingly, the College of Physicians and Surgeons of Ontario and the Ontario Medical Association expressed concern over the possible introduction of legalized midwifery into the province. As we have seen, though, CPSO opposition was fairly weak; they dropped it later in the review process. The OMA, however, remained unhappy about the whole idea of autonomy for midwives, indicating that an assistant role – or as one author put it, a 'glorified obstetrics nurse' role[111] – would be more acceptable to them. It should be kept in mind, however, that there have always been a number of supportive individual doctors in the province, some of whom have long provided emergency back-up for the midwives practising prior to 1991.

Opposition coming from the medical profession seemed to stem partly from fears of the family physicians with regard to their potential loss of entrepreneurial territory, although the number of GPs attending births had been steadily declining in the 1980s.[112] One Ontario physician commented in 1988, 'I believe that if midwives function in a hospital setting, it will simply provide our specialists colleagues in obstetrics with the perfect opportunity to take over the care of all of the obstetrical patients in Canada, to the exclusion of the family doctor, because they have someone else to do the low-risk obstetrics, and they can look after the complications.'[113] This was clearly not an issue of clinical expertise; it seems some GPs were afraid that their elite colleagues would, in effect, do to them what their predecessors had done to the midwives.

There had also been some early opposition to the independent regulation of midwifery from the nursing leadership. Earlier in the HPLR process the College of Nurses of Ontario argued against the midwives' independence on the grounds that they would best be included under the Nursing Act as nurse–midwives.[114] But once it was made clear to them that this was not in line with the intentions of the minister of health (at that time, Murray Elston), they acted in cooperation with the midwives. In fact, the minister deflated any serious opposition to midwifery by his early announcement in 1986 that it was slated for self-regulatory status. By this action, he removed midwives from the reach of all of their enemies. Although there was still the occasional letter to the editor in the major Canadian newspapers in the mid-1990s commenting, inaccurately, on the 'backwardness' and 'danger' of midwifery,[115] these sporadic attacks are probably useless, and today tend to come from outside Ontario.[116]

After the relatively smooth introduction of midwifery into the Ontario health care system, including the hospital sector, representatives of both the midwives and family physicians (who are replacing GPs as the latter are phased out) commented on the good relations between the two groups.[117] Midwives were also working in consultation with medical specialists in obstetrics and pediatrics, and despite some difference in clinical opinion or normal protocol, midwives commented that both medical doctors and nurses, 'to their credit, have been able to adapt their style of practice to work with our clients and us.'[118]

Nursing Specialists

The dominant relationship for nurses, that with the medical profession, has, as we have seen, become increasingly tense as nurses, more and more, fought their subordinate role to medicine. From the nurses' perspective, 'the contrast between [historical] and [contemporary] views of nursing toward medicine is startling. In contrast to the old deference there is often open antagonism and conflict.'[119] Overall, though, what stands out in the HPLR submissions with regard to this historically important relationship is the very little mention either group made of the other – it was as if there were some sort of truce. Perhaps, the 'cooperation message' from the policy planners got through here. Nonetheless, signs of tension between the nursing profession and the medical profession can still be seen when one reads through enough statements and literature by and about the two practitioner groups. For example, the nurses' college refers to the two roles of nursing, as the independent role and as the interdependent or collaborative role,[120] while the Canadian Medical Association refers to the three roles of nursing, the independent role, the interdependent role, and the dependent role, the latter of which refers to 'carrying out duties under the orders of the physician.'[121]

During the HPLR and RHPA processes the medical profession agreed to some expansion of limited independence for the registered nurses, but they were clearly wary.[122] Whenever nurses have presented any threat to medicine's practice turf by their increased scientific training or independent practice,[123] the medical profession tends to take on the substantive characteristics of the enemy. In contrast, in 1987 the British governing body for general physicians advocated 'nurses working for family physicians to be allowed to prescribe a limited range of items and to use their professional judgment to adjust the dosage of pain killers.' Canadian physicians appear to be more wary of nurses becoming 'pseudo-doctors.'[124] Overall though, despite periodic threats to small segments of their turf by the registered nurses,[125] doctors have not really had to concern themselves to any great extent with this encroachment. As the push for professionalization continues, registered nurses are seeking to carve out mostly new scope-of-practice territory, rather than presenting any great threat to that already held by the medical profession. Their success in doing so will determine the quality of their relationship with the medical profession. If they fail, they will remain in their historic paternal relationship; if they succeed, they will likely face less than friendly relations with their old patrons. One hint of possible future dissent comes from a concern voiced in mid-1998 by a representative of family physicians: there may be disputes over territory associated with the contemporary move towards community care, especially home care – which nurses' tend to view as their territory, but which will increasingly involve family physicians as their patients are moved there.[126]

Any serious turf competition for overall medical territory from nursing, however, will likely come from the new extended class nurse practitioners. It is they who have won the coveted primary contact and diagnosis, and it is they who present an alternative for cheaper (but still good quality) medical services. While the extended class nurse practitioners are careful to define their role as complementary to medicine's role,[127] in reality they could, in the future, be used to perform a fair number of the (many) common tasks of the family physician. For all the talk about cooperation and collaboration, extended class nurse practitioners do think that physicians are overtrained to meet with patients for common conditions, and family physicians do think nurse practitioners ought to be 'helping to cover the same patient population,' that is, not working independently.[128]

The nursing leadership may also trigger changing relations with both the institutional managers, under whom most nurses work, and the other levels of nursing and assistants found in the institutional health care facilities. Were the elite nursing factions to succeed in their bid to elevate their educational requirements, in the hospital or institutional setting, where tensions between employees and their managers are being exacerbated by today's cost-containment strategies, they may simply end up pricing their beneficiaries right out of their jobs. One of the repeated concerns of the Ontario Hospital Association in its submissions to the review was that of the cost-efficient use of less formally trained workers to do the many simple tasks involved in institutional health care.[129] In the mid-1990s Ontario hospitals began advertising for 'generic hospital workers' to work at much lower salaries than a well-educated nurse.[130] By the late 1990s, a nursing representative was referring to the practice of hiring cheaper 'non-regulated workers' as 'pervasive.'[131]

As we saw in Chapter 6, the current market down-sizing climate which pits professionals against each other has further exacerbated the friction between registered nurses and the registered practical nurses. It has also heightened the tension between the regulated practitioners and non-regulated practitioners, as we saw with regard to the RPNs and generic workers who are moving up behind the RPNs. As the institutional managers and the hospital medical staff[132] continue to trade off one worker for another, or their own benefits for those of their fellow practitioners, tensions will continue to grow.

Dental Hygiene Specialists

The other assistant-turned-technique specialist group, dental hygiene, had as

Continuity and Realignment of the Positions of Connection 165

much difficulty as the nurses in winning a greater degree of independence, so the tension between them and their elite provider group of dentistry was high. Dentists reacted negatively towards independence of practice for dental hygienists; they preferred the old relationship which they described as follows: 'It is the College's position that the proposed general statement with regard to dental hygiene should be altered to ensure that the legislation clearly indicates the relationship between the dental hygienist and the dentist which in law must be that of employe—employer.'[133] It is clear that the old employee–employer relationship is now threatened. It is unlikely that the animosity of dentists will abate if dental hygienists do begin to make any serious progress towards entrepreneurial independence. The more equal they become, the more the former paternal relationship will be replaced with that of enemies.

Other Technique Specialists

The story of the 'positions of connection' for the remaining technique–specialist groups who were included in the Regulated Health Professions Act, the mental and social health, diet, and speech–language specialists, simply repeats the dynamics of those stories already told here. Positioned in the middle, between the elite professions and the new groups coming up after them to fill the space they themselves have vacated as they climbed the ladder to professional status, all technique-specialist groups fought off the pressures from above and below – reinforcing old animosities from both.[134]

Technology and Assistant Group Connections

The relationships of importance to both the medical and dental technologists are those with the elite professions of their field, the laboratory bosses over them, and the assistant groups under them.[135] The medical profession raised no objection to the attaining of professional status by the medical technology groups, having little to lose by it; whereas, the dental profession was ever watchful for any move by its ancillary groups which might result in any decline in the dentists' income. Dentists had, as we have seen, repeatedly attacked the break-away technology-group-turned-merchants, the denturists, but the remaining technologists, appearing content to work under the direction or supervision of the dentists, were considered safe. Their inclusion in the new legislation would, in fact, help dentists offset the rising power of denturists.

From the perspective of registered dental technologists, for whom the relationship was a dependent one and the role of professional was new, the HPLR process did elicit questions of boundary, for example, in their questioning of the ability of dentists to work with the materials with which technologists have expertise. It was pointed out that dentists used to have this training but did not now receive it – which also raised the question of why a dentist is allowed to supervise a dental laboratory.[136] Most of the conflict in the relationships which are of importance to dental technologists is related to entrepreneurial crossover. Because there is no laboratory governing legislation in the dental field, as exists in the medical field, conflicts of ownership and supervision are more difficult to settle.[137] There is also some cross-over between the dental technologist and denturists – with joint membership held by some. This too has resulted in questions of jurisdiction.[138]

Competition for the registered dental technologists work also comes from the cheaper labour of the less educated, unregistered technicians, who are supposed to work under the supervision of a dentist. Here the RDTs are concerned about 'basement labs' which fail to meet supervision requirements. The role and level of training of the dental assistant presents the same problem here as it does in nursing, namely, the use of cheaper (perhaps inadequately trained) labour to replace the work of their more expensive, more educated coworkers.[139] Medical laboratory technologists are also concerned about the use of cheaper labour to perform their functions. For example, although MLTs have the controlled act for drawing blood, there is an exemption in the Laboratory Licensing Act for anyone working in a laboratory.[140] Here too there are concerns about the number of technicians and laboratory assistants being brought in to 'undermine' the role of the MLT.[141]

The tendency for technologists, as for nurses, has been to argue against direct supervision by those higher up the status hierarchy, while at the same time arguing for the authority to supervise directly those below them, the 'laboratory assistants.'[142] But those assistants are at the same time arguing that technologists are overtrained for some of the tasks they are performing – as practical nurses claim of registered nurses, and registered nurses claim of medical doctors. Ironically, for all their attempts to control the assistant group below them, technologists, technicians, and nurses themselves perform a great number of assistant-type tasks for the medical and dental professions. Respiratory technologists and therapists, for example, defined themselves as 'an allied health discipline devoted to the scientific application of technology in order to assist the physician.'[143]

Respiratory therapists also found 'a bit of friction' caused by the development of new specialties within the profession. Questions of regulatory jurisdiction and delegation have arisen between these specialists and both the traditional respiratory therapists and other practitioners, such as nurses, who also train in these specialties.[144] A representative of the respiratory therapists also spoke of the college's 'good' relationship with the provincial association, and 'bad' relationship with the profession's national association which has tended to view itself as a national regulatory body, especially with regard to the setting of practice standards – a role which obviously conflicts with any provincial governing council role.[145]

Medical radiation technologists are also experiencing problems with cross-trained practitioners and the employment (in clinics) of workers without MRT qualifications, although the employment of assistants to do their work has not occurred in the hospitals, primarily because of and/or the care taken with radiation.[146] With regard to cross-training, however, developments have not all been problematic. The profession is also looking at cross-training or 'multi-skilling' as a means to save and/or coordinate jobs during the present downsizing in public health institutions.[147]

One theme running throughout the story of the technological groups is that of the difficulty of their dual role as both professional and employee of an institution. Despite their status as professionals, as one association put it, 'Administratively and professionally the ... technologist will be directed, and the responsibility of the technologist will be controlled by, department/hospital/clinic policies and procedure manuals ... provided by: health administrators, medical directors, and/or designated departmental managers.'[148] Two medical laboratory technologists I spoke to seemed little concerned about the new regulatory legislation, although they resented the annual fees they now had to pay to their new governing body. They doubted that the new legislation was going to be very important to the rank and file of their profession. As hospital and laboratory employees, their real concerns were with their managers and supervisors, and their new professional governing body was not under any mandate to fight those managers and supervisors for the labour interests which were uppermost in the technologists' minds.[149]

Another institutional technology or assistant group of practitioners vying for position is that related to diet or nutrition. Dietetic 'supplementary personnel'[150] consist of either those referred to somewhat misleadingly as 'dietetic technologists,'[151] or 'food service supervisors.' Both are assistant groups to dieticians and therefore work mostly in hospitals and other health care institutions under the direct supervision of dieticians. Dietetic assistants or technologists did not request inclusion in the new legislation, but food service supervisors did. The HPLR team denied the request of the latter on the grounds that they did not fit the 'nine criteria,' mostly because they are already closely supervised by dieticians and therefore do not constitute a danger to public health – interestingly, this argument was *not* used against most other groups, such as physiotherapists, dental hygienists, nurses, and so on.[152] The biggest competition for dieticians, though, comes from the unregulated practitioners and merchants, such as the many nutritional consultants and health club 'experts,'[153] who want a piece of the 'diet and nutrition' action. Relations here are less than friendly.

The primary relationship for all assistants is, of course, that with their supervisors. As long as the assistant group remains friendly with its elite provider group, there will likely continue to be, 'No disputes anticipated.'[154] The dental nurses and assistants association (ODNAA), for example, appeared during this policy process to be quite co-opted by the Royal College of Dental Surgeons; not only did they repeat the dentists' positions in relation to their own situation in all of their submissions, but they also took the dentists' position in relation to both denturists and dental hygienists.[155] All this was done even though the dentists argued not only for complete regulatory control of dental assistants but also for their silence.[156] It remains to be seen just how long this assistant group will retain its passive attitude. If its counterpart in the medical field, that is, nursing, is any example of what might occur in the future, it is likely that these nurse–assistants, too, might eventually find their voice; but like nursing, this might simply open up new space for assistants to the assistants. Regardless of the gains of particular groups, the disputes which continued throughout, and beyond, this policy process over the 'supervision' of the assistant- or ancillary-type workers and the 'delegation' of labour or controlled acts from one group of practitioners to another will not likely disappear.

Conclusion

Overall, the patterns of connection in the Ontario health sector have undergone some interesting shifts in the course of the HPLR/RHPA process. In the recognition of its sovereign authority in the agency relationship of professionalism, the state has now been positioned more neutrally with regard to all practitioner groups, shifting it more towards the centre of relations – away from both the overly friendly position and the overly antagonistic position it has long held with the elite and the non-elite of the sector, respectively. The state is also more visibly present now with its enhancement of the role of the governing body within each profession. That is, the agency relationship held by the health professionals has also undergone a reinterpretation. It would appear that there are two elements to the agency relationship found here. One, which is emphasized by economists and professionals, might be referred to as private or market agency, and the other, which is emphasized by political and public actors, might be referred to as public or legal agency.[157] Private or market agency tends to focus on the more autonomous privileges bestowed on the agent (that is, the health practitioner) by virtue of her or his superior knowledge to that of the principal (that is, the patient) with the obligation of good service being held for the individual consumer or patient. Public or legal agency tends to focus on the collective obligations of the agent (through its professional governing body) which is acting as a political–judicial proxy for the state which is itself an agent of the same principle (that is, the public or patients as a whole).[158]

Both types of agency have been called upon in the formulation of the professional relationship. It would appear that there has now been a shift in emphasis in health policy away from the predominance of the private or market agency between the health practitioner and the individual patient towards the public or legal agency between the health practitioners and the public or body of patients – which is mediated by the state. The limited obligation of the private agency relationship between the practitioner and the patient for the provision of service based on superior knowledge is still important in the health sector, but as this case study shows, it is being increasingly joined by the obligations concomitant to a more public agency. In the latter, the role of the state as the guardian of the public interest under the rule of law is respected, and with this comes a more demanding set of political and judicial obligations which must be ensured from the subgovernment of professionalism. During the development of the RHPA, the obligations of governance within the subsystem of health care were held up to the standards of our broader legal–political system and adjusted to better fit the principles and blueprints found therein. With the strengthening of the public agency relationship came a shift in the positions of connection inside the professional groups. The obligations of this agency rest with the professional governing body, so an emphasis on that relationship is an emphasis on its role. The professional associations will continue to voice their union-type concerns loudly in the contemporary climate of cut-backs, but it is clear that the voice of the professional college will also be prominent in the decisions of the future.

Patterns of connection among the practitioner groups were sometimes reinforced and sometimes disrupted by this policy process. One noteworthy shift in relations seen during the RHPA policy process was that initiated by the medical profession, particularly the CPSO, with regard to other health practitioners. With the exception of specific medical specialties, such as ophthalmology, medical opposition was aimed primarily at the whole body eclectics and empirics. The medical profession displayed a surprising degree of cooperation and in some cases support for the many practitioners who were successful in their bid to acquire full professional status under the RHPA. Given the power of the medical profession in the health policy sector as a whole, this alone might signal a significant expansion for the future of the dominant mode of expertise long upheld in the sector – particularly as it has been followed by a high degree of cooperation and support for the new professionals from the family physicians.

The alternative whole body practitioners were largely unsuccessful at winning or maintaining relationships of support with other practitioners; even old relationships of support, such as that between naturopaths and chiropractors failed to hold up under the pressure of the policy dynamics at work. Naturopaths were successful, however, at gaining the support of a vocal public constituency and occasionally their politicians, and they may yet use that success to win inclusion as professionals in the new legislation.

Positions of connection among the merchant–service providers continued along the old lines of animosity, as illustrated by the relationship between dentists and denturists. Dental hygienists, whose bid for increased autonomy threatened the dentists' already shaky entrepreneurial hold in the dental market, were repositioned both more antagonistically with regard to the elite practitioners of the field and somewhat more sympathetically with regard to a state oriented towards the principle of egalitarianism. Dentists, in contrast, did little to garner the support of state actors adopting a stance which was strongly out of step with the climate of ideas in good repute with both the HPLR team and the state. In fact, dentists went some way towards antagonizing both decision-making bodies. Pharmacists, on the other hand, were considerably more diplomatic although they are also under entrepreneurial threat. They made small advances into medical territory without antagonizing either the medical profession or the policy makers – although that could change as physicians become increasingly concerned with what they see as fragmented and uncoordinated patient care. Where pharmacists did elicit less than friendly relations was in their attempt to maintain their market overlap with the unregulated practitioners in the sale of prosthetics, orthotics, hearing aids and monitors, and botanic or herbal products, thus eliciting antagonism only from the weakly positioned health practitioners – those without many connections.

Within the merchant–service specialist category of health care there were divisions related to the practitioners' connection or lack of connection to the medical profession, as in the chiropody and podiatry split, where the former defined itself as complementary to medicine and the latter as independent of it. Here, the group in complement to the medical type of care, chiropody, was successful in its bid for recognition. In the field of eye care, however, it was the independent practitioners, the optometrists and opticians, who did well despite opposition from the medical specialist in the field. In the neuro–

muscular–skeletal field of care, physiotherapists and massage therapists played on their medical connections in order to enhance their legitimacy, while chiropractors and midwives did the opposite. In this case, all four groups made substantial gains, so it might be assumed that one's medical connections were not overly relevant here – with the exception of the major loss chiropractic incurred with regard to protecting its 'spinal manipulation' turf from invasion by the medical profession and its physiotherapy and massage complements.

The primary relationship for nurses has, of course, always been that held with the medical profession, and here a rather calm wariness prevailed on both sides. It may be that the relationship of importance for nurses in the near future will be that between them and the managers and other employees of the cost-cutting institutions in which they work. Likewise, the dependent technology and assistant groups also expect the relationship between them and their institutional administrators and managers to play an increasingly important role in their future, particularly with regard to any form of cheaper labour which might be justified as their replacement. The employer–employee relationship between dental hygienists and the old elite of their field, the dentists, will likely continue to cause tension in the future, particularly if dental hygienists succeed in establishing entrepreneurial independence from dentists. Lastly, the unregulated practitioners were more likely to find support among their fellow practitioners if they were offering alternative services, such as shiatsu therapy, acupuncture, reflexology massage, kinesiology therapy, and so on, rather than offering alternative products, such as corrective footwear, diet products, and botanic products. The connections of importance or influence for the alternative product providers lay more with their 'big business' partners than with their fellow health practitioners.

8

The Regulated Health Professions Act of 1991[1]

The legislation which now largely governs Ontario's health professionals was the product of a decade-long process of assessment, reinterpretation, and restructuring. The embedded ideas associated with health professionalism were once again being challenged by contemporary principles and blueprints for change. In Chapter 6 we saw the key ideas which had informed the original mandate of the 1983–9 policy review. The main purposes for reviewing and redesigning the existing legislation governing health professionalism were (a) to coordinate the health practitioner groups, and hopefully diffuse many of the long-standing conflicts among them, and (b) to align the rules and regulations of professional governance with the broader economic, political, and judicial standards of the day, or what I have referred to earlier as a realignment of the benefits and burdens of professional self-governance. The question to consider, then, concerns the manner in which the Regulated Health Professions Act fulfils this mandate.

Practitioner Coordination and Cooperation

With regard to the coordination of the health practitioner groups, the new legislation constitutes a considerable improvement over previous legislation. There is now one body of legislation with a consistent set of legal and procedural provisions for all health professionals as well as individual acts laying out each profession's legal range of clinical and often entrepreneurial activity. In Chapters 6 and 7 we saw that difficult decisions were made about who was to be included or excluded from the new legislation – summarized in Table 6.1. Despite the ongoing debates over the defined scopes of practice and authorized acts of the new legislation, there are now clearer working definitions of each profession's functions and range of expertise. Many outstanding legal issues such as the restricted use of professional titles have been settled, and those that remain have been given an avenue of redress. More generally, ongoing adaptation of the legislation is now possible in that the statutory amendment process has been simplified and made more easily adjustable by the statutory separation of the main body of legislation and the individual professional acts, as well as in the making of regulations and bylaws.[2]

The policy process also made progress with regard to improving communication throughout the sector. There was a considerable amount of dialogue and 'policy learning'[3] on the part of both the state representatives and the practitioner representatives of the health sector during the course of the policy development. Assumedly this enhanced understanding, even if only at the level of clarification of positions on issues, will help in the coordination of the sector in the future. For the smaller, historically less powerful practitioner groups, exposure to this policy process has helped teach them the rules of the game and the contemporary ideas in good repute, so that they might participate more fully in future policy debates. There are still issues of contention among the provider groups which will continue to affect the coordination of and relationships within the health sector; however, many issues have been settled and those that remain have at least been openly debated with considerably more understanding of the underlying causes of contention than previously existed. Some of these disagreements, particularly those related to entrepreneurial competition, will likely never be settled, once and for all, but in many cases lines have been drawn and practitioners working in competition with each other are learning to adjust to the new reality.

Cooperation also developed among the professions grappling with difficult regulation issues. Many groups commented on the enhanced interaction with other practitioner groups with whom they had previously had little or no contact prior to the review. At one point a working group of college officials was instigated to share information about the more difficult issues on which decisions had to be made. The original meetings were so useful for participants that an ongoing organization called the Federation of Health Regulatory Colleges of Ontario was set up with a monthly newsletter, the *Federation Exchange*, to discuss issues, such as sexual abuse, quality assurance, fitness to practice, delegation, and so on.[4] The exchange of information and ideas has been particularly helpful for the new or smaller colleges lacking the research and legal resources of the larger established colleges. One such college official referred to the federation as 'a life line.'[5] It allowed the colleges 'to work as a group' in their discussions of, and submissions for, the government's recent Red Tape Reduction Act.[6] One participant claimed, overall, that the federation had 'increased the level of trust and communication between the [practitioner] groups,' while others commented that it provided a coalesced approach with which to communicate with the government.[7]

Aside from particular discussion groups, such as the federation, the entire legislative process, as one participant noted, 'got people talking,' and in so doing, resulted in more cooperation, better understanding, and, 'incidently, more referrals.'[8] Whether or not this new communication will result in any serious structural changes in the health sector remains to be seen, however. As another participant put it, 'RHPA has given groups a platform, but real changes [in terms of power] have been minimal.'[9]

Realignment of the Rules and Regulations of Self-Governance

The second major element of the review and redesign of the health professions legislation was that related to the rules and regulations of professional self-governance. As we saw in Chapter 6, earlier reports on the state of Ontario's health care sector had argued against its anachronistic and uncoordinated legislation, lack of control mechanisms for the minister of health, and general lack of public scrutiny and accountability measures. The HPLR report reinforced these concerns, emphasizing the restrictive nature of the existing legislation in economic, political, and judicial terms.

The Economic Blueprint and Critique

The old legislation was considered economically restrictive largely because of the practice monopolies which were maintained through the exclusive licensure of the various professional groups' scopes of practice. These monopolies, as we have seen, were granted on the basis of arguments of expertise, so any attempt to open them up to increased competition necessarily ran up against arguments of quality of care. Backing the anti-monopoly arguments, however, were the widely accepted blueprints of market liberalism, such as 'pro-competition, pro-freedom of choice, and suspicion of government regulation,'[10] which the Professional Organizations Committee had emphasized and HPLR had reinforced, as well as the increasing concerns over the fiscal state of the sector as an economic recession continued to affect the province. Despite disclaimers at the beginning of the legislation review that the mandate was not economic,[11] by the end of the review the HPLR report was giving prominent mention to its recommendations for 'more efficient and cost-effective ... services.'[12]

Overall, the new legislation has, in effect, 'restored [some] market forces'[13] back into the health care system. Health professionals no longer own their skills in the way they have since the late nineteenth century. Each profession now has to be granted the right to engage in risk-related activities via its authorized acts rather than defining its own range of activities. And although those groups which held the monopolies of concern to the policy designers, that is, the elite professionals, seem to be doing much the same work they always did, space has now been created for others to perform a range of activities for which they used to risk prosecution. Even more important, perhaps, new institutional space for change was created with the adoption of an ongoing advisory body, the Health Professions Regulatory Advisory Coucil (see below), for decisions related to new health practices and practitioners which might develop in the future. With both this and the newly sanctioned professionals, the elite monopolies have been eroded somewhat. From the perspective of the non-professional practitioner groups, the professionals may appear to own the property of their controlled acts, but it is a property on lease. Any incidental monopoly could at any time be broken by the granting of those monopolized functions or acts to other practitioners – which is, of course, why the established professions fought vigorously right to the end of the policy process against the design of the controlled acts. With the erosion of their monopoly, or what Tuohy has argued was a form of property right over a particular field of knowledge,[14] the elite health professionals no longer own the products of science and technology in the sense that they no longer have as much privilege of exclusion over them. As Tuohy predicted, state stewardship of this form of knowledge is more and more becoming the norm.

With regard to the policy reviewers' intent to open the sector to a more efficient use of labour, the new legislation does allow for the utilization of a greater range of practitioners in the various tasks of the health care institutions; for example, midwives can now be employed in hospitals. It remains to be seen, however, whether these new professionals will prove to be any less expensive than their counterparts. As we saw in Chapters 6 and 7, there was some attempt made to allow previously exclusive tasks to be performed by cheaper labour (a nurse rather than a doctor, for example) by the granting of these tasks as controlled acts to a broader range of practitioners, but on the whole there was little of this done. There was also a concern for the push for unwarranted qualifications or credentialism but, again, this did not seem to translate very directly to cost-containment measures. The fear of overriding regulatory requirements for the maintenance of standards of quality by an emphasis on cost[15] appears to have limited the degree of interference the policy designers and makers were willing to engage in with regard to the embedment of legislative means to greater 'market efficiencies.'

The objective of opening the existing labour arrangements to a more efficient use of cheaper labour may also have been hampered by the 'free market / suspicion of government regulation' orientation of the policy designers. Given that the health sector is a mixed economy sector with a public-private balance rather than a free market sector, free choice of practice within the sector leaves the state and institutional managers little room to offset the practice decisions of health providers. That is, if an expensive medical physician, for example, chooses to perform a clinical practice which could be performed more cheaply by a qualified non-medical practitioner, such as a physiotherapist, she or he is free to do so regardless of the inefficiency of cost this presents for the public purse.[16] As we saw in Chapters 6 and 7, during the HPLR process physicians were challenged by nurses for an unnecessarily broad scope of practice. They were also challenged by psychologists, optometrists, audiologists, speech–language pathologists, podiatrists, chiropractors, and midwives for practising techniques for which they have little training. Dentists were challenged by denturists and dental hygienists for the same lack of comparative training. Pharmacists were challenged by prosthetic and orthotic practitioners, as well as the hearing aid dispensers. The latter also challenged the audiologists. Even at the technical and assistant levels, the less educated practitioners, such as technicians, lab assistants, and nurses, argued that they were often better able to do particular tasks than their supervisors. The policy reviewers lacked the time or, perhaps, clinical expertise to properly investigate these claims; however, even had such claims been found valid,[17] it is not certain that the facts would have swayed the policy designers from their free market orientation.[18] It may also be the case that the time and resources required for this sort of clinical analysis are only available to the research centres, staffed with epidemiologists and statisticians, which are being given high priority throughout Canada today.[19] The question remains, however, whether this new legislation will be able to allow for the sort of recommendations for efficiency coming from these research centres, or whether it will hamper them.

The Political–Judicial Blueprints and Critiques

The restrictive character of the pre-1990s' legislation, with regard to the legal or political–judicial standards it upheld, related predominantly, according to the HPLR, to its statutorily outdated, closed, and unresponsive nature.[20] Echoing the recommendations of the reports of the 1960s and 1970s, the legal recommendations of the 1980s' policy review took the form, predominantly, of (a) increased mechanisms of control for the professional governing bodies over the practitioners and (b) increased mechanisms of control for both the minister of health and the public over the practitioners and their professional governing bodies. Most of the recommendations were taken up in the new Regulated Health Professions Act of 1991, where the obligations attached to the privilege of self-government were clarified and strengthened. It was made clear, for example, that professional associations and professional governing bodies do not carry the same privileges of self-interest: what is acceptable practice for a unionlike body fighting for its representatives' benefits or privileges is not acceptable practice for a governing body which has been granted the ultimate state function of the rule of law. According to the rules of the social contract, on which all social governance in Western society is based, the only justification for the state transfer of its governing powers over to a 'subgovernment' lies in its demanding that that government act in the best interests of the public – the ultimate site of sovereignty in a liberal democratic system. The duty of the professional college was clearly stated: to 'serve and protect the public interest.'[21]

Many of the enhanced controls targeted at the professional governing council focused on extending the colleges' powers over incompetent members. They included increased power for the college registration committee to refuse to register applicants deemed unfit; increased requirements for reportage by those who employ or associate in practice with health professionals for whom they have 'reasonable grounds' for suspicion of professional misconduct, including sexual misconduct; the granting to colleges of effective authority to deal with physical or mentally incapacitated members; enhanced powers of, and funding for, the college registrar's investigation of professional misconduct or incompetence; and a statutory requirement for a fitness-to-practice committee to look into cases of practitioner 'incapacity,' as well as a quality assurance committee to look into cases of questionable competence or means of improving the prevailing standards of competence.[22]

In general, the medical profession raised little opposition to proposed changes meant to enhance its obligations of self-regulation – even proposing many itself.[23] Whether this was because of pragmatism, that is, their seeing the inevitable, or out of genuine concern for their patients, is indiscernible. Both factors were probably at work here; but it is notable that their concern for the public interest seemed a great deal stronger when it came to strengthening their own governing body's control over its own and its competing professionals than it did when it came to strengthening the mechanisms of control coming from outside the profession – those from ministerial control and those from public scrutiny.

Increased mechanisms of control over all health practitioners by both the minister of health and the public were incorporated into the new legislation in order to bring the professions more in line with the broader political–judicial

178   Health Care Practitioners

standards of the day. We saw in Chapter 4 how the broader political blueprint of public participation and consent set within a representative, responsible, and accountable governing system operating under rules of judicial fairness had helped shape the health professional legislation of the nineteenth and twentieth centuries. The same was true of the Ontario health professions legislation of the 1980s and 1990s. We have seen how extensive the public participation was in the RHPA policy-process in the form of both interest group participation and access for the general public. Organized interest groups participated in an unprecedented manner during both the policy-designing and policy making stages of the process.[24] Likewise, the general public was given direct access to the HPLR submissions, and press releases were issued to keep the public informed as decisions were made. There seemed, however, to be little public interest in this policy process – probably because of the legal and technical nature of most of the debates.

Interest groups involved in the process carried a considerable amount of the cost of participation. The direct cost of production as well as the indirect costs of time and energy it took to prepare the submissions to the review were borne by the practitioner groups themselves – with the exception of midwifery whose government-funded task force supplied ample back-up resources for the mid-to-late stages of the policy process. The larger and richer practitioner groups hired consultants, usually legal experts, to help prepare their HPLR submissions, and this in the standard interest group theory of power ought to have given them a distinct advantage. That advantage, however, did not appear to get translated into any substantial advantage of outcome. Many excellent submissions came from groups, such as the dental hygienists and massage therapists, who prepared their own submissions on a meagre budget. Their submissions were thoughtful and honest, as well as providing the opportunity for the group's leadership and members to think through the gamut of difficult problems presented by professional regulation.

Where the general public did respond to the policy process as it developed, the response was often practitioner-led. Patients of disaffected practitioners were encouraged to write letters to their political representatives, and in one case at least, that of naturopathy, this response did play an important role in staying a previously committed decision. The organized practitioner groups were also backed, in some cases, by related interest groups. Merchant groups tended to have business interest support. The 'natural therapists,' for example, were part of a coalition, the Natural Therapies and Products Coalition, which included the manufacturers of herbal or natural drugs or therapeutic products, as well as the health food and Chinese herbal retailers. This group played a major role in the letter-writing campaign to protest the HPLR recommendations which it felt threatened the ability of alternative therapists and retailers to provide their treatments and products to the public.

Midwifery, with its practitioners and clientele all being female, was clearly a health area concerning women, and with the history of female midwives' subordination to male medical doctors, it was also a feminist issue. Throughout the review and legislation process, midwives had the backing of influential women's groups and the Women's Health Bureau of the Ministry of Health – a backing which probably contributed to their high level of success.

There was some public input from interested organizations, such as the Canadian Jewish Congress, the Coalition of Major Christian Denominations, the Ontario Teachers Federation, and the supporters of the disabled, but this centred around specific concerns, such as pastoral or educational counselling. Broad consumer advocacy groups also made submissions to the HPLR. The Consumers Association of Canada (Ontario branch) was quite supportive of the review's recommendations and came out in agreement with the proposed harm clause which remained an object of concern for consumer groups, such as the Association of Concerned Citizens for Preventive Medicine, whose basis of support came from the advocates of alternative care. The latter had sponsored a parliamentary lobby and tricycle ride across Ontario[25] to protest the HPLR recommendations, but they were unsuccessful in their attempt to have the harm clause deleted – although as we saw earlier, it was weakened in modified form. These groups continued to bring forth their concerns throughout the legislative process.

Two other non-practitioner groups represented an interesting interplay of public interests in the policy process leading up to the Regulated Health Professions Act. The Patients' Rights Association[26] and the Ontario Hospital Association represented the legal–ethical perspective of the individual patient and the economic cost–benefit perspective of the aggregate body of patients, respectively. The actual influence of the two associations is impossible to measure, but it is notable that all practitioner group participants in the HPLR process were required to address the claims made by both, and in doing so, to justify any actions which would violate the interests of 'the patient' or 'patients' as seen through the eyes of these representatives.

New structures of public participation were embedded in the 1991 Regulated Health Professions Act. Indirect public participation, that is, the public's access through its elected representative responsible for health issues, the minister of health, was enhanced. As we saw earlier, all of the reviews of the health care system from the 1960s on had strongly emphasized the need for the minister to gain access to further controls both within the health institutions and over the health professionals. Ad hoc policy reactions to regulatory needs had resulted in an uncoordinated and uncontrolled system. The HPLR team made several recommendations which would ensure that 'the ultimate authority reside with the Government,'[27] and most of these were incorporated into the RHPA giving the minister the power to:

(a) Inquire into or require a council to inquire into the state of practice of a health profession in a locality or institution
(b) Review a council's activities and require the council to provide reports and information
(c) Require a council to make, amend or revoke a regulation under a health profession act
(d) Require a council to do anything that, in the opinion of the minister, is necessary or advisable to carry out the intent of this act, and the health profession acts.[28]

The wording of the new legislation with regard to the minister's duty reflects the climate of ideas within which it was developed. Section 3 of the Regulated Health Professions Act states: 'It is the duty of the Minister to ensure that the health professions are regulated and co-ordinated *in the public interest*, that appropriate standards of practice are developed and maintained and that individuals have *access* to services provided by the health professions of their *choice* and that they are treated with *sensitivity and respect* in their dealings with health professionals, the Colleges and the Board.'[29] It is within this climate of ideas that the colleges (and the Health Professions Board and Health Professions Regulatory Advisory Council; see below) are to submit their mandatory annual reports to the minister on 'their activities and financial affairs'(with each of the colleges' seven mandatory committees: executive committee, registration committee, complaints committee, discipline committee, fitness-to-practice committee, quality assurance committee, and patient relations committee, in turn submitting mandatory reports to the college councils).[30] In this way a line of internal professional scrutiny and accountability leads up to the minister of health and thus indirectly to the public.

Mechanisms for the enhancement of *direct* public input and scrutiny of the professions were also put forth by the HPLR. The 1973 Health Disciplines Board was recommended to be continued as the Health Professions Board. The HDB had been a public body of appointees assigned to conduct hearings and to review decisions of the complaints and registration committees when requested by a complainant or defendant to do so. Some changes were suggested in order to make the work of the new board more effective,[31] and, as recommended by the review, it (the Health Professions Board of public appointees)[32] was set up with a mandate 'to hold a review of [a registration committee] application and the documentary evidence in support of it, or a hearing of the application,' as well as to 'review ... a) the adequacy of [a complaints committee] investigation conducted, or b) the reasonableness of the decision.'[33] Through the continuation of this mechanism, direct public scrutiny is brought to bear on the internal professional processes for the benefit or scrutiny of both applicants and practising members of the profession, as well as for the protection of the public interest.

The HPLR team also recommended the creation of a policy advisory body of five to seven (non-college or ex-college members, non-civil servant) persons who would be appointed on the recommendation of the minister. This Health Professions Regulatory Advisory Council, which would report directly to the minister, would act 'as an open forum for balancing the competing claims of various professions,' while at the same time 'give currently unregulated professions *controlled* access to express their claims for regulation.'[34] 'Controlled' here meant 'through the minister,' that is, the new practitioner access would not be direct, rather it would be channelled through the minister's office. This recommendation was taken up almost verbatim in the RHPA. The advisory council's duties are to advise the minister on,

(a) Whether unregulated professions should be regulated
(b) Whether regulated professions should no longer be regulated
(c) Suggested amendments to the act, a health profession act, or a regulation under any of those acts, and suggested regulations under any of those acts
(d) Matters concerning the quality assurance programs undertaken by colleges
(e) Any matter the minister refers to the advisory council relating to the health professions, including any matter described in clauses (a) to (d).[35]

The new council, or H-PRAC as it is pronounced, is *advisory* only.[36] Aside from the annual report to the minister 'on its activities and financial affairs' (mentioned above), it was also given the mandate to report to the minister within five years of its formation with regard to the 'effectiveness' of 'each college's (new) patient relations and quality assurance programs, and each college's complaints and discipline procedures with respect to professional misconduct of a sexual nature.'[37] These mandatory reports are to be submitted by the minister to the legislative assembly for political scrutiny.[38] It was later decided that HPRAC would conduct a five-year review of the Regulated Health Professions Act.[39] Preliminary studies were commissioned with regard to quality assurance and (sexually abusive) patient relations,[40] and the advisory council released the first of their public discussion papers in December

1995 'designed to start discussion with regulatory bodies, patients, associations, community groups, unions, and the public,' and then conducted a workshop requested by the colleges (through the Federation of Health Regulatory Colleges).[41] As of 1999 these reviews were all still in process. (For 1997 and 1998 preliminary assessments by the colleges of the RHPA, HPRAC, and the new mandatory college committees and programs for patient relations and quality assurance, see the section entitled 'Practical Assessments' near the end of this chapter.)

Other recommendations of the HPLR which would enhance the public participation in, and scrutiny of, the professions were,

(a) Increasing the number of public members on governing councils and statutory committees to 'reflect the principle that no distinction be drawn between public and professional members'[42]
(b) Opening council meetings, discipline hearings, and complaint reviews to the public
(c) Giving aggrieved patients access to the record of a college's complaint investigation
(d) Giving the public greater access to specified information on college registers
(e) Requiring colleges to publish disciplinary decisions and reasons.[43]

There was considerable opposition from the established professions to both the indirect public scrutiny measures (via the minister) and the direct public scrutiny measures proposed by the HPLR team. The five professions that had been regulated under the 1974 Health Disciplines Act were still arguing as late as 1987 that the 'transfer of power to the Minister of Health' indicated by the proposed legislation changes, represented 'the dilution of the principle of self-government.'[44] Had they had the power to do so, they would have prevented the new legislative design which allowed for the inclusion of separate professional acts for other practitioners. There was particularly strong opposition to the opening of council meetings, discipline hearings, and complaint hearings to the public. A few provider groups, midwives, for example, strongly encouraged any move in the direction of enhanced public input and scrutiny, but not the traditional elite groups.[45] Dentists argued about this throughout the entire policy process. In fact, the dental profession remained opposed to much of the proposed legislation throughout the review and the ministry process that followed. The dentists' governing body (RCDSO) objected to the overall design of the new legislation,[46] the creation of an advisory council,[47] the proposed quality assurance measures,[48] the opening of hearings to the public,[49] the public availability of discipline hearing transcripts,[50] and numerous legal details over the proposed college council and committee rules and regulations.[51] Aside from a few details, the dental association (ODA) submissions were in 'substantial agreement' with those of the college.[52] The medical profession argued against the proposed open (public) discipline committee hearings, in 1985,[53] and again (along with the other practitioners subject at that time to the Health Disciplines Act) in 1987, at which time they also argued against making the transcripts of discipline hearings available to the public, as well as disclosure of documents during complaints reviews and open council meetings.[54]

The established health professions were unsuccessful in these requests to limit public scrutiny of the health professions. The RHPA (and its regulations), with some legal caveats, did increase the number of public members on governing councils and statutory committees to just under 50 per cent of the total composition. Council meetings, discipline hearings, and the review by the Health Professions Board (of registration and complaints decisions) are open to the public.[55] Aggrieved patients are now given access to the record of a college's complaint investigation which is under review by the HPB (with some exceptions, such as public security, integrity of process, where disclosure of financial, personal, or other matters will cause undesirable effects, prejudice of a criminal or civil suit, or jeopardy of the safety of a person).[56] The public has been given greater access to specified information on college registers, and the decision and reasoning of discipline hearings is to be published in the college's annual report.[57] Very little was won by the elite professions here.

The degree to which the participation mechanisms of either the policy process itself or the new governance of the professions translates into the actual consent of the participants, or at least an acceptable degree of consent, is difficult to assess. Just how much consent the various participants of the HPLR/RHPA process, including the public, actually gave to its final product is not clear. It is clear that the HPLR team and ministry officials gave voice to a wide range of practitioners and interested parties. It was hoped that as many of the practitioner groups as possible would come on board with the legislation, and many groups did come out in support of it. The degree to which this wide consent was freely solicited rather than quietly coerced is not so clear, however. For example, the consensus over the nine criteria used by the review team as the measure of fitness for self-regulation for all practitioner groups remains as rhetoric only. All nine of these criteria may have been 'universally endorsed by the participants' as claimed,[58] but there was no evidence to this effect produced for public scrutiny; in fact, comments by the head of the review would suggest otherwise.[59] It does seem rather suspicious that those practitioner

184   Health Care Practitioners

groups fighting for the privilege of self-regulation would have agreed to criteria which would have excluded them from the RHPA. When asked in 1997 about their overall access to decision makers in this policy process, one practitioner college representative said, 'access, yes, but what the Ministry wants, it gets.'[60]

Aside from the democratic means of participation and consent used to check the power of the decision makers and governors, other governing mechanisms commonly used in the broader political sphere have been enhanced in the subgovernment of health care professionalism. We have seen the enhanced public representation on the councils and committees of the professional governing bodies; but at a more general level, just as representation in the broader political sphere has expanded to include previously excluded social categories of people, so too has it done in the health sector. The inclusion in the RHPA of previously excluded or marginalized health practitioners, such as midwives and massage therapists, is itself evidence of an expanded attitude towards 'others.' As we saw, many of the newly included groups come predominantly from the historically underrepresented of society. All of the seven previously unregulated practitioner groups who were allowed into the RHPA were predominantly female in composition.[61]

Aboriginal peoples were also treated, or rather they insisted on being treated, as a group requiring special consideration because of a history of oppression. Aboriginal healers and aboriginal midwives were given exemption from the legislation[62] – partly because they refused to participate in the same way as the others had. Empowered with expectations emanating from a broader political milieu in which they were being granted special status as 'First Nation' during the Canadian constitution talks, they simply refused to negotiate with health ministry officials, seeing the RHPA process as having no relevance to them.[63] The climate was right for their attitude, and so it prevailed.[64]

Other categories of social discrimination which were not dealt with in this policy process[65] may prove problematic in the near future. At a time when the gender divisions between nurses and doctors are becoming somewhat diffused or perhaps confused[66] by the rise in the number of women doctors working in the system, race and class tensions are taking on a more focused and openly confrontational character. For example, as white middle-class women move into both the medical hierarchy and the management hierarchies of nursing and institutional administrative positions, women of colour and working-class women tend to move in under them to take the subordinate positions they have vacated.[67] Race tensions showed up during the review process, for example, in the public complaints made by two black nurses regarding colour discrimination in relation to the composition of the nursing governing bodies in Ontario.[68] An Ontario court case, in 1985, resulted in recommendation of an investigation into 'whether the College of Nurses of Ontario has disciplined a disproportionate number of non-white nurses and thus practised racial discrimination.'[69] An Ontario Human Rights Commission decision regarding a 1990 complaint of racial discrimination filed against a Toronto hospital by one Filipino and seven black nurses came out in favour of the nurses' claims.[70] These race-related issues will continue to be brought to the fore, particularly under the present atmosphere of cost control,[71] but issues such as racial discrimination are notoriously difficult to regulate given their subtle and somewhat hidden nature, and the RHPA does little to help here.

Even the recruitment of diverse membership within a practitioner group can present subtle difficulties. A Registered Practical Nurse's Association representative commented that it has been difficult to recruit males to the profession as well as provide a more balanced association membership and leadership. Associations are voluntary, their boards are elected by nomination and, therefore, composition cannot be mandated. The present composition of the contigent of registered practical nurses of both the association and the college, for example, is all white (with the exception of some of the appointed members), and the leadership of both organizations is struggling with what to do about this structural impediment to diversity.[72] Midwives have also run up against difficulties in their attempts to encourage diversity in their profession as a whole, for example, male practitioners face bias, not with the profession, but 'with the consumer group,' which is difficult (and would be expensive) for midwives to address – except possibly by public education. Despite 'targeted special access for Aboriginal and Francophone women' by the NDP government, and some success at elevating the number of women of colour and Aboriginal women in the midwifery profession,[73] structural problems presented themselves here as well. As one midwifery representative put it:

> The very model of practice [of midwifery] and the commitment to continuity of care ... creates barriers. Midwifery is not an easy profession to practise, you need tremendous family support. If you are a woman with children and are going to be leaving in the middle of the night for your job, it takes a very autonomous self-reliant woman with lots of family support to do so. In a very traditional patriarchal family where the woman is supposed to do all of the child care, that may create problems ... In order to be an autonomous care provider, in order to be someone who sees herself as a collaborator with the medical profession, it takes an enormous amount of self-esteem and we know that women sometimes have issues with self-esteem because of the society we live in.[74]

Here we see some of the difficult structural and ideational barriers that potential health practitioners and practitioner group leaders come up against. The practitioner colleges and associations will need to give more thought as to how they might best identify and deal with these barriers to broad representation and equity within the profession.

With regard to our prevailing standards of responsible governance, the idea of responsible government as representative of the interests of the public it serves was one which was repeated over and over to the self-governing professionals during this policy process. As we have seen, during the review and the Ministry of Health follow-up, concerted effort was made to establish the link between responsible governance and the protection of the public interest, particularly with regard to the common confusion about the distinction between the responsibility of the governing body and that of the professional association. The professional record with regard to protecting the interests of the public was, as we have seen, less than satisfactory. However, after the review process most of the group representatives commented that the purpose of a professional governing body was clearer now.[75] Whether or not the strong dose of moral suasion received over the decade-long policy process will affect action, however, remains to be seen.

Public accountability measures taken from our broader legal blueprints were adopted and enhanced in the new policy design. The Health Disciplines Act of 1974 had embedded some accountability measures in the governing of the professions, but the HPLR and RHPA processes dramatically extended them: administrative, political, and financial accountability[76] have been enhanced in the RHPA. Administrative accountability, as the following of set regulations or laws, has become important in terms of bureaucratic coordination, scrutiny, and input, originating from, and being translated by, the government and its bureaucratic wing. The enhancement of administrative accountability is also important today in that its fuller definition contains the command to 'efficiency and effectiveness,'[77] so central to cost and quality control.

Political accountability, while providing the necessary governmental and bureaucratic input for a system in need of central coordination, is also useful rhetorically. It is always difficult for a Western government to move into entrepreneurial territory, and in this case it is a territory with a history of clinical autonomy based on scientific and technological expertise. This expertise is situated in a very powerful private area championed by liberalism, and the champion of the private can best be countered with democratic references to the public, using terms, such as 'public participation,' 'the public interest,' and 'egalitarianism.'[78] It is no accident that the HPLR report is laced with such references.[79]

Financial accountability has taken on new importance in today's climate of scarce resources. As Tuohy predicted, governments have redefined the obligations of the professions to include a responsibility for cost-control.[80] During both the review and legislation-making process there was a great deal of emphasis put on the idea of institutionalizing a continuous check on the quality of health care, and, while this emphasis on quality was overtly directed at the effectiveness of health care treatments and diagnostic instruments, it is also intricately tied to cost control. Good quality care includes an assessment of the strain particular health procedures place on the resources available for the whole. Direct talk about cost was considered inappropriate; it had to be hidden in talk of political accountability rather than financial accountability (as the public's right to good quality health care). This is not to say political accountability itself was taken lightly – only that this emphasis had a nicer ring to it. Of course, the professionals knew full well the importance of the cost element of their work.[81] They were, and continue to be, rightly, quite threatened by reference to financial accountability or 'affordability.'

The enhancement during this policy process of the legal aspects of the professional's role carries other more general implications or commitments. The policy process was rather highly influenced by the presence of lawyers, and with these lawyers came their ideational baggage, that is, their legal concerns, perspectives, and language, resulting in what Russell refers to in the broader context as 'a general transformation of the nature of political life' – a judicialization of that life.[82] The subsystem of health care has become increasingly judicialized. The best illustration of this here probably is a complaint voiced to me by one of the authors of the 1960s' report by the Committee on the Healing Arts, that the Health Professions Legislation Review could hardly be called a review at all. He quite rightly pointed out that rather than being a comprehensive report reviewing the state of the health professions legislation, which the former committee report had been, it was merely a volume of draft legislation written up in legal language with scant explanation of any kind – much less a good political and ethical review.[83] This is not to say that the lawyers, under whose supervision and creation it was placed, were thoughtless or theoretically unsophisticated, but rather that its thoughtfulness, if there, was fairly well hidden from the democratic eye.[84]

The legalization of the HPLR report did have its advantages, especially with regard to bringing the legal procedural elements of the new legislation into line with the legal norms of the rest of our society, as well as providing participatory access to the actual design and wording of the legislation. There is much to be said for work which has done the difficult task of translating policy analysis and concerns into concrete, precisely worded recommendations which are then made available as draft legislation throughout the consultation process for the various affected interests to argue about while there is still some hope of alteration. However, it is difficult to assess the intentions which lay behind a series of conclusions without access to the thinking which went into the development of those conclusions. Legal language needs to be exact, so by the time we non-lawyers see it, its precision has obfuscated the path by which it has arrived. The world of politics and health care, on the other hand, does not entirely lend itself to exactitude. Difficult concepts like 'quality of life' or 'professional competence' are concepts that need to be debated. Furthermore, concerns have been raised about the risk of 'overly "judicializing" the system by subjecting too broad a range of decisions and activities to procedural constraints, providing another mechanism whereby well organized groups may challenge and frustrate the implementation of policy when political action has failed them.'[85]

Practical Assessments of the New Legislation

Regulated Health Professions Act, 1991

The Health Professions Regulatory Advisory Council was given a ministerial directive in 1999 to review the effectiveness and impact of the RHPA and profession-specific acts. This 'five-year review' was in its early stages at the time of this writing. However, during the course of college interviews conducted for this work in 1997 and 1998, there were opinions voiced which indicate some of the concerns which will likely be brought to light during the HPRAC review. In summary, the new RHPA and accompanying health professional acts, received good, bad, and neutral reviews. One participating civil servant had this to say: 'Overall the professions feel it is working; it enlarged the scopes of practice and moved away from the exclusive and monopolistic control of acts by single groups ... and if this is any indication, other provinces are consulting with us, such as British Columbia, Quebec and Alberta.'[86] Comments from college representatives (which will remain non-attributed because of the sensitive nature of the decisions still in process) were positive: 'The RHPA has worked well ... is fine ... The Procedural Codes [section] is good.' Some of the older, more established regulated groups thought the new legislation was 'not much different from the old Act' (in terms of understanding and using it). One established group commented, 'It was generally a good experience. There was a lot of due process, but we have a lot of people here ... on staff. Generally, we are quite content with the RHPA, there is more openness and accountability now, for example, with public members. [The process] allowed for dialogue between the parties.'

Some of the colleges were positive in broad terms while still expressing concern over specific issues. They said: 'It is a good start, but there are grey areas open for interpretation, e.g., delegation ... and loop-holes left.' '[It is] workable. It is a quantum leap from the Drugless Practitioners Act. We do like the controlled acts ... [but the RHPA] does have some difficulties.'; 'We find it workable, except [for] appeals.'; 'The act is well set out and it establishes what we have to do ... [but] it is a difficult act in that it encompasses a mandate for twenty-three different colleges each with its own unique problems and concerns and that in and of itself is the prime criticism in that any one of the twenty-three colleges might say they would rather have an act specific to [their] own requirements and needs, but having said that, it is a compromise that seems to be working well.'

Some of the colleges were more critical, although some of this criticism came from the difficulties of the transition period when regulations, and later bylaws, were still being drafted and approved. Comments were made, such as, 'There was a lot of work left to be done by the colleges and it was difficult to operate during this transition time.' 'There was a lot of work for the new colleges.' 'How do you operate [as a college] with things [so much] in process?' Other, more general criticisms were made of the new legislation. Some said: 'The RHPA is an expensive Act to administer.' 'It is 'extremely cumbersome ... wordy ... confusing ... written by lawyers for lawyers ... compared to B.C. and Alberta legislation which is "easy to understand."' 'It is scattered ... difficult for members to follow and understand ... difficult to read. Our members have trouble understanding it.' 'It is really confusing, especially [when you are also dealing] with other acts ... You need a lawyer to help you get through this. [Plus] standards vary with colleges; we need standard standards.' The RHPA 'is difficult administratively.' 'There are problems with the model itself. It is new and not tested, with no precedent. [Also] there is a problem with enforcement. There is no [mechanism] set up for unauthorized people using controlled acts and going into the scope of others.'

There were also comments that the burden and costs and work of RHPA 'should decrease ... our members have complained about the fees' (and what they get for them). One representative commented on the post-proclamation process: 'There was an element of composing the symphony on the night of the performance.' Many voiced concern over the controlled acts: 'We still disagree with the [concept of] controlled acts.' 'There is still too much left to the public domain. We need more controlled acts.' 'We were concerned with the tasks approach [to controlled acts].' 'Controlled Acts are a challenging concept. This is confusing still ... We have unwieldy wording ... and end up with problems in application.' 'Our key problems relate to delegation [of controlled Acts] and what is in the public domain. Unless a college fails to disallow it, any member can delegate to anyone.' Long-term concerns for the integration of both health care and health practitioner relationships were also expressed. One influential college commented, 'I don't think there is enough integration, everybody is doing their own thing and therefore it creates fragmentation of care ... [There are] integration and communication issues, especially the integration of the professions in terms of working cooperatively in teams – and quit playing turf wars.' While another said, 'Our issues [of concern] are mostly related to multidisciplinary relations and RHPA doesn't deal with these.'

Overall, then, the new RHPA and its accompanying legislation is seen by the regulated colleges which will be administering them to have some broad and some particular attributes at the same time as it has some broad and some particular problems. The new advisory council (HPRAC) made some interesting comments on the RHPA in a discussion paper released in late 1996:[87]

- Harm is the overriding principle of the RHPA.[88]
- It is not possible to eliminate the potential for harm. The aim, instead, is to minimize the risk of harm by ensuring adequate training, competency and ongoing monitoring.
- The centrality of the controlled acts to the concept of harm and thereby to the rationale for regulation raises the question of whether health professions who do not perform any controlled acts need to be, or even should be, regulated under the RHPA [which some are now].
- We need to determine the minimum levels of training necessary to perform an act safely, rather than relying on maximum levels of training as the standard ... [Safeguards here could include] the requirement that the profession establish mandatory indicators for referral ... limits on the body parts on which the act can be performed ... limits on the circumstances under which the act can be performed, or limits on the types of patients/clients on whom the act can be performed.
- One of the challenges of the RHPA is to protect and enhance choice while minimizing risk of harm ... including choices in primary care ... [One important question remains.] Should choice be limited by encouraging or requiring standardized approaches to each controlled act, such that those professions that share controlled acts will perform them in the same way?
- It is our view that the RHPA is flexible enough to include non-western/non-allopathic medical systems and approaches ... The RHPA will be required to

The Regulated Health Professions Act of 1991   191

accommodate forms of health care practice that are not based on the western medical model.
- Access to safe health care is another fundamental tenet of the RHPA. While the RHPA speaks generally in section 3 about this access and the right of all people to be treated with sensitivity and respect, and while the RHPA has gone to considerable lengths to address sexual abuse of patients, other forms of discrimination and abuse have not been sufficiently addressed by the RHPA.
- There is considerable variation in the specificity of the authorized acts ... [Our] approach is that authorized acts ought to be specific where possible.
- There is no consistent approach to delegation. It occurs: on an individual basis; under inter-professional agreements; or in accordance with facility or professional guidelines and standards ... The RHPA should be amended to explicitly require that any delegation of controlled acts by a regulated health profession must be provided for by a regulation ... On the question of to whom controlled acts are delegated: Should the group that is being delegated to have the controlled acts authorized to them? On the other end of the spectrum there is the issue of delegating to people who are not capable of performing the act.
- While all controlled acts should be reviewed as part of the Five Year Review of the RHPA, [we] would like to flag the first controlled act, communicating a diagnosis, for particular discussion.
- [We] have been asked on numerous occasions to consider the economic implications of different options when developing advice on referrals, [but we] have not been in a position to gain access to or develop data that could provide a real foundation for such an appraisal of fiscal implications ... Nor have we been able to deal directly with issues around OHIP coverage ...
- The fact that professionals work in many types of settings raises the level of complication and implications for regulation and advice on regulation ... We believe professionals must be able to exercise their responsibility to refuse to be put into positions where the public interest is in jeopardy.

Among these statements and recommendations of the advisory council (HPRAC) we hear some familiar issues of the past – some couched in new language and some taking on a more contemporary dynamic – but still there to be dealt with.

Health Professions Regulatory Advisory Council

The new Health Professions Regulatory Advisory Council is itself an interesting addition to the mechanism of regulation of the health professions. Despite some very interesting work coming out of the advisory council, the unregulated practitioner groups 'have not had the access they expected.'[89] Events also proved that the council could be used by the minister of health as an effective holding body. HPRAC deals only with issues referred to it by the minister and therefore has no formal power of initiation. During the late 1990s, important issues which had been dealt with by the council were being held up by the Conservative government, that is, neither the advisory council reports, nor the minister's decisions regarding them, were being released to the public. Nor, as it stands now, would they ever legally have to be released, since the HPRAC report is confidential.[90] Aside from the potential waste of resources and the frustration of groups, such as the naturopaths and regulated practical nurses, who had invested heavily from their sparse resources in the HPRAC review of their cases,[91] this backlog clearly shows the limited power of the advisory council. Not only does the government in power control the council's research agenda, but it also controls the release of its output.[92] In their 1996 discussion paper, HPRAC itself 'developed a number of recommendations to ensure the ongoing credibility, usefulness and public interest foundation of HPRAC ... including changes to the RHPA ... to clearly indicate the following: a time frame for referral by the Minister of legitimate requests for referral to HPRAC for public review of a regulatory issue; an ongoing mandate to make recommendations on legislative reform as a matter of self-initiation; and the advice provided by HPRAC shall be made public after a specific period of time.'[93] As of mid-1999, there had been no changes of this nature to the RHPA.

Opinions expressed by the colleges about HPRAC varied from neutral to positive to mixed. Some said: 'We have not had much dealing with them.' 'Our relationship is a distanced relationship. They are advisers to the minister.' 'We haven't had a lot of dealings with HPRAC except by the federation.' 'We are neither happy nor unhappy, it is too soon [although] we are in agreement with their principles.' Positive comments, both weak and strong, were made: HPRAC 'is fine' or 'okay.' 'The information [they generate] is good.' 'We were impressed with HPRAC – even before [we had any dealings specific to our profession] with them.' 'Our experience has been very positive, particularly around scope-of-practice issues. I don't know what we would have done without HPRAC for issues like this ... We [had] questioned [the plan for a new advisory council] as another layer of bureaucracy, but it has stood the test of time.' Some of the positive comments were conditioned by concern. College representatives said: 'They have a role to play, but their time lines are too tight. New small colleges with few resources ... get overloaded.' 'HPRAC are doing what they can, but there is difficulty in understanding the act, for example, with controlled act definitions: they are not through the courts yet [so] opinions vary as to what they are.' One informant said:

It is a mixed bag ... it was created – as they politically stated to us – to deal with or deflect groups from the minister and it is used for that by some. They are generally good people with good motives. I am not sure they are equipped or fully staffed enough to do the very complex job they have to do. I am not sure you always get the best decisions from having a wide array of stakeholders. Plus they are only advisory and the decisions are generally political at the end of the day. Each issue gets exposure, but I don't know if the result is much different [because of it]. I appreciate what they are trying to do, but when it gets into their hands it is a real drain on time and money, for the colleges ... It was difficult in getting them to understand what it is we do. They ask questions that really can't be answered, at least not the way they want them answered, and they think that we are being evasive. We have had a lot of difficulty with technicalities, e.g., diagnosis, what is a disease/disorder/dysfunction? But these issues are terribly important from a practice point of view.

One college representative commented (in mid-1997): 'Lately, HPRAC is less valuable.' Others thought the advisory council was 'trying to do too much' with their current reviews. 'The evaluation plan looks [too] ambitious, but especially since [we are all] very much in the learning process.' It should be noted that, the above comments are largely relevant to the original HPRAC, the composition of which has recently changed (see below).

The politics around the advisory council showed a tension between the role of merely advising the minister on specifically referred issues and furthering the minister's duties – in section 3. On the one hand, the original council 'saw a wasted opportunity for important work ... tagging of problems, recommendations, etc. ... coming from their consultation role with various stakeholders in the sector, while on the other hand, a change in government ... to a Conservative government ... resulted in a lot of "reigning in the council" talk.'[94] The original advisory council was appointed under an NDP government, and its composition reflected the ideology of that party, although the chair, Ms Christie Jeffries, was 'interviewed by an all-party committee to make sure [the position] was not partisan' (and there were disagreements between HPRAC and the NDP government during their term).'[95] There was some question of the survival of the council, but it was kept – with the backing of the Ministry of Health, Professional Relations Branch, which argued for its continuation because of 'the need for this independent [judgement] ... [saying] the HPLR had proven the value of objective assessment.'[96] The incoming advisory council (appointed under the Conservative government after a two-year period of holding the original council in stasis), while not making any disparaging comments about the outgoing advisory council – indeed, referred to its independence – did point out the 'blue ribbon ... highly educated' composition of

194 Health Care Practitioners

the new council, who see their role as 'autonomous ... arm's length ... [while still] aware of what is going on within the Ministry and with the minister so that we are not making off-the-wall recommendations.'[97] It will be interesting to see just what 'arm's length' comes to mean under the new regime. The minister is already receiving advice through the normal governing channels of her or his civil service. For example, the Professional Relations Branch of the Ministry of Health played an important role throughout this whole long review, legislation-making, and now legislation-adaptation and -assessment process. Although it defines its role as providing 'advice in the broader context,'[98] it is a very knowledgeable player and, as such, carries considerable influence on issues which inevitably get translated down to the level of detail we have seen repeated throughout this story. I would not underestimate its importance.

Quality Assurance Programs of the Colleges

The new quality assurance programs of the colleges, as mentioned earlier, are under (legislated) scrutiny in the HPRAC review processes. Quality assurance is a very complex goal in its definition, planning, and implementation – as can be seen in the framework for its evaluation which was developed for HPRAC by Harry Cummings and Associates.[99] As expressed by the colleges, QA has roughly come to mean 'quality assessment' (standards of practice with comprehensive practice audits) and 'quality improvement' (adult learning and reflective practice).[100] One college group defined its main QA components as '(1) The Professional Portfolio (prior learning assessment), (2) Self Assessment (self critical process), and (3) Technical Testing ... (of a practitioner's skills).'[101] When asked for their opinions about their QA programs in early 1997, when they were still in the relatively early stages of development, the college representatives spoke of early problems: 'At first MOH was very general, that is, one version for all, but groups said, "We are each unique, we need our own [QA program]." In the end [with collaboration among the groups] there was a fair bit of commonality ... colleges need to get together to develop a generic model and then add specifics ... Early [membership] opposition was more about confusion, that is, they needed clarification.' Another college representative said, 'It is surprising that there wasn't greater direction. We ended up with various models for the [practitioner] groups ... the research shows that mandatory continuing education is not linked to outcome, but [some groups] went with it, despite the evidence.'

Colleges recognized the importance of the QA program. One representative said, 'QA is a very important committee. It [represents the] gist of the existence of the college.' While another commented, 'QA has been absolutely indispensable ... [This] is good work which had to be done.' And another said: 'This is a big concern with members.' But most colleges and their practitioner groups also had both general and specific difficulties emerge. Some said, 'QA has been an incredible amount of work. We got bogged down with regulations not passed and then we were told we had to have random pure assessments – a couple of groups came up with this – and we had to go back to our design.' 'QA was a lot of work, for example, the Comprehensive Practice Audits.' 'QA will be very expensive. All colleges have had to raise fees, especially for the practice review component.' One college representative expressed concern about the possibility of a shift in focus from quality to cost. 'Quality is difficult to evaluate – especially while also meeting MOH goals ... An economic evaluation would be good – re: public money versus return – we need to go beyond the regulatory role of the college.' Another said, 'We have to show changes in competence do improve patient outcome, re: stats, ... [but this is] expensive. [Plus] we work with others, therefore, cause and effect is difficult. I would recommend more calibration ... [All this] will take a lot more time than the three-year time line.'

By 1998, despite some lingering problems, the colleges had become more comfortable with their programs. For example, one college representative said, 'QA is our big issue right now. We want to see legislation passed to allow for mandatory peer review that is initiated without needing a member of the public to complain, rather each [practitioner] would be required to go through a peer review. This can be done in a non-threatening way in areas like infection control, and we will try and get the [practitioner] to upgrade through quality assurance.' Another said, 'The QA program here at the college is in full force. [What we have now, in mid-1998] works on routine random selection, but we are looking at how it is going to be used by other committees [for example] complaints ... We are getting lots of good results, but we are getting results [including negative results] we expected to see ... We found [our practitioners] still were not comfortable with the lifelong learning process ... They cannot lose their license for failing the QA program (under RHPA) ... [but] if the results were really bad it would be referred to the executive committee [of the college].'

New training programs, such as that for the extended class nurse practitioners indicate that the QA requirements which will likely be required of any new groups (or old groups with extended authorized acts) in the future. 'The RN(EC) must be an RN who takes a Nurse Practitioner course test, then goes through a year long Quality Assurance monitoring program where they are evaluated at the end of the year, or simply takes an NP course through the universities that offer RN(EC) education ... which includes RN education, the College RN(EC) exam and a year of Quality Assurance review.'[102]

A representative from the Registered Nurses Association of Ontario added an interesting note on the broader influence of the quality assurance programs: 'The QA program helped to improve the quality of nursing, and inadvertently, the quality of the health care institutions. There is often a conflict for nurses between the needs of the clients and the demands of the college, employer, labour laws, and union. Although the college has no jurisdiction over the workplaces of nurses, there is a moral expectation for managers to make changes when the college calls. No health care institution wants the college calling them, they don't want to be known as a poor or inadequate provider of health care ... [Although] the RHPA did not create the problem (of the utilization of casual, transient nursing labour) ... it highlighted it, [through] its quality assurance requirements.'[103] That is, questions of quality which were brought forth by the new legislation have brought these new labour practices into the formal debate. Questions of quality will continue to play an important role in shaping the dynamics of health care. This is where key questions about the necessity for the existing distribution of controlled acts might begin to be addressed. For example, medicine was authorized to perform all of the controlled acts, but can all MDs actually perform each one of them competently? There are a lot of actors in the health care sector interested in QA findings, and the results will be important to the sector's decision makers.

Patient Relations Program

The other new program for which there was a mandate for review by HPRAC was the patient relations program. During the late development stages of the RHPA, the patient relations program had become defined predominantly in terms of sexual misconduct and the patient relations review was thus targeted.[104] Some of the colleges expressed concern over the narrowness of this interpretation of patient relations. One said of the new committees in general, '[There is a] tendency to compartmentalize, rather than using general principles ... [such as] the public interest.' Another said, 'The PR focus on sexual abuse is too narrow. [It has] tended to overcome [the importance of] other issues, such as communication [between health practitioners and their patients].' And another said, 'There has been a problem going beyond sexual abuse.' It will be interesting to see if these broader concerns result in a future broadening of this program, particularly since the concern for patient relations is such an interesting new addition to the legislation.

On the patient relations program (and accompanying committee), college representatives expressed some positive and some negative views, while others explained its relative lack of pertinence to their health practices. The latter was mainly because some professional groups, such as opticians, 'have never had a complaint or referral for sexual abuse,' or registered dental technologists who 'have little or no direct contact with patients.' Some of these colleges said the PR committee 'makes life really difficult ... [because as one commented] we [were] told, if we don't have patients, we don't need the committee, but we had to set it and the program up [and] it doesn't work.' Others had related problems of relevance, such as the midwives, who 'are all women providing health care for only women.' A dietician's college representative said, 'Sexual abuse is not a big issue with our college. We are mostly women.' Regardless of relevance, however, all colleges had to set up programs similar to those of the colleges where the issue was of considerable relevance.

Opinions of the relevant practitioner groups were sometimes positive and sometimes critical. For example, one college representative said, '[The PR program] has been very useful for us. We have a travelling road show for our membership, with brochures and booklets. The first day is ethics; the second day [we deal with] patient – professional boundary issues. We have to be particularly careful about this. The issue needed to be addressed, although we are getting a bit of backlash from this. It seems overdone [to our members].' And another said, 'We have developed behavioural guides: a code of ethics, rules of conduct, and conflict of interest.' Other comments included, 'It will be useful, and '[We have done] significant work on prevention, public education, and targeting groups.' One college saw it as unproblematic. Its representative said, 'The PR committee has been very useful, especially for sexual abuse guidelines, but without any problems. We participate via a bi-monthly journal, public meetings, and a public relations program.' Others said, 'It is hard to say whether the [PR and QA] committees are going to be valuable.' '[PR] was needed as a start up, rather than ongoing.' 'In my opinion, it will be redundant in the future.' One college representative commented, 'We would like to see changes ... in the minimum mandatory sentencing for sexual abuse, which is five years revocation. I have a problem conceptually with a minimum sentence. It limits us in doing our job and doing it well as a disciplining organization.'

In 1998, one college admitted to having found 'members not well informed on what the RHPA means and the sexual abuse regulations surrounding that, including the penalties.' While another said, 'Patient Relations has been a struggle. Even the Federation of Health Regulating Colleges struggled [with this one]. Like with complaints, the mandate is not as clear-cut as it seems '[plus] the criminal code standards are very high ... Therefore there was not much focus [to the PR committee].' 'The PR committee has not been productive ... We [could not] even get a public relations brochure out on this' (by February 1997). 'The relationship with the QA program is hard to know.' This college also asked, 'What about sexual abuse of unregulated practitioners? ... In twelve states in the U.S. it is a crime in the case of [either] regulated or unregulated practitioners.'

Complaints and Discipline Committees

Complaints and discipline committees, which are not new committees having been made mandatory in the previous Health Disciplines Act, were not much criticized in these interviews with the colleges. The main complaint was the 'lack of authority to deal with frivolous and vexatious complaints made to the college.' The Health Professions Board, to which unsatisfied complainants can appeal a decision of a college's complaints committee, does, however, have the power to deem a review as unnecessary based on these grounds.[105] One college representative explained the reason for the concern: 'Frivolous complaints are time consuming and utilize our [limited] resources ... The [complainant] only needs the price of a stamp. We prepare a background file [for HPB] and have to send out investigators every time. [When we are thus tied up] we cannot deal with new complaints – and there is a 120-day limit for the college dealing with a complaint.'

On the problem with discipline, one college representative had this to say, 'Discipline ... deals with only extreme cases. For example, continuous quality improvement is not best achieved by discipline ... alternative dispute measures may [work here] ... The problem with discipline, kicking people out of the profession, is that it does not solve most cases, for example, a guilty [professional] gets a reprimand and suspension, but in terms of prevention it does little or nothing, and courts are not very comfortable revoking professional licences and tend to reduce the penalty.'

One interesting statement on an overarching problem with these details of regulatory control was made as follows: 'There are two classes of care givers; people who are self-employed, and people who are institutionally based. These are two different worlds with different means of accountability. We can talk to each other, for example, about regulations on advertising, conflict of interest, or professional misconduct, but the requirements are completely different. The difficulty is that the [MOH] Professional Relations Branch has created guidelines/regulations which can be customized to some extent, but they run into problems, for example, [with regard to] professional misconduct: there is no supervision in the field but there is supervision in institutions and [the policy makers] are not taking this decision seriously enough.' About the mandatory college committees in general, one college representative had this to say: 'They are too many, too long – compare the college of teachers.'

These early assessments of the RHPA and its bodies and programs give us a sense of what will likely come out in the reviews now in progress. It is an important body of legislation to assess. It has broken new ground and attempted a regulatory model for a complex and conflict-ridden sector.

Conclusion

Overall, the new Regulated Health Professions Act has made considerable strides towards both of its main objectives: to increase the coordination and cooperation of the health professionals and to align the rules and regulations of professional self-governance with the broader economic, political, and judicial standards of the day. The new legislation has resulted in better coordination of both the old sets of practitioner groups and the regulatory legislation under which they are governed. The whole process of defining each profession's scope of practice and authorized acts constituted an exercise in coordination. We have seen many issues of dispute remaining, but many were also resolved. This is a very difficult area, and questions will necessarily continue to arise over issues of expertise. Now, at least, there is a process to draw on in settling further disputes. Coordination of the regulatory statutes for each profession into one body of legislation constitutes a first step in creating an overall design for the regulated groups to replace the ad hoc developments of the past. It is not clear, however, what effect this will have on the outcome of the details of either the governance of the professions, or the everyday working relationships of the sector. In fairness, this latter type of institutional or workplace coordination falls outside the mandate of a policy-making process, such as the HPLR/RHPA, but in some way the latter may well contribute to the former. The review and development of the new legislation did set up a process of dialogue between the practitioner groups which would necessarily form the starting point of any attempts in the near future to enhance the cooperation of health practitioners in the workplace.

The new act has succeeded in updating its predecessor legislation with regard to the economic, political, and judicial standards or blueprints in good repute in Ontario today. With these changes comes a shift in the privileges and obligations of the key actors of the sector. Political–judicial control mechanisms for both the professions' governing bodies and the public (including those via the state) were enhanced. Our broader blueprints of governance – participation, consent, representation, responsibility, and accountability – were brought to bear on the subgoverning system of professional self-regulation. And while they remain considerably weaker in the privileged sphere of professionalism than in our broader society, the latter's more demanding blueprint is now more clearly positioned as the model of good governance. Only time will tell what these shifts truly entail. The new ideational investments in Ontario's health care subsystems have only just begun to show us both their potential for growth and adaptation and their potential for new sets of problems in need of resolution.

9

Conclusions from the Story

At the formal end of this health policy event, as in all policy events, a restructuring had taken place. Like the new 'Snakes and Ladders' board game, at the end of the game ideas which once sat outside the institution (the game board) were now embedded in it; positions were now altered; old relationships had been sustained or severed and replaced with new ones.[1] There is freedom for change in a restructuring process but the game is never played as freely as it might appear at first glance. There is always continuity as well, or as William Faulkner put it, 'The past isn't dead; it isn't even past.'

We watched a political story unfold while key principles and blueprints were either embedded, marginalized, or excluded during important policy events in the Ontario health sector. What makes this story a political story is its telling of the *relationship between* the ideational and the institutional – a relationship between ideas and institutionalized power. As particular principles and blueprints were taken up with each restructuring event, they became part of a process which translated into structured benefits and burdens for the actors there. Manifest benefits or privileges of economic monopoly, political self-governance, and internal judicial processes were joined by obligations such as public accountability. There were also both manifest and latent benefits and burdens of institutionalization in which some actors were left better positioned in terms of their power or potential power than were others.

As an essential part of any political story, the dynamic under investigation was played out within the context of public organization, both its degree and its mode. The degree of acceptable public organization is reflected in the role the state plays in the story; while the mode of public organization is reflected in the nature of the organized rationality found there. In the health care story presented here, the public organization was constituted by the politics of interpretation around the degree of professional governance and the mode of scientific, bureaucratic rationalism which would become embedded in the workings of the sector. Various actors fought for various interpretations of good governance and good health care, and as they won or lost their preferred interpretations, so too did they win and lose the accompanying benefits and burdens.

The Embedment in the Old Legislation

The earliest organization of the health practitioners in Ontario saw the acceptance of a new blueprint for health care – self-governing professionalism – wherein the state turned over considerable governing authority to those practitioners who fit the new mode of scientific, bureaucratic rationalism. Those who were unable to represent themselves as falling within this paradigm were excluded. Divisions within health practice were given institutional sanction as whole body, specialist, merchant, and assistant practitioners were positioned or sanctioned as professionals, semi-professionals, and non-professionals under the terms of the health professions legislation of the nineteenth century. Once linked to regulatory limitations and status, these divisions carried tensions of economic monopoly and competition as well as a set of institutionalized positions of power or authority.

During the early to mid-twentieth century these patterns were both continued and expanded. Further divisions of health practice developed inside and outside this public organization of self-governing professionalism as whole body practitioners, merchant–service practitioners, technique specialists, technology specialists, and assistant groups continued to develop in the sector (see Table 6.1). Society's mode of public organization, which encouraged institutionally sanctioned hierarchies of gender, class, and race, had also been given representation in the public organization of the health practitioners.

Prior to the 1980s' Ontario policy review of the health professions, benefits of authority and connection had accrued for some of the health practitioners but not others. Medical and medical-like practitioners were given considerable statelike authority; and while the non-medical semi-professionals were given less of the same, neither were held up to much accountability for this authority. The regulatory function of almost all the groups' governing bodies was legally distinguished from the unionlike functions of their voluntary associations. In practice, however, relations between the two were sufficiently good to bring the former's regulatory attitudes into question. Positions of authority within and between practitioner groups had also been realigned by regulatory legislation. Relations between practitioner groups began to take on the potential for future disagreement as some practitioners were given authority over others in, for example, prescription, supervision, and delegation of goods and services. Likewise, patients' relations were now complicated by their 'double agents': the practitioners and the state, both of whom wished to be the voice or agent of the patient in policy decision making.[2]

Supportive, neutral, and antagonistic positions of connection (as in being well-connected or poorly connected) had also developed in the sector. The elite science-based professions of medicine and dentistry maintained friendly or neutral relations with those professional or semi-professional practitioners who did not threaten either their clinical or their entrepreneurial territory. The marginalized practitioners of the Drugless Practitioners Act had developed a hierarchy which conformed to both society's science and gender biases. The institutionally excluded practitioners operated in a sphere of their own unless they crossed into the less than friendly whole body practice territory of the medical profession. All of these positions embodied tensions which would be taken directly into the 1980s' restructuring of Ontario's healthcare practitioners.

Public funding of health care services and delivery in the 1960s and 1970s only served to reinforce the divisions and tensions among the practitioners and between the practitioners, the state, and the public. The public–private (state–professional) tension was exacerbated by the introduction of a 'medicare' blueprint which left the responsibility for payment with the state at the same time as a considerable amount of control was left in the hands of the medical profession. Tensions over governance and expertise issues, which had developed during the introduction and workings of the practitioner regulatory system, were both embedded in this new institutionalization and exacerbated by new dimensions, such as the role of institutional managers, the labour concerns of the rank-and-file institutional employees, and the changing nature of the provider–patient relationship.

The external economic, political, and judicial climate was also drawn nearer the sector with the enhanced role of the state. Health policy reports of the 1960s and 1970s began to document the lack of fit between the principles and blueprints found in our larger Canadian context and those of the health sector. When held up to the standards set within a liberal, democratic, market society, the economic blueprint of the free market was considerably hampered by the monopolies provided by the exclusive licensure of particular health professionals; the professional blueprint of self-governance was rather light on the burdens or obligations set by our broader political standards of public participation and consent set within a representative, responsible, and accountable governing system; and the judicial processes found within the self-governing system were rather biased towards the interests of the professionals rather than their patients. Tensions developed over time because of this misfit between the economic, political, and judicial parameters of the healthcare sector and the broader organized society in which it sat – remaining to be addressed in any health care restructuring plans of the future. Calls for enhanced coordination, ministerial control, public accountability, public participation, judicial fairness, and so on, were heard from the critics, and although their advice was acted on only in a limited sense in the 1974 Ontario Health Disciplines Act, it was a sign of impending reinterpretations in the sector as a whole.

The New Legislation

The 1983 Ontario Health Professions Legislation Review was brought about, essentially, by the tensions embedded in the sector by this time. Ironically, as the *degree* of public organization in the broader realm of Canadian governance shifted and brought new ideas to the forefront, it began to challenge not just professional self-governance but also the embedded *mode* of public organization. That is, the mode of formal (objective, universal) rationality, specialized expertise, and hierarchy came up against the public tenets of market liberalism, participatory democracy, and procedural fairness which set the standards of good governance in the broader milieu. The anti-monopoly orientation of market liberalism, the egalitarian thrust of both participatory democracy and judicial fairness, and the public interest orientation of democratic governance served as particularly strong challenges to the hierarchies of clinical expertise (and its concomitant entrepreneurial monopolies) which had become embedded in the health care sector. As this broader milieu brought pressure to bear on the policy review and design process, it also created the possibility that previously excluded ideas might come to be incorporated into the existing structures of professionalism. The opening of the sector to these prevailing ideas would result in a realignment of its ideational and structural base.

By targeting the health sector's ad hoc legislative developments, lack of central direction, convoluted practitioner relationships and internal hierarchies, and the proliferation of increasingly educated and costly practitioner groups, the HPLR team set out to make sense of the existing roles and relationships among the practitioners and between them and the state. For this, they had to investigate the practitioners' claims to both health care expertise and good governance. Not surprisingly, the health practitioner groups fought hard to maintain or enhance the old benefits accrued from their favoured interpretations of expertise, while containing or minimizing the burdens associated with self-governance.

Conclusions 205

Expertise

The turf wars over expertise in the 1980s and 1990s were fought over the technical and legal details of the practitioners' authorized acts or procedures and scopes of practice. We have seen the details of these expertise turf wars where the practitioner groups 'fought and fought for a word on a page.'[3] This policy process brought these embedded tensions to the fore, highlighting the themes which will remain central to the sector, such as the balance between science and empiricism, or heroics and low intervention; clinical expertise and entrepreneurial ownership, or the service function and the merchant function; primary patient contact and secondary patient contact, or diagnosis and assessment; whole body health care and specialization; autonomy of practice and prescription, orders, supervision, and delegation; 'over-credentialism' and 'under-credentialism'; and infusing all of the above, the difficult balance between both limiting the risk of harm to the recipients of health care and ensuring a broad range of choice of health practitioners and therapies to the public. These are the central themes of contemporary health care expertise. They will continue to mould the policy debates and strategies of the sector.

In this policy round, medicine retained its control over whole body practice with the exclusion of the alternative non-medical competitors. Merchant expertise remained suspect. Those merchant–service practitioners who had made gains towards independence in the twentieth century were joined only by those able to emphasize a service function rather than a merchant function in advocating their health care expertise. The previously marginalized semi-professionals or non-professionals in the areas of technologist specialists or technical or nursing assistants were granted professional status only if they had managed to win regulatory gains in the past. The most dramatic indication of the willingness of the policy makers to break down some of the hierarchies of the old professional expertise turf came from the substantial gains of many of the contemporary technique specialists. Of those who had historically been *dependent* technique specialists, physiotherapists won both professional status and clinical and entrepreneurial independence from the elite profession under whom they had always practised, while dental hygienists and registered nurses made smaller gains in both. The *independent* technique specialists who have long been derided by the dominant practitioners as quacks also made impressive gains – chiropractors and midwives especially. It is interesting to note that contrary to the common assumption that interest groups with the greatest resources (of money, status, or numbers) will win the greatest gains, the biggest winners in this policy process, that is, those who gained the most ground, were the smaller groups with considerably fewer of these concrete resources. Their resources were more ideational – having better fit with the ideas in good repute with the policy makers.

More generally, the lengthy open forum of discussion made possible by the HPLR/RHPA policy process allowed for both a new set of communications between the practitioners and a questioning of the underlying ideational assumptions of the sector. Practitioner group communication was mandatory in both written and verbal form. The organizers of the policy process deliberately set up a 'hermeneutical' environment with at least the potential for the 'sympathetic placing of oneself in the position of the other.'[4] Groups were asked to comment on each other's submissions with all polemic clearly discouraged, as well as meet face-to-face to discuss their differences and, hopefully, come to better understand the other's position. The signals from the state officials were clear: everyone was expected to do their part in relieving the tensions among the practitioner groups. The HPLR team gave equally clear signals of the same commitment, and both, as we have seen, made constant reference to egalitarian principles. Any politically astute group would have to have been uncharacteristically imperceptive to have refused to give in to some of this pressure and come to an agreement. Some did, others did not, and still others laid a groundwork of communication which might enhance cooperation in the future. The evolution of the groups' submissions to the HPLR suggests that they were engaged in the process of 'policy learning':[5] not only were they picking up the aforementioned signals from the policy makers, but many also appeared to be genuinely listening to the concerns and arguments of the other practitioners.[6] This can only benefit the climate of communication which will be necessary for today's restructuring within the sector.

Aside from learning to communicate better with each other, practitioner groups – especially those not overly familiar with the policy process – learned the language, reputable principles and blueprints, and strategies of the process itself, that is, they learned to talk to the policy makers. With the exception of naturopathy, which thereby gave up a chance to join the profession (at that time), even the small, previously policy-unlearned groups showed signs of learning how to play the game. In this sense, even losing had some element of winning: next time, they will better understand the process – and there is the possibility of a next time since the new legislation built in mechanisms for ongoing attempts at entry for the excluded.

The policy process itself also allowed for questioning the underlying assumptions of the clinical and entrepreneurial monopolies which had grown up in the sector. Interesting questions were raised about the nature and use of expertise. The problematic link between health care expertise, which provides the foundation for health care service, and health care expertise, which provides the foundation for the selling of merchandise, will remain a source of tension in the sector. The designers of the RHPA attempted to minimize the potential distortion of the practitioners' clinical judgments with their entrepreneurial interests by accepting only the former as the basis for any new regulation of practitioner groups, but this proved to be a difficult task, as Tuohy predicted some time ago. Debates over this rather interwoven 'line' between the clinical and entrepreneurial will continue to be central to the regulation of health professionalism – especially because this debate is important to the issue of public reimbursement (via OHIP) of entrepreneurs, such as medical practitioners, optometrists, chiropractors, and others. There is a lot invested in these border disputes.

One of the problems for policy making in the health care field lies in the changing nature of health care knowledge itself. A large part of the story of health care practices and practitioners is one of constant adaptation to a changing knowledge base. We have seen the development of ladders of specializations, specializations-within-specializations, new whole body practitioners, new merchants, new technologists, and new assistants. This presents a serious problem for policy makers, since they must update new legislation to fit present-day conditions at the same time as they design adaptive legislation and structures which will be able to respond to ongoing change. The policy makers here made one important change in this regard: the new legislation was designed such that new practitioners and new practices could be added over time. Just how responsive the new structures set up for this accommodation (such as the Health Professions Regulatory Advisory Council) will be, or how forthcoming ministerial authorization of change will be, remains to be seen. It is significant, however, that the health professions have now been left open for adaptation.

Another central expertise question highlighted by this policy process is that of the opening of an established, institutionalized sector to alternative concepts of expertise. While science and technology based expertise has clearly been of great importance to contemporary health care, the two do not preclude the use of techniques and compounds (by medical and non-medical practitioners) which, while not scientifically credited, appear to provide relief from suffering without undue harm. The fairly large overall presence of alternative practitioners and their techniques and patients over time has argued for a broader definition of health care expertise than had been institutionally acceptable in the past. The policy outcome itself does lend a certain legitimacy to the fringe critiques of the dominant paradigm of knowledge. The process has resulted in the inclusion of a broader range of groups (with different ideational blueprints) within the regulatory structure and allowed for an expansion of the roles of several types of practitioners. The general 'live and let live' attitude adopted towards the non-regulated practitioners by the decision makers, although it may not hold up in court, was also indicative of a new climate of acceptance of this broader expertise. That is, beyond the concrete or visible level of letting alternative practitioners into the system, there is a potentially important ideational shift here.

If you look at this story from an institutional perspective, on the whole the most successful practitioner groups were still those who could situate themselves solidly within the scientific paradigm of health care. There was little institutional change in terms of who continues to hold power in the sector.[7] If you then take account of the role of ideas as some institutionalist analyses do, it can also be noted those who were somewhat scientifically suspect – at least when using medicine as the standard – also bettered their former positions if they were able to tap into the economic, political, and judicial ideas in good repute during the policy process. But if you go even further in investigating the complex and subtle relationship between the institutional and the ideational you see that beyond this visible, strategic 'getting in' of alternative groups, there are interesting ideational implications for the sector as a whole. What the new legislation says is that other practitioners know how to make people healthy or guide them safely through life experiences, such as pregnancy, or illness prevention. That 'knowing' is what the HPLR and RHPA processes have lent legitimacy to, and this legitimacy could prove to have wide, long-term implications.

The 'getting in' of outsider groups can work in two ways: one, it may signal the beginning of a process of assimilation into the dominant paradigm or embedded ideational climate of the sector; two, it may signal the beginning of a process of paradigm shift or redefining the embedded ideational climate of the sector. Chiropractors may represent the former, since their acceptance often came at the price of down-playing or abandoning their less acceptable characteristics of difference – holism, subjectivity, contextualization, and empiricism – in order to represent themselves as closely linked to the scientific bureaucratic ideal as possible.[8] In this sense they have entered and reinforced the establishment. Midwives, in contrast, represent, at least partially, a redefining of the establishment. While they did make use of any scientific data they could find to substantiate their application for inclusion in the established health professions, beyond this policy strategy, once inside, they have slowly and apparently fairly successfully, moved to redefine the established practices of childbirth, both in the institutionalized hospital setting and in the institutionally unsanctioned and hitherto, for them, illegal location of the home.

It can be argued that previously excluded or marginalized practitioners have eroded the dominant knowledge base of the health sector by what might be seen as an attempt at reasserting the role of empiricism in health care: first, by seeing health care knowledge as existing on a continuum from empiricism to science; second, by seeing empiricism as a check on scientific abuse; and third, by seeing empirical observation of, and by, the patient as playing an important role in healing and health maintenance. Ironically the new evidence-based research or outcome analyses being advocated by today's health care analysts and policy makers may be just the establishment boost the alternative practitioners need. Since evidence here appears to be strongly weighted towards patient outcome or perceived outcome, this places empiricism in a new and improved light. Empirically based health care has always had to take into account the wellness or perception of wellness of the patient rather than the results of the controlled, reproducible clinical trials of science. Regardless of how scientific chiropractic (for example) may prove to be after the fact, they were present to fight for inclusion in the RHPA because their empiricism had been sound: their patients kept coming back because they felt better (or their friends or family had felt better) after chiropractic treatment. This is the sort of standard most of today's alternative practitioners have already met.

It remains to be seen whether the previously marginalized or excluded practitioner groups will continue to redefine health care's ideational base or whether they will predominantly be assimilated within the dominant paradigm. It is interesting to note how little the efforts of preventive health care were rewarded during this policy process.[9] It is inevitable, however, that the present-day debates will continue for some time over the efficacy or worth of heroic scientific health care versus the conservative empiric approach to care, or the eclectic mix of the two found in complementary medicine.

The central problem with the new term 'complementary care' is the power relations implicit to it. Complementarity implies complementary-to, and that 'to' refers to 'medicine.' There is nothing complementary about two distinct diagnoses, prognoses, or treatment recommendations coming from, say, a medical surgeon and a chiropractor, or a dentist and a dental hygienist, or a general (medical) practitioner and a naturopath, or an obstetrician and a midwife. There are cases where the ideas of separate practitioners are complementary, and there are cases where they are contradictory, or alternative to – there are probably even cases where they are relatively neutral. This fundamental contradiction will not go away. As we saw during this policy story, the question of who has the requisite expertise for first contact (or diagnosis) of patients has long been and continues to be the cause of much debate and strife in the sector. The alternative, conservative practitioners are still saying 'try us first, before you resort to surgery or drugs,' and the medical or medical-like practitioners who are not opposed to alternative practices are still saying, 'I suppose you might as well try them after you have exhausted all medical avenues.' The answer to the question, 'Who comes first?' is nowhere near settled, or 'in complement.'

Complementary health care suffers the same problem as its earlier manifestation as eclecticism; it represents the dance of the elephant and the mouse, with little doubt as to which partner is most likely to get stepped on. As we have seen, eclecticism has had a long history of failure. As we have also seen, old animosities between practitioner groups die hard. Emotional complementarity may be as crucial as clinical complementarity. Even assuming that radically different groups could set aside their personal history or animosity, I would argue, the dynamic offered by alternative practitioner groups is healthy – at least up to a degree. The advantage of alternative health care is its willingness to fight the established ideas of health care. This is not to say it is necessarily right and the embedded ideas wrong, since it too will need to be assessed for 'harm,' only that its attitudinal approach is healthy. It ought to be kept in mind that the science-based medical profession was itself once the voice of change, that is, the alternative to the status quo. New ideas have long played an important role in the development of both science and society. Likewise, the twentieth-century alternative practitioners who have now entered the system have again shown us that radicals represent important critical ideas. For, as Pross puts it, 'We must contain and channel the energies of pressure groups without destroying the vitality and creativity they contribute to modern democracy.'[10]

Lastly, the biggest expertise question for the sector, one which has been forced to the forefront by today's cost-control blueprints, is 'Who can do what? Or rather, who can do what the most efficiently and effectively?' We have seen the challenges among the practitioners to 'overcredentialism' and unnecessary monopoly. A recurrent criticism from those previously marginalized or excluded in the sector was that the categories of disease commonly used for making distinctions among the health practitioners are too gross, that is, they would be better broken down into 'normal or recurring minor deficits' (normal births, colds, eye deficiencies, laboratory tests, and so on) and 'major or more difficult pathologies' (which the crisis personnel are best at). The new legislation gives legitimacy to this claim in that it recognizes the role of midwives in 'normal' births, opticians in normal eye degeneration, chiropodists in normal minor foot disorders, and so on. More recent trends continue this redefinition of expertise with, for example, the move to expand the role of the extended class nurse practitioner into the area of recurring common illnesses with readily discernible patterns – areas where nurse practitioners, as we saw earlier, have demonstrated their abilities.

The HPLR/RHPA policy designers and decision makers did not have the resources to properly investigate the many claims made during this policy process, of both underutilization and overutilization of various practitioners in the health care system, but today's climate of evidence-based policy debate necessitates such investigation. What the Ontario review did uncover was evidence such as that we have seen for midwives, nurses, and dental hygienists, which lends credence to their claims of underutilization and therefore unnecessary expense to the system. Some of this investigation is now proceeding throughout Canada in the form of epidemiology studies, health practice utilization assessments, and some review of practitioner substitution. The HPLR/RHPA story, I would argue, provides at least five important caveats to that work: (1) It is not enough to know what the clinical capacity of the various practitioner groups might be (although this in itself presents a considerable challenge). Who can work with whom and why (in clinical, legal, and historical relationship terms) is also key to understanding practice potentials. (2) The evidence here suggests that the practitioners themselves, especially the more powerfully positioned practitioners, are not reliable 'objective' policy makers. What this story shows is the overwhelming tendency of practitioner groups to guard both their clinical, entrepreneurial, and legal territory against any and all intrusion by others. This long history of turf wars and emotion-laden relationships constitutes considerable evidence of bias. Difficult 'border disputes' need to be investigated externally as well as internally. (3) Internal critiques from health practitioners outside the specific group under investigation ought to be given serious consideration. (4) External investigation ought to include both scientists per se (which none of the practitioners are) and non-scientists willing to investigate the evidence of favourable results obtained by the empirically based practitioners. In the best of policy situations one might also find former or critical practitioners who would be willing to admit to unnecessary territorial practices, overcredentialism, over- and underutilization, inefficiency, and waste in the system. (5) Improved investigation of health and illness needs to take more notice of an undervalued source of information, the patient. There is a wealth of knowledge in the 'sense' of health, illness, or cure experienced by the patient. If practitioners, particularly the medical profession, have anywhere proven their inability to act as objective scientists it is here. Disappearing patients have never been followed up to find out whether they never returned because they were cured or because they were not cured; this is a truly non-scientific practice. This is not to say that the patient alone should determine health care practices, only that it is time to take the intelligence or informed judgment of the patients more into account, giving them credit for considerable knowledge of their own bodies. After all, they too are gatekeepers in a universally accessed system.

Relationships

As practitioner expertise was called into question, the relationships among the practitioners, and between them and the state and the public, were also subject to adjustment. The state has now distanced itself further away from the former elite of the sector, at the same time as it has moved to a closer relationship with the formerly marginalized groups and a more neutral relationship with the excluded groups. The agency relationship held by the health professionals has also undergone a shift from the predominant private entrepreneurial agency, with individual 'consumers' of health care, to one which now includes both this private agency (with the individual practitioner as agent and the patient as principal) and public agency (with the professional governing body representing the agency of the state towards the public as principals). With this public agency relationship has come increased obligations of governance (to which I return soon) and therefore a closer association with, and accountability to, the ultimate site of public sovereignty, the state. This double agency held for the patient or public by both the practitioner and the state-via-the-professional governing body is, of course, a source of continued tension simply because it endorses more than one decision maker. In effect, there are three decision makers under this agency arrangement: the individual practitioner, the professional governing body, and the state. When the three disagree on the best interest of the patient, someone has to give in, or at the very least, confusion results. This agency relationship is made even more difficult by the rise of the autonomy of the patient per se who is less and less willing to delegate agency or proxy to anyone, and therefore becomes a fourth decision maker in the processes of health care. It is difficult enough to find out who is actually making key decisions in an organization as complex as health care, but when this is overlain by legitimate questions of who ought to be making key decisions in health care, the dynamics get more and more complex.

This complexity is made all the more confusing by another distinction of roles within the recipients of care which is utilized by the agents above, that is, the three-way division of the patient–patients–public, once the patient becomes more than an individual entering the office of a practitioner. Each recipient of health care services is all three at one and the same time, that is, a patient, part of a group of patients, and part of the public which both uses and

Conclusions 213

pays for health services; and each role can carry different and sometimes contradictory interests. It is in my interest as a patient that I have access to any and all diagnostic and treatment technologies and therapies regardless of cost. However, as a member of a patient group with a rare disease which has not been targeted for many health care dollars, for example, I have an interest in syphoning off some of the funds supporting general technologies and treatments. Likewise, as a member of the public I may wish to further displace funds for other social services or simply to reduce overall funding in order to lower my taxes. Each of these roles can be highlighted in argument such that a person gets divided and pitted against herself or himself. The tensions and confusions caused by this three-way health care recipient distinction being acted out within a dual-agency relationship (with three actors – the individual professional, the professional governing body, and the state – representing the interests of the patient–patients–public) are predictably difficult, particularly when placed in the context of restructured roles and relationships. As time goes on there will be an increasing need to settle on, or at least gain some clarity towards, an open and fair allocation of patient–practitioner–state roles and responsibilities: one which is more in keeping with today's principles regarding the contemporary needs for patient or client autonomy, as well as the acceptance by the state of its obligation towards the public interest in all policy sectors, including those historically designated as professional subgovernments.

The relationships of the practitioner groups towards each other did show improvement in some areas during this policy process. The tone from the College of Physicians and Surgeons of Ontario, for example, was decidedly more cooperative towards other professional–practitioner groups than in the past, with the exception of the alternative whole body practitioners. More importantly perhaps for future relations, the review process introduced an important blueprint of communication among the practitioners within the sector. Forced to represent themselves to both the policy designers and their fellow practitioners, each group spoke of its intentions and perceived position within the sector at the same time as its members listened to the same from others – including the state, representatives of the public, and to a lesser extent institutional managers, such as representatives of the Ontario Hospital Association. Despite ongoing disputes, a platform of communication now exists, with considerably more understanding among the sector's participants than had ever before existed. From communication and understanding sometimes come better relationships.

With regard to the politically strategic relationships of the sector, historical connections to the elite, like historical connections to the state, were not sufficient indicators of success in this policy process. Ophthalmologists, for example, were not successful in using the traditional weight of the medical profession to reduce the gains of optometry. Nor were the medical opponents to midwifery successful in rallying any significant opposition. While the whole body enemies of the medical profession were kept off medical territory, this was probably more the result of their relationship to the scientific paradigm of health practice than to their relationship with medicine. Where the non-medical whole body practitioners failed was in their ability to provide any proof of their claims to expertise. The intense opposition of the elite of the dental field to the competition of denturists failed to meet with success. Nor were registered nurses able to block the independence of midwives, although they did succeed in doing so with the practical nurses – the latter, however, was influenced by the policy-makers' reluctance to split 'a profession.' The merchants were only successful in keeping out the new lower-level competitors, such as hearing aid dispensers, from the protection of professionalism, but this probably had more to do with state reluctance to generate monopoly than with interest group influence. The pressure to extend entrepreneurial monopolies was resisted for all professions, regardless of their connections.

Neither were historical connections of friendship necessarily good indicators in this policy process. This was most dramatically illustrated by the desertion of the naturopaths by their long-term friends and associates, the chiropractors. But, neither were the old friendly or, at least, non-hostile relationships of dependency or paternalism to remain intact: positions of authority held between health practitioners in the form of prescription, supervision, or delegation were continued in many cases under the RHPA – although the fight for independence from direct supervision was won by new professional groups, such as midwives, physiotherapists, and denturists; softened for others, such as nurses; and left to be fought over in either the political or judicial realm for others, such as dental hygienists. Here, the medical profession, if not necessarily initially enthusiastic, in the long run was supportive of the technique specialists, particularly the physiotherapists, whose body of knowledge did not directly clash with theirs. They were less supportive of anything but the most minimal of intrusion into their clinical territory by the pharmacists and the nurses. The dental supervisors of dependent technique and technology specialists and assistants of the field quickly reversed any support of their former friends, when the same began to fight for any independence which would cut into the elite practitioners' profits.

Gender, race, and class-based biases were interwoven into the relationships of the health sector, and they too carry their own tensions and future difficulties. The RHPA did gain considerable ground in enhancing gender equality in the professional legislation, exemplified in both the inclusion of seven new predominantly female professions and the special treatment of midwifery. Yet, aside from the unique treatment of natives (who were allowed some measure of internal control), race and class relations were given little attention, even though they continue to affect the sector, for example, in the long sought after Bachelor of Science requirement for registered nurses which would make accessibility to this level of the nursing profession more difficult for the socially disadvantaged as university tuition continues to rise. More generally, while the effects of down-sizing tend to fall heavily on the poor,[11] the cheaper, more accessible categories of practitioners, such as registered practical nurses become more attractive to budget conscious institutions, providing more employment for these categories of workers – although the work is generally less attractive with regard to issues like hours or benefits.[12] Doubtless, the fight between credentialism and economy of service delivery will continue to affect relations in the health sector, at the same time as claims to injustices of gender, race, and class relations are brought to bear via the political and judicial routes of public influence.

Most of today's restructuring blueprints for the health sector are advocating multidisciplinary teams or at least a much higher degree of cooperation among the various health practitioners. But cooperation and team work imply a high degree of compatibility, and this study of the relations and tensions among the practitioners leaves little doubt that there will be some serious barriers to implementing such everyday cooperation. The battles over 'Who does what?' will continue, with both entrepreneurial and clinical arguments being couched in the language of expertise. At the very least, any attempts to further coordinate the provider groups in the health sector will need to take into account the history of conflict-ridden interaction laid bare by this policy process. Unless policy makers understand the underlying justifications for the arguments made and positions held, by all of the practitioner groups, they will be ill-equipped to come up with well-designed teams – ask any student of Canadian federalism.

Economic Issues

We have seen how many of the tensions still present in the practitioner relationships are linked to economic interests. Where there is money to be lost, there is continuing conflict. This is not to say that this conflict is not couched in the language of, and inevitably inseparable from, clinical expertise, only that if one were looking for sources of conflict one would necessarily consider market and/or employment overlap among the practitioners. Perhaps the

RHPA was inevitably unable – as regulatory legislation – to overcome the tensions here, but perhaps also, the original mandate was too naive to have resulted in better clarification of these age-old entrepreneurial and/or labour disputes. The early emphasis on the importance of separating regulatory control from economic interference posited a dichotomy that never existed. Regulation of the practitioners' services and merchandise has unavoidable consequences for their cost, as the expertise and the conditions of its provision become interwoven. As we continue to search for a better health care system, we will necessarily look to the *relationship between* the clinical and entrepreneurial or, in a larger sense, between quality and affordability.

The health sector's overall economic blueprint provides considerable room for tension over the relationship between quality and affordability. The restructuring of the Ontario health professions in the 1980s and 1990s brought forth ideas of free competition and suspicion of government regulation, but the self-regulation blueprint which already existed in the sector severely constrained any new interpretation brought in via free market ideas. Since an alternative (complete) deregulation blueprint of the health professions was never seriously countenanced, free market ideas were being grafted onto a highly regulated sector. This, of course, resulted in a necessarily specific interpretation of 'the market' within this particular sector. This interpretation, which became embedded in the RHPA, decreased monopoly forces by (1) refusing to grant professional regulation to any previously unregulated merchant of health care products, (2) licensing health practices rather than health practitioners – under a regulatory design which allowed for ongoing modifications to the 'leasing out' of these practices to various practitioners who could now present a case for their ability to expand the list of procedures allowed their profession, and (3) the introduction of more rather than fewer regulated groups in the sector in order to disperse the monopoly effects of professional regulation via oligopoly. That is, the historical monopolists were joined by more competitors. This new market in the health sector will be tested in the restructuring currently under way. Whether enough room has been opened up for the utilization of a broader band of practitioners capable of performing new or previously disallowed health procedures will likely be put to the test.

It is necessary to keep in mind, however, that these anti-monopoly assumptions of reduced cost are here being applied to a health care blueprint combining public funding with considerable practitioner control over services. So while efforts to break down the monopolies of the sector might be expected to reduce costs, this is offset by the free choice of practitioners to provide their services to the public despite inefficiencies of cost. This is, of course, most relevant to the (almost) fully funded practitioners of the sector who are also allowed the widest range of entrepreneurial choice within the system, the medical practitioners. Even if cheaper practitioners were found to be capable of providing quality services, the current public–private blueprint of the sector would not guarantee their utilization.

A related aspect of economic relations taking on considerable importance in the current restructuring of the health sector concerns labour issues. We have seen how many of the rank and file of the professional groups expressed more concern about labour relations within the institutions in which they work than they did about professional issues. Such concerns can only be enhanced by the current trend to down-size, especially in the hospitals. Analysts and practitioners have expressed concerns about the treatment of institutional practitioners as restructuring takes place. The utilization of lowest cost care providers (LCCP) or 'generic workers' has led to concerns about worker lay-offs, poor working conditions, the trade-off of quality health care for cheaper labour, the ethical and legal conduct of poorly trained practitioners, and equity and fairness issues.[13]

Interestingly, despite these valid labour concerns,[14] the current changes in the health sector may well provide the first real impetus for a major restructuring of practitioner roles which would work to the advantage of many previously disadvantaged groups. A long history of the state's 'collegial accommodation' with the medical profession has resulted in 'relative structural and institutional stability' in the Canadian health care system.[15] Now that that stability is threatened, so too might be the long-embedded barriers to expansion of practitioner roles. Practitioner groups positioned at the top of the hierarchy, such as general practitioners and dentists, would stand to lose some work to the middle-positioned practitioners, such as nurses, dental hygienists, or technologists, who in turn would lose some work to the lower-positioned practitioners, such as assistants and technicians, who in turn would lose work to groups (probably unregulated labour groups), such as orderlies and new assistant groups, who in turn might lose tasks to volunteers. Only those at the top would be placed in a position of loss; the rest would be placed in a win–lose position. Unfortunately, as we have seen in this story, everyone wants to win–win, so they expend a great deal of energy trying to make sure that they do not lose anything to the group below them, when they might be channelling that energy towards redesigning their profession in a manner that (at the same time as addressing labour abuses) would give serious consideration to handing over some of its old tasks in order to take up new ones.

Practitioners who stand to lose most from this upward mobility are the ones at the top. Within medicine, losses would fall mostly on family physicians or general practitioners, and they will, of course, fight to maintain their ground.

However, it may well prove to be true that the history of accommodation to medicine has resulted in a wide range of ownership of relatively simple tasks easily performed by another, less costly practitioner; and this, of course, is what the nurse practitioners of the North (or today's extended class nurse practitioners) have demonstrated. It may be that family physicians and general practitioners are somewhat outmoded in both clinical and economic terms: it may be time for all of medicine to move up the ladder and specialize in more complex, difficult illness care, gradually phasing out the simpler tasks and technical gatekeeping and leaving them to the extended class nurse practitioners.[16] Any such suggestion coming from the policy makers would likely be strongly opposed by family physicians who would argue, as they have all along, that it is only the physician who is capable of *the* gatekeeping and coordinating role. But as we look across the whole spectrum of health practices and their historical patterns, this is essentially what has taken place throughout the health sector over time, that is, an evolutionary process whereby practitioners gradually move from simpler to more complex tasks with new practitioners moving in to fill the vacated position. Almost all of this movement, as we have seen in this story, has been and continues to be vigorously contested by any practitioner group with clinical monopoly or entrepreneurial profits at stake.

Certainly all of this begs further investigation. One seasoned civil servant predicts that the combination of institutional (especially hospital) economics, patients' rights, competing professions, and today's Ministry of Health policy direction will put considerable pressure on the question of 'Who does what?'[17] However, it should also be kept in mind that investigative results and reasoned argument are sometimes no match for interest groups with well-embedded positions of power and strong public support. If serious restructuring of the tasks within the health professions takes place, it will likely only come as the result of a long slow process backed by considerable state determination and public education – and I did say 'if.'

Political–Governance Issues

The RHPA contains a new balance between the public and the private. The privilege of professional self-regulation, with the control it entails over a group's authorized acts as well as the implications held by a group's scope-of-practice statement, was won at the price of an enhanced set of obligations commensurate with that governance. That is, the balance has shifted away from much of the automatic trust of the professionals to a more publicly exposed and accountable system of governance.

As we saw in Chapter 8, means of direct public input, indirect public control via elected representatives (the Minister of Health), and internal professional governing control (via colleges or college councils) were laid out in the new legislation. Some of the previous measures developed in the 1974 Health Disciplines Act were enhanced, and some new modes of input or control were introduced. It will be interesting to see what effect these measures have. The ability of an interest group to self-regulate has long been questioned by analysts. However, given the prohibitive cost of direct state regulation of the professions, professional self-regulation has been seen as necessary. Here, it might be countered that the state is having to more and more 'interfere' in the sector precisely because the overall effect of self-regulation (rather than the specific costs of regulation per se) has been to ensure higher costs of services because of the monopoly privileges it promotes.[18] Despite this, however, professional self-regulation does appear to be here to stay, and given the fact of its acceptance, the important questions relate to its efficacy and fairness. In particular, whom does it protect, the public or the professionals? It was made clear during this policy process that the governing bodies of the professions are meant to represent the interests of the public. But the 'public interest' is a notoriously slippery concept, and it remains to be seen just what interpretation the new professional colleges place on this obligation.

The emphasis placed on the public interest both during the policy process itself and in the new design of the legislation runs up against the contemporary problem of how to define and operationalize an enhanced public role. During the HPLR/RHPA process itself, direct public participation was low. This hardly seems surprising since it was a legalistic process involving complex regulatory and scientific details. It may be that policy processes such as this one, where the political issues are couched in highly technical debates, will tend to remain the necessary domain of the interest groups who can translate the technical into the political, leaving the state to act as representative of the public-as-citizenry. It may also be that the cost of eliciting broad public involvement in complex policy debates is prohibitive.

The details of the measures taken to enhance the presence of the public in the everyday workings of the health sector's professional governance were provided in Chapter 8. Further study of these measures is needed to assess their efficacy. Are they fulfilling their intended purpose? If not, why not? For example, one particularly interesting new body to watch is the mandatory patient relations committee and program in the professional colleges. Thus far, the patient relations focus has been targeted at 'vulnerable client abuse,' particularly that related to sexual misconduct, but it will be interesting to see if this agenda broadens,[19] or if it begins to be led by the patients or clients themselves. That is, will there be mechanisms put in place for patient-led investigation into, and recommendations for, a broader interpretation of good patient relations?

The way in which these new participatory mechanisms are handled by both the professional governing bodies and the ministry will provide us with clues as to their commitment to fulfilling the principles which were meant to be contained within the RHPA. We saw the opposition of the elite practitioners to the enhancement of (a) direct public input from lay members on their committees and hearings, as well as the opening of these to the general public, and (b) indirect public input from the Minister of Health. Regarding the opposition to opening committees and hearings to the public, my sense here is that the old elite professions were less concerned with lay representatives of the public on their committees and hearings than they were with open (that is, media) access to their proceedings and decisions. The lay participants of the past proved little threat, but the latter were a lot less likely to be susceptible to professional pressure. Media access could prove to be considerably more threatening, especially coupled, as it would now be, with increased ministerial input.[20] It will be important for outside analysts to follow these processes and see just how much public voice they appear to allow.

It is always difficult to assess the degree to which public participation actually reflects public consent in political processes. In the policy process itself, for example, we saw the crucial determining factor of practitioner accessibility to the new legislation, the nine criteria put forth by the HPLR as participation based, but no evidence was produced (aside from the fact that this participation came from practitioner groups only, rather than the general public). Here is a case where the lack of explanation in the HPLR Report leaves us without the ability to explore the nature or ideational foundation of its decision makers. The nine criteria form the basis of legitimation for the inclusion and exclusion of all health practitioners in the province, and yet they were never justified or even explained to us.[21] The brief introduction to the HPLR Report does not disclose its reasoning, only its position. The Ministry of Health follow-up meetings with practitioner groups were all done in secret, with no disclosure of the basis of the decisions made there either, so the answers to our questions about consent cannot be garnered. For a process that promised public access, this seems a rather serious omission, especially since it made the single most important determining criterion of the whole process inaccessible.

More generally, the knowledge gap between the public and the professional has concerned analysts interested in the efficacy of direct public participation in the structures of professional self-governance – in terms of both the lay participant and patient input. In both, there is a problem of lack of complementarity between the hierarchy of health care organization and the egalitarian intent of participation and consent. Egalitarian participation and informed consent[22] are made problematic by both the dichotomy between the dominant medical knowledge base of health care and that of lay participants or patients, as well as the dichotomy between the social status of the providers of health care and that of the majority of the recipients of health care. A long history of medical hierarchy and paternalism has deeply embedded a complex system of both formal and informal rules and roles which will provide subtle and not-so-subtle resistance to the public.[23] To complicate matters further, the traditional private agency of the professional-to-patient relationship is being undermined, as we saw in Chapters 4 and 5, by both the desire of state to lay claim to this agency as an obligation to the public, and the desire of patients themselves to replace it with their own autonomy.[24] The two are not necessarily incompatible, as the public members could use the power of the state to overcome the power of the professionals, while still retaining a fair degree of autonomy from the state. This does appear to be happening, particularly as the state has moved to increase the power and numbers of the public members on the councils and key committees of the professional governing bodies.[25] New interpretations of the requisite knowledge for decision making in the health sector might find their way into the sector, and as these interpretations shift to include the knowledge of the public, so too will the status of the public bearers of knowledge likely increase. Any bid for more autonomy and authority on the part of public members, however, will still have to overcome historical barriers to participation and consent.

With regard to the practitioner groups themselves, access to research information is decidedly skewed in favour of the medical and medical-like practitioner groups. Both our publicly and privately funded health science research institutions have long been dominated by the medical orientation to health. If the alternative practitioners are to be given a fair chance to participate in a redesigned health care system, this bias ought to be alleviated. The ability to research and prove one's foundational ideas or disprove and move on from them is central, as we have seen, to participation in today's health sector. As the state invests in a broader commitment to participation and consent in the health sector, it will need to bring that commitment in line with its research funding commitments.

The RHPA, however, did provide, both in process and outcome, much more information and access than has been made available in the past.[26] Draft legislation in this instance was provided well ahead of the actual legislation, and concerted effort was made towards enhancing understanding of the implications of that legislation.[27] The new legislation continues along these lines with its measures for increased participation and consent, but just how well these measures translate into *effective* participation and *informed* consent in the everyday workings of the sector remains to be seen. One body to keep an eye on, perhaps as a barometer, will be the new advisory council. The Council (HPRAC) was set up as a means of channelling health practitioner input. Whether or not it becomes a participatory and informative body of access for practitioner groups or a means of shuffling input off to infinity remains to be seen. As it is now structured, the system presents a long road from interest group participation to observable outcome – with as many roadblocks as the government chooses to construct. In broad policy terms this serves as a reminder: advice is only as valuable as its recipient perceives it to be.

Some of the public participation in the health professions comes, as we have seen, from representatives of the public involved in ongoing relations with the professional governing processes. Public members on the council, committees, and hearings of the colleges face the same problems of representation as those in the broader political structures. Just as our political representatives in parliament are caught between a commitment to their voters and a commitment to their party, so too are both the practitioners and the public representatives of the professional governing organizations faced with a confusion of purpose. Are the practitioner representatives there to represent their fellow practitioners or their patients? Are the public representatives there to represent the individual patient, the aggregate of patients, or the public at large – or even themselves? It is important that the obligations commensurate with the service be clearly articulated. If the state's expectations for representation have changed over the past several decades, those expectations need to be pointed out, and in some cases assisted,[28] in order to avoid confusion and tension. Again, more study of the actual (rather than legislatively intended) role of these public participants is needed.

Representation taken in its broader sense, of course, includes giving voice to disparate social groups. Gender and race or ethnicity representation will continue to present a challenge to health care institutions – as class has in the labour relations discussed earlier. Historically, the social hierarchy has been reproduced or embedded in these institutions, but today the logic of that hierarchy is increasingly challenged by our broader social commitment to democratic egalitarian principles. More work needs to be done in consultation with social groups to assess their representation within the process of professionalism and to consider new means of addressing the problems which are presenting themselves as particular to the mechanisms of self-governance – as we saw in the case of midwifery.

Mechanisms of responsible and accountable governance were enhanced in the new professional legislation. The former revolved mainly around the principle of popular sovereignty or, in words of the policy designers, the obligation to 'serve the public interest,' which was clearly meant to be interpreted by the professional governing bodies as an indication of their objective relationship with the practitioners – unlike the association's subjective relationship. The colleges do appear to be committed to the 'public interest' but, of course, this term can be interpreted in a great many ways, as indicated in our broader climate of governance by the fact that all political parties and all interest groups lay claim to this moral high ground. What the coupling of this obligation with greater ministerial scrutiny and enhanced mechanisms of accountability means, however, is that the government is more than likely to be providing the colleges with help in their interpretation of the public interest. This is likely to remain true for the current restructuring process.

Earlier administrative accountability measures were enhanced and joined by new measures of political and financial accountability in the new professional legislation. The working effects of these new measures will need to be assessed with regard to their own mandate as well as larger questions about self-regulation. On the former, for example, the new mandatory quality assurance committee and program of the professional colleges, while ostensibly meant to assure quality, also has the added benefit of providing a measure of financial accountability. This is because of the new interpretation of quality assurance, which goes beyond the college's traditional role of investigating questionable practitioner competence to a mandate which includes the examination of means of *improving* standards of competence within the profession.[29] This entails a shift of standard from the norms of the profession to the much broader question of how to improve on those norms. It also brings into account not only the practices of a 'few bad apples' of the profession, but also the collective activity of the profession as a whole. This activity can then be held up comparatively across the country in a way which questions not only the clinical standards of a particular practitioner, institution, or province,[30] but also necessarily begs the question of wasted financial resources.

Assessment of these accountability mechanisms also highlights larger questions about self-regulation which have been asked, but never really answered. For example, Can we trust professionals to discipline themselves? When does professional regulatory responsibility become clinical and entrepreneurial harassment of other practitioners? What is self-regulation really costing the public? and so on. These questions will stand a better chance of serious consideration now that the accountability of the health professions has been enhanced – particularly as this accountability comes under closer scrutiny as the sector undergoes restructuring.

It is probably safe to say, that Ontario's health professions will never again enjoy the kind of trust-based autonomy they have had in the past. There is always a difficult balance between too much control and too much trust in any semi-independent relationship. Too much trust weakens the bond of obligation commensurate with privilege, while too much control threatens the cooperative nature of the trust relationship. But neither are these alternatives themselves static: each side interprets control and trust into their preferred definitions. Up until now, it might be argued, the professions have had considerable interpretive power over these terms, but they are beginning to lose that power. As the health sector shifts into the glare of the broader system of governance, disparities between the citizens' government and the sectoral subgovernment become available as tools of reinterpretation.

It could be pointed out that, for example, when compared with the accountability and responsibility measures of the broader political sphere, the health professionals remain relatively protected from the checks on potential abuses of their power: there is no equivalent to the exposure of these governors in a parliamentary question period, although the press is still free to expose bad governance within the professional bodies on an ad hoc basis;[31] there is no Opposition to challenge this government; there is no possibility of overthrow by a disillusioned public since elections are internal, and ministerial appointments are not open to public scrutiny; and there is no firing of unethical governors by the public. In all, it is still a rather protected institution. For all their complaining about 'outside interference,' these governors, one might say, get off rather lightly.

Likewise trust appears to be undergoing a reinterpretation by the public's representatives. In a rather startling comment on trust, Ontario's health minister recently noted, 'The logical relationship between a government and a hospital system that is largely financed by it is one of partnership characterized by candour and *trust based on facts and evidence.*'[32] Considering that a trust relationship has always, by definition, precluded the need for facts and evidence, this is clearly a radically new interpretation of the concept. What this reinterpretation signals is, of course, a power struggle. The winning definition of any principle inevitably has considerable influence over ensuing blueprints for action. The professionals' definition of trust, for example, requires little in the way of blueprints for accountability, it being assumed within the definition of the principle itself. While the minister's definition necessitates blueprints not only for accountability mechanisms but also for the collection of, and justification for, 'facts and evidence' – which itself will constitute the next terrain for competing interpretations.

It is difficult to say whether a radical new interpretation of the trust relationship between the health professionals and the state could survive. Today we see provincial governments across the country struggling to deal with collective action, including strike action, from the medical and nursing professions.[33] The practitioners are taking the war of words to the streets, vying for public support, and they may well win here, at least for now. The state, however, may also learn to talk 'better talk' to the public. Important concepts can be ever so slowly reinterpreted.

Judicial Issues

Another set of opposing interpretations, which will affect the future blueprints and dynamics of the health sector, are those brought forth in the judicial sphere. Contemporary critics have raised concerns over our Western judicial interpretation of justice and fairness, particularly with regard to its bias towards individual or group rights rather than collective concerns or individual obligations and compassion. Not surprisingly, given the rights orientation of contemporary society, one sees health interest groups, like those in other policy areas, learning the language and tactics of rights discourse.[34] Likewise, arguments of a right to health care have been put forth by consumer advocates inside and outside the bureaucracy or government.[35] These consumer rights then come up, as Tuohy has argued, against the provider 'corporate property rights' mentioned earlier.[36] What gets lost in the fight over rights, however, is the context of the human condition; the rights orientation, while providing access for those groups who can make claim to it, is a partial interpretation of the human condition. The individualistic rights dominated orientation to health policy best fits the individual-oriented medical and technical specialized approach to health care; thus, both disfavouring the alternative holistic approach, and consequently encouraging the alternative approach to abandon its ideals in order to speak in the dominant legal voice. We have seen in this story how some practitioners learned to adapt to the policy requirements and the language of the process itself. The problem with this kind of buying in is that we lose our alternatives. As Rein and Schon comment, 'If people see the world as different and act on their different view, then the world itself becomes different.'[37]

The critique of the disassociated nature of the judicial sphere becomes particularly important to health care policy as the vital relationship between the care provider and patient begins to be reconstituted. The old paternal relationship between the medical profession and her or his individual patient has come increasingly under attack and may well be replaced by the judicial relationship between rights-bearing individuals, particularly as the patient or client fights for more autonomy and choice. What such a shift would imply for this and other important relationships for the patient or client will need to be monitored and assessed in the future. The judicial orientation towards individualism is also of importance in relation to the rising need for macro-allocation and micro-allocation (or triage) decision making in a time of severe cost restraint, since it necessarily calls for collective as well as individual patient orientations to the provision of services. We need to decide as a society what to keep and what to give up in an increasingly zero-sum game. It is difficult to find the language or the ideational milieu necessary for the discursive process of tough resource allocation when few of the key participants are comfortable with the basic words of collectivity and holism; and those few who are have been relegated to the fringes with their holistic orientation either denigrated or subsumed.

Ironically, in their embrace of judicial pragmatism, health policy officials may find that they have distanced themselves from their public and practitioner allies in a political project to which they themselves are increasingly giving voice. Today's state officials and advisers in health policy are increasingly turning to communitarian or holistic appeals.[38] That is, the embedded judicial orientation favouring individualism, freedom, rights, private property, adversarial confrontation, defence, and conservatism[39] are being challenged by alternative ideas of the collective good, social obligation, compassion, stewardship, cooperation and consensus building, patient outcome, and innovation. This is not a new orientation or new language for many of our alternative (or as of recently ex-alternative) practitioner groups; we have seen here, for example, a fundamental compatibility between this broader appeal and the long-established holistic orientation of alternative practitioners.[40] Whether or not this orientation can survive the move of its carrier groups into the mainstream organizations of the health sector, or the relegation of those groups to the fringes, remains to be seen – we also saw here how little attention was paid in this policy process to the advocates for the prevention of ill health. One of the most important practitioner groups to keep an eye on will be midwives, since they represent the strongest and most successful attempt, to date, to counter the norms of our health care institutions from inside those institutions. They quite rightly perceive their success in maintaining their practice of allowing women the choice of home birth to be a radical position to hold. They may lead the reinterpretation of good health care.

It is also important not to romanticize the alternative. It too will have its problems and outdated but embedded aspects which will need to be critically assessed. Big ideas about holism and collectivity are a lot easier to voice than to practise in institutional or institutionalized settings. Nor is it an easy task to translate these ideas and practices into the legislation, regulations, and bylaws needed to govern a highly complex, technical set of practices and practitioners while still maintaining integrity to principle. This is only to say, we have a creative potential here, and we should make use of it.

In general, in our broader public interpretations, the existence of the objective, universal observer is now being questioned in the light of human subjectivity and contextualization. Formal rationality, with its historically developed standards of proof, is being challenged by the alternative of wisdom, common sense, or empirical knowledge. Specialization is being criticized as limited in the light of a more holistic alternative. Hierarchy is being challenged not only by a broad-based commitment to egalitarianism, but also by an acknowledgment of the creative potential of difference. What is most telling in the story presented here is that all of the ensuing issues of knowledge and governance form an integral part of contemporary professionalism issues. This story has shown how the technical, legal details of specialized legislation contain ideational commitments and positions of power which impede efforts to make changes to the whole package captured in that institutionalization – a package which includes interpretations of principles such as equality and fairness, which then go into the designing of blueprints such as self-regulation and accountability, which contain benefits and burdens which affect the living of the story.

When set within the rich stories of our health practitioners' historical and contemporary political struggles, the new health professions legislation and the review which preceded it can be seen in the context through which it has passed, and within which it will continue to grow. It will remain a most interesting and important story.

Methodological Conclusion

I mean for the story told here to justify itself: if it is a good telling, and it is useful to those interested in understanding the dynamics of contemporary health professionalism, that is enough. Despite resistance in social studies to the idea that social 'scientists' are 'mere' storytellers – which I might point out, is itself an interpretive struggle – I would argue, we ought to give more respect to the difficult and admirable art of storytelling. We would do well to heed the words of a political analyst who has long been held in good repute: 'We must be well content if we can provide an account not less likely than another's; we must remember that I who speak and you who are my audience are but human and should be satisfied to ask for no more than the likely story' (Plato, *Timaeus*). This story does, however, raise some interesting questions of methodology or thoughts for those interested in interpretation, ideas, and institutions. The following notes are not meant as dictums; they are 'only' ideas.

Methodological Notes

Interpretive Analysis

Interpretive analysis is, as I interpret it, a hermeneutical pursuit whereby one attempts to immerse oneself in the story or stories of others after first suspending judgment of or analytical organization for that story, as discussed in Chapter 1. For this, at least in policy analysis, larger stories have to be 'decomposed' or broken down into the various stories contained within the larger one. Deciding what the larger story really is is a rather subjective process. For a policy analyst, the policy or policies of concern will necessitate a certain degree of contextualization; for example, the regulation of health professionalism necessitates a look at the health professionals themselves, and the specific regulatory legislation of health professionalism (for example, the 1991 RHPA) in one jurisdiction (Ontario) narrows the story to more manageable proportions. However, there is no particular rule here. There is still considerable room for the analytical subjectivity which is of considerable concern for the post-positivist analyst.

The hermeneutical process of 'getting a reading' with minimal distortion is a difficult one. No one can enter a policy world without taking some of her or his ideas with them. One can, however, attempt to suspend judgment and frame making in the early stage of story gathering. Here I was fortunate to have had access to not only the policy process itself, but also to a large set of documents (the HPLR submissions) which gave voice to any interest groups (or individuals) which considered themselves to be health practitioners, that is, any groups whose interpretation of their work was that it constituted legitimate 'health professionalism.' This was a gold-mine for interpretive analysis. In it, key actors were asked *the* interpretative question, that is, how they saw (interpreted) themselves, others, and their relationships to one another, and why? I was able, through these submissions, to get a reading on a rather large 'whole' of health professionalism. The catch here is that these interest groups were not giving a personal 'narrative' with no objective other than the telling of the story itself; rather they were aware that this was a political process and so theirs was a strategic presentation. They were given specific questions (see

Appendix 6), and for the most part they answered them carefully. Still, they did constitute each group's interpretation of both their role in the organized health sector and their fit with the policy agenda and the politics of the day. They gave us an interpretive *political* story, and that is what I have tried to capture here.

Excess subjectivity in either the actor's telling or the analyst's interpretation of those tellings can be guarded against, as discussed in Chapter 1, by providing a balance between the particular stories gathered in the early stages of the process and historical documentation of, and by, those same actors. Here the literature was most helpful with regard to the larger dominant groups in the medicare organizations, particularly medicine and nursing. Other groups, however, generally had some historical documentation with which to balance their HPLR 'submission stories,' as well as more recent claims and concerns to be found in internal sources such as practitioner group's newsletters. What the historical investigation helped provide – following the hermeneutical immersion – was a richer ideational context over time.

Other guards against the subjectivity of the groups' portrayal of themselves can be provided by (a) comparing their words and claims with their deeds, (b) looking for contradiction in their claims about themselves and others, and (c) the presence of supporting data. The HPLR team played an important role in this check on the practitioners' claims. As we have seen, the first submissions to the review were scrutinized carefully and any unsubstantiated statements by the practitioner groups were returned to them for explanation, and if none could be provided they were 'encouraged' to drop those claims from later submissions. There was a noticeable improvement in the quality of the storytelling in the submissions thereafter. We also saw how some groups, midwives in particular, made use of comparative data from other countries to back up their interpretation of themselves as having been unfairly excluded from the established health care system.

One of the problems, perhaps *the* problem in weighing the groups' clarifications, evidence, and so forth was the set of standards by which the recipients of these submissions, the review team, were assessing the worth of the substantiating arguments and data being provided. This story is one of two deeply embedded and deeply opposing definitions of fact or data or evidence based on either science or empiricism; there could be no easy answer to which version was truth. In the end, as we have seen, the science-based practitioners benefited more than the empirics-based or science-plus-empirics-based practitioners, but to their credit, the review team must have allowed for considerable withholding of judgment (the standards of their Ontario community clearly being science-based overall), otherwise the alternative practitioner groups would have been shut out altogether. There is no right approach for the policy analyst faced with more than one version of good evidence or data, except perhaps for that illustrated here: open-mindedness and common sense; the former was necessary to even allowing the 'other stories,' and the latter was demonstrated in the decision to weigh patient outcome (or lack of harm) against the trump card of science.

Another broad standard for limiting the subjective nature of story gathering is that of holism. The exposure to and analysis of a broader more holistic story helps in both the early reading of broad context and the recomposition of a frame within which to tell the larger story to others.[41] Larger stories contain smaller stories, and the more smaller stories listened to, the better the quality of the larger story told. Thus, for example, the more interest group stories understood, the more the claims made by friends and enemies can be held up for comparison. In this sense, holism is a guard against the 'untruth' of partiality. The big story here also demonstrates the value of including both powerful 'political' actors and less powerful quiet actors in the telling, in that when each group is set off against the others, a richer understanding of both ensues.

The holistic inclusion of other actors, such as the state and the public, also enriches the story in both its institutional aspects (what is) and its ideational aspects (what the ideational climate has been, is, and might be). A better telling would have included more actors than I have chosen to include. Finally, the more holistic orientation helps guard against framing the larger story in a too narrow frame. My designation of group types (whole body, merchant–service, technique specialist, technology, and assistant groups), and their ideational commitments (to science or empiricism or both), came from moving the focus beyond the traditional set of health policy actors, medicine and nursing predominantly, to a more inclusive set. It is here in a story which includes the marginalized and the excluded that we see the power of the embedded and the wide range of alternatives exerting pressure on that embedment.

Lastly, the subjectivity of this process might also be minimized by returning one's large written story to the people whose stories are being captured and moulded into the frame of that telling. Assumably, they will tell you if your version rings false to them and over time a better story will emerge – as in the assumption of the value of peer review in academia. I did, however, encounter a problem here: in the process of 'returning' with my story, the practitioner groups I approached quite correctly viewed me as having potential influence on decisions made in the future (with the publication of a book about them), and therefore they moved to convince me of their reinterpretations of both my smaller stories about them and my larger story about all of them in relationship to the state and the public over time. Unfortunately their more favourable

Conclusions 231

interpretations of the stories contained enough rewriting of history, and enough attention to that in my story which did not suit their current policy agenda (coupled with little or no attention to that which did), to make me suspicious of their preferred revisions. So, 'going back' to the subjects of one's story is itself a politics of interpretation and therefore in need of its own interpretive analysis. Interpretation is a difficult process, and there is a lot remaining to learn and discuss as we each make our attempts at it. Aside from limitations on our resources (of time and money), we will have to watch the subjects of the story for their subjectivity: in both their strategic presentations in the earlier immersion process and their strategic reinterpretation of the larger story after its telling. In interpretative theory we can never have proof of good judgment, we can only guard against our subjects' subjectivity and our own subjectivity in pursuit of the 'likely story.'

The Interaction between the Ideational and the Institutional

The framing of one's story can either come out of one's imagination or out of the story itself. Interpretive analysis suggests we do the latter. If one is telling a story based on the realities of an organized social system, that system is by definition, already framed by that organization. Within it, the ideas of the story or stories are organized into the embedded, the marginalized, and the excluded. As we saw in tracing the historical developments of ideas in Chapter 2, some ideas have won a better placement in the organization of health professionalism than have others, that is, in the process of organization, the ideational engages that organization or institutionalization. This story illustrates the continuous nature of the interaction between the ideational and the institutional or structural. In keeping with the claims of the institutionalist analysis in contemporary policy studies, we have seen in the story presented here how 'institutions constrain and refract politics.'[42] The emphasis placed on embedment and the importance of organizational characteristics, in this work, speaks to the same concerns as those focused on by the historical institutionalists. Historical patterns developed in the organization or institutionalization of the practitioners and practices of the health sector played an important role in the development, many years later, of the 1991 Regulated Health Professions Act. This history of institutionalization did indeed 'structure political interactions.'[43] Just as the institutionalists are now moving on to broaden their approach 'to illuminate the distinctive patterns of policy innovation and change,'[44] so too has been the attempt of this study: policy change has been understood here in both its ideational and institutional manifestations.

The placement or displacement of the ideational as it engages with the process of organization or institutionalization involves a power struggle. Even before 'things' come into being, the ideas associated with those things have to fight for placement, have to be interpreted as positive or worthy of pursuit by those designing and implementing the organization. We have seen how the interpretation of good health care and science-based health care was central to the power struggles engaged in during the organization of health professionalism, and how this interpretation has remained important to today's organized health professionalism. Yet, we have also seen how old interpretations do not sit in stasis, how they are in continuous process, and how affected actors will fight to either maintain or incur the benefits and burdens which accompany the winning interpretations of institutionalization. Policy restructuring processes only highlight (and heat up) a placement or displacement process which is never far below the surface of the seeming stasis of organization – much like the structures of the adult human body which appear relatively unchanged for long time periods but are actually undergoing continuous cellular decomposition and recomposition.

The HPLR/RHPA policy process began mid-stream in an advanced process of ideational and institutional interaction, but its introduction also brought, as any policy process does, the possibility of bigger, more rapid interaction and even the potential of an interpretive shift. It paused to pull out and examine the old interpretations of good health care and good governance. It held them up to the light of their broader ideational and institutional environment – an environment which was constitutive at that particular point in time of its own ideas in good repute, both embedded in the institutions of that larger environment and free-floating. The policy process itself started another round of 'Snakes and Ladders,' so to speak. Most of the interested parties engaged in that process began by assessing their position, *vis-à-vis* this new climate, and then responding to the questions of the decision makers on the basis of that assessment. Since some of the then-established health practitioner groups (in the 1980s) had played an important role in the original professional legislation (of the nineteenth to mid-twentieth centuries) – having pushed the government for regulation and then having been allowed to basically design it – they had their interpretations of good health care and good governance built into the original legislation. Essentially, they had had the power to see that their interpretations were protected by law. This is a likely reason why, for example, there were signs of complacency from the elite in the early submissions to the HPLR – in their largely unsubstantiated claims to the necessarily exclusive gatekeeping or supervisory roles. As it became apparent, however, that the old interpretations would not be allowed to go uncontested by the HPLR team, almost all of the practitioners involved in the policy process began to bring forth ideas or interpretations of themselves which would help them obtain a good position in, first, the policy process itself, and second, and linked to the first, its outcome. They knew the political importance of linking the ideational to the institutional.

We have seen how the policy actors entered this policy process on a spectrum from the well positioned to the ill-positioned. We watched them 'fight and fight' over the exact wording of the new legislation because of the manifest and latent positions, and therefore power, it would entail. Some gained positions of authority over others; some an independence from the authority of others; and some only degrees in between; but no one was unaffected. Some positions carried enlarged benefits and some only potential benefits (for example, in the case of the latter, a better seat at the table for the next round). Some made new relationships among the practitioners, and some broke old relationships among the practitioners. At the very least, all of the practitioner groups, the patients or public, the state actors, and others not necessarily even heard from in the process have a new ideational and institutional climate in which to continue their engagement. As policy analysts, attention to this new climate will give us both a sense of what is and what might be. For example, to understand the potential successes and failures of the new health practitioner teams being advocated today, a policy analyst would have to consider the ideational and institutional history of each participating practitioner group *since it is still being played out today.* Aside from the difficult questions about expertise, simple questions would need to be asked: Who has long resented the authority of whom, and why? Are any of the practitioner groups longstanding enemies, and why? Are the members of the proposed teams capable of trusting each other? There may be no particular institutional reason why a team could not work well together, but there may be a more human reason based on long-held ideas and the emotions attached to them.

Interests

Interest group politics, in general, provides examples of the embodiment and transport of the ideational. The case of health care is particularly important because it, like the case of environmental policy, or women's policy, provides a study of ideas sitting in direct opposition to each other, where the previously excluded ideas have come to play an important role in the policy dynamic. It also provides a study of ideational survival and revival over a long period of time – of ideas which remained unacceptable to the mainstream organization of the sector, but still remained. In the story presented here, the history of the emergence of the various types of health professional groups – whole body, merchant–service, technique specialist, technology specialist, and assistant – illustrates the embedment of ideas associated with science, bureaucracy, and governance at the same time as it illustrates the marginalization and exclusion, but not destruction, of alternative ideas.

Clearly the story presented here is an interest group story, so some of my readers may wonder why in my methodological elements I refer to the ideational and the institutional rather than the 'ideas, interests, and institutions' elements common to contemporary policy literature. The answer is as follows. I do not see the need for a separate methodological element here for interests. The term 'interests' generally refers to (a) people, as in 'interest groups' or 'the interested,' and, (b) goals, as in 'interested in getting something.' Both of these appear in this analysis. In the first reference, any social analysis, political or otherwise, refers to people (as state actors, the public, stakeholders, and so on); they are, in the broadest sense, the whole point of the analysis and therefore are necessarily present without needing their own methodological category so as not to be forgotten, unlike ideas and institutions which are *deliberately brought into* the analysis. No one, to my knowledge, is arguing that we should not be wasting our time talking about people (as interest groups or otherwise). Aside from this, there is no ideational analysis without people; behind every thought is the thinker. In the second reference, what interest groups are interested in is also included in my analysis by the simple fact that these interests have to be voiced in ideational form to be considered political interests. They have to say what they want – and this I have told. Lastly, my treatment of the ideational and institutional as not only what and who gets embedded, but also what and who gets marginalized and excluded necessarily covers the interests (as both people and ideas) that did not make it into the policy process. So, I see no interests left out and therefore requiring a separate methodological category to necessitate inclusion in the analysis or story.

The people of our institutions (as key actors or interests) provide us with one of the means to examine the role of ideas in change, in that they are ideational conduits. As we saw here, the broader the range of actors taken into account, the richer the analysis. We also saw how the interpretive investments of institutionalized actors either encouraged or discouraged change in the system over time. For example, if particular groups are allowed to design the institutionalized system in light of their favoured interpretation of themselves as gatekeepers of that system, they will have a vested interest in fighting change to those institutions, since change might throw that favoured interpretation up for question. Likewise, the opposite is true for those left out or marginalized by the early institutional design. The creative potential of interest group dynamics does not generally lie with the long-favoured.

Notably, the traditional parameters of interest group or interest analyses, such as the power and resources of interest groups or the history of relationships of authority, while useful to a certain extent, were not adequate predictors of outcome, here. That is, they were more useful when situated within the ideational context of the political interaction. What was often more telling than the old embedded structures and relationships of power was the relationship of that embedment to the ideational climate in which it sat. Where the ideational climate was conducive to change, the old embedded patterns tended to be undergoing a shift; and where the policy participants were able to succeed or were willing to retain old relationships it was more often because of the compatibility of their policy positions and relationships to the ideas in good repute than to any history of dominance per se.

The Importance of the Ideational Per Se (or Value Added)

What appears embedded at any set point in time may, in fact, be undergoing subtle change. In this story we saw, for example, how the early liberal logic of Canadian society left the dominant professionals with a high level of clinical and entrepreneurial freedom which, in turn, has led to the need for today's state actors to draw on communitarian logic to counter the costs of that liberty. Likewise, the freedom of the utilizers of science and technology to define their direction has led to a backlash against their abuses and a call to public stewardship or control over the utilization of science rather than the freedom of the claim to science and technology as private property. Even the call to freedom of public participation has opened access routes for citizen and group critique of the excesses of freedom – entrepreneurial and scientific freedom – as well as resulting in the need to contain that participatory input within manageable parameters. Liberty and the progress of science and technology may have begun to undermine themselves by their own excesses.

A focus on the ideational per se helps us think about change and stasis. As we saw in this story, no sooner were things 'set,' than they began to be pressured for both a change to that stasis (a bringing on of the new) and a continuity of that stasis (a keeping of the old); such pressure, which is present in any sector at any time, is based on ideas. By including the propositional or alternative ideas in the ideational (rather than only those attached to or associated with the institutional), the analyst is encouraged to think about forces for change which are likely, less likely, and even unlikely (ideas associated with the 'surprising' fall of communism, for example). It is through this full ideational focus that we might best take seriously a much broader range of potential outcomes to political interactions.

A focus on the ideational also allows us to think more broadly about the 'community' being referred to in policy community literature. While the term is generally used in this literature to describe a specific interaction around a specific process, there is in fact a real living community involved in this policy process. A community per se tends to be defined by its dominant or shared ideas, but within any community there are always those ideas which sit at odds with the dominant ideas embedded in it. This unshared nature of a community, coming from those who do not fit the logic on which that community has been built, provides us with an opportunity to examine the changing nature of our communal life. Since it is in the interaction between our shared and unshared values or ideas that the agency of change is often found, the analyst must look at the relationship, or interplay, between a community's shared values and its unshared values and ask what tensions lie behind the social contract and how those tensions help shape the community's ideational and institutional evolution.

The ideational, as here presented, also allows us to move beyond the focus on dominant ideas common to the role of ideas literature. This focus provides us with only part of a policy story, with any turn from that dominance leaving us surprised. Most surprises in politics are probably more foreseeable than they might first appear: a richer story, one which includes the voices of dissent both within and surrounding the policy sector, might well provide a clue to its possibilities for change – as we saw in the latent potential of the 1960s' critique. Nor is it enough to look at alternatives once they have already become dominant ideas. Historical institutionalists, such as Hall, are concerned with the role of ideas in shaping change, but they tend to look back from the present, tracing the genesis of ideas which were once alternative but which came to dominate policy.[45] This analysis is useful but it has limited predictive power; for that we need to look at the relationship between today's dominant ideas and today's pool of possibilities. Everyone can spot the dominant ideas once they become dominant. The trick is to see them coming.

An ideational analysis also helps provide us with a means of dealing with obscure or diffuse actors, such as the public, or the experts. Contemporary policy studies have been noticeably inattentive to the 'attentive public'; nor have we had much success in following through on Heclo's concern for the rise of the experts.[46] It is not that these people have proven unimportant, rather our methodologies have proven incapable of dealing with them. To place them in policy community diagrams, for example, would be to make those diagrams look like 'Where's Waldo?' pictures. For this reason they tend to be dropped out of contemporary institutionalist analyses. These analysts tend to see the public through interest group analysis and therefore miss the inattentive public, or differently attentive public, who may only be represented ideationally. It is interesting to note what happens under an ideationally attentive approach where these actors are translated into the ideas they represent. In this political story, members of the public played an important role in ideational translation, for example, as 'the public interest,' as did the experts as 'expertise' (of, for example, heroic science versus conservative empiricism). Here the public and the experts are being used as representative of communal ideals and goals rather than embodied people per se. This is actually more true to the political role the public often plays in policy decisions. Certainly during the HPLR/RHPA process, despite the low showing of public participants at open meetings, they were ever present in the use of the public interest as a balance against health practitioner interests. The 'striking a balance' of the, thus-entitled, final report of the HPLR was as much a balance between the practitioners and the public as it was a balance among the practitioners. Likewise, that same balance was as much struck from a manageable number of interpretations of expertise, as from the competing arguments of the more than one hundred *experts* involved in the process.[47]

The ideational approach also allows for a splitting of 'individual people' where their political roles warrant it, for example, into the three-way distinction used here for the patient–patients–public. That is, rather than drop these actors off, we might better approach their input from an ideational analysis in which one person can be all three at the same time, particularly since this is the way persons were treated in this policy process. In general, judicial arguments tended to focus on the individual patient; economic arguments on aggregates of patients; and political arguments on the collectivity or public. More particularly, we also saw how specific actors such as practitioner groups or government actors had a tendency to draw on the distinction which best suited their arguments of the moment. This is, I think, an important tactic to keep an eye on in policy analysis in general. Certainly in health care policy debates there is considerable slipping back and forth between individual, aggregate, and collective orientations without much consideration of the implications of this: the people of health care policies have an interest in being represented at all three levels. Also, we have choices to make between the three. More clarification of this distinction, via an interpretative ideational analysis, would be helpful to the recipients and the providers of health care as well as its policy makers.

Principles and Blueprints

Another tendency of the role of ideas focus in policy analysis is that of seeing ideas as principles. It is interesting to consider the role principles played in this policy story. Despite the argument by some analysts that a focus by political analysts on principles is futile because political actors cannot be assumed to be sincere in their claims to principle, what we saw here illustrates the limitations of such a critique. First, actors must work within the bounds of ideas in good repute; they all make ample use of calls to principle, and those principles cannot simply be plucked out of thin air.[48] Second, there are costs to this usage, that is, even if actors are using and/or abusing political principles, such as egalitarianism, they still set a direction with this usage, particularly if it is the state doing so. We saw in this political story how the principles of concern to the government were contained in the words and intent of the HPLR mandate, report, and ensuing RHPA legislation,[49] and how these principles played an important role in policy decisions about the new legislation.

The other thing we saw happening to these principles was that once they had been articulated by the policy makers or people understood to have some control or power in the policy process, these principles then became engaged in an interpretive process whereby policy participants began interpreting their past actions and translating their future intentions in a manner which fit with them. Two interesting things happen in this interpretive process of key principles: (1) Once proponents of a principle begin to accentuate it or prove their adherence to it, they will, as Archer argues, in all likelihood get caught up in the logic of those principles,[50] (2) The interpretation involves moving from an ideational principle per se to an application, or plan – what I have referred to here as a blueprint (see Chapter 1).

If you claim to value democratic participation and representation, for example, certain things should follow from this, particularly when concrete policies are being examined and restructured. In this health policy story, we watched the public interest asserted over and over by the decision makers as a principle of democratic governance in our larger society which would now be considered fundamental to professional self-governance. At some point or other, every practitioner group (and most other interested actors) began to take up this principle, with most attempting to demonstrate the connection between it and their policy positions, and some simply claiming their policy positions already reflected their commitment to it. Interestingly, although there is no way of knowing whether the practitioner groups really were as concerned about the public interest as their arguments claimed, in a strange way it is not really necessary to know whether they were or were not committed to principle. Their approval or disapproval of the principle per se did not much affect the policy process. No one, not even the policy makers, had to 'mean it' to illicit political action and reaction to a principle. Intent is not what was important here, but interpretive usage was.

What followed from this usage of principle(s) involves the second distinction I am proposing, that between principles and blueprints (as introduced in Chapter 1). Although a blueprint or plan can come from an original principle or set of principles, this is not always true. Some blueprints come not from ethical or communitarian concerns for the good, but from desire, greed, imagination, revenge, forgotten history, and so on (the free market blueprints come to mind). For this reason it is necessary to think of ideas as *both* principles and blueprints. The separation here can be difficult. Is democracy a principle or a blueprint? It seems to me to be a blueprint which has become so established as to be now thought of as a principle – which indicates considerable interpretive power on the part of those who have sold it as such. The point here, however, is not to get bogged down in argument over exact category distinctions. What I propose is more a primary emphasis on separating the two categories *analytically*, even if separation is difficult in reality. We might ask ourselves, How do people or governments or institutions appear to have interpreted the ideas in use in a policy story, as principles or blueprints? And what has followed from this? The point of this analytical dualism is not precision of naming, but rather the ability it then gives us to see the two elements in relationship to each other, or each in relationship to other elements or actors. We saw earlier in this chapter how the principle of trust appears to be undergoing a reinterpretation within our contemporary health care institutions in order to better fit the new blueprints in good repute. That is, trust based on honour and respect is being redefined as 'trust based on facts and evidence.' Where did this rewriting of meaning come from? The answer appears to be the new cost-control blueprints of the policy makers which are emphasizing performance measurements in an attempt to reinterpret good health care. Interestingly, the minister of health is using a blueprint to reinterpret a principle. This is a difficult task: blueprints are more easily changed by governments since the nature of political representation has already primed the public to accept revised political party blueprints as part of the electoral process, but principles have more staying power. For example, the principle of equality is a difficult one to argue against in contemporary Western society, so that what we tend to see happening is rather than attempt to redefine the principle of equality per se (or fundamental human worth), actors will more likely attempt to reinterpret the ensuing blueprints, thus resulting in debates over strategies or plans based on either equality of opportunity or equality of outcome. That is, the principle is left intact but reinterpreted into favoured blueprints for political action.

This relationship between principles and blueprints is important to watch. How is one being used to boost or destroy the other? Who is doing the questioning or attempting the reinterpretation, and why? We saw, for example, how the maintenance of the interpretation of good health care as necessitating a blueprint based on the utilization of science and technology provided considerable benefits for the science-based practitioners of the sector. But, notice also how adherence to this blueprint has affected the actors' own ideational politics. Practitioners' groups get caught up in the logic of the ideas that they have so carefully preserved for many years. Adherence to an idea of science and technology as good has locked its proponents into a logic which has made it difficult to view health care in any other way. Likewise, the same is true for the proponents of empiricism and nature's healing mechanisms. This reluctance goes beyond personal persuasion within the groups and their patients or clients as it enters and gets played out in the policy process; here the ideational becomes political.

Once an ideational commitment is made (as either principle or blueprint), its beneficiaries have a vested interest in defending it (with either principles or blueprints); but they may also, of course, have a sincere commitment to their ideational base and be forced into difficult choices because of this commitment. Midwives, chiropractors, naturopaths, and other alternative practitioners entered this policy process with all the fervour of previously excluded policy participants ready to fight the good fight. But they were soon faced with choices to be made between their historical interpretations of the principles and blueprints of good health care, as they had learned to define and practice them outside the organized sector, and the principles and blueprints deeply embedded in the relationships and institutions they would be joining if granted inclusion in the new legislation. They will continue to be faced with these difficult choices. We saw, for example, how midwives are now juggling the delicate balance of an interpretation of good midwifery care based on a blueprint of low intervention, low technology health care, but set in a hospital environment based on an opposing blueprint of science and technology based care. Fortunately for midwives their preferred blueprints, although not in keeping with that of the hospital environment, are in keeping with the results expected from the state's new cost-control blueprints for the sector, in that, as we have seen, the new midwifery practices have resulted in such evidence-based, good performance indicators as reduced hospitalization.

In this policy story we also saw the principles and blueprints of a sector being thrown up for question by the breadth of the policy review itself. Key elements of the old embedded blueprints, such as the gatekeeper roles of medicine and dentistry, were in danger of being reinterpreted and redesigned. All of a sudden the elite of the sector were put in a defensive position where previously no defence had been necessary. They called on whatever ideas they and their lawyers could think of to shore up this old blueprint, and for the most part succeeded. But the ideational fight is not over. The governments' broad new fiscal blueprints are no longer aligned with those long ago embedded in the health sector, when cost control or evidence-based decision making were not ideas in good repute. Both the government's new fiscal blueprint and its newly polished democratic blueprint require an adjustment of the blueprints of the health sector such that they are brought more in line with the contemporary idea of the state, and therefore 'the people,' as the gatekeepers of the sector – thus all call to the 'public interest.'

There are some interesting things to think about here. (1) Organized or institutionalized society draws lines between acceptable and unacceptable principles and blueprints and then goes on to fight over those lines. (2) Blueprints give us the winning interpretations in the fight over principles and plans, that is, *the* blueprint, the one that gets used or institutionalized, signifies our ideational trade-offs, our pragmatism. (3) Institutional restructuring holds the old embedded principles and blueprints up to the light of either or both the principles and blueprints in good repute at the time of the restructuring process. (4) One indicator of the power of specific policy actors is their ability to sell a blueprint without the backing of principles (for example, the state's fiscal blueprints in good repute today) or their ability to provide a non-sensible interpretation of a principle which then wins credence (as the government's new interpretation of trust may do). (5) Policy analysts have to ask: Are the proposed blueprints of a policy change sensible in light of the principles and blueprints already institutionalized there? Or would a questioning of that embedment be a good thing in itself? (6) We need to stop and ask who certain ideas attract and why? Then we need to go on to investigate the range of options and alternatives in both our principles and our blueprints.

In the end, a careful interpretive analysis ought to provide a likely story, but that story would only be enriched by a frame which grew out of attention to both its ideational and institutional elements, as experienced by those living that story. Attention to ideas as they are played out within the power dynamics of institutionalized positions and relationships, or as they are drawn in from outside those institutions, can only give us a better understanding – or an even more likely story.

Notes

1 Introduction

1 For the positions of authority see the scale referred to in Figure 3.1, of autonomy – negotiation – consultation – audience – exclusion. For the positions of connection, see the scale referred to in Table 3.1, as supportive – non-supportive or neutral – antagonistic.
2 Ruth Hubbard, CBC Radio Interview, 1996.
3 This is apparent throughout Offe's work, of course, but he does make reference to Lockwood in his article (co-authored with Gero Lenhardt and first presented in 1976). Claus Offe, 'Social Policy and the Theory of the State,' in John Keane, ed., *Contradictions of the Welfare State* (Cambridge, MA: MIT Press, 1984), 103. David Lockwood, 'Social Integration and System Integration,' in George K. Zollschan and Walter Hirsch, eds., *Explorations in Social Change* (New York: Houghton Mifflin, 1964).
4 A good discussion of 'constitutive meanings' rather than 'causal determinants' can be found in Ronald Manzer, *Public Schools and Political Ideas: Canadian Education Policy in Historical Perspective* (Toronto: University of Toronto Press, 1994), 6.
5 Gibbons provides a good discussion of the 'hermeneutics of recovery ... of everydayness' as well as the 'hermeneutics of suspicion.' Michael T. Gibbons, *Interpreting Politics* (Oxford: Basil Blackwell, 1987), 3.
6 This separation (in Chapters 2 and 6) has made my story at times repetitive, but it also allows readers interested in particular groups to think of each group or type of group as having a discrete context and story. It also allows the practitioner groups themselves to more easily critique my interpretation of their story and their fit of that discrete story with the story of the whole.
7 For reasons of time and expense, these were predominantly leadership interviews.

These were done following the enacting of the new legislation, again in 1997 when most of the regulations had been developed, and again in mid-1998. Appendix 1 provides a methodological outline of the interview techniques used.
8 Nelson Goodman, *Ways of World-Making* (Indianapolis: Hackett, 1978), 7.
9 Goodman refers to 'resorting.' Ibid., 7. Rein and Schon refer to 'frames.' Martin Rein and Donald Schon, 'Reframing Policy Discourse,' in Frank Fischer and John Forester, eds., *The Argumentative Turn in Policy Analysis and Planning* (North Carolina: Duke University Press, 1993), 146.
10 Gibbons, *Interpreting Politics*, 3.
11 D.C. Paris and J.F. Reynolds, *The Logic of Policy Inquiry* (New York: Longman, 1983), 212.
12 This was best illustrated during this policy process by the way all but the most obtuse of the practitioner groups learned to present their clinical and entrepreneurial interests as being 'in the public interest,' once it became clear this was a key criterion for the policy makers.
13 The ultimate hermeneutical compliment would have to be one such as that which Jane O'Reilly gave Jane Mansbridge on the jacket cover of *Why We Lost the ERA*: 'This book ... answers all the questions that have haunted me since the ERA failed ... I understood at last the politics ... of the fight I could only try to understand as I reported on it during those long years.'
14 An interesting text which appears to be applicable to this work, but which I came upon after having developed my methodological approach, is Jaber F. Gubrium and James A. Holstein, *The New Language of Qualitative Method* (New York: Oxford University Press, 1997).
15 Guy Maupassant, 'The Piece of String,' in *Selected Short Stories*, trans. Roger Colet (Harmondsworth: Penquin, 1985).
16 Carolyn Heilbrun, *Writing a Woman's Life* (New York: Ballantine, 1988), 18.
17 I should note that because I think the term 'cultural' is somewhat misleading – at least for my purposes – I would prefer to use the term employed by Margaret Archer in her discussions of culture and agency, i.e., the 'ideational.' Here the focus rests on ideas and beliefs, rather than the grab-bag implied by the word 'cultural,' much of which in common parlance refers more to the manifestations of the ideational than to the ideational itself. Margaret S. Archer, *Culture and Agency: The Place of Culture in Social Theory* (Cambridge: Cambridge University Press, 1988).
18 This is, of course, why the definitions themselves (of structure and culture) have become so awkward in contemporary policy analysis. The 'structural' in particular has become so laden as to become an almost meaningless word. It is being asked to conjure up pictures in our minds of almost everything political. I do not see the sense in this.

19 For a good review of the U.S.-based 'new institutionalists' literature, see Sven Steinmo, Kathleen Thelen, and Frank Longstreth, eds., *Structuring Politics: Historical Institutionalism in Comparative Analysis* (Cambridge: University of Cambridge, 1992). Canadian case studies are presented in Michael Atkinson, ed., *Governing Canada* (Toronto: Harcourt Brace Jovanovich, 1993).

20 Ronald Manzer, *Public Policies and Political Development in Canada* (Toronto: University of Toronto Press, 1985), 185. This work also *demonstrates* the importance of the role of ideas in policy making, where careful attention to the Canadian ideational history has necessitated equally careful attention to the ways in which the ideational has been structured or institutionalized into our social systems. As well, one can see here (in my language) attention to the role of the non-embedded ideational as it comes to impact and ultimately restructure the embedded.

21 Sol Worth explores what a 'picture means.' Sol Worth, *Studying Visual Communication* (Philadelphia: University of Pennsylvania Press, 1981), ch. 7.

22 The old physics, e.g. could not say 'dead cat / live cat' as one in the same, until the advent of quantum physics.

23 Archer, *Culture and Agency*, xii.

24 The importance of policy community relationships and the necessity of taking into account the role of the state was emphasized in William D. Coleman and Grace Skogstad, eds., *Policy Communities and Public Policy in Canada: A Structural Approach* (Mississauga, Ont: Copp Clark Pitman, 1990), and while I have benefited from their work, I would wish to take it still further.

25 Paris and Reynolds, *The Logic of Policy Inquiry*, 181–2.

2 Historical Patterns of Ontario's Health Professions Legislation

1 Corinne Lathrop Gilb, *Hidden Hierarchies: The Professions and Government* (New York: Harper and Row, 1966), 6.

2 The story of contemporary professional protectionism sits at odds with the general story of Western entrepreneurial activity, in that professional regulation provides an example of an economic policy sector where the entrepreneurial interest groups have pressured for, and generally won, regulatory legislation of their sphere of activity.

3 David C. Naylor, *Private Practice, Public Payment: Canadian Medicine and the Politics of Health Insurance, 1911–1966* (Montreal: McGill-Queens's University Press, 1986), 16. The medical men were so labelled because of their utilization of medicinal drugs to treat diseases or dysfunctions.

4 This act, plus others which followed in Upper Canada, in 1791, 1795, and 1815, 1818, and 1827 were either inconsistently applied, repealed, never enforced, or simply flaunted by those they had excluded. The first licensing board in Upper

Canada was not even appointed until 1818. Ronald Hamowy, *Canadian Medicine: A Study in Restricted Entry* (Vancouver: Fraser Institute, 1984), 18. Evidence of the effectiveness of the (mostly scientifically unsubstantiated) clinical arguments date back to the legislation of the 1700s when the new 'scientific' practitioners argued for examinations of the credentials and expertise of any newcomers. Naylor, *Private Practice*, 17. A 'syphilis epidemic' provided the spur for the 1788 ordinance. Ibid., 11–13.

5 Ibid., ch. 2. See especially, 'The Apathy of Parliament,' p. 56, and 'Parliamentary Resistance,' p. 58.

6 The new scientific practitioners who wanted this protective regulation were somewhat scarce, especially in the more isolated areas. Elizabeth MacNab, *A Legal History of Health Professions in Ontario: A Study for the Committee on the Healing Arts* (Toronto: Queen's Printer, 1970), 5. Hamowy notes that the 1806 act was likely repealed because of the shortage of birth attendants it produced by limiting the practice of midwifery to physicians. Hamowy, *Canadian Medicine*, 15. It was not until 1887, after the protective legislation had been won in Upper Canada, that the faculty of medicine at the University of Toronto was reorganized to allow for the 'extensive equipment and necessary staff' required of a laboratory-based scientific education for medical students. In 1882, after students had been examined on the basis of the scientific knowledge their peers felt requisite for graduation from a medical program, the number of graduates dropped from thirty-two to ten. J. Heagerty, *Four Centuries of Medical History in Canada*, vols. 1 and 2 (Toronto: MacMillan, 1928), 85.

7 For the broader Canadian context, see, Ronald Manzer, *Public Policies and Political Development in Canada* (Toronto: University of Toronto Press, 1986), 23. More specifically, Tuohy discusses how '[professional] groups ... have appropriated certain aspects of ... technology ... [by the] establishment ... [of] property rights in particular technological resources.' Carolyn J. Tuohy, 'Private Government, Property, and Professionalism,' *Canadian Journal of Political Science*, 9/4 (1976), 672–3. In the U.S. context, Ehrenreich and English also argue that medicine was made into a market commodity by its practitioners. Barbara Ehrenreich and Diedre English, *For Her Own Good: 150 Years of the Experts' Advice to Women* (New York: Anchor, 1979), 45.

8 The term 'licensure' tends to be referred to rather loosely in the health care literature, but licensure, as I will be referring to it here, means exclusivity of practice. Only those with a licence to practice can legally practise. Certification merely reserves a name, like 'physiotherapist.' Registration occurs when a central agency (private or public) keeps records of those who meet certain qualifications. So a register can contain the names of those licensed or those certified. The most powerful tool is licensure, since it legally excludes non-licensed practitioners. Registration and/or certification leave the onus of discrimination up to the service

receiver; the public is supposed to recognize, and check for, these qualifications. It is therefore, in effect, a rather weak measure of control against turf invasion, since the public seems little inclined, or educated, to check a practitioner's qualifications, unless, as has happened with a limited number of groups, health care institutions use such qualifications as their minimum requirement for practise within its organized structures, such as hospitals and nursing homes.

9 Hamowy discusses this legislative history in detail in *Canadian Medicine*. MacNab provides a more cursory summary in *A Legal History*, although Hamowy does make some corrections on her work there. Even briefer summaries can be found in the Ontario CHA Report, vol. 1 (Toronto: Queen's Printer, 1970), 57, 60, 72.

10 I am using 'empirical' here as non-scientific, i.e, 'relying or based on practical experience rather than on scientific principles.' *Webster's New World Dictionary*, 2nd ed. (Cleveland: William Collins, 1979). As Cartwright put it, 'The physician depended, and continued to depend for many years to come, upon his five senses.' F.F. Cartwright, *A Social History of Medicine* (New York: Longman, 1977), 20. Scientific health care is constituted by the practice of applying the findings of controlled scientific studies of the human and animal body – its normal anatomy and physiology, as well as its pathologies and malfunctions – to the purpose of healing. The hallmark of the scientific method is the controlled, reproducible laboratory experiment where outside factors are either eliminated or accounted for as much as possible in order to understand the scientific laws at work in the development of disease and malfunction. Having thus understood the various stages of disease and illness, the same scientific procedure of controlled experimentation can be utilized to investigate potential cures. An interesting collection of articles on the history and philosophy of the laboratory technique with a good introduction to some of the well-known authors in this subject area can be found in Andrew Cunningham and Perry Williams, eds., *The Laboratory Revolution in Medicine* (Cambridge: Cambridge University Press, 1992).

11 'Even in 1900, a date at which the laboratory revolution was effectively accomplished, the roster of acknowledged practical pay-offs attributed to laboratory researches remained sparse in diagnostics and prognostics, and yet sparser in therapeutics, as clinicians opposed to laboratory education and laboratory practices in medicine continued to protest well into the present century.' Nicholas Jardine, 'Rhetorical and Aesthetic Accomplishment,' in Cunningham and Williams, *The Laboratory Revolution*, 306. Chen comments on the 'puzzling' fact that penicillin, which was discovered in the late 1920s, was not widely promoted even by its discoverer, Fleming, until fourteen years had elapsed. Wai Chen, 'The Laboratory as Business,' in Cunningham and Williams, *The Laboratory Revolution*, 247. Latour asks, 'How come laboratories were believed to be essential, years or even decades before doing anything of value for medicine?' Bruno Latour, 'The Costly Ghastly Kitchen,' in Cunningham and Williams, *The Laboratory Revolution*, 207.

12 The new scientific healers were not, and are still not, themselves the scientific investigators of disease and disorder. They applied medical theory, they did not themselves produce it. Given the paucity of life sciences at the time, they were often guessing and for that they had, of necessity, to make use of empirical observation, which they combined in unpredictable mixtures with medical beliefs of the day. An influential example of the sort of backward 'scientific' reasoning that came out of medical empiricism (and in which Canadian physicians played a key role) is referred to by Bliss. Observation of the tendency towards masturbation by the wards of mental institutions led to the '*post hoc propter hoc* fallacy' that 'as much as 50 percent of mental illness stemmed from masturbation.' Because of their conclusions, generations of sexually healthy people were instilled with totally unnecessary fear and guilt. Michael Bliss, 'Pure Books on Avoided Subjects,' in Cunningham and Williams, *The Laboratory Revolution*, 266–7.

13 The 'wicked pretenders' held other scientific beliefs, which the medical men claimed were merely empirical, and the 'quacks' relied on a history of experience and observation to guide their practices. Hamowy's excellent historical review of Canadian health practitioner legislation contains a number of quotes to this effect. The terms used here are taken from pages 12 and 29. Hamowy, *Canadian Medicine*. Gevitz provides an interesting and entertaining account of the origin and usage of the term 'quack' as it was applied by the orthodox medical group to those they deemed unqualified to practice health care. Norman Gevitz, ed., *Other Healers: Unorthodox Medicine in America*. (Baltimore: Johns Hopkins University Press, 1988), ch. 1.

14 Homeopathy had originated in Germany from the work of Hahnemann (1755–1843), a disaffected medical physician who had developed an alternative method of treatment after having surveyed his lack of success in the, by then, orthodox means of medical treatment. Rather than using medicines meant to treat the symptoms of disease, as orthodox medicine does, Hahnemann advocated the use of medicines which, when introduced into the body, would produce the same symptoms as the disease did, thus stimulating the reactive power, or 'vital force,' of the body itself (a force which medical practitioners also believed in despite the lack of scientific basis for such belief; see Bliss, 'Pure Books,' 266–7). Hahnemann died in 1843, 'a successful and wealthy physician.' Martin Kaufman, 'Homeopathy in America: The Rise and Fall and Persistence of a Medical Heresy,' in Gevitz, *Other Healers*, 99–100. Eclectics were, just as the word indicates, eclectic in their practices. They borrowed from any practitioners those techniques which appeared to be effective.

15 As one dean of a medical school put it, competing practitioners had become 'an obstacle to the financial success of the respectable medical practitioner.' Quoted in E. Richard Brown, *Rockefeller Medicine Men: Medicine and Capitalism in America* (Berkeley: University of California Press, 1979), 64.

Notes to pages 17–18 249

16 Contention arose over the efficacy of the minute dosages of medicine being used (up to 200 times the original concentration). Problems also arose because of the heavy demand placed on the homeopathic practitioner by both the burdensome pharmaceutical knowledge required and the holistic homeopathic treatment regiment which called for lengthy consultation with patients which were to include discovery of their present and past psychological state – the body's healing forces believed to be affected by its emotional state.
17 Kaufman gives examples of this with regard to opposition from the American Medical Association and the American Food and Drug Administration agency. Kaufman, 'Homeopathy,' 106–7, 113–15, 117–20.
18 Hamowy says the eclectics were Thomsonians, but Gevitz, whose research specializes in the details of 'other healers,' refers to the eclectics as 'medical sectarians' like the homeopaths, rather than the 'popular health crusades, religious healing, and folk medicine' of the Thomsonians, Grahamians, and Christian Scientists. Hamowy, *Canadian Medicine*, 24; Gevitz, *Other Healers*, 10–11. Gevitz refers to a founder of eclecticism, Wooster Beach, who originally practised as an orthodox medical practitioner. Ibid., 12. Ehrenreich and English also refer to eclectics as practising a mix of orthodox medical therapies and unorthodox therapies – which, of course, makes more sense of the name. Ehrenreich and English, *For Her Own Good*, 59.
19 CHA Report, vol. 1, 58. Hamowy discusses the debates surrounding this legislation in detail. Hamowy, *Canadian Medicine*, 100–17.
20 Hamowy, *Canadian Medicine*, 107.
21 Those practitioners we would refer to today as medical professionals, homeopaths, and eclectics, respectively, were all referred to at this time as 'medical.' To avoid confusion, however, I have used the three-way designation here.
22 CHA Report, vol. 1, 59.
23 Hamowy, *Canadian Medicine*, 114. The eclectics never applied for registration under the new act. CHA Report, vol. 1, 59.
24 Their use of both homeopathic science and medical science was also incompatible in practice because homeopaths called for minute drug doses with no other bodily intervention, while orthodox medical practitioners called for heavy drug doses with extensive bodily interventions.
25 Hamowy, *Canadian Medicine*, 114.
26 Canada had never set up homeopathic training institutions to any extent, receiving its supply of homeopathic practitioners from the U.S., so the demise of that supply (following the Flexner Report in the U.S.) obviously exacerbated the demise of the Canadian practitioners as well. Only recently has homeopathy begun to be revived in both countries.
27 Jardine links the promulgation of the scientific (laboratory-based) medicine to the

use of both 'rhetorical incitement' and 'aesthetic incitement.' The former consists of 'an entire range of persuasive strategies: appeal to ideals of rationality and morality, appeal to authority, and appeal to social and factional interests.' The latter consists of 'the whole range of ways in which perceptible things, such as, gestures, works, representations, instruments, preparations, displays and demonstrations, move persons through their appeal to the senses, the imagination and emotions.' Jardine, 'Rhetorical and Aesthetic Accomplishment,' 321–2.

28 Although anaesthetic for surgery was available in the mid-1800s, antiseptic for surgery was not available for general use until the turn of the century. Diagnostic radiation was also developed at the turn of the century, and penicillin was not readily available until the 1940s. Cartwright, *A Social History of Medicine*, ch. 8.

29 D.W. Gullett, *A History of Dentistry in Canada* (Toronto: University of Toronto Press, 1971), 50.

30 'With stiff competition ... and a dismal demand for services from a frightened public [these new dental professionals] ... were hard put to make a living. In consequence, the belief in the value of sharing professional knowledge [was soon] forgotten, and secrecy kept communication and goodwill among dentists to a minimum.' James W. Shosenberg, *The Rise of the Ontario Dental Association: 125 Years of Organized Dentistry* (Toronto: ODA, 1992), 8. The free market approach was not tolerated for long with regard to the educational component of the dental profession, either. 'The only effort ever made in the country [in 1869] to operate a private dental school for profit ... was not a financial success.' So the idea was quickly abandoned. A school set up in the late 1800s by the directors of the new professional governing body was closed after its trial year when the two students enrolled managed to sink the school into the apparently unforgivable deficit of $125. Gullett, *History of Dentistry*, 50.

31 In Jan. 1867 a Toronto meeting of Ontario dentists was called and the nine attendants decided to set up the ODA which then drafted a proposed legislative bill. Ibid., 42.

32 RCDSO was created and was granted full powers of licensing and regulating dentistry. A licensed dentist could have that licence cancelled, e.g., 'if the Board were satisfied that its holder was guilty of acts detrimental to the interests of the profession.' MacNab, *Legal History*, 62–4.

33 Gullett, *History of Dentistry*, 39–42. It is assumed that the state was influenced in this general decision and in the form the legislation took by the relationship already established between the state and organized medicine. The latter group supported the dentists.

34 R.J. Clark, 'Professional Aspirations and the Limits of Occupational Autonomy: The Case of Pharmacy in Nineteenth-Century Ontario,' *Canadian Bulletin of Med-*

ical History, 8/1 (1991), 43–63, 44. The Pharmacy Act also established the profession's governing body, the OCP. This original act has been amended and re-enacted over the years making governing changes as well as regulation limitations and adjustments to the retail aspects of pharmacy.

35 Ibid., 45. Patented drugs were treated like any other patented materials, i.e., they were under the control of the patent holder, not any state body.
36 Ibid., 48.
37 Ibid., 45–7. CHA Report, vol. 2, 216.
38 In 1904 Ontario nurses formed their first formal association, the Graduate Nurses' Association of Ontario, which succeeded in having the first Nurses Act passed in 1922. The name of the association was changed at this time to the RNAO. Hoping to obtain professional status, nurses had pressed for an internally run governing council similar to that of medicine, dentistry, and pharmacy. They succeeded only in attaining further registration measures. (Under the 1912 Hospitals Charitable Institutions Act, nurses working in hospitals had been granted the right to register their members.) A government department, rather than the nurses themselves, was made responsible for the registry. They had won a minor extension of their certification rights, rather than licensure; licensure, because it legislates exclusivity of scope of practice, would entail the monopoly privilege so highly valued by all professionals. CHA Report, vol. 1, 64, 76, and vol. 2, 154. For further elaboration see the MacNab volume of the CHA reports.
39 In 1951, under the Nurses Registration Act, the board of directors of the RNAO was given regulatory powers concerning the 'education, examination, registration and discipline of nurses.' This control was later transferred to a separate governing body, the CNO, in 1962. Ibid., vol. 1, 77; vol. 2, 154.
40 The first input regarding their own educational standards came with the 1924 amendments to the Nurses Act of 1922, when an appointed council of nurses education of 'inspectors of hospitals and training schools' included three nurses, as well as two physicians. The 1951 Nurses Registration Act gave regulatory power over education to the nurses themselves, but 1963 legislation removed this control by setting up an educational advisory committee with representatives from the medical profession, the hospital administration, and the health bureaucracy. It also removed the power to approve nursing schools from the nurses' college and returned it back to the lieutenant governor in council. Ibid., vol. 1, 76–8. In the late 1960s, a report described nurses as 'having little power to influence their conditions of work.' It recommended that they be given their share of influence in the institutional decision-making processes. Ibid., vol. 2, 161, 169.
41 Coburn refers to the motherhood role. David Coburn, 'The Development of Canadian Nursing: Professionalization and Proletarianization,' *International Journal of Health Services*, 18/3 (1988): 444. Moloney refers to the role of 'physician's

handmaiden.' Margaret M. Moloney, *Professionalization of Nursing: Current Issues and Trends* (Philadelphia: Lippincott, 1986), 31.
42 Former registered nurse, interview by author, 11 Aug. 1992.
43 Nursing assistants (now called practical nurses) were included in the 1951 Nurses Act.
44 For further discussion of those who failed to gain the benefits of legislation, see the section in this chapter on 'The Excluded.'
45 There were twenty-one specialties being practised within medicine in Ontario by the mid-twentieth century. J.W. Grove, *Organized Medicine in Ontario: A Study for the Committee on the Healing Arts* (Toronto: Queen's Printer, 1969), 153.
46 The specialties of dental care, eye care, and ear–speech care, e.g., developed a particular internal division of clinical territory (see their sections in this chapter).
47 In the former, there were, e.g., British-trained chiropodists, massage therapists, physiotherapists, nurses, dieticians, psychologists, and dental hygienists. In the latter, there were, e.g., American-trained chiropodists, chiropractors, osteopaths, and masseurs.
48 Optometry managed to be included with only four other practitioner groups in the 1974 HDA.
49 This was after the inclusion of the latter in the Medical Act (under a system of registration) had proven unworkable. CHA Report, vol. 1, 78.
50 The drugless practitioner groups were granted registration rights, but they failed to win the licensure which the nineteenth-century health practitioners had been granted. They were given a joint governing body, the board of regents, but its members were externally appointed rather than internally elected. When the board of regents (which governed all of the drugless practitioners together) was changed to separate boards of directors for each drugless practitioner group, in 1952, the board members were still externally appointed. Educational control (direct via specific educational programs and indirect via entrance exams) was given to the board of regents (later directors). Disciplinary power was given in 1925 to the board of regents for 'incompetence, ignorance, or misconduct.' Note this 'incompetence' provision predates the same for the medical profession by forty years. Ibid., vol. 1, 78–9; vol. 2, 477.
51 Looking at the story of the drugless practitioners' legislation, one gets the sense that the policy makers were not very interested or threatened by these alternative provider groups, i.e., that the legislation was a grab-bag of more or less harmless healers who had to be put somewhere. Two of the practitioner groups, osteopaths and chiropodists, were not drugless practitioners at all. More telling was the fact that the new legislation permitted a practitioner to be registered under more than one of the five provider categories, as if their scopes of practice were interchangeable. A barred registrant could simply resume practice under another of the cate-

gory designations – a move unthinkable among the elite professional groups. Ibid., vol. 2, 453.
52 The German physician Benedict Lust is credited with its founding here. Elaine H. Gort and David Coburn, 'Naturopathy in Canada: Changing Relationships to Medicine, Chiropractic and the State,' *Social Science Medicine* 26/10 (1988), 1061; Robert Posen, 'Naturopathy,' *On Continuing Practice*, 16/2 (1989), 27.
53 That is, the Mills's study, done for the Canadian RCHS (1964–5).
54 Posen, 'Naturopathy,' 27. At the time of the CHA report in the late 1960s, the board of directors of drugless therapy (naturopathy) described their approved methods as 'consisting of a complete order of natural therapeutics, embracing the use of nature's agencies, processes, and products; and including the application of physiotherapeutical (electrical, mechanical, manual, adjustive, manipulative, orthopaedic [minor surgery]) procedures; emphasizing the treatment of prophylaxis; nutrition, vitamin–mineral, tissue salts; phyto-therapeutics; and psychological [psychotherapeutics – remedial psychology].' Quoted in CHA Report, vol. 2, 482.
55 The former by Andrew Taylor Stills and the latter by D.D. Palmer.
56 See Walter I. Wardwell, 'Chiropractors: Evolution to Acceptance,' in Gevitz, *Other Healers*; Gevitz, 'Osteopathic Medicine: From Deviance to Difference,' in *Other Healers*. Gevitz comments that 'all the originators of these oppositional movements considered their own approach to be the very embodiment of scientific thinking.' Gevitz, 'Three Perspectives on Unorthodox Medicine,' in *Other Healers*, 18.
57 Gevitz, 'Osteopathic,' in *Other Healers*, 146–53. The term 'parallel profession' is taken by Gevitz from Wardwell, 'Chiropractors,' in *Other Healers*, 1.
58 At the time the DPA was passed, there were only 100 osteopaths in Ontario. CHA Report, vol. 2, 445. This number had dropped to five by the beginning of the latest policy round which resulted in the 1991 RHPA.
59 One of the arguments put forth in Ontario against the expansion of the osteopaths' scope of practice is that they would then merely duplicate a service already available through the existing medical profession – as they do in the U.S.
60 Wardwell, 'Chiropractors,' in Gevitz, *Other Healers*, 157.
61 The publicly funded OHIP is meant here. Boase has documented this highly efficient and effective campaign (although they only won partial insurance coverage). Joan Boase, 'Regulation and the Paramedical Professions: An Interest Group Study,' *Canadian Public Administration*, 25/3 (1982), 335–42.
62 Like the hypotheses of all health practitioners, theirs were continuously moulded according to their rates of success, but these adjustments were based on empirical observation rather than controlled experimentation.
63 They continue to this day to see themselves as applied scientists; see Chapter 6.

64 Massage practitioners apply manual manipulation to the soft tissue and joints to maintain or rehabilitate physical function or to relieve pain.
65 Educational standards were also established, and limitations were placed on their scope of practice. They now had to graduate from a nine-month course at a school of massage. They were not allowed to make adjustments to any bony structures of the body, that being chiropractic territory. CHA Report, vol. 2, 383–4.
66 Ibid., 385.
67 This was even though, as one group of health policy reviewers pointed out, 'masseurs as a group are not highly regarded by many physicians.' Ibid., 385, 388.
68 Ibid., 374.
69 OSOT was established in 1921. In 1934 a national voluntary association was established under the name of the CAOT. The first training course was offered at the University of Toronto. In 1950 the course was combined with physiotherapy and placed within the faculty of medicine. Ibid., 373.
70 Boase says this concession was not opposed, or sufficiently opposed, by the medical professionals because they considered the physiotherapists to be 'easily controlled.' Joan Price Boase, 'Public Policy and Regulation of the Health Disciplines: An Historical and Comparative Perspective' (PhD dissertation, York University, 1986), 105. Only physiotherapists with these pre-1964 agreements can submit to OHIP for reimbursement. CHA recommended 'that the services of licensed physiotherapists in private practice be covered under publicly financed health insurance plans wherever the treatments were provided.' CHA Report, vol. 2, 364.
71 MacNab, *A Legal History*, 56; CHA Report, vol. 2, 341.
72 CHA Report, vol. 2, 336.
73 U.S. 'chiropodists' refer to themselves more correctly as podiatrists. The term 'chiropody' includes reference to the hand, but the term 'podiatry' relates only to the foot.
74 A 1958 private act gave the dieticians' voluntary association, the ODTA, the authority to grant the title 'registered professional dietician' to those members meeting its entry standards; but, no governing mechanisms were developed at that time. Psychologists were given their own body of legislation in 1960, the Psychologists Registration Act, which allowed them a governing body which could register, standardize, and discipline its members. MacNab, *A Legal History*, 149.
75 This shows up, e.g., in the psychologists' recognition of the importance of the psychotic and antidepressant drugs in the treatment of mental disorders, while at the same time they discourage unnecessary use of drugs as well as the need to complement them with the science of psychological counselling. Ontario Board of Examiners in Psychology, 'Submission to the Health Professions Legislation Review (HPLR)' (June 1984), 15–16.
76 They worked out of mail order houses using 'machines with which a customer

could test [her or] his own eyes and order the indicated spectacles by mail.' CHA Report, vol. 1, 80.
77 Technicians and technologists are often confused by outside writers in the health care literature as one and the same thing, but technologists receive more training than technicians, so the distinction is important to them. This educational gradation developed through the college system later than the legislation I am referring to here, when the single designation of technician was used, so legislation drafters have tended to maintain the old nomenclature of 'technician' as all-inclusive. Today the hierarchy has been recognized in legislation, so I will adopt the more appropriate terminology throughout this work.
78 To avoid confusion I will refer to this latter group as opticians rather than both opticians and ophthalmic dispensers – as the literature does. They are now referred to legally only as opticians.
79 By then, independent merchants were excluded via formal educational requirements which had been put in place by the Board of Examiners of Optometry. Retail merchants had won a partial victory by exemption from this act; however, they were now hampered by a provision which prohibited them from supplying any vision-testing device, except the standard eye chart, with which customers could assess their own eye device requirements. Ibid., vol. 1, 79–80.
80 As had been the case for the earlier demand by pharmacists for protective legislation, the state was reluctant to grant a monopoly to what it perceived to be a merchant group. Three bills presented in Ontario in 1911, 1912, and 1913 failed to pass on the grounds the legislature was opposed to the creation of 'closed corporations.' Success, however, was helped by the fact that the optometrists and opticians, although they themselves represented monopolistic tendencies compared with a free market, also represented a breaking up of the medical monopoly on merchandise sales (of glasses) into an oligopoly, introducing more price competition than would have existed under the complete control of the medical profession. Ibid., vol. 1, 18, 79; MacNab, *A Legal History*, 56.
81 General practitioners are allowed to perform this function, but a specialty within medicine, ophthalmology, has now developed. The latter tends to specialize in pathologies of the eye.
82 Prior to the Second World War, in North America, audiology and speech therapy had been labelled as handicap specialties, but with the expansion of facilities and treatments for war veterans, programs were set up in the U.S. to train personnel in these fields. By 1958 the University of Toronto had set up a two-year diploma course which combined the training of both audiology and speech pathology. CHA Report, vol. 2, 391.
83 The wide distribution of hearing aids did not come until later, and when it did, it set up the same type of divisions as had the merchandise profits of vision care, with the

development of hearing aid dispensers, who then sought inclusion in the health practitioner legislation.
84 Dental technicians (as denturists were then called), e.g., were given registration but not licensing; their governing body, or college, was externally appointed rather than internally elected; and, most telling of all, the act allowed for veto from the *dentists'* governing body on any proposed regulations from the dental technicians' college. See, for elaboration, CHA Report, vol. 1, 73–4; MacNab, *A Legal History*, 81–3.
85 Shosenberg, *The Rise*, 184. This organization followed earlier attempts to win self-regulating legislation for all dental technicians – which would include the group later calling themselves dental therapists or denturists.
86 Shosenberg documents the back-and-forth gains and losses of this battle between the two groups and their state supporters and detractors. Ibid., 184–98.
87 See the Denture Therapists (Denturists) Act of 1974. As we shall see, the sale of partial dentures was to become a contentious issue.
88 Attempts by the federal government in 1942 to include dentistry in the impending medicare bill had been successfully fought by the CDA. Limited public funding of dental care, mostly for schoolchildren and recipients of general public welfare programs, was all that was ever introduced in Ontario as well as the rest of Canada. This story is well documented in Gullett, *History of Dentistry*.
89 The provincial premier publicly blamed the dental profession for making denticare impossible because of the high fees the professionals charged for their work. This, coupled with the fact that low-cost dental clinics, which had been attempted by the dentists as a response to this criticism, were considered by the government to have had disappointing results, helped sway attitudes towards the freeing up of denturists to once again provide less expensive dentures. Shosenberg, *The Rise*, 198.
90 They were granted certification for their members, e.g., rather than licensure; the new BRT registered its practitioners, set training and examination standards, and was empowered to revoke registration for 'unprofessional conduct, incompetence, fraud, or misrepresentation,' but as MacNab points out, the composition of the board reflected both the internal power of the group's voluntary association, which was to nominate four members of the board, and the 'subordinate status' of the group, which, unlike the elite professions, had to accept three external members, all of whom were medical doctors. In addition, any recommendations for regulatory changes to the act were allowed a thirty-day scrutiny period by the CPSO with their recommendations, or counter-recommendations, to be submitted to the government. MacNab, *A Legal History*, 150–2.
91 The medical laboratory technologists were placed under the Laboratory and Specimen Collection Centre Licensing Act, regulation 845, which regulated the overall performance of the laboratory, rather than the technologists per se.

Notes to pages 28–30 257

92 This was probably because of the success of the optometrists in moving into the service aspects of their occupation.
93 However, there is also an occupation referred to as dental nurse. See n95.
94 A 1947 act allowed the dental college to make regulations with respect to dental hygienists. There was no representation of the hygienist group on the 'joint' council of the dental college. Later legislation continued the dentists' control. CHA Report, vol. 1, 74.
95 There are now many medical specialists' assistants, such as ophthalmologists' assistants. The nomenclature of dental assistants is confusing. One might also hear reference to dental nurses, preventive dental assistants, level two dental assistants, expanded duty dental assistant, dental auxiliaries, dental prosthetic therapists, and children's dental auxiliaries. These are all just some form or other of nurselike dental practitioners, up to and including the level comparable to that of the independent 'nurse practitioner.
96 For discussion of the U.S. origins and success of the Thomsonian movement, see Ehrenreich and English, *For Her Own Good*, 53–5. As Ehrenreich and English point out, 'Thomson's system was little more than a systematization of [the healer/midwife's] combination of herbs and steam, which in turn was derived from Native American healing lore.' Ibid., 53. For discussion of the success of this movement in Canada, see Hamowy, *Canadian Medicine*, 24–5.
97 In the U.S., where most of Canada's nineteenth- and twentieth-century alternative practitioners originated and trained, Sylvester Graham founded the Hygienic Movement in the early nineteenth century. Like the European health movement of its kind, this one was based primarily on a vegetarian diet supplemented by measures we associate with the idea of 'rest cures' (fresh air, exercise, and so on). It was for this diet that he invented the 'Graham cracker.' Ehrenreich and English, *For Her Own Good*, 54.
98 The history of medicine literature utilizes this term to refer to the dramatic techniques of, e.g., bloodletting, purging, and surgery used in the eighteenth to twentieth centuries.
99 The Christian Scientists had 'overcome medical opposition and won for its exponents the legal right to practice on the faithful its distinctive form of mental healing.' Gevitz, *Other Healers*, ch. 1, and p. 11.
100 Ehrenreich and English, e.g., point to evidence that 'a sizable faction within Thomsonianism began to hanker for respectability and something very much like professionalism – even though this meant reversing the original tenets of the movement. If Thomsonianism was going to fit with the personal ambitions of these upwardly mobile healers, it would have to break with the old "do it yourself" philosophy and rag-tag collection of radical causes which had kept company with the early movement.' Ehrenreich and English, *For Her Own Good*, 55–6.

258   Notes to page 30

101 CHA Report, vol. 1, 9; Hamowy, *Canadian Medicine*, 125.
102 I have documented this story elsewhere. Patricia O'Reilly, 'Midwifery and the Medical Monopoly' (MA dissertation Queen's University, 1986). Some of the examples used there were taken from the following: Donnegan, who points out that male birth attendants worked partially blind because the mother's body was covered in order to preserve her modesty. Jane B. Donegan, *Women and Men Midwives: Medicine, Morality and Misogyny in Early America* (Westport, CO: Greenwood Press, 1978), 82. Shorter refers to the effects of the European hospitalization of birth (which utilized medical men rather than female midwives) at the time when puerperal fever raged, 'Hospital birth was roughly six times more dangerous than home birth in the 1860's.' (Note the date in relation to the granting of the Upper Canadian licences to physicians whose scope of practice included midwifery.) Edward Shorter, *A History of Women's Bodies* (New York: Penguin, 1982), 130. Wertz and Wertz comment: 'Young [American] doctors [of the early 1800s] rarely had any clinical training ... Many arrived at a birth with only lectures and book learning to guide them ... [Many] were embarrassed, confused and frightened ... [but] they had to use their arts because they were expected to "perform." Walter Channing, Professor of Midwifery [Obstetrics] at Harvard Medical School in the early nineteenth century remarked about the doctor, in the context of discussing a case in which forceps were used unnecessarily, that he "must do something. He cannot remain a spectator merely, where there are too many witnesses and where interest in what is going on is too deep to allow of his inaction."' R.W. Wertz and D.C. Wertz, *Lying-In: A History of Childbirth in America* (New York: Schocken, 1979), 63–4. Biggs refers to the same for Ontario doctors 'wishing to show that they were really doing something.' C. Lesley Biggs, 'The Case of the Missing Midwives: A History of Midwifery in Ontario from 1795–1900,' *Ontario History*, 75/1 (1983), 33. Biggs is quoting an Ontario medical doctor writing in 1892.
103 Prior to that a 1795 Medical Act, which prohibited midwives from practising in Upper Canada, proved unworkable and publicly contentious, so it was overturned in 1806. An attempt by the medical profession to control midwifery in 1808 also failed, and an 1839 Medical Act which did place midwives under medical control was soon repealed. Hamowy, *Canadian Medicine*, 14–15. Ontario, *Report of the Task Force on the Implementation of Midwifery in Ontario* (Toronto: Queen's Printer, 1987), 31.
104 See, e.g., O'Reilly, 'Midwifery and the Medical Monopoly,' 2, 5, 7, 18, 25, 38, 52, 162, and n56. There are many good historical reviews which refer to these biases throughout their texts. I would recommend (for our historical influences from Britain) Jean Donnison, *Midwives and Medical Men: A History of Interprofessional Rivalries and Women's Rights* (New York: Schocken, 1977); (for our his-

torical influences from the U.S.) Wertz and Wertz, *Lying-In*; as well as Ehrenreich and English, *For Her Own Good*; (for a Canadian writer on midwifery and related topics) Shorter, *A History of Women's Bodies*; (for the story of midwifery in Canada) Elinor Barrington, *Midwifery Is Catching* (Toronto: NC Press, 1985); and (for an account of the history of midwifery in Ontario) Biggs, 'The Case of the Missing Midwives.'

105 A *Globe and Mail* editorial in defence of midwifery recommended practising midwives circumvent the law rather than get a medical education in order to continue practising midwifery because as women they would have to 'endure the almost insupportable ordeal, opposition and prosecution' of an education system run by and for men. Biggs, 'The Case of the Missing Midwives,' 26.

106 J. Heagerty, *Four Centuries of Medical History in Canada*, (Toronto: MacMillan, 1928), vol. 2, 134.

107 Strong-Boag says of this atmosphere, 'Like lawyers and ministers, many doctors were determined to close their ranks on female candidates.' Women's fight for 'professional prestige and power' offended the male professionals' 'conservative defence of an idealized womanhood' which was, among other things 'uniquely susceptible to a multitude of emotional and nervous disorders.' Veronica Strong-Boag, 'Canada's Women Doctors: Feminism Constrained,' in S.E.D. Shortt, ed., *Medicine in Canadian Society: Historical Perspectives* (Montreal: McGill-Queen's University Press, 1981), 208–9.

108 An example of a typical statement of this kind came from the Medical Board of 1838 which claimed: 'Quacks are an intolerable nuisance in any and every country, but especially in this, where empiricism and radicalism go hand in hand. It is a monstrous grievance that our Government should allow the Province to swarm, as it does, with these pestilent vagabonds, every one of whom is a Yankee loafer, and makes his occupation a cloak for inculcating Jacobinical principles. All know how numerous have been the self-styled "doctors" implicated in rebellion, but perhaps all may not know that they were almost one and all Yankee Quacks. We are truly glad to see that the Medical Board are active in setting about means to annihilate the dirty birds, nest and all; we trust the legislature will second their efforts.' Hamowy, *Canadian Medicine*, 29.

109 See, e.g., Hamowy, *Canadian Medicine*; Joseph F. Kett, 'American and Canadian Medical Institutions, 1800–1870,' in Shortt, *Medicine*; and Hilary Rose, 'Gendered Reflexions on the Laboratory in Medicine,' in Cunningham and Williams, *The Laboratory Revolution*.

110 See, e.g., for Canada, Agnes Calliste, 'Women of Exceptional Merit: Immigration of Caribbean Nurses to Canada' *Canadian Journal of Women and the Law*, 6/1 (1993); for the U.S., Ian McMillan, 'Rough Justice,' *Nursing Times*, 87/3 (1991), 20–1.; for Britain, Marina Lee-Cunin, *Daughters of Seacole: A Study of Black*

Nurses in West Yorkshire (West Yorkshire: West Yorkshire Low Pay Unit, 1989); for South Africa, Shula Marks, 'Class, Race and Gender in the South African Nursing Profession' (public lecture, Political Science Department, University of Toronto, Nov. 1989).

111 Calliste, 'Women of Exceptional Merit,' 85–102.
112 Brown, *Rockefeller Medicine Men*, 146–56.
113 The infamous Flexner Report of 1910 included inspection of some Canadian medical schools and was to become influential in Canada as well as the U.S. Ibid.
114 Kett, 'American and Canadian Medical Institutions,' 197.
115 Historians point to the importance of class prejudice, e.g., in the nineteenth-century rise of homeopathy. The Western upper classes of the mid-nineteenth century had taken a liking to homeopathy. As Brown notes: '[John D.] Rockefeller, a life-long follower of homeopathy, objected to any move [via his immensely wealthy philanthropic organization] that strengthened the regular profession in its conflict with homeopathists ... Rockefeller and homeopathy were both products of the nineteenth century. From the mid-nineteenth century on, homeopathy in the United States appealed primarily to the upper classes. It was safer than the heroics of regular medicine, and it was a sign of affluence and taste since it was very fashionable among the European nobility and upper classes, who were aped in many ways by wealthy Americans.' Brown, *Rockefeller Medicine Men*, 109–10. Likewise, in Canada, the fact that the English aristocracy had taken to homeopathy, after its introduction there in 1827, lent a definite air of respectability to it. CHA Report, vol. 2, 108–9.
116 Naylor quotes an OMA president's complaint against the 'obnoxious opposition' from the Patrons of Industry, a rural populist party which won legislative representation in Ontario in 1894, 'to all kinds of class legislation.' Naylor, *Private Practice*, 21. Hamowy captures another medical leader's nineteenth-century class sentiment in the following quote: 'not a few young Canadians [says the CMA president], disinclined to do manual work, as their fathers had done, cast aside the home-spun clothes, donned a broadcloth suit and kid gloves, hung up a shingle and announced themselves to be 'Doctors' according to the doctrine of Thompson.' Hamowy, *Canadian Medicine*, 25. It is hard to say which was more annoying for this influential medical physician, the practice of Thomsonian medicine, or the nerve of the lower class.
117 Timothy Lenoir, 'Building Institutions for Physiology in Prussia 1836–1846,' in Cunningham and Williams, *The Laboratory Revolution*, 17–18.
118 Sutherland points to an area of health care where class prejudices were overridden, i.e., in the area of public health an egalitarian treatment of all children was fought for by professionals and non-professionals alike. (Although, these children certainly represented no entrepreneurial threat to medicine; quite the opposite.)

Neil Sutherland, 'To Create a Strong and Healthy Race: School Children in the Public Health Movement, 1880–1914,' in Shortt, *Medicine*, 361–93.

119 Strong-Boag, 'Canada's Women Doctors,' 209. Cunningham and Williams also point out, 'Hilary Rose calls for us to ask how far the laboratory vision, the particular manual and mental skills taught by the teaching laboratory, was the product not merely of a specific class but of a gender within that class.' Cunningham and Williams, *The Laboratory Revolution*, 9. Science historian Rose also refers to scientific health care, especially medicine, as 'men's studies,' or 'gendered research,' 324–42 and 329. Some practitioners, many midwives, e.g., crossed over several categories of discrimination, including that of age. One might have been an elderly, female, French-Canadian or Afro-American, working-class midwife, which would, in the eyes of the medical profession, have made you dirty, ignorant, and dangerous (Biggs, 'The Case of the Missing Midwives,' 31.), irrational and emotional (Donegan, *Women and Men Midwives*, ch. 7), 'meddlesome old women' (Biggs, 'The Case of the Missing Midwives,' 28), 'illiterate ... gossips' (ibid., 23, 26), and 'old ... quacks' (Barrington, *Midwifery Is Catching*, 26).

120 Boase discusses the female–male power relations impacting on the occupation of physiotherapy. Boase, 'Public Policy,' 113–17. The directors of physiotherapy training schools have historically usually been male, while the enrolment was predominantly female. Ibid., 115–16.

121 As MacNab put it, 'By far the greatest handicap for nurses was that they were a feminine profession seeking power in a world still dominated by men.' MacNab, *A Legal History*, 116.

122 Tania Das Gupta, 'Anti-Black Racism in Nursing in Ontario,' *Studies in Political Economy*, 51 (Fall 1996), 100–1.

123 In the 1920s a Canadian doctor was rebuked by his medical colleagues for having compiled maternal mortality statistics which showed a mother's chances were better with a non-professional attendant than they were with the professional doctors and nurses. Barrington, *Midwifery Is Catching*, 28. An Ontario study done in 1933 found that maternal deaths under hospitalization were double the rate of that for home births. Jo Oppenheimer, 'Childbirth in Ontario: The Transformation from Home to Hospital in the Early Twentieth Century,' *Ontario History*, vol. 75 (1983), 54–5. A 1960 California study of the replacement of the obstetrical staff of a hospital with nurse–midwives showed the neonatal mortality rate and the prematurity rate dropped considerably. Barry S. Levy, Frederick S. Wilkinson, and William M. Marine, 'Reducing Neonatal Mortality Rate with Nurse–Midwives,' *American Journal of Obstetrics and Gynaecology*, no. 109 (1971), 177. A 1973 survey conducted in the Netherlands, where midwives attend over half of all births, showed that country as having the third-lowest infant mortality rate in the world; Canada was ranked fourteenth. Jennifer Trachera, 'A Birth Right: Home

Births, Midwives, and the Right to Privacy,' *Pacific Law Journal*, no. 97 (1980), 101. These are only some of the examples I have documented in an earlier piece of work. For more, see O'Reilly, 'Midwifery and the Medical Monopoly,' 104–14. Also, see *Report of the Task Force on the Implementation of Midwifery* (Toronto: Queen's Printer, 1987), 81; and the references to the MC submissions to the HPLR in Chapter 6 of this work.

124 A 1989 Task Force found evidence of unfair, culturally biased treatment of foreign-trained persons wishing to practice a profession or trade in Ontario. Ontario, Ministry of Citizenship, *Report of the Task Force on Access to Professions and Trades* (Toronto: Queen's Printer, 1989). For the colour bias of Canada, the U.K., and the U.S., see James Walker, *Racial Discrimination in Canada: The Black Experience* (Ottawa: Canadian Historical Association, 1995); Louis Kushnick, 'Racism, the National Health Service, and the Health of Black People,' *International Journal of Health Services*, 18/3 (1988), 457–76; and Woodrow Jones and Mitchell F. Rice, *Health Care Issues in Black America* (New York: Greenwood, 1987).

125 Critical literature has, of course, been coming up with examples of these various types of discrimination for some time. Macpherson has argued that the liberal democracy of the contemporary Western nations has itself been designed to fit onto the class-divided society so essential to the workings of our whole system. C.B. Macpherson, *The Life and Times of Liberal Democracy* (Oxford: Oxford University Press, 1977). For more recent work on the Canadian social and political environment, see Ronald Manzer, *Canada: A Socio-Political Report* (Toronto: McGraw-Hill Ryerson, 1974); Daiva K. Stasiulis and Yasmeen Abu-Laban, 'The House the Parties Built: (Re)constructing Ethnic Representation in Canadian Politics,' in Royal Commission On Electoral Reform and Party Financing (Toronto: Dundurn 1991), 1–99; also, see some of the articles on women's participation in the report.

126 It might be argued that these proponents of scientific method were guilty of no more social prejudice than the majority of their fellow citizens. To this I would reply that they themselves fought hard for the privileges awarded them on the basis of their self-asserted objectivity and scientific impartiality.

127 See Table 2.2.

128 Pharmacy and nursing were also included in the professional legislation (the HDA of 1974), but as we have seen, they were not then, nor had they ever been, autonomous professionals.

129 Independent technology specialists, e.g., denturists, became, once independent, merchant–service specialists (which is why there is no category for them in Table 2.1.)

130 Medical science was growing by leaps and bounds throughout the twentieth century. By mid-century it was 'estimated that an article on medical science was published somewhere in the world every 23 seconds.' Grove, *Organized Medicine*, 1. Also, see n45.
131 It should be noted that it is also not clear that they were interested in the elaborate business of proving their claims scientifically.

3 Benefits and Burdens of the New Regulatory Blueprint

1 Grove refers to the 'hallmarks of the new professions' as 'organization, a tendency to monopoly, mutual self-defense, and ... restrictive practice.' J.W. Grove, *Organized Medicine in Ontario: A Study for the Committee of Healing Arts* (Toronto: Queen's Printer, 1969), 16.
2 This latter function gave the professional governing body the authority to perform the state's policelike functions of search and seizure and its judicial-like functions of legal judgment and discipline with its own members as well as other health practitioners it deemed intrusive on its profession's practice territory.
3 Our Western free market blueprint assumes that 'the competitive drive to maximize one's welfare stimulates people to be very resourceful, creative, clever, and productive, and ultimately raises the level of economic well-being of society as a whole.' Deborah A. Stone, *Policy Paradox and Political Reason* (Glenview, IL: Scott, Foresman, 1988), 13.
4 C.E.S. Franks, *The Parliament of Canada* (Toronto: University of Toronto Press, 1987).
5 The original grounds for disciplinary action from the college, e.g., were minimal. The licence of a physician, a homeopath, or an eclectic could only be revoked if he had been convicted of a felony. Nor did the professional colleges seem much concerned with the carrying out of their obligations. The dentists' college, e.g., was given disciplinary powers in 1868 but failed to set up any formal process for enacting this obligation until 1908. CHA Report, vol. 1, 59–61, 72–3.
6 Medicine in 1965, dentistry in 1966, and pharmacy in 1953. Ibid., vol. 1, 72, 73, 75, respectively.
7 A situation the 1970 CHA referred to as 'a lack of central control.' See, e.g., ibid., 89.
8 College officials moved readily into 'seeking greater benefits' for their members, e.g., monetary benefits. Elizabeth MacNab, *A Legal History of Health Professions in Ontario: A study for the Committee on the Healing Arts* (Toronto: Queen's Printer, 1970), 41. State actors often themselves confused the lines of authority – to the point of granting regulatory powers to a profession's union-type organization,

its professional association, whose only goal is the protection of the self-interests of the professionals themselves, rather than the protection of the public's legal interests. Pharmacy, e.g., despite the fact that it, like medicine and dentistry, had won professional legitimation on the basis of its claim to 'esoteric technical knowledge,' was originally governed by its business interests which took control of the profession from the start. Strange as it sounds today, the original 'governing body,' the OCP, was set up and run by the wholesale drug dealers. R.J. Clark, 'Professional Aspirations and the Limits of Occupational Autonomy: The Case of Pharmacy in Nineteenth-Century Ontairo,' *Canadian Bulletin of Medical History*, 8/1 (1991),' 43–63, 47–50, 59; quote from p. 59. Even as late as 1951 the Nurses Association of Ontario was granted the powers of a governing body. CHA Report, vol. 1, 77.

9 There was no ministerial accountability. (While the minister of health later became, at least theoretically, an avenue of public input into the inner governance of the professions, the general isolation in which the colleges operated left them without this check on their power – there being no 'minister' inside the college itself.) Nor was there any exposure of the governors to a question period or all-party debates in parliament, or any ultimate means of accountability via the overthrow of the governors by public election.

10 The literature on alternative health practitioners often portrays the elite practitioners, especially the medical profession, as unfairly 'going after' other practitioners. While there may be a moral case to be made against this zeal, it ought to be kept in mind that legally they were not only allowed to do so, they were, in fact, obliged to do so. If blame for the injustice of such prosecution is to be placed anywhere, it would have to be on the heads of the legislators who passed this obligation into law.

11 The college, or more specifically, its executive council, appointed an official prosecutor who was to prosecute quacks. (Individual physicians could do the same – with instructions given out by the council on how to do so.) The Prosecutor was paid in fines. MacNab, *A Legal History*, 19, 36.

12 Ibid., 36.

13 When the CPSO brought a case against an acupuncturist in 1981, the court decided in the acupuncturist's favour because his practice could not be deemed to be in contravention of the Medical Act since acupuncture could not be considered a part of medicine, not being taught in medical schools. Joan Price Boase, 'Public Policy and Regulation of the Health Disciplines: An Historical and Comparative Perspective' (PhD dissertation, York University, 1986),' 111–12.

14 Legal control over members of the profession had been limited until 1887 by the fact that the only grounds, or ground, as it was, for council action had been the (external) conviction on a felony offence. Prosecution of medical practitioners after 1887 was related mostly to misleading advertising (exaggerated claims by profes-

sionals constituted 'improper conduct'), although working with an unorthodox (non-medical) health practitioner or utilizing one drug company exclusively was also considered to be improper conduct for a medical professional. MacNab, *A Legal History*, 23, 34.
15 Ibid., 23.
16 Ibid., 26.
17 Ibid., 104. As Grove comments, 'The very character of a profession militates against discipline or regulation of its members.' Grove, *Organized Medicine*, 161.
18 It should be noted that the excluded practitioners enjoyed a certain degree of autonomy from the state because of their exclusion. Although they were not protected as entrepreneurs or clinicians, their exclusion left them rather 'out of sight, out of mind,' and, as we shall see, this freedom was something a fair number of them were reluctant to give up when it came time to decide whether or not to press for inclusion in the professional legislation of the 1980s and 1990s.
19 Carolyn J. Tuohy and Alan D. Wolfson, 'Self-regulation: Who Qualifies?' in Philip Slayton and Michael J. Trebilcock, eds., *The Professions and Public Policy* (Toronto: University of Toronto Press, 1978).
20 G.H.L Fridman, *The Law of Agency*, 7th ed. (Toronto: Butterworths, 1996), 11.
21 Some of the earliest formal professional associations did not come into effect until after legislative gains were made; in those cases, individual practitioners or informal groups of practitioners lobbied the politicians.
22 See Chapter 2. In the U.S., which supplied many of Canada's alternative practitioners, 'physicians violated the American Medical Association code of ethics if they consulted with sectarian physicians [such as the homeopaths and eclectics] or female or black doctors.' E. Richard Brown, *Rockefeller Medicine Men: Medicine and Capitalism in America* (Berkeley: University of California Press, 1979), 88. Likewise, when these alternative practitioners emigrated to Canada, physicians here violated the medical profession's code of ethics if they cooperated with any care givers other than their own kind, regardless of the circumstance of the unfortunate patient. Ronald Hamowy, *Canadian Medicine: A Study in Restricted Entry* (Vancouver: Fraser Institute, 1984), 100.
23 The medical profession had developed a symbiotic relationship with the pharmaceutical companies which were beginning to develop some of the tremendous profits and clout that they enjoy today. Coulter argues that it was the combined forces of the American Medical Association and this pharmaceutical industry which destroyed homeopathy. Elaine H. Gort and David Coburn, 'Naturopathy in Canada: Changing Relationships to Medicine, Chiropractic and the State,' *Social Science Medicine*, 26/10 (1988) 1062. In Canada a similar relationship had developed. CHA Report, vol. 2, 108.
24 Barrington quotes a journalist's comment in 1981: 'There is no better index of the

political power of the medical profession than the fact that it put midwives out of business, even where there was no doctor to provide service.' Elinor Barrington, *Midwifery Is Catching* (Toronto: NC Press, 1985), 30.
25 David R. Kennedy, 'One Hundred Years of Pharmacy Legislation.' Seminar titled '1867–1967, One Hundred Years of Pharmacy in Canada,' for the Canadian Academy of the History of Pharmacy, Toronto, 15 Aug. 1967, 27–8.
26 Dentists, like physicians, strongly resisted any autonomy on the part of the dental semi-professionals and would-be-professionals, even when evidence suggested that the latter were perfectly capable of performing certain tasks. A pilot project in Saskatchewan, e.g., found that 'the work of dental auxiliaries,' who performed many of the routine duties normally performed by dentists, was equal to or better than that performed by dentists.' Boase, 'Public Policy,' 209–10.
27 Brown, *Rockefeller Medicine Men*, 145–56. Johns Hopkins Medical School provided Flexner with a standard, 'without which in the back of my mind [he said] ... I could have accomplished little.' Ibid., 145.
28 This is a term used by a leading Canadian doctor to refer to alternative practitioners. Hamowy, *Canadian Medicine*, 107.
29 CHA Report, vol. 2, 450–1.
30 Ibid., vol. 2, 451.
31 Norman Gevitz, 'Osteopathic Medicine: From Deviance to Difference,' in Gevitz, ed., *Other Healers: Unorthodox Medicine in America* (Baltimore: Johns Hopkins University Press, 1988), 144.
32 Ibid., 134.
33 The MacNab study for the CHA found 85 per cent of the 309 naturopaths in the province held dual registration with chiropractic in 1953. Referenced in Gort and Coburn, 'Naturopathy in Canada,' 1064.
34 On the one hand, naturopaths made use of the chiropractic training schools to teach courses in naturopathy at a time when there were no naturopathic schools in Canada – which was the situation until quite recently. (In a cooperative move with the American naturopaths, Canadian naturopaths had set up a joint U.S.–Canada naturopathic school, but it was located in Portland, Oregon. It was not until 1978 that a Canadian training program was established in Ontario.) On the other hand, complaints were made that once the chiropractors had won inclusion into the public health insurance program, naturopathic services were also being billed 'under the table' by dual registrants who were able to bill only for their chiropractic services. CHA Report, vol. 2, 486.
35 It allowed them to make use of the expanded list of 'drugless therapies' which had been allowed naturopathy under the DPA: e.g., homeopathic and herbal remedies, colonic irrigation, and acupuncture. Gort and Coburn, 'Naturopathy in Canada,' 1068.

36 For an expanded version of this story see ibid., 1067–9.
37 Chiropractors opposed the physiotherapists' bids in the 1980s for primary patient contact, arguing, just as the medical profession does about them, that physiotherapists are not sufficiently educated for such autonomous practice. See Chapter 6. It is debatable whether the physiotherapy–chiropractic alliance is tenable. The former are educated strictly according to 'medical knowledge' which the latter clearly finds remiss. Chiropractors have been less threatened by massage therapists whose scope of practice is much further removed from theirs. Although some chiropractors make referrals to masseurs, as we saw in Chapter 2, OAMT rejected this potential alliance for one with medicine.
38 Joan Boase, 'Regulation and the Paramedical Professions: An Interest Group Study,' *Canadian Public Administration*, 25/3 (1982), 346–7.
39 CHA Report, vol. 2, 385. Masseurs have been legally prohibited from using the technical instruments used by physiotherapists.
40 As we have seen, the nurse's role of 'physician's handmaiden' as well as the gender hierarchy between the female nurses and the male doctors contributed to a relationship of that of a subordinate to a superior. As the CHA reported at the end of the 1960s, 'The traditional subservience of the nurse to the physician is one of the most fundamental relationships in the health services field.' Ibid., 168.
41 Grove refers to the code of 'professional ethics' of medicine as 'in truth, a brand of business morality; the code gave a gentlemanly patina to what was essentially a matter of business like anything else.' Grove, *Organized Medicine*, 17.
42 After reading through the early medical journals, Hamowy is not inclined towards the idea that the medical profession was acting in the best interests of its patients in its attack on its competitors. He concludes, 'We are asked to believe that it was not out of a "more self-interested desire" to protect themselves that the established profession attacked eclectic practitioners who were winning away their patients and reducing their incomes. But it is difficult to believe that any reader of the medical journals of the day could have thought otherwise.' Hamowy, *Canadian Medicine*, 65.
43 This was indicated during the health professions review of the 1980s.

4 The 1960s and 1970s

1 My intent here is merely to situate these institutional developments within the framework of this analysis. Detailed policy analyses of the development of hospital care and state funding have been provided elsewhere. For hospitalization, see the CHA Report, vol. 2, ch. 7; and Grove's contribution to that report J.W. Grove, *Organized Medicine in Ontario: A Study for the Committee on the Healing Arts* (Toronto: Queen's Printer, 1969), ch. 5. For the medicare story, see esp. Malcolm

Taylor, *Health Insurance and Canadian Public Policy: The Seven Decisions That Created the Canadian Health Insurance System* (Montreal: McGill-Queen's University Press, 1979). David C. Naylor, *Private Practice, Public Payment: Canadian Medicine and the Politics of Health Insurance 1911–1966* (Montreal: McGill-Queen's Press, 1986). Robert G. Evans and Greg Stoddart, eds., *Medicare at Maturity: Achievements, Lessons and Challenges* (Calgary: University of Calgary Press, 1986). Michael B. Decter, *Healing Medicare: Managing Health System Change the Canadian Way* (Toronto: McGilligan, 1994).

2 The relevant 'Medicare' legislation was the 1957 Hospital Insurance and Diagnostic Services Act, and the 1966–7 Medical Care Act, followed by OHIP extensions to other than medical practitioners in the 1970s.

3 'The medicare system put in place in the 1960s and early 1970s ... combined "centralized" and "public" payment ... with "decentralized" and "private" decision making about the pattern and volume of health care delivery.' Carolyn J. Tuohy, *Policy and Politics in Canada: Institutionalized Ambivalence* (Philadelphia: Temple University Press, 1992), 112–13. For a discussion of the 'institutionalized ambivalence' of the health care sector, see ibid., ch. 3.

4 State bureaucratic structures were set up at the national, provincial, and local levels. The main function of the federal government has been to provide advisory services to the provinces and financial assistance. At the provincial level, it is the MOH and its agencies which are responsible for health matters. At the local level, responsibility for health is concentrated on public health programs, but a growing number of linkages have begun to be developed with the provincial system through the expanding role of local district health councils and community clinics. For details see CHA Report, vol. 1, ch. 4. For a good (short) discussion of the relationship between the national and provincial institutions, see Malcolm Taylor, 'Health Insurance: The Roller-Coaster in Federal–Provincial Relations,' in David P. Shugarman and Reg Whitaker, eds., *Federalism and Political Community: Essays in Honour of Donald Smiley* (Peterborough, Ont: Broadview, 1989). Likewise, for Tuohy, *Policy and Politics*, ch. 3, 109–12, 129–30.

5 A report released in 1970 comments, 'One of the chief characteristics of Ontario's health care system is the diversity of institutions which have some role and influence in the provision of health care, among which there has been minimal communication or cooperation.' CHA Report, vol. 1, 91.

6 T.D. Hunter, 'Self-Run Hospitals,' quoted in Grove, *Organized Medicine*, 65.

7 Although price and volume allowances were set, these 'limits' were negotiated between the state and the medical profession's association (OMA) in an atmosphere which resulted in their being set at whatever level the medical profession considered to correspond to the free market level. As a result, they remained quite high, or open-ended, until recessionary times hit the province in the 1980s.

Notes to pages 54–5   269

8 Even today, high volume service providers such as chiropractors have much more restriction on price (with less than half of the price of their services reimbursed by the state) and volume (with a limit of approximately twenty-two visits per year regardless of the severity of the injury or disability of the patient) than do their medical counterparts. This situation exists despite the uncovering of facts such as the efficacy of chiropractic treatment and the inefficacy of very high volumes of general (medical) practitioner treatments. Pran Manga, Douglas E. Angus, Costa Papadopoulos, and William R. Swan, 'A Study to Examine the Effectiveness and Cost-Effectiveness of Chiropractic Management of Low-Back Pain,' funded by the Ontario MOH (1993). It is also estimated that $400 million per year is paid by the Canadian government to GPs/FPs for the useless 'treatment' of the common cold. CTV Televison, W5 with Eric Malling, 14 Apr. 1995. Rachlis and Kushner have also done extensive research into the need for 'house-cleaning' in health care. Michael Rachlis and Carol Kushner, *Second Opinion: What's Wrong with Canada's Health Care System and How to Fix It* (Toronto: Collins, 1989).
9 They were chiropractors, osteopaths, chiropodists, and optometrists.
10 The patient's expectation that the entrance into her hospital room of the white man, with the educated grammar of a 'good family,' marked the arrival of her doctor rather than her nurse or technician was in all probability correct – as was her inclination that the woman of colour attending her needs was more likely to be a nurse's assistant than a registered nurse or the head nurse of the ward.
11 Hunter, 'Self-Run Hospitals,' 65.
12 Grove, *Organized Medicine*, 21. Grove is referring here to Oswald Hall's discussion of sponsorship.
13 Nurses were needed in government-operated institutions such as hospitals, old age homes, and psychiatric institutions, as well as for the implementation of public health projects.
14 At the top are registered nurses who have passed registration standards set by the College of Nurses. They include both the university educated elite and the nurses educated in community colleges who are further down on the hierarchical ladder. (There is also a category of '"trained" but not registered nurses ... usually from abroad.') Then there are registered nursing assistants, renamed in the latest legislation as registered practical nurses, who perform routine nursing functions, often under the formal supervision of an RN, and who have had less education than the RNs, although they also have to meet standards set by the governing College of Nurses. Moving on down the hierarchy, the lowest ranks are the 'least "formally qualified" ... the orderlies, nurse's aides [what used to be called] "practical nurses," and psychiatric aides who perform a wide and ill-defined range of housekeeping, manual and other routine tasks in hospitals.' CHA Report, vol. 2, 158.
15 ONA was created by court order in 1973 as a separate bargaining unit for the origi-

nal association (RNAO). A split between it and the RNAO in 1975 represented a split between the elite and the rank and file: the former made up of management nurses and nurse educators with university degrees and a 'professional project'; the latter group made up mainly of rank-and-file nurses with community college or hospital training who continued 'to feel alienated and intimidated.' The quotes are taken from M.S. Larson and P.M. Jensen respectively in David Coburn, 'The Development of Canadian Nursing: Professionalization and Proletarianization,' *International Journal of Health Services*, 18/3 (1988),' 449.

16 Ibid., p. 448: 'Anything that smacked of unionization was the antithesis of the carefully nurtured image of professionalism that the nursing leadership had so painfully tried to construct. However, among many of the working nurses of the 1950s and 1960s the traditional orientation to nursing and the continual cries to be professional had become hollow in the face of economic and work pressures. The push for collective bargaining was thus part of a revolt by nurses against the timidity and the interest of their own leaders and associations.' See also Karen McSwain, 'If We Are Professionals, Why Are We on Strike?' *Canadian Nurse* (Dec., 1991), 17.

17 Carolyn Hughes (Tuohy), 'The Saskatchewan "Medicare" Crisis in 1962: A Case Study,' in Grove, *Organized Medicine*, 303–20; Carolyn J. Tuohy, 'Medicine and the State in Canada: The Extra-Billing Issue in Perspective,' *Canadian Journal of Political Science*, 21/2 (1988), 267–95.

18 An MOH representative had been placed on the professional council by a 1932 act, Elizabeth MacNab, *A Legal History of Health Professions in Ontario: A Study for the Committee on the Healing Arts* (Toronto: Queen's Printer, 1970), 43. But this had changed little.

19 Decter, *Healing Medicare*, 118.

20 Audience and consultation are difficult to distinguish because of the knowledge of intent they imply, but I am using the distinction here as an analyst who can look retroactively at the before and after of the relationship and judge which category best describes what went on, rather than trying to discover intent on the part of the director of the relationship. That is, the state actors appear to have given audience to certain groups when I look at the outcome of their relations.

21 These shifts became more important during the cost-control days of the 1990s. I will be returning to this spectrum in later discussion.

22 Dentists, or more correctly, oral surgeons, were also allowed to work in the hospitals, but theirs was not the position or the power of the medical professionals.

23 Ontario, *Report of the Royal Commission Inquiry into Civil Rights* (McRuer), (Toronto: Queen's Printer, 1968); POC, Report (Toronto: Queen's Printer, 1980); and the CHA Report. Causality cannot be proven here, of course. These earlier reports, however, are often quoted by policy designers in argument for particular ideational orientations. In the case of Ontario's most recent provider legislation, the

Notes to pages 58–9 271

1991 RHPA, references were made to these earlier reports in the discussions of mandate and guiding principles in its introductory draft form. HPLR, *Striking a New Balance: A Blueprint for the Regulation of Ontario's Health Professions* (Toronto: Queen's Printer, 1989).

24 One also hears this derision from the participants of these reports. This is mainly because of the lack of attention that the mid-1970s' 'revamping' legislation paid to the broad sweep of recommendations these reports had made – legislation which did very little overall revamping of the system, aside from measures which were taken to increase public accountability – which will be discussed later.

25 I am using the 1960s here rather loosely, as is often done in discussion of this period of change. Ideas generally have a complex developmental path, and I do not wish to imply otherwise by this usage. The 1960s' critiques, of course, had their proponents, such as Max Weber, Karl Marx, Gandhi, Jesus Christ, and so on back through time.

26 In 1960, Wolin comments, 'Among nineteenth-century writers the idea of organization was partly associated with economic or technological considerations, but in its mature form, such as we know it today, it has meant far more. Organization also signifies a method of social control, a means of imparting order, structure, and regularity to society.' Sheldon Wolin, *Politics and Vision: Continuity and Innovation in Western Political Thought* (Boston: Little, Brown, 1960), 364–5.

27 When a national medical insurance plan began to appear inevitable by the mid-1960s, Ontario set up its own inquiry into its provincial health care system and legislation. It announced the creation of the CHA in June 1966. Its term of reference was 'to enquire into and report upon all matters relating to the education and regulation relevant to the practice of the healing arts.' Its extensive reports were tabled in the legislature, April 1970. CHA Report, vol. 1, vii.

28 Grove, *Organized Medicine*, 13.

29 CHA Report, vol. 2, 249, 271.

30 Boase documents the lack of both bureaucratic and political will to implement the many CHA Report recommendations. With regard to the bureaucratic will, she quotes one official as admitting, 'No one knew what to do with it.' And with regard to the political will, she points out, 'The Report, which followed four years of extensive input from organizations and individuals and was a comprehensive analysis of the state of health care in Ontario, led to further study, increased interest group activity and a policy paper.' Joan Price Boase, 'Public Policy and the Regulation of the Health Disciplines: An Historical and Comparative Perspective' (PhD dissertation, York University, 1986), 74, 75.

31 Many of our health care practitioners have emigrated from the U.S.

32 It makes reference, e.g., to the 'illness and curative' orientation of the system which tended to override the alternative emphasis on 'states of health and an emphasis on

preventive measures.' Its authors also commented on the heavy influence of science and technology on the health sector. CHA Report, vol. 1, 8. See also ibid., vol. 3, 6.
33 Grove, *Organized Medicine*, 282.
34 Ibid., 11, ch. 9.
35 McRuer argued, e.g., with relation to dental hygienists and nursing assistants, regarding the 1960 Dentistry Act and the 1961–2 Nurses Act, 'No self-governing body should have statutory control over others who are not members of the body.' McRuer, Report, vol. 3, 1211. 'We see no justification for the present situations, which are thoroughly undemocratic.' Ibid., vol. 3, 1205. CHA had agreed in principle, but the HDA of 1974 had continued the practice.
36 See, e.g., Grove's chapter on the medical schools where, as he says, 'they socialize as well as train doctors.' Grove, *Organized Medicine*, 82, ch. 6.
37 The market mentality has, of course, been much criticized for its narrow interpretation of human interaction. At the time of the 1960s' and 1970s' critique, Macpherson translated these concerns into political analyses of the Canadian/Western situation. C.B. Macpherson, *The Life and Times of Liberal Democracy* (Oxford: Oxford University Press, 1977). Strong concerns remain about the liberal/market mind-set of contemporary society. Try as we might to view ourselves as economic units, the argument goes, we would never be able to act as apolitically as the logic implies. See, e.g., Deborah A. Stone, *Policy Paradox and Political Reason* (Glenview, IL: Scott, Foresman, 1988), 6–7, 53–65. Also see, e.g., Ronald Beiner, *What's the Matter with Liberalism?* (Berkeley: University of California Press, 1992); and Michael J. Sandel, ed., *Liberalism and Its Critics* (New York: New York University Press, 1984).
38 POC, in particular, focused on the need to open up health care to more competition, or deregulation. One academic participant in the POC study explained that there had been a legal and economic focus in the 1970s' academic literature on the professions: 'The central issue was anti-trust, and therefore deregulation, or pro-competition, [although] many were willing to admit health care might be one area of professionalism which needed [minimal] regulation.' So there was an assumption that POC principles would be set within an emphasis of minimal regulation. Interview with academic participant of POC, 8 Oct. 1992. Trebilcock's contribution to this school of thought is perhaps best summarized in his 1975 title 'Winners and Losers in the Modern Regulating System: Must the Consumer Always Lose?' *Osgoode Hall Law Journal*, no. 13 (1975). See also Michael J. Trebilcock, 'The Professions and Public Policy,' in Philip Slayton and Michael J. Trebilcock, eds., *The Professions and Public Policy* (Toronto: University of Toronto Press, 1978), 3–14.
39 Sylvia Ostry, 'Competition Policy,' 18–19; James Younger, 'Competition Policy,'

39; Ostry, 'Competition Policy,' 21; all in Slayton and Trebilcock, *The Professions and Public Policy.*
40 Carolyn J. Tuohy, 'Private Government, Property, and Prefessionalism,' *Canadian Journal of Political Science*, 9/4 (1976), 679–80.
41 We have seen this for the CHA in the above discussions, although there were also signs of elitism in its recommendations to limit the 'proliferation of professionalization,' restrict the title 'doctor,' and group all but the 'senior [or elite] professions' under one form of blanket legislation. CHA Report, vol. 2, 348, 251, 479. The authors also made reference to a more pluralist approach to health care, Ibid., vol. 1, 11; vol. 3, 7. The POC Report recommendations had emphasized the principles set forth by its participating academics; these had pointed to the importance of considering not only the interests of the elite professionals, but also those of the semi- or para-professionals and those of the public. For this, see the academic study for the POC Report by Michael J. Trebilcock, Carolyn J. Tuohy, and Alan D. Wolfson, *Professional Regulation* (a staff study of Accountancy, Architecture, Engineering and Law in Ontario, prepared for the POC, Jan. 1979.
42 As it stood, government policies could not be implemented without the concurrence of the governing body of a profession; disputes between professions could not be resolved; and coordination of the health professions was problematic.
43 The report referred to the need to balance individual rights with 'social needs.' CHA Report, vol. 1, 8–10, 12. It also drew on contemporary liberal welfare/market arguments related to principles of both redistribution and 'economy and efficiency ... [set in a world of] scarce resources.' Ibid., 11, 12; also see ibid., 89 and ch. 5; vol. 3, 49.
44 See, e.g., their discussion of the need for 'protection of vulnerable interests.' POC Report, 7–11.
45 CHA Report, vol. 1, 5; vol. 3; appendices 3–5.
46 POC, Report, 14.
47 The same has been true in the U.S. DeVries refers to 'the problem of consumer absence in the decisions and proposals of creative solutions for regulating health personnel [in the U.S.].' Raymond G. DeVries, 'The Contest for Control: Regulating New and Expanding Health Occupations,' *American Journal of Public Health* (Sept., 1986), 1147.
48 This is, of course, further complicated by the fact that various interest groups claim to represent portions of the public, but I am referring here to representation of the public or the patient body as a whole.
49 I am using Frank's three-way distinction here C.E.S. Franks, *The Parliament of Canada*, (Toronto: University of Toronto Press, 1987), 233.
50 McRuer Report, vol. 3, 1162.

274   Notes to pages 62–4

51   See the 'Guiding Principles for the Regulation and Education of the Health Disciplines' released by Ontario Minister Wells, in 1971, after consultation with his bureaucracy and the provider groups. It also recommended the establishment of a 'Health Disciplines Regulation Board.'
52   POC Report, 7–11; see also, Alan D. Wolfson, Michael J. Trebilcock, and Carolyn J. Tuohy, 'Regulating the Professions: A Theoretical Framework,' in Simon Rottenberg, ed., *Occupational Licensure and Regulation* (Washington: American Enterprise Institute for Public Policy Research, 1980), 182–4.
53   HPLR, *Striking*, 6. RHPA, c.18. Furthermore, I heard this often from the ministry officials and the minister.
54   CHA Report, vol. 1, 10, 9. One of the mechanisms suggested for the more direct public voice was a health commissioner's office which would function as a public ombudsman 'with broad jurisdiction and wide powers of investigation.' Carolyn J. Tuohy, 'Public Accountability of Professional Groups: The Case of the Legal Profession in Ontario,' in R.G. Evans and M.J. Trebilcock, eds., *Lawyers and the Consumer Interest* (Toronto: Butterworths, 1982), 109.
55   Tuohy, 'Public Accountability,' 108.
56   I am referring to their fourth 'principle' here. POC Report, 15–17.
57   Tuohy, 'Public Accountability,' 131.
58   Tuohy has discussed these recommendations and the ensuing failure to incorporate most of them into the 1974 HDA, see ibid.
59   Ibid., 107–8.
60   CHA Report, vol. 1, 7.
61   Tuohy, 'Public Accountability,' 108.
62   Ibid., 109; also POC Report, 7–11.
63   Malcolm Taylor, 'Health Insurance,' in Shugarman and Whitaker, eds. *Federalism*, 80.
64   These particulars are explained in a clear and concise manner in Carolyn Hughes Tuohy, *Accidental Logics: The Dynamics of Change in the Health Care Arena in Britain, the United States, and Canada* (Toronto: Oxford University Press, 1999), ch. 7.
65   Tuohy foresaw this shift some time ago when she argued that governments were 'redefining the social responsibilities of the professions to include financial responsibility, a responsibility for cost control.' Tuohy, 'Private Government,' 678. For a recent discussion of this concern from a former Ontario Deputy Minister of Health, see Decter, *Healing Medicare*.
66   Trebilcock, Tuohy, and Wolfson, *Professional Regulation*. A good discussion of the reasoning behind this and other principles utilized by the POC academic staff can be found in Wolfson, Trebilcock, and Tuohy, 'Regulating the Professions,' in Rot-

tenberg, *Occupational Licensure*; and for a discussion of the importance of efficiency see ibid., 186; also, POC Report, 15.
67 CHA Report, vol. 1, 11–12.
68 Tuohy, 'Public Accountability,' 109. Tuohy has summarized the developments of the HDA in this article, as well as in Carolyn J. Tuohy, 'Conflict and Accommodation,' in Evans and Stoddart, *Medicare at Maturity*, 408. A more detailed analysis can be found in Tuohy, 'Private Government.'
69 Tuohy, 'Public Accountability,' 110.
70 That is, the minister of health could review these regulations as well as recommend new ones, while the lieutenant governor in council could approve the professional regulations or enforce the passing of regulations that the minister had initiated. Tuohy argued that these mechanisms of governmental input ought also to have been held up to democratic scrutiny via accountability mechanisms linked to our broad political channels of the executive and legislature. Ibid., 113, 134.
71 Ibid., 109–10. One-quarter of the members of the governing council and one member of each college committee were to be public members.
72 Ibid., 134–5. In these recommendations, Tuohy was, of course, sometimes reinforcing earlier recommendations (already discussed) of which she had been a part in the POC process.
73 CHA had recommended repeal of the DPA and the Chiropody Act – with the chiropodists (recommendation 191), physiotherapists (rec. 206), massage therapist (rec. 225), chiropractors (rec. 289), and osteopaths (rec. 275) to be given licensure under a new Health Disciplines Regulatory Board. It had also recommended the naturopaths be given exemption under the Medical Act, an exemption which encompassed a broad scope of practice for the naturopaths, if they complied with the requirement of notification of their practice to the MOH (rec. 291). The committee had also recommended the certification (by the same board) of occupational therapists (rec. 217), remedial gymnasts (rec. 222), speech–language pathologists and audiologists (rec. 240), and health technologists (rec. 263). The five practitioner groups included in the new legislation were medicine, dentistry, pharmacy, nursing, and optometry.
74 Tuohy refers to these changes as 'largely symbolic in effect.' Tuohy, 'Conflict and Accommodation,' 408. One of the key players in the development of the RHPA referred to the existing model, i.e., the judicial-like structures of the HDA as 'not even being particularly effective in preventing unauthorized practice' (supposedly its most highly pursued 'obligation'). Linda Bohnen, 'In Defense of the Health Professions Legislation Review,' *Health Law in Canada*, 10/2 (1989), 164.
75 This is a term Archer uses. Margaret Archer, *Culture and Agency: The Place of Culture in Social Theory* (Cambridge: Cambridge University Press, 1988), xv. A library is meant here as an active place where books are used.

276 Notes to pages 70–1

5 Overview of the 1980s' Ontario HPLR Process

1 This section is meant only to provide an overview with which to understand the discussions of the following chapters; more details will be provided throughout the remainder of this work. For an excellent detailed legal account of the resulting legislation, see Linda Bohnen, *Regulated Health Professions Act: A Practical Guide* (Aurora, Ont: Canada Law Book, 1994).
2 Bureaucratic and government insiders commented in interviews with me that the minister was 'sick and tired' of not being able to get anything done because of the constant meetings with disaffected health provider groups and companies. According to an official report, Minister Larry Grossman had 'met with some 80 different special interest groups' prior to the HPLR process. Ontario, MOH, *Health Care in the 80's and Beyond: Seeking Consensus* (Toronto: Queen's Printer, 1983), 6.
3 The oft-repeated justification for the huge sum of money spent on this external review, a mere decade after the costly and lengthy review by the CHA was that such delicate matters required 'objective analysis.' There was a widely held assumption in the bureaucracy that all the health practitioners, other than the medical profession and dentistry, considered the bureaucracy so biased in favour of the two dominant groups (medicine and dentistry) that any fair assessment would have to be done outside the ministry.
4 The founder and managing director of Canada Consulting Group Inc. (CCG) was James D. Fisher who had previously done consultant work for the Ontario MOH, as well as other federal and provincial ministries and legislative select committees. According to the acknowledgments of Schwartz's report, Fisher 'provided a strong conceptual framework for the Review.' The senior associate consultant of CCG was Morrey M. Ewing. He analysed the many participant submissions to the review (ibid). Also working on various aspects of the project were Daphne Wagner (a lawyer), Derrick Milne (the database and information system coordinator of CCG), Matt Holland (who worked on the scope-of-practice issue), and Linda Bohnen (a lawyer who joined the HPLR in its last year but then went on to work as the legal counsel for the MOH branch which was handed the review's report).
5 Ontario, MOH, 'A Proposal to Modernize and Restructure the Legislation Governing the Health Professions,' 13 Sept. (1982), 15–17.
6 The HPLR report notes that the review team 'was made fully aware of the Ministry's policy objectives' throughout the process. HPLR, *Striking a New Balance: A Blueprint for the Regulation of Ontario's Health Professions* (Toronto: Queen's Printer, 1989), 5. Also, MOH policy coordinator Paul Gardner played a not unimportant role in the whole process.
7 Interview with review team member, 8 Dec. 1992.
8 Ontario, MOH Management Consulting Services, 'Request for Proposal: Health

Professions Legislation Review' (Project I – Tender No.: 17-302, Project II – Tender No.: 17-303), 6.
9 HPLR, *Striking*, 5.
10 Ibid.
11 CCG, 'Renewing the Regulatory Framework: A Response to Pressure and Change in a New Health Environment' (May, 1983). Tuohy and Trebilcock had acted as research directors for the project, and Dupré had been one of the three committee members who produced the report.
12 Interview with review team member, 8 Dec. 1992. I was also told these ideas were reinforced by Wagner who was a member of the HPLR who had formerly been a student of Trebilcock.
13 Interview with review team member, 8 Dec. 1992.
14 Ibid., 21 Jan. 1992.
15 HPLR, *Striking*, 2–17. It should be noted that this introduction was written at the end of the process by *one* of the participants – albeit a rather influential one, in that she (Bohnen) was to provide a key link between the review process and the actual drafting of the legislation itself. See Appendix 3 of this work for a list of the ideas which dominate that report.
16 See Appendix 4 for a list of these criteria.
17 HPLR, *Striking*, 9–10.
18 Ibid., 9, 13.
19 The first three questions concentrated on self-regulation (Was it advisable? And, if so, what form should it take?), while the last nineteen concentrated on specific regulatory issues, such as scope of practice and discipline.
20 Cover letter sent out with '22 Topics' package.
21 The longer list is available in HPLR, *Striking*, and the shorter list is given below.
22 Other responses had come from 'public interest groups and advocacy organizations ... health care institutions and unions,' but my focus here will be the practitioner groups. HPLR, *Striking*, 6.
23 There is no clear-cut list (at least not in the papers allowed the public) of all the 'approximately 75' aspiring health care professionals. I have made up this list from a number of participant lists and any other information that I came across in my research. It may not be perfectly accurate, but it should be close.
24 HPLR, *Striking*, 6.
25 Ibid.
26 Ibid.
27 Osteopaths were included under a special provision of the Medical Act in the 1991 version of the legislation, however, by final proclamation in 1994 they had been taken out of the Medical Act at the request of the medical profession and have since remained outside the RHPA, once again governed under the DPA.

278 Notes to pages 78–83

28 The former would establish each profession's (or cluster of two professions') regulation-making authority, the size and composition of its governing body committees, any title protection given the profession, and the scope of practice and licensed acts of the profession (explained below). The latter uniform or omnibus statute would establish common organizational, legal, and procedural provisions for all of the professions, as well as lay out the role of the minister, the Health Professions Board, and the HPRAC (explained below).
29 Ibid., 8. The most basic principle was that the '[state] grant of self-regulatory powers ... [was] limited in many ways ... [in order] to provide the public with an assurance that its rights and interests are protected and also to protect the rights of individual practitioners.' HPLR, 'Legal and Procedural Issues,' 1–2. That is, the traditional influence and responsibility of the professional governing body was to become more balanced by the public interest, and by due process for offending or aspiring professionals. The other so-called principles were really just blueprints, such as lay representation on governing councils, and so on, to ensure compliance with the basic principle (above). Quotes are taken from HPLR, *Striking*, Introduction.
30 HPLR, *Striking*, 8.
31 Ibid.
32 Ontario, MOH, public communication.
33 It also ensured a strong legal focus, since she is a lawyer.
34 The legislation went to first reading on 2 Apr. 1991, 2nd reading on 29 May 1991, 3rd reading on 21 Nov., 1991, royal assent on 25 Nov., 1991, and proclamation on 31 Dec., 1993.
35 Although Conservative Minister Larry Grossman initiated the project, Liberal Minister Elinor Caplan did the bulk of the labour during her tenure, and she continued to shape the legislation in her role as Opposition Health Critic when her party left power. She also sat on the parliamentary committee which examined the proposed legislation.

6 Expertise Turf Wars

1 Tuohy quotes this from a member of a labour union commenting on a similar process in another province. Carolyn J. Tuohy, 'Institutions and Interests In the Occupational Health Arena: The Case of Quebec,' in William D. Coleman and Grace Skogstad, eds., *Policy Communities and Public Policy in Canada* (Mississauga: Copp Clark Pitman, 1990), 260.
2 Ontario, MOH, 'A Proposal to Modernize and Restructure the Legislation Governing the Health Professions' (13 Sept. 1982), 15–17.
3 The existing legislation comprised of the HDA for some, the DPA for others, and group-specific legislation for still others.

Notes to pages 83–5   279

4 HPLR, *Striking a New Balance: A Blueprint for the Regulation of Ontario's Health Professions* (Toronto: Queen's Printer, 1989), Introduction.
5 Ibid., 15.
6 Ibid., Introduction.
7 Ibid.
8 See below for modifications made to this definition.
9 Ibid., Introduction.
10 I am returning here to the practitioner practice categories I have designed for this work (see Table 2.2).
11 As late as Feb. 1987 (the final hour of the HPLR), the CPSO had joined with the colleges of other health professionals controlled under the 1974 HDA (dentistry, pharmacy, nursing, and optometry) to present a joint submission, arguing, among other things, against the HPLR's 'concept of defined scopes of practices and licensed acts for each profession.' RCDSO, CPSO, CNO, COO, and CPhO joint submission to HPLR (Feb. 1987).
12 They also paid little heed to the old elitist claims such as that made by the OMA, in its June 1984 submission, where it referred to the physician's 'sacred trust' which asserts 'that a person who holds this [medical] professional standing must exercise a higher standard of moral conduct than might be the societal norm'; although that same submission indicated this higher standard did not imply that the medical professional was to be held as accountable for her or his actions as the rest of society. OMA submission to HPLR (June 1984), 19, 20.
13 RHPA, c.18–39.
14 Ibid., c.18 s.30(1).
15 The definition of diagnosis contains a long struggle which continues today. The RHPA, 1991, defines it as 'Communicating to the individual or his or her personal representative a diagnosis identifying a disease or disorder as the cause of symptoms of the individual in circumstances in which it is reasonably foreseeable that the individual or his or her personal representative will rely on the diagnosis.' Ibid., s.27(2.1).
16 OMA submission to HPLR (Dec. 1983), 6, 11, 12; ODA submission to HPLR (Dec. 1983), 4, 23, 24, 30.
17 Chapters 6 and 7 give examples of claims and evidence suggesting that many less-elite practitioners are more capable of performing specialized tasks than are the medical practitioners, especially the non-specialist MDs (GPs or FPs,) who are allowed to cross over into the areas of practice of most of these other practitioners.
18 Pran Manga, and others, 'A Study to Examine the Effectiveness and Cost-Effectiveness of Chiropractic Management of Low-Back Pain' (funded by the Ontario MOH, Aug. 1993). Manga and Angus released a second report on 28 Apr. 1998. http://www.chiropractic.on.ca/execsummary.html

280 Notes to pages 85–7

19 OMA backed up its arguments for medicine's exclusive primary contact and undifferentiated diagnosis (except in the area of dentistry) by emphasizing the advantage of continuity of care provided by physicians. But again, policy analyses from the 1960s on have all emphasized the increasingly fragmented nature of medical care. OMA submission to HPLR (June 1984), 14. J.W. Grove, *Organized Medicine in Ontario: A Study for the Committee of the Healing Arts* (Toronto: Queen's Printer, 1969), 11. One of the important arguments made by advocates of midwifery, e.g., was that medical supervision of the birth process has become so fragmented that the mother might have to deal with a dozen different health practitioners during its course; while midwives, in contrast, provide continuity of care throughout the entire birth process. Elinor Barrington, *Midwifery Is Catching* (Toronto: NC Press, 1985), 130–4. The 1987 Ontario Task Force on midwifery also found that continuity of care would be enhanced over that of the medical profession through the implementation of midwifery care in Ontario. *Report of the Task Force on the Implementation of Midwifery in Ontario* (Toronto: Queen's Printer, 1987), 13, 15. See n20 for the family physician's position on this.
20 FPs argue that they 'not only have the best picture of the patient, but also of the total health care system.' Interview with family physicians college official, 16 June 1998. (The GP, who was required to have one year of postgraduate training, is being phased out in Ontario for the FP, who is required to have two to three years of postgraduate training.)
21 By 1998 midwives and nurse practitioners were also being allowed to 'communicate diagnoses.' Interview with nurse practitioner coordinator, 2 June 1998.
22 Although all of these definitions underwent constant adjustment or revision, the term 'assessment' was defined as 'the evaluation of a patient's physical or mental state in order to determine whether a treatment within the health professional's scope of practice is appropriate to the patient's condition and if so, in what manner it ought to be applied or administered, and includes communication of the evaluation to the patient and his or her representative.' HPLR, *Striking*, 120.
23 The dissatisfied practitioners might ultimately be proven right in their scepticism, since there can be no guarantee that the courts will not distinguish, unfavourably for them, between diagnosis and assessment.
24 Interview with HPLR team member, 21 Jan. 1992. Any idea that the HPLR 'was just another study' was soon put to rest, particularly when the practitioner groups received the review team's replies to their first submissions replete with demands for clarification and proof of the exaggerated claims of those submissions.
25 HPLR, *Striking*, Introduction.
26 For elaboration of these comments to the medical profession, as well as similar ones made in Grossman's public announcement of the HPLR process, see Joan

Price Boase, 'Public Policy and the Regulation of the Health Disciplines,' (PhD dissertation, York University, 1986) 178–82.
27 HPLR team member interview, 11 July 1986; HPLR, *Striking*, Introduction.
28 See, e.g., CPSO submission to HPLR (Dec. 1983), 5, 16; or OMA submission to HPLR (Dec. 1983), 21.
29 Linda Bohnen, 'In Defense of the Health Professions Legislation Review,' *Health Law in Canada*, 10/2 (1989), 166.
30 RCDSO, CPSO, CNO, COO, CPhO joint submission to HPLR (4 Feb. 1987).
31 Chiropractors, historically, and still to some extent today, also saw themselves as whole body practitioners. I have categorized them as technique specialists, however, because that is the form their practices tend to take.
32 See Board of Directors of Drugless Therapy (BDDT), e.g., submission to HPLR (Dec. 1983), 3, 4–5, 9–10, and (June 1984), 13–18, 26. Although the association makes the claim, in the opening lines of its initial brief, that 'the profession of naturopathic medicine does not advocate a position as an alternative of existing medical practices utilized and provided by licensed physicians and surgeons,' they then go on to speak of their profession in exactly the same terms as their licensing board does, ending with the exact same 'wish list.' ONaA submission to HPLR (Dec. 1983), 1–5, 11–12, and (June 1984), 2–7, 12–15.
33 RCHS concluded that the naturopaths were 'not scientifically oriented to the extent they should be included as providers of services to be paid for under comprehensive health services.' RCHS Report, vol. 2 (Ottawa: Queen's Printer, 1964–5), 80. CHA recommended that the naturopaths be deregulated and left to practice a limited range of relatively harmless activities as long as the public was willing to pay for them. CHA Report, rec. 291. Grove, however, recommended that they be placed 'under a firmer measure of public control.' Grove, *Organized Medicine,* 283. Gort and Coburn give some good examples of the ineptitude of the naturopaths in their attempts to portray themselves as medical scientists. Elaine H. Gort and David Coburn, 'Naturopathy in Canada: Changing Relationships to Medicine, Chiropractic and the State, *Social Science Medicine*, 26/10 (1988).
34 BDDT submission to HPLR (Dec. 1983), 1; ONaA submission to HPLR (June 1984), 5.
35 The HPLR team, MOH officials, and ministers did appear to put considerable effort into allowing the naturopaths leeway to argue their case. It was not for lack of opportunity that they failed to do so during the HPLR/RHPA process. See Appendix 7 for the other problematic criteria.
36 Ontario, MOH, *News Release* (3 Apr. 1986).
37 Lorrie Goldstein, 'He's Out of Breath,' *Toronto Sun*, 8 Sept. 1987, 46.
38 The penalty for doing so was set at a fine of up to $25,000 and/or imprisonment for up to six months. RHPA, c.18 s.40.

39 Patricia Wales, CBC Radio, *Morningside*, 'Special on Alternative Medicine,' 3 Oct. 1989.
40 The potential for other (regulated) practitioners to move into the unregulated practitioners' practice territory was exacerbated by the fact that the new legislation was open to evolving scope-of-practice statements and controlled acts. RHPA groups could push to license even more of the unregulated practitioners' expertise territory in the future.
41 The NDP, which is sympathetic to the underdog and was politically indebted to left-wing interest groups for their rise to power in the province, tends to support alternative or fringe health practitioner groups, such as the naturopaths.
42 There is a transcript of the public meeting held prior to the HPRAC report. HPRAC, 'Transcript of Public Meeting: Naturopathy' (3–4 Nov. 1995).
43 Interview with naturopathy association official, 29 May 1998.
44 Minister of Health, letter to OANaD president, 31 July 1998.
45 Follow-up conversation (interview) with naturopathy association official, 18 Aug. 1998.
46 Minister of Health, letter to OANaD president, 31 July 1998. It is also noted here that HPRAC had only recently been restored to its statutory minimum number of council members, which accounted for some of the delay.
47 They had, however, been granted limited OHIP coverage. CHA had recommended, in 1970, that osteopaths be reimbursed by OHIP for the same type of manipulative services for which physicians and physiotherapists were being reimbursed. CHA Report, rec. 274. They aslo recommended that the licensing of osteopathy (with a repeal of the DPA) with a scope of practice which did not 'extend beyond that which is presently permitted osteopaths under the Drugless Practitioners Act' – in other words, with a very limited scope of practice compared with that allowed in the U.S. Ibid., rec. 275, 276.
48 In the U.S. osteopaths have been trained in the same manner as students of the medical profession, with the addition of courses on muscular–skeletal 'manipulative therapeutics' and 'palpatory structural diagnosis.' Submission to HPLR (June 1984), 2. There is some suspicion among policy analysts who have looked at the U.S. osteopathic profession that it is well on its way to becoming either amalgamated into the orthodox medical profession, or becoming more 'medicine' than Medicine. Norman Gevitz, 'Osteopathic Medicine,' in Gevitz, ed., *Other Healers: Unorthodox Medicine in America* (Baltimore: Johns Hopkins University Press, 1988), 149–56. In a 1998 inverview with a Canadian MD, who has also trained in osteopathic therapy, I was told that in the U.S. most osteopathic MDs practice predominantly as MDs (using drugs and surgery) and practice very little osteopathic manual therapy; some rural GPs combine general medicine with osteopathic; some medical specialists combine osteopathic with their specialties (e.g., surgery); and,

Notes to pages 91–3   283

lastly, about 10 per cent of osteopathic doctors practice predominantly osteopathic manual therapy. Interview with Canadian osteopathic doctor, 18 June 1998.
49 OOA submission to HPLR (June 1984), 3.
50 This was in keeping with the recommendations of both their association (the OOA) and their governing body (the board of directors of osteopathy, BDO. OOA submission to HPLR (Dec. 1983), 8; BDO submission to HPLR (Dec. 1984), 8; The Medicine Act, 1991, S.O., c.30 s.9(1)(3).
51 An inspector for the CPSO found the Canadian standards of training for osteopathy to be far below those of osteopathic training facilities in the U.S. (with which an American-trained Canadian osteopath who had formerly been a member of the BDO of Ontario, concurred). Interview with former member of the BDO, 30 Jan. 1997. This was coupled with the fact that a decision during the drafting of the legislation had been made not to allow further registration of U.S.-trained osteopaths as physicians under the CPSO.
52 A BDO was appointed in 1993. However, its members' term expired in April 1995, and no new members had been appointed as of July 1999.
53 Graduates are not allowed to use the title 'osteopath' since it is a protected title. They must refer to themselves as 'practitioners in manual practice.' Telephone conversation with Osteopathic Centre of Canada student, 28 May 1998 and 9 July 1999. Enrolment and graduate numbers were given as 204 in mid-1999.
54 Interview with member of 'Transitional Council for the College of Osteopathic Manual Practitioners of Ontario, 18 June 1998.
55 Ibid.
56 Homeopathic representation on the council of the CPSO had ceased in 1960 with the death of a long-standing homeopathic representative. CHA Report, vol. 2, 109.
57 During the CHA study, the homeopaths made submissions under the name Homeopathic Laymen's League, 'which consisted of twelve to fifteen individuals striving to promote homeopathy in Ontario.' Ibid., 109.
58 Interview with OAH member, 18 Jan. 1994. It is interesting to note that of the twelve-member faculty teaching their courses, five have MDs, one a PhD in physiology, and one an MSc in pharmacology, with the rest designating themselves as 'doctors of naturopathy.' Courses consist of 600 hours of homeopathic instruction and 730 hours of training in the sciences – 'focusing on Environmental Medicine.' This information is taken from the course literature available from the International Academy of Homeopathy and Toronto Homeopathic Clinic (Toronto, 1994).
59 Follow-up interviews of the leadership of Ontario's naturopathy, homeopathy, and osteopathy after the enacting of the RHPA still elicited enthusiastic responses to the idea of their joining the establishment.
60 Ernst W. Stieb, *One Hundred Years of Organized Pharmacy* (Toronto: Canadian Academy of the History of Pharmacy, 1967), 22.

61 In practice, they hold such a monopoly, but legally in Ontario physicians and dentists can also dispense drugs to their patients. OCPh submission to HPLR (Dec. 1983), 2.
62 One of the problems with the legislation covering pharmacy which was looked at by the CHA involved the fact that a retail pharmacy could not open its drug dispensary without a pharmacist present, although a hospital pharmacy was not even required to employ a pharmacist. Despite questioning of this practice by the CHA, the HDA did not change it. CHA Report, vol. 2, 526. During the HPLR process, this contradiction was again brought up by the pharmacists. OCPh submission to HPLR (Dec. 1983), 5, and (June 1984), 2; OphA submission to HPLR (Apr. 1984), 6. Since many hospitals did, at the time, employ pharmacists, the point here must have been to close off the option of budget-slashing hospital managers replacing hospital pharmacists (of which there were 700 practising in 1982) with cheaper, non-pharmacist personnel. The number comes from an MOH policy conference paper presented by the OCPh in Apr. 1983, and included by them in their Dec. 1983 submission to HPLR. OCPh, 'A Background Paper on the Role of Pharmacists in Health Care,' submission to HPLR (Dec. 1983), 1.
63 'These [hospital] pharmacies [they said], operated by "not-for-profit" institutions, compete with privately owned community pharmacies and have an unfair competitive advantage over them. Hospitals do not pay taxes. They buy drugs at prices considerably below those at which community pharmacies buy them [etc] ... If it is not corrected quickly ... this very serious problem ... [could] bring about the closing of many *free enterprise community pharmacies*' (emphasis added). OphA submission to HPLR (Apr. 1984), 6.
64 These measures are contained in the RHPA, the Drug Pharmacies Regulation Act (sec. 118), and the Public Hospitals Act. Pharmacists also won title protection against pharmacy PhDs working in a pharmacy as a 'doctor.' Interview with pharmacy college employee, 29 Sept. 1994.
65 Health Disciplines Act, 1974, S.O. s.138.
66 CHA Report, vol. 2, 241–2; HPLR Report, 295.
67 Drug Pharmacies Regulation Act, s.142.
68 OPhA submission to HPLR (Apr. 1984), 3–5.
69 Pharmacy Act, 1991, S.O. c.36 s.3.
70 OCPh submission to HPLR (June 1984), 3; also see, OCPh, 'A Background Paper on the Role of Pharmacists in Health Care,' presented at an MOH Policy Conference, Apr. 1983, and included in the OCPh, submission to HPLR (Dec. 1983). There was also some concern for the overlap of this function with the same by the nurses. Ibid., 2.
71 See, e.g., the 'Health Watch Reminder' provided by Shoppers Drug Mart, or the 'Patient Advisory Leaflets' provided at the Boots Drugstores. Ellen Roseman,

'Drug Factsheets: A New Approach to Prescriptions' *Globe and Mail*, 23 Jan. 1984, B3.
72 OPhA, 'A Background Paper,' 2–3; interview with pharmacy college employee, 18 Feb. 1997.
73 Philip Isbister (college solicitor, OCPh), 'Patient Counselling – Professional Liability,' *On Continuing Practice*, 16/3 (1989), 2. The overkill lies just over the line between educating and frightening the patient. Some medical practitioners do not themselves inform their patients and so are reluctant to have someone else performing this function. Interview, with pharmacy college employee, 18 Feb. 1997.
74 OCPh, *Member's Dialogue* (Summer 1996).
75 The college and association have been involved, on and off (along with medicine's college and association), in a Drug Utilization Review Steering Committee set up in 1993 to look at drug utilization regarding eligibility, dispensing, prescribing, and manufacturing. Interview with pharmacy college employee, 18 Feb. 1997. The pharmacy association has also been involved with the MOH in a memorandum of understanding (linked to the government's drug benefits program) to look at 'appropriate use of medications ... to review patient's education and counselling by pharmacists and the appropriate use of prescription drugs and medications ... and to study the possibility of creating a trial prescription plan.' OPhA, *News Release* (26 Sept. 1996).
76 HPLR Report, 295.
77 Pharmacy Act, 1991, S.O. c.36 s.3 and s.4.
78 See, e.g., their interpretation of professional judgment, in OCPh submission to HPLR (June 1984), 3.
79 OCPh, 'A Background Paper,' 4.
80 Interview with pharmacy college employee, 29 Sept. 1994.
81 Interview with pharmacy college official, 14 Aug. 1998.
82 Laurel Leff, 'Pharmacists to Prescribe Drugs: Florida's Druggists Will be First to Write Prescriptions,' *Miami Herald*, 29 Dec. 1985, F1.
83 Ibid. There has also been a move in some states to 'grant [pharmacists] the authority to begin "therapeutic substitution" of [similar but not chemically identical] drugs prescribed by physicians.' Editorial, 'Should Pharmacists Have the Right to Second-Guess You?' *Medicine Economics* (20 Feb. 1984), 15.
84 Leff, 'Pharmacists.'
85 Follow-up conversation with pharmacy college official, 14 Aug. 1998 and 9 July 1999.
86 Ibid.
87 Pharmacists, e.g., would have discretion to give out a bit more medication for which a prescription has expired on, say the Friday of a long weekend. OphA submission to HPLR (Dec. 1983), 3.

286 Notes to pages 96–7

88 The Drug Interchangeability and Dispensing Fee Act (previously the Prescription Drug Cost Regulation Act) allows for this sort of professional judgment with regard to the dispensing of smaller quantities – without mention of larger quantities.
89 Interview with former senior civil servant, 28 Apr. 1994. Another insider commentator put it more crudely, referring to the 'less-than-a-dollar professional fee' corporations as 'the whores of pharmacy practice.' Editorial, 'Those Whores of Pharmacy: Creative Tactics Needed to Root Out This Evil,' *Drug Merchandising* (July 1989), 8.
90 See, e.g., Arnold S. Relman, 'What Market Values Are Doing to Medicine,' *Atlantic Monthly* (Mar. 1992), 99–106.
91 Two of the largest in Ontario in the mid-1990s were Meditrust and Pharmex. Both the association and the college spoke out against them. City TV, *Eye on Toronto*, Toronto, 29 July 1993; CBC Television, *Marketplace*, 'Special on Mail-order Pharmacies,' 25 Jan. 1994.
92 Whereas a standard pharmacist's fee at a community drugstore was approximately $11–$12 (in 1994), the mail-order companies first reduced this to about $5, then, with the giant drugstores following suit, dropped it again, and so on. Interview with former senior civil servant, 28 Apr. 1994. In early 1999 the Pharmacare Drugstore chain purchased Meditrust. Global Television, *Global News*, 25 Jan. 1999.
93 These companies do employ pharmacists, but, of course, working as an employee of a large company does not allow for the same independence as running one's own business. Assumedly the mail order companies would also employ far fewer pharmacists as supervisors than a company that has its pharmacists counting pills and doing other unskilled activities. On the positive side of the new developments, though, one Meditrust pharmacist did say, in a television interview, that her work there was much more satisfying than any of her previous traditional-type pharmacy jobs. She said, 'We do more counselling here than I ever have anywhere else.' The mail-order customers interviewed for the same television program said the Meditrust pharmacists were more helpful than any they had ever had, plus they liked the fact that they could tell their 'embarrassing medical problems' to someone over the phone in the privacy of their home, rather than shouting them over the counter of a crowded store. CBC Television, *Marketplace*, 'Special on Mail-order Pharmacies.'
94 Mail-order pharmacies have been trying to convince some doctors to send their patients directly to the mail-order system, with a dispensing fee being paid to the doctor and absorbed by the company. This would not entail any extra work, aside from some paperwork for the doctor, so it may just prove attractive, especially if the medical doctors perceive the pharmacists to be invading their prescription territory. The medical profession's college, however, may not like the idea of the physician sullying her or his professional reputation with merchant activities.

95 Carolyn Tuohy and Patricia O'Reilly, 'Professionalism in the Welfare State,' *Journal of Canadian Studies*, 27/1 (1992), 74. Tuohy has also pointed to the importance of this distinction in her earlier work.
96 Political analysts would refer to this as 'symbolic politics,' where the myth of, say authority, takes on a certain reality, at least for a time. For general political science discussion, see, e.g., Murray Edelman, *Symbolic Uses of Politics* (Urbana: University of Illinois Press, 1964). For health care politics discussion, see Carolyn J. Tuohy, 'Medicine and the State in Canada: The Extra-Billing Issue in Perspective,' *Canadian Journal of Political Science*, 21/2 (1988), 267–95.
97 Conversation with civil servant, 21 Mar. 1990. These concerns could only have been reinforced during this policy process by a series of articles in a major Canadian newspaper, in 1985, concerning the violation of the HDA by pharmacy *College Council members* who were found to be acting illegally (along with many other pharmacy professionals) by overcharging consumers for prescription drugs by means of a higher dispensing fee than allowed by law. The officials of self-governance were themselves ignoring the laws of that governance. See, e.g., Duncan McMonagle and Ann Silversides, 'Minister to Call in Druggists on Inflated Dispensing Fees,' *Globe and Mail*, 25 Sept. 1985, 1; and Ann Silversides, 'Drug Overcharging Surprises Watchdog,' *Globe and Mail*, 26 Sept. 1985, 2.
98 OPhA, Press Release (26 Sept. 1996).
99 http://www.newsworld.cbc.ca/archive/html/1998.01.19/pharma98 0119e.html
100 RCDSO submission to HPLR (Jan. 1987), 59. To the denturists' claim that they can, and do, refer the necessary patients to dentists, the latter replies, 'To suggest that a denturist will refer a patient whose remaining natural teeth may be compromised begs the question of the lack of competence of a denturist to recognize a contingent threat to the remaining natural teeth.' RCDSO submission to HPLR (June 1984), 16.
101 To avoid confusion, I am using only the term 'denturist' here, because that is the nomenclature now in use. The denturists were, however, still legally referred to as 'denture therapists' (under the Denture Therapists Act of 1974) at the time of the HPLR, although the term 'denturist' (preferred by its bearers) had also been in popular use for some time. The new legislation prohibits the use of the old term, 'denture therapist.'
102 Ibid., 15; GBDT submission to HPLR (June 1984), sec. II, 4.
103 DAC submission to HPLR (Aug. 1984), 20.
104 GBDT submission to HPLR (June 1984), 7, 23.
105 Done by a respected legal academic, Prof. Bernard Dickens, in Jan. 1981, the report was entitled 'Report of a Review of Denture Services Related to the Denture Therapists Act, 1974.' DAO submission to HPLR (Jan. 1984), 6.
106 Ibid., 17.

288   Notes to pages 99–100

107 These products are used throughout Canada. The association referred to a B.C. Denticare program, where the public were free to obtain the services of either a dentist or a denturist, and they chose 60 per cent of the time to obtain their dentures from a denturist despite the fact there are ten times as many dentists as denturists in the province. DAC submission to HPLR (Aug. 1984), 2. In a 1986 article on denturists, Anne Murphy points to a survey in Ontario which indicated that approximately 50,000 partial dentures were installed by denturists between 1976 and 1978. In a price comparison, she notes that in 1986, while a denturist charged $400–$600 for a complete set of full dentures, a dentist charged $784 plus lab fees of $200–$300. Murphy goes on to point out that all complaints against denturists installing partial plates which were received in 1984–5 (the time under study) came from dentists or dental associations, with not one coming from the consumers of their product. The dentists reply that dissatisfied customers take their complaints to the dentists rather than to the proper licensing authorities. Anne Murphy, 'Denturists Fear for Professional Freedom,' *London Free Press*, 10 July 1986, C2.

108 Denturism Act, 1991, S.O. c.25 s.3. HPLR had recommended this expanded scope of practice. HPLR Report, sec. 2.01, p. 172. The denturists also failed to sway the review team on some of their recommendations (e.g., their governing body argued against the proposed advisory body, as well as council committee annual reports) but these, one can only assume, were of little concern compared with their long-standing territorial battle. GBDT submission to HPLR (June 1988), 3, 5. They did agree with the idea of open complaint and discipline hearings. GBDT submission to HPLR (Dec. 1983), 12.

109 This, aside from losing their autonomy altogether, which seemed unlikely, was 'the issue' of concern for the denturists. In their initial submission, the denturists' association 'breezed through' the first twenty-one topics, getting to 'Topic 22 – Other Matters of Concern?' Here they began, 'There is one absolutely critical, over-riding issue [for us] ... If, in this Health Professions Legislation Review, we were restricted to but one item, the right to do "partials" would be our consuming focus.' DAO submission to HPLR (Jan. 1984), 6. In addition, the denturists had reason to fear the dentists. The latter group had shown itself in the past to carry considerable political weight. As we saw earlier, they had succeeded once in having the denturists' hard-won gains overturned, and they had also, more recently, succeeded in reversing the decision which had come out of the Dicken's Commission in favour of the denturists. GBDT submission to HPLR (June 1984), 14.

110 GBDT submission to HPLR (June 1984), 13 (emphases added).

111 Ibid., 17, 19, 20, respectively (emphases added).

112 See Table 2.2 for a summary of their positions.

113 The speech–language pathologists will be discussed in a later section on the technique specialist groups.

114 In an attempt to get rid of the confusing double nomenclatures, the new legislation restricts the optician/ophthalmic dispensers to the term 'optician.' Opticianry Act, 1991, S.O. c.34 s.9. I will keep with the official usage where possible.
115 For their formal definitions (scope of practice) see Appendix 8.
116 As OSHA put it, 'The concept of *dispensing*, along with *prescription* has caused the Review much concern.' OSHA submission to HPLR (Jan. 1988), 12. The optometry profession is obviously quite aware of the tension created by this ambiguity. In 1970 the CHA's commented on the fact that optometrists were obliged by their college to, in effect, hide the merchant component of their fees under service charges reported for reimbursement under the OHIP plan. CHA Report, vol. 2, 528–9. In a minority opinion attached to the 1970 report, Dowie (chairman of the CHA) argued this restriction should be discontinued.
117 See, e.g., COO submission to HPLR (Dec. 1983), 2–3, and (July 1988), 2–6; OAO submission to HPLR (Dec. 1983), 16–18, and (Aug. 1988), 1–11. OSHA (later referred to as the Ontario Association of Speech–Language Pathologists and Audiologists or OSLA submission to HPLR (June 1984), 5, and (Jan. 1988), 3, 11–14.
118 Optometry Act, 1991, S.O. c.35 s.3 and s.4(1). RHPA, c.18 s.33(2).
119 Audiology Act, 1991, S.O. c.19 s.3(1). RHPA, c.18 s.33(2).
120 It is interesting to note just how much the ideas of the iridologists comply with those put forth by the ophthalmologists in their OMA submission. OMA (Section on Ophthalmology) submission to HPLR (June 1984), 7.
121 The optometrists were concerned about 'the growing number of non-specialized physicians [GPs] with undemonstrated qualifications who are performing eye and vision examinations often in cooperation with retail optical outlets.' OAO submission to HPLR (Dec. 1983), 17. The audiologists and speech–language pathologists argued that GPs are under-educated in the area of auditory function – having received little training in that area of expertise. (Physicians prescribe hearing aids. Some refer to audiologists; some use minimally trained staff assistants to do testing; and many issue a generic prescription and rely on the hearing aid dispensers to determine the most suitable hearing aid.) OSHA submission to HPLR (June 1984), question 7, 2–4.
122 OAO submission to HPLR (Dec. 1983), 5. Optometrists take five years of university-level courses. Ophthalmologists are trained first as general physicians and then specialize in surgery and abnormal pathologies of the eye, i.e., above and beyond the 'normal' age-related diminishing eyesight of most people.
123 OMA (Section on Ophthalmology) submission to HPLR (Sept. 1984), 3. This claim had also been made repeatedly in their initial submission to HPLR (June 1984).
124 AHAD submission to HPLR (Dec. 1986), 1–4.

125 Vision Care Council of Canada submission to HPLR (July 1989).
126 Boase, 'Public Policy,' 208.
127 BOD submission to HPLR (June 1984), 8. Based on this domination, the board claimed that the (fair) election of board members 'is not possible' and went on to make the unusual request for the appointment of these members instead. Ibid.
128 OAO submission to HPLR (July 1984), 23; OADO submission to HPLR (June 1984), 5.
129 See, e.g., BOD submission to HPLR (July 1988), 1.
130 Ibid.
131 Opticians Act, 1991, S.O. c.34 s.3–5(1). The opticians also wanted authorization in their act to 'duplicate, replace, reproduce and repeat' original orders without further prescription orders (another piece of the process). OADO submission to HPLR (June 1984), 9. Although the wording was not put into their statute, they continue to 'duplicate' based on prescription. Opticians Act, 1991, S.O. c.34. Interview with optician college official, 5 Mar. 1997.
132 This was still of concern to the opticians in 1997. Interview with optician college official, 5 Mar. 1997.
133 See, e.g., BOD submission to HPLR, section on the OCLA (June 1984), 5–6. This dispute shows up over and over throughout the ensuing submissions.
134 A representative of the college claimed that OCLA members who had submitted to the review now belong mostly to the OOA. Interview with optician college official, 5 Mar. 1997.
135 Chiropodists were fully insured in the institutions in which they predominantly worked, and podiatrists were partially insured in the same manner as chiropractic practitioners.
136 Although they are both referred to in the old and new legislation under the general heading 'chiropody,' the podiatrists were allowed to submit their comments to the HPLR independently of the chiropodists' submissions.
137 BRC submission to HPLR (Dec. 1983), 3–4; through to their Sept. 1988 submission, no pagination given. (Similarly for the OSC.)
138 Chiropody Act, 1991, S.O. c.20 s.4 and s.5(1). The surgery here cannot be the 'bone surgery' done by the podiatrists. Interview with chiropody college official, 28 Sept. 1994.
139 Agreement was finally reached with the podiatrists that they be allowed to practice with a wider scope of practice than the chiropodists (see the movement from Bill 45, 'communicating a conclusion' and 'cutting into tissues of the foot,' s.5 (2.1 and 2.2), to the Chiropody Act, 1991, S.O. c.20 'communicating a diagnosis' and 'cutting into subcutaneous tissues of the foot and bony tissues of the forefoot,' s.5 (2.1 and 2.2).
140 Chiropody Act, 1991, S.O. c.20 s.3(2).

141 It makes little sense to train in the U.S. under a more lengthy, rigorous, and expensive program, only to practice a limited version of your skills in Ontario.
142 The podiatrists pointed, e.g., to the fact that 'the podiatrist is defined as a physician within the meaning of a variety of [U.S.] federal and state laws.' OpoA submission to HPLR (Dec. 1983), 3. The Ontario podiatrists were infringing on two key areas of medicine: surgery and drugs. They had won an earlier decision on surgery in the courts (OpoA submission to HPLR (July 1986), 5), but when the CPSO again prosecuted them for intrusion on medicine's licensed territory, they were ordered by the Ontario Supreme Court, in a Dec.1987 decision, to stop performing surgery (on the foot). The podiatrists appealed, but the appeal was stayed pending the decisions made by the policy makers in the new RHPA legislation – at that time HPLR had recommended they be given this licensed act.
143 Comparing in-hospital foot surgery for three common procedures, bunion removal, hammertoe correction, and toe nail removal, to the same procedures performed in the podiatrist's office, they calculated the government would save $12.9 million (1986) were the podiatrists to perform the surgery. Ontario Podiatric Medical Association (which they were then referring to themselves as) submission to HPLR (Apr. 1986), Table 1.
144 OpoA submission to HPLR (June 1988), 1–3. There was some concern about the grandfathering of the students-in-process at the time.
145 The governing body (BDC) and the association (OCA) were in basic agreement over their requests to the HPLR. CMCC (their Canadian training facility, located in Toronto) also presented submissions to the review – again in general agreement.
146 BDC submission to HPLR (Dec. 1983), 4(a), and (July 1986), 7.
147 See, e.g., BDC submission to HPLR (Jan. 1988), 2–9; OCA submission to HPLR (Jan. 1988), ii.
148 The new scope of practice reads: 'The practice of chiropractic is the *assessment* of conditions related to the spine, nervous system, and joints and the *diagnosis*, prevention and treatment, primarily by adjustment, of, a) dysfunctions or disorders arising from the structures of functions of the spine and the effects of those dysfunctions or disorders of the nervous system; and b) dysfunctions or disorders arising from the structures or functions of the joints.' (emphases added). Their licensed acts also included the act of 'diagnosing' specific 'causes' of a 'person's symptoms.' Chiropractic Act, 1991, S.O. c.21 s.3 and s.4(1).
149 I am including the optometrists in this elite now, since they had managed to join the club in 1974 with their inclusion in the HDA.
150 Chiropractic Act, 1991, S.O. c.21 s.4(2).
151 The chiropractors wanted to be allowed to diagnose and treat problems of the

joints of the extremities and be given the licensed act of going beyond the anal verge for the purpose of manipulating the tail bone. The extension of their scope beyond that of the spine was strongly resisted by the medical profession. The OMA argued that the scientific theory on which chiropractic is based does not provide a foundation for treatment of this nature. The chiropractors countered that (a) the medical profession was not equiped to make such a clinical judgment, (b) OHIP was already allowing for billing by chiropractors for treatment of 'any extremity,' and (c) these services were needed in small communities lacking orthopedic specialists. The HPLR report had not recommended either the 'extremities' or the 'anal verge' areas of scope or authorized acts. HPLR, *Striking*, 144. But in the end, the chiropractors did win both these clinical activities in their scope of practice and licensed acts. Chiropractic Act, 1991, S.O. c.21 s.3 and s.4. The medical profession had held out in their opposition to the extremities territory extension, infringing as it did on medical territory, and it looked for some time as if they would win, but the NDP government which made the final-hour decisions went with the chiropractors.

152 OCA submission to HPLR (June 1984), 19. Some chiropractors do their own testing on site, and others send their samples to the U.S. for analysis. In 1981 the CMCC was ordered by the MOH to close a laboratory it was operating without a licence. This raised a number of questions related to invasive techniques (e.g., the drawing of blood) and the use of lab test results for purposes of diagnosis and prescribed treatment – questions which the HPLR was dealing with in relation to its concern to license all 'harmful [clinical procedural] acts.'

153 BDC submission to HPLR (July 1986), 12.

154 CHA Report, rec. 286. The other legislation referred to was the Healing Arts Radiation Protection Act, the Laboratory and Specimen Centre Licensing Act, and the Public Hospitals Act. Under the RHPA the technologists who would be performing these procedures are under order to perform them only for medical doctors and dentists.

155 Interviews with a representative from the chiropractic college and the chiropractic educational institution, 28, 29 Sept. 1994 and 5 Feb. 1997. X-rays were not listed as a hazardous form of energy under the RHPA regulations, so they do not require a licensed act (under the RHPA) to be performed. Another college official explained in 1998 that because chiropractors can now diagnose they ought technically to be able to order lab tests, but since they do not themselves have laboratory facilities, 'It really is an issue of dollars and cents, the ministry of health does not want to have more health care providers ordering lab tests.' Interview with a chiropractic college official, 4 June 1998.

156 A flyer dated 1988, which was being distributed before the enacting of the new legislation by Ontario chiropractors at public demonstration sites such as shop-

ping malls, clearly referred to all chiropractors as 'doctors.' CCA, 'Which of These Doctors Are Chiropractors?'
157 BDC submission to HPLR (July 1986), 8; OCA submission to HPLR (Dec. 1986), 16.
158 CHA Report, rec. 289. CHA had been opposed to any extension of the title 'doctor' beyond that of the medical and dental professions. Regarding the RHPA, there was no evidence of serious opposition.
159 Psychologists are also legally recognized as 'doctor,' but this title had already been held by the psychologists as graduates of PhD programs of a university. HPLR, *Striking*, 144; RHPA, c.18 s.33(2).
160 CMCC submission to HPLR (Dec. 1983), 2.
161 Interview with CMCC official, 6 July 1999. Although the chiropractors had won earlier approval from several universities, the government had failed to come up with the funding for the new programs. Interview with chiropractic college employee, 28 Sept. 1994. The senate of York University, Toronto, has 'agreed to create a degree for chiropractors as Doctors of Chiropractic Medicine.' Interview with chiropractic college official, 4 June 1998.
162 Within chiropractic there was an attempt made by 'straight chiropractors' (a more traditional type of chiropractic) to gain separate regulation from that of the majority 'mixer' chiropractors (see discussion on chiropractic in Chapter 2). The HPLR team, however, recommended against this on the grounds that there were too few 'straight' chiropractors to qualify for self-regulatory status. The decision was upheld by later officials.
163 Pran Manga et al. 'A Study to Examine the Cost-Effectiveness of Chiropractic Management of Low Back Pain' (Toronto: MOH, 1993). For a U.S. study, see, e.g., Paul G. Shekelle and Robert H. Brooke (both MDs), 'A Community-Based Study of the Use of Chiropractic Services,' *American Journal of Public Health*, 81/4 (1991) 439–42. The report by Manga, and others, estimated that with the proper utilization of chiropractic care for low-back pain, the Ontario government could save $600 million a year in OHIP billing, and provincial employers could save $1.4 billion per year in lost work time. They also reported, 'In our review, we came across many studies that support the effectiveness of chiropractic care for headache and migraine, neck pain, referred and radiated pain, and a variety of other ailments.' Manga et al., 'A Study to Examine,' 83.
164 Ibid., 12.
165 Manga and Angus estimated: 'Expenditure to improve access to chiropractic services, and the changed utilization patterns it produces, [would] lead to very substantial net savings in direct and indirect costs. Direct savings to Ontario's health care system [might] be as much as $770m., [would] very likely be $548m., and [would] be at least $380m. The corresponding savings in indirect costs – made up

of the short- and long-term costs of disability – [would be] $3.775b., $1.849b., and $1.255b.' These figures are quoted by the OCA, 'Enhanced Chiropractic Coverage under OHIP as a Means of Reducing Health Care Costs, Attaining Better Health Outcomes and Achieving Equitable Access to Health Services,' http://www.chiropractic.on.ca/execsummary.html (28 Apr. 1998).

166 They had fought for, and like many others, failed to win inclusion as a full profession with a governing college granted the power of exclusive licensure, in the 1974 HDA.

167 They had adopted the same educational upgrading strategy as that of the nurses, i.e., university undergraduate and graduate degrees and research. Boase, 'Public Policy,' 110.

168 Physiotherapy Act, 1991, S.O. c.37 s.3 and s.4; BDP submission to HPLR (Dec. 1983), 16–23, and (June 1984), 12–16. OPA submission to HPLR (Dec. 1983), 5, and (June 1984), 28–9. This decision may well have been influenced by the fact that similar requests were being granted to physiotherapists in the U.S. (The HPLR group was aware of international decisions being made on these professional issues.) The other legislation mentioned was the Public Hospitals Act, the Workman's Compensation Act (now called the Work Place Safety and Insurance Act), and the Long Term Care Act. Interview with physiotherapy college employee, 28 Sept. 1994.

169 Despite this, as of 1997, there were 'hundreds of [new] independent clinics/ practises' in Ontario. Interview with physiotherapy college official, 20 Feb. 1997.

170 Interview with physiotherapy association official, 5 June 1998.

171 Physiotherapy Act, 1991, S.O. c.37 s.3. The governing board was still fighting for this in their eighth (and final) submission. BDP submission to HPLR (Jan. 1988), 2–3. The association was still fighting for this in their ninth (and final) submission. OPA submission to HPLR (Aug. 1988), 5.

172 Cover letter accompanying the OPA submission to HPLR (Aug. 1988). All of the groups who did win the diagnosis fight belonged to the traditional elite and newly elite male professions: medicine, dentistry, chiropractic, optometry, and psychology. While the gender composition of these groups is moving more towards balance, the leadership and clinical elite of the professions is still predominantly male, but, more importantly for my point here, the composition of the 'non-doctor' groups is still predominantly female.

173 By 1997 the college had developed guidelines for practise with regard to practitioners' primary contact, but practising physiotherapists were still concerned about the legality of their assessment/diagnosis of patients. Interview with physiotherapy college official, 20 Feb. 1997.

174 The review team had only recommended they be given the 'spinal manipulation'

Notes to pages 109–10   295

(HPLR, *Striking*, 316), but they were also given 'tracheal suction' during the ministry processing of the review recommendations. Physiotherapy Act, 1991, S.O. c.37. s.4. Those that failed to be included were 'diagnosis,' 'performing procedures on tissue beyond the dermis,' 'manipulating ... peripheral joints beyond the individual's usual range of motion,' 'correcting irregularities in teeth, jaws and contiguous and adjacent structures,' 'administering substances by inhalation,' 'performing invasive instrumentation,' 'ordering diagnostic applications of ionizing radiation,' 'dispensing [limited] prescription drugs' (by which they really meant the application and dermal insertion of prescription drugs during treatment procedures), 'dispensing [limited] dental appliances [to patients with jaw disorders, and those without the use of their hands],' 'labour' (by which they meant prenatal education and assistance in 'managing' labour pain), and 'ordering laboratory investigations.' BDP submission to HPLR (Jan. 1988), 2–5. They would still be able to perform these procedures as long as they were not licensed to other health practitioners, such as was the case for labour which was licensed to the midwives. The physiotherapists, like others, also failed to dissuade the review or ministry against either the idea of expanding the minister's powers over health professionals, or the idea of setting up an ongoing independent advisory body. BDP submission to HPLR (Dec. 1983), 1.
175 OPA submission to HPLR (Aug. 1988), 8.
176 Physiotherapy Act, 1991, S.O. c.37 s.8(1).
177 Interview with physiotherapy association official, June 5, 1998. Their position may yet be improved as a result of the considerable concern over the shortage of physiotherapists in the province, and throughout North America, in the past decade, partly because of the projections of increasing needs in this direction in the near future. OPA Executive Director Signe Holstein sees 'an aging population, the trend toward "deinstitutionalization" and increased home care, integration of handicapped children into regular schools, and medical advances that are keeping head injury victims alive longer' as some of the important factors contributing to this rising demand. Dana Flavelle, 'Physiotherapy "In a Crunch,"' *Toronto Star*, 7 Jan. 1988, A18.
178 At the time the HPLR decisions were being made, one enterprising massage therapist who had worked hard to win over a collection of medical doctors for patient referrals to her clinic (after receiving no reply from the 100 letters she sent out to doctors in the late 1970s) said she thought that the considerable number of doctors (30) now willing to refer patients to her was atypical. Paul Marshman, 'Massage: Many People See Masseurs on Physician's Advice Now,' *Medical Post* (Feb. 1986), 13. Chiropractors and psychologists also refer patients to massage therapists. Barbara MacKay, 'The Right Touch,' *Canadian Consumer*, 13/7 (1983), 38.
179 BDM submission to HPLR (Feb. 1986), 1, 4. See also the earlier submissions by

both the board and the association; BDM submission to HPLR (June 1984), 1–4; OMTA submission to HPLR (June 1984), 3. The CHA had recommended the massage therapists be licensed in a manner similar to that of the physiotherapists. CHA Report, vol. 1, rec. 228. (They were also found by the HPLR to be weak in the 'knowledge' and 'public interest' categories; see Appendix 7.)

180 Several pages of discussion of the issue of sexual impropriety were allotted space in the board's first submission to the HPLR. BDM submission to HPLR (Dec. 1983), 24–8.

181 The CHA recommended making a clear distinction between the medical or therapeutic massage practitioners ('massage therapists') and the non-medical ones ('masseurs'). That is, the masseurs would be 'controlled by a government agency other than the Department of Health'; and the massage therapists would be licensed and required to 'practise on the prescription of a qualified physician or under the direction of a registered physiotherapist.' *CHA Report*, vol. 2, 388. The 'credentialist' masseurs, or 'massage therapists' seeking this distinction, broke off from the general association (SRRMO) to form their own OMTA in 1965, who 'have agreed to work only on referral from physicians.' CHA Report, vol. 2, 385. It is interesting that physicians, who knew virtually nothing about massage, were given supervision over its specialized practitioners.

182 BDM submission to HPLR (Dec. 1983), 11. OMTA submission to HPLR (June 1984), 4.

183 Massage Therapy Act, 1991, S.O. c.27 s.7 and s.3; BDM submission to HPLR (Dec. 1983), 1. The association had also argued for the protection of the word 'massage' in order to further clarify the distinction between themselves and others, but this they did not win. OMTA submission to HPLR (Dec. 1983), 10, and (June 1984), 4.

184 Interview with massage therapy college official, 19 Feb. 1997.

185 BDM submission to HPLR (Dec. 1983), 10, 13; OMTA submission to HPLR (Dec. 1983), 4, 16. The board was not, however, very hard-line on the issue of medical referral. At one point, they said, 'Because this [therapeutic massage] is a specific skill requiring a thorough and specific training, outside supervision by other health professionals of any of the modalities is not indicated. This does not mean that an Registered Massage Therapist (RMT) will not treat on referral, or that there are not conditions that an RMT should not treat except on referral, or that the input of another professional may not be crucial for proper treatment.' BDM submission to HPLR (Dec. 1983), 10. My sense here is that the board was trying to prevent any mandate for outside interference in the practise of massage therapy, at the same time as they recognized the importance of voluntary cooperation among the health professions.

186 BDM submission to HPLR (June 1984), 10.

187 BDM and OMTA (joint submission, not dated, but making mention of a prior meeting of Jan. 1987), 1.
188 Interview with massage therapy college official, 19 Feb. 1997.
189 Massage Therapy Act, 1991, S.O. c.27. Their scope also included 'manipulation,' a word which the chiropractors had tried to prevent the massage therapists from getting.
190 The massage therapists were concerned to have included in, first, their scope, and, later, their authorized acts, mention of the therapeutic treatments and equipment which they used in their practises. Their old scope of practise had included mention of the use of electric or vapour baths and thermal or ultraviolet lamps, and they proposed their new scope include mention of the use of 'hydrotherapy – the use of water in any form for therapeutic purposes; actinotherapy – the use of infrared and ultra-violet lamps; mechanical modalities; remedial exercises; and health counselling – home care, e.g., hydrotherapy and exercises.' OMTA submission to HPLR (Dec. 1983), 11. The governing body included 'thermotherapy' and 'electrotherapy' to the list for inclusion in the scope-of-practice statement. BDM submission to HPLR (July 1986), 1. They also argued for licensed acts for massage therapy. Ibid., 1.
191 Their concern here, which continues today, is more about restricting the practise of therapeutic massage by untrained practitioners. Because they did not win the argument to restrict therapeutic massage to massage therapists (via its inclusion as a controlled act licensed only to massage therapists), they have limited grounds with which to control its general usage (aside from that provided by title violation). Interview with massage therapy college official, 19 Feb. 1997.
192 OSHA submission to HPLR (Dec. 1983), topic 7.
193 No one can perform the controlled or authorized act of another profession unless she or he has been given the same authorized act.
194 OSLA submission to HPLR (Aug. 1988), 5–6, and cover letter.
195 Interview with audiologists and speech–language pathologist college official, 27 Sept. 1997.
196 Audiology and Speech–Language Pathology Act, 1991, S.O. c.19 s.8(1). Generally, unregulated providers are prone to advertising their skills with loose terminology, such as 'speech therapy,' or in other areas, 'massage' or 'physical therapy.'
197 The occupational therapists had argued for licensed status in their submissions to the CHA, but it had recommended only certification for this group. CHA Report, vol. 2, 378. CHA also recommended 'improved salary schedules ... by OHIP' and that 'greater efforts be made to recruit more men into this occupation.' Ibid.

198 This took the form for the occupational therapists of an ongoing fight between the college-level educators and the occupational therapists' association which preferred to have the educational programs restricted to the more elite institution, the university. The association limited its members to degree holders and foreign-trained practitioners who met the standards of the governing college. In the institutions the expectation of the university standard still prevailed although the Canadian Hospital Association had changed its accreditation standards to comply with diploma accreditation. The national occupational therapists association carried out its own unapproved assessment of the Mohawk College program in Hamilton, Ontario (the only college program for occupational therapy in Ontario at the time) and failed to accredit it. So there was a fair bit of tension here. At the time of writing, the field had developed into a university degree educational standard. Interview with occupational therapist college official, 5 Mar. 1997.

199 They also made the common request for diagnosis rather than assessment, and they were not happy with the implications of the wording of their scope-of-practice statement with regard to the distinction between function and dysfunction.

200 Occupational Therapy Act, 1991, S.O. c.33.

201 Psychology Act, 1991, S.O. c.38 s.3 and s.4. RHPA, c.18 s.33.

202 OBEP submission to HPLR (June 1994), 2. Here the OBEP refers to a 1982 study which found that 88.4 per cent of psychologists do some form of 'research as part of their work.'

203 There is growing concern within the profession with the fact that the publishers for student testing have set criteria which include interpreting tests by people with Master of Education credentials rather than or as well as members of the psychology profession. Interview with psychology college official, 20 Feb. 1997.

204 OBEP submission to HPLR (June 1984), 18.

205 Interview with practising psychologist, 11 Apr. 1995. The drug treatment issue is rather odd in that while psychologists are opposed to what they refer to as the over-medication of the medical practitioners in the mental health area (themselves advocating a balance of psychological counselling with necessary drug treatments only), they are also engaged in the research of these drugs. Interview with academic psychologist, 17 Dec. 1995. Ibid., 15–16. This could, therefore, become an area of contention between the two professions.

206 Interview with psychology college official, 20 Feb. 1997.

207 OBEP submission to HPLR (Dec. 1983), 13–16. Note: A psychologist or psychological associate could be practising as a psychometrist (doing psychological testing), although the psychometrists per se were not included in the new act.

208 Psychology Act, 1991, S.O. c.38 s.8(1). The 'psychological associate' must have

Notes to pages 114–16 299

both an MA in psychology from an accredited university and a number of years of practise in the field in which she or he specializes.
209 Interview with psychology college official, 20 Feb. 1997.
210 I did ask around about this, at the time, but was never given a very satisfactory answer.
211 Interview with social work college official, 29 Sept. 1994. The latter interviewee informed me that the Ontario social workers were the only social workers in North America without state regulation. Ontario social workers also have a governing mechanism in place, to which some of the new RHPA groups looked, as an example of how best to organize the details of their own governance.
212 See the website of the Ontario CCSW, http://www.ocssw.org
213 The profession of psychology argues that the psychometrists ought to be 'supervised' by a psychologist. Interview with psychology college official, 20 Feb. 1997.
214 The word 'mental' was also dropped from the harm clause. Earlier wording had referred to physical or mental harm, but only physical remains. RHPA, c.18 s.30(1).
215 In Canada, lay midwives and nurse–midwives (often British- and European-trained) practised in remote areas of northern Canada and in Newfoundland, as well as in some of the non-Anglo-Saxon communities of major cities. Barrington, *Midwifery Is Catching*, 30–2. Small communities, like the one I grew up in, in Ontario, often had a community woman who was not necessarily referred to as a midwife, but who acted as a family or community midwife. My husband's family, from that same small community, were all born in the 1950s under the guiding hands of their grandmother.
216 Ibid., 32.
217 MC submission to HPLR (Dec. 1983), 1. The childbirth organizations mentioned were the Childbirth Education Association, the Toronto Birth Centre Committee, the Lamaze Association, Choices in Childbirth, and the International Association of Parents and Professionals for Safe Alternatives in Childbirth. The women's groups mentioned were the Provincial Council of Women and the National Action Committee on the Status of Women.
218 MC submission to HPLR (Dec. 1983), 3–4; and (June 1984), 12–14, 42, 68.
219 MC submission to HPLR (Dec. 1983), 3–4, and attached appendices. Note these studies showed up the higher level of competence of midwives in attending *all types of births*, not just the low-risk births that they were asking to be allowed to attend in Ontario today. I have also referred to some of these studies in my earlier discussion on midwifery in Chapter 2. One study was done in the case of a lengthy doctors' strike in California.
220 Ibid., 2. 'Normal' birth is given *by the OMA* to be 85 per cent of all births. Patients

Notes to pages 116-17

'presenting identifiable risks at a moderate level' constitute 12 per cent, leaving only '2-3% of pregnancies at high risk' (emphases added). OMA 'Discussion Paper on Directions in Health Care Issues Relating to Childbirth' (1984), 15.
221 See, e.g., MC submission to HPLR (Dec. 1983), 36.
222 There were also 'pilot projects' being run in Canada at the time of the review. The one at Vancouver's Grace Hospital, e.g., where the midwives who had been providing full maternity care including the delivery had already obtained very impressive results with lower than average infection rates, episiotomy and Caesarean section rates, and utilization of forceps and epidurals. They had also had 'superb patient satisfaction,' so much so that the hospital could not keep up with the demand for their services, despite the fact those services had never been advertised to the public. Elinor LeBourdais, 'Despite CMA Misgivings, Support for Midwifery Appears to be Growing,' *CMA Journal*, no. 139 (Oct. 1988), 770.
223 'The training physicians receive in obstetrics would not, by international standards, be considered broad-based training in midwifery.' MC submission to HPLR (June 1984), 61. The midwives even claim that the CPSO, in discussions encouraged by the review team to settle differences between the two groups, was of the 'opinion two reasons for this [leaving of obstetrics care by GPs] are that there is a lack of adequate training for GP's in obstetrics and the volume of births they attend is insufficient to maintain their skills.' Ibid., 59.
224 MC submission to HPLR (Dec. 1983), 4, 4 and 39, 37, 5. I do not mean to imply they were being false or obsequious. These positions on issues were in keeping with their historical commitments.
225 Ibid., 4-5, 37. Here they pointed to the existing system of maternity care for the North where expecting mothers are routinely flown to southern hospitals well before their delivery dates; families are separated for long periods of time, and women are thrown into an alien culture regardless of whether their birth is high or low risk. Although they do not mention cost here, it would certainly be on the minds of the ministry officials behind the scenes. This is a very expensive program, and any safe means of reducing its costs would, assumedly, be welcome.
226 Ibid., 2. They also point out that 'private health insurance plans in the U.S. are increasingly covering midwifery care because of its cost-effectiveness, despite opposition from the medical profession.' MC submission to HPLR (June 1984), 68.
227 This is what other groups who did not fit the criteria were being advised to do. Interview with HPLR team member, 11 July 1986.
228 The Task Force was announced Jan. 1986, along with the MOH's intentions to regulate midwifery. The *Report of the Task Force on the Implementation of Midwifery in Ontario* was released Oct. 1987 (Toronto: Queen's Printer). Both the

Task Force and an Interim Regulatory Council for Midwifery (1989) were chaired by Mary Eberts (a well-known, well-connected, feminist, Toronto lawyer). The interim council set up committees to investigate particular areas of concern with regard to the introduction of midwifery into the mainstream health care system. There was a bylaws committee, a public education committee, and an equity committee. The latter was set up to investigate the access all potential patients would have to midwifery care in Ontario.

229 Midwifery Task Force Report, ch. 5, rec. 8, 19–22.
230 As of mid-1999, there were 150 practising midwives (in 41 practices). Interview of CMO official, 7 July 1999. For home births see Ontario Regulation (on Registration) 867/93, e.g., s.4(1)2ii(d) which refers to births 'in a residence.' Home births constituted (between 1994–8, approximately 38% of all midwifery births in Ontario, and I was told 'hospitals do not put pressure on midwives not to assist in home births.' Interview with midwifery college official, 18 Feb. 1997 and 7 July 1999. For drugs, see Ontario Regulation (on Designated Drugs) 884/93. Some are to be administered under the midwife's discretion and some on 'order' by a member of the CPSO. In 1997 there were also some planned changes to the Federal Narcotics Act with regard to specific schedules of drugs to be released for use by provincial health practitioners – including the Ontario midwives. (This had been given momentum by the push to expand the role of the nurse practitioner.) Ibid. As of mid-1999, this was still in process.
231 Interview with midwifery program director, 9 June 1998.
232 I had done an earlier set of interviews for a previous project on midwifery in 1985–6. At that time, the midwives were still quite ambivalent about whether or not they ought to be engaging in the HPLR process, although they were then participating. Interviews with Toronto midwives, 1985–6.
233 This was referred to over and over in the midwife interviews. It seems to be a very strongly held conviction. 'Informed consent,' here, meant considerable effort towards patient or client education, followed by acceptance of the patient's (client's) decisions in the end. The best example of this was the mother's choice to have her baby at home; after lengthy education on all the potential risks involved, it was the mother's decision to make, not the care giver's.
234 Interview with a practising midwife, 11 July 1986.
235 This concern showed up, e.g., in the midwives' push to have more public representatives involved in the self-regulation of the profession of midwifery. Interview with midwifery college official, 3 Aug. 1994. The quote is taken from an interview with a member of the Toronto MC, 30 Aug. 1985.
236 Interview with a member of the Toronto MC, 30 Aug. 1985.
237 A member referred to the midwives as holding 'a unique position' and went on to say, 'They need help.' Interview with a member of the HPLR team, 11 July 1986.

302   Notes to pages 118–21

This unique position was believed to be the result of the illegality of their practise. Because of it, they could not just be left to develop on their own, as other small provider groups might; they needed protection from criminal prosecution.
238 Interview with midwifery program director, 9 June 1998.
239 Ibid.
240 Ibid.
241 Ibid. She explained, 'Basically how it works is if a woman chooses a hospital birth, we first go to her home, we bring her into the hospital very late in the labour, she is in there on average a few hours before the baby is born and a few hours after.'
242 Other groups involved in this legislative process could also be seen as posing a problem for this standard political science theory.
243 Less than half-a-dozen energetic Toronto midwives, with little or no resources or ties to the few scattered midwives throughout the province, formed the midwifery 'pressure group.' Compared with the organization, resources, and connections of their opposition pressure group, the medical profession, they could hardly be called a pressure group.
244 They suggested, e.g., a 'scope' which included 'nutritional counselling for *normal and therapeutic needs*' (emphasis added) as well as protection of the title 'nutritionist.' ODtA submission to HPLR (Dec. 1983), 22–3.
245 Ibid., HPLR (June 1984), 6. Further, their next submission dealt almost exclusively with this delineation. ODtA submission to HPLR (Oct. 1985). A late submission reiterated their request for exclusive rights to the prescription of therapeutic diets. ODtA, 'Supporting Document for the Licensure of Dietician Nutritionists to Prescribe the Formulation of Parental and Enteral Nutrition' (Feb. 1988).
246 Dietetics Act, 1991, S.O. c.26 s.3 and s.7(1). See Appendix 8 for the dieticians' scope-of-practise.
247 Interview with dietician college official, 4 Mar. 1997. An example was given during this interview of an insurance company (which should have known better) referring people to 'registered nutritionists,' who do not legally exist.
248 Many of these participants belong to the National Health Food Association which made submissions to the HPLR under the name of the National Health Products Association.
249 Interview with a nurse's assistant, 13 Jan. 1992. Her opinion was that many ordinary nurses and nursing assistants had not given much thought to the legislation. It seemed too removed from them.
250 See the section on nursing in Chapter 2 for reference to the double association group in nursing. RNAO tended more towards professional concerns – its submissions were much like those of the college – while ONA acts more as a labour

Notes to pages 121–2   303

union, as was reflected in the concerns it submitted to HPLR. ONA has also tended to represent the RNs rather than the RPNs; the latter are now, in the late 1990s, represented by the Practical Nurses Federation of Ontario and broader unions such as, the Canadian Union of Public Employees and the Ontario Public Services Employment Union.

251 CNO submission to HPLR (June 1984), Introduction, 1–2.
252 Ibid., (Jan. 1984), 15, 6–7; (June 1984), 11; (Jan. 1984), 7, 9, 24; (June 1984), 17; and (Jan. 1984), 31.
253 RNAO submission to HPLR (Dec. 1984), 9; CNO submission to HPLR (June 1984), 37. ONA also disagreed with the RNAO recommendation.
254 CNA submission to HPLR (Dec. 1984), 4. This merely states in answer to the HPLR team's 'Topic 2' regarding 'the ability of the profession to regulate itself effectively,' that 'nursing has shown it is able to regulate itself effectively.' The college took the statement to indicate ONA support of the status quo. The college then felt that ONA had back-tracked on this support when it took a position favouring RNA's requests to get out from under the authority of the college. CNO submission to HPLR (June 1984), 38.
255 The college later agreed.
256 ONA submission to HPLR (Dec. 1984), 2, 4–5, 8–14, and (June 1984), 1–8 (discussed the last concern in more detail).
257 Nursing Act, 1991, S.O. c.32 s.5(a). The specific licensed acts allowed to be performed without authorization from another health profession are contained in the regulations, see Ontario Regulation 116/96.
258 HPLR, *Striking*, sec. 2.01A. The practitioners who might now order a procedure from a nurse are physicians, dentists, chiropodists, and midwives. Nursing Act, 1991, S.O. c.32 s.5(1b).
259 Nursing Act, 1991, S.O. c.32 s.5(1a). Ontario Regulation 115/96. Not all of the RNs' authorized acts are included within reg. 115/96. They cannot initiate the 'administration of a substance by injection or inhalation' (authorized act 4(2)); but, they can initiate with regard to 'preforming a prescribed procedure below the dermis or below a mucous membrane' (authorized act 4(1)).
260 Ibid., c.32 s.11(1). The only exemption to the 'nurse,' 'registered nurse,' and 'practical nurse' titles are 'Christian Science nurse' and 'graduate nurse.' Ibid., s.11(2).
261 Ibid., c.32 s.3.
262 Ontario, MOH and Ontario Ministry of Colleges and Universities (MCU), 'Government of Ontario Position Regarding Entry to Practise as a Registered Nurse in Ontario' (Nov. 1983), 1. Reports from the U.S. have indicated 'growing employer dissatisfaction with baccalaureate nurses. Marjorie Meehan, RN, Operations Division Director for the Denver Department of Health and Hospitals, complains:

"They come to us with credentials that are supposed to ensure competence, but often they cannot do the work without significant orientation. They are trained in the ivory tower, where they are supposed to be able to provide total patient care and to know all there is to know. Instead they enter a world of budget cuts and shortages."' Emily Friedman, 'Nursing: New Power, Old Problems,' *Journal of American Medical Association*, 264/23 (1990), 2981.

263 Ontario, MOH and MCU, 'Government of Ontario Position Regarding Entry to Practise as a Registered Nurse in Ontario' (30 Nov. 1983), 1. Their investigations indicated that, while 'baccalaureate nursing programs were initially developed to provide the base for public health nursing and for management and teaching positions ... over 50% of university-educated nurses are employed in hospitals where their functions generally are not differentiated from those of diploma-prepared nurses' (p. 2). They argued that 'various levels and types of nursing practise' were needed (p. 2)

264 Interview with nurses association official, 2 June 1998. This official also pointed out that any educational changes would have to be Canada-wide, since no province can create barriers to the mobility of a professional group.

265 RNAO, 'Support for New Nursing Competencies from Provincial Nursing Organizations,' *News Release* (10 Dec. 1998).

266 She went on to say, 'I don't think I was an exception – to feel this way. Others seemed to [feel the same] but still stayed.' Interview with former RN, 11 Aug. 1992. Sister Marie says the same of U.S. nurses: 'Nursing education is producing a problem. Nurses come out of university programs with a smattering of technical skills and little skill in caring for people. It takes them 2 or 3 years more to learn who they are and what they are doing as nurses. It is so traumatic for many of them that they leave nursing.' Friedman, 'Nursing,' 2981.

267 'Ontario Nurses,' interview by *Global News*, television, Canwest–Global Broadcasting System, 7 May 1990. One registered nurse said, 'We are supposed to be health *professionals*. They keep telling us that anyway ... and then we have to lug laundry.'

268 Interview with nursing assistant, 13 Jan. 1993.

269 The interviewee added, 'The nurses don't feel that they will be taking much more delegating power from doctors; we can only delegate within our scope-of-practise.' Interview with registered nurses association official, 2 June 1998 and 7 July 1999.

270 One author points out, 'Nursing is in such an early stage of theory development that no one model could be identified as the most suitable.' Jacqueline Bridges, 'Working with Doctors: Distinct from Medicine,' *Nursing Times*, 87/27 (1991), 43; also, see K.A. Noble and Richard Rancourt, 'Administration and Intradisciplinary Conflict within Nursing,' *Nurse Administration Quarterly*, 15/4 (1991),

36–42, for a discussion of some of the problems with these theoretical models. Also, according to the then-president of the RNAO, there seems to be 'a move towards de-professionalization' in nursing, e.g., 'community nurses are being replaced by volunteers.' Kathleen MacMillan, President, RNAO, *Briefs*, interview by Rogers Cablecast, Toronto, 26 Nov. 1993.

271 Elizabeth Peter and Ruth Gallop, 'The Ethics of Care: A Comparison of Nursing and Medical Students,' *Image: Journal of Nursing Scholarship*, 26/1 (1994), 47–51.

272 A 1997 article reported on the return of the 'parish nurse' as a move by the church to 'reclaim some of its old turf ... the apostolic mandate of the church to preach, teach and heal.' Paul Marck, 'Churches Hire Nurses to Fill Gaps in Health Care,' *Toronto Star*, 18 Jan. 1997, H14.

273 In a late interview, one nursing official said, 'There is a science to caring that is foundational of nursing based on limits to what works and what does not work with helping patients. There is scientific research being done on this.' Interview with registered nurses association official, 2 June 1998.

274 One dissatisfied ex-nurse said she had never been able to convince her mother there was any other kind of nurse but the old 'vocational' nurse who was 'very care-giving and other-oriented, and who aimed to please.' She laughingly said, 'To this day my mother thinks that's what nursing is.' (Despite her daughter's attempts over the years to explain the 'higher status' of today's university educated nurses.) 'Lots of patients are looking for this [she went on to say], the soothing, calm, mother-figure. Particularly older patients; that is really all they want.' Interview with former RN, 11 Aug. 1992.

275 CNO submission to HPLR (Jan. 1984), 7, 15, and (June 1984), 13, 19, 21. ONA submission to HPLR (June 1984), 13; RNAO submission to HPLR (June 1984), 5. The college newsletter often refers to these orientations to nursing care. For example, 'a nurse assessing the health status [functional competence] of an individual would consider, not only his physiological status, but such other factors as his emotional status, his goals, his perceptions of his health status, his coping strategies, and his growth and development.' *College Communiqué*, 8/4 (1983), 6. In arguing with the HPLR for a broadly defined scope-of-practise, they claimed 'a broad scope would ... allow for a holistic, multi-faceted approach to the concept of nursing.' Ibid., 9/6 (1984), 2. One summary of theories related to nursing claimed, 'All of these nursing theories agree that the purpose of nursing is the promotion of health or functional competence and that the focus of nursing is the care and study of the individual(s), family and groups in their environment.' Ibid., 12/5 (1987), 6.

276 As one medical member of the CMA board of directors put it, 'We don't agree that nurses look after patients' health while we just concentrate on disease.' Charlotte Gray, 'What Do Nurses Want?' *CMA Journal*, no. 136 (1983), 985. In 1998

the president of OCFP, in expressing concerns over recent trends towards 'fragmentation of health care,' said, 'I think family physicians are the only ones trained to see the broad spectrum of health care.' Interview with family physicians college official, 16 June 1998.

277 For example, MOH, 'Deciding the Future of Our Health Care System,' 32. But as one Ontario nurse pointed out in a 1993 interview, 'Nurses have a lot to offer in terms of long-term planning, but we are often not consulted. Nurses were not mentioned in the [recent MOH] Long-Term Care document [for example].' 'Ontario Nurses,' *Good Afternoon Television*, interview by Rogers Cablecast, Toronto, 26 Nov. 1993. While 'rank-and-file' nurses have, in recent years, been given input into hospital decision-making committees, upper-level management nurses have been reporting some less than satisfactory behaviour on the part of hospital management. Christie McLaren, 'Ontario Gives Ordinary Nurses a Place on Hospital Committees,' *Globe and Mail*, 16 Feb. 1989, A5. One Toronto head nurse returned from a six-week leave to find her ward had been shut down. No one had seen fit to notify her of this draconian measure whereby she and all of her nursing staff lost their jobs, much less consult her about it prior to its happening. At the time of the interview this woman had been unable to find another job for some time. She kept being told that she was too highly qualified. Interview with a former RN, 11 Aug. 1992.

278 Public Hospitals Act, 1990, S.O. c.P40 s.12(1), Ontario Regulation 83/89. The mandate of the 1996 research unit (jointly conducted at McMaster University and the University of Toronto) includes questions such as, 'How many and what kind of nurses we need, the knowledge and skills nurses should have, and how registered nurses and registered practical nurses can work better with other health care providers.' Ontario, MOH, *News Release* (2 Dec. 1996). The Task Force report was released January 1999. It is entitled, 'Good Nursing, Good Health: An Investment for the 21st Century.'

279 Interview with nurses college official, 6 Feb. 1997.

280 Interview with registered nurses association official, 2 June 1998 and 8 July 1999. The 1998 interviewee also mentioned: 'They work on "call" on short notice; they often work at six or seven institutions on a rotating basis; they [tend to] have no commitment to any one institution; and there is no continuity of care for patients because they see different faces every day they are in the hospital or health care institution.'

281 Robin S. Phillips, 'Nurse Practitioners: Their Scope of Practise and Theories of Liability,' *Journal of Legal Medicine*, 6/3 (1985), 391.

282 At the time the HPLR process began, one author notes, 'It has long been recognized both here and abroad that acceptance of the nurse practitioner as part of the multi-disciplinary health care team often results in more comprehensive health

care, increased accessibility to the public and a continuity of more personalized care than has been available until now.' Evelyn Zohar, 'Nurse Practitioners,' *Globe and Mail*, 6 Sept. 1983, D6. Like many involved in the Northern nurse practitioner system, Roberta Hildebrand, director of nursing services at Health and Welfare Canada, 'sings praises of the nursing-station system.' David Silburt, 'Nursing the Right Convictions: The Nurse Practitioner as Primary Care Giver – Heresy or Prophesy?' *Canadian Doctor* (June 1987), 4. Nurse practitioner experiments in Ontario, Newfoundland, and Saskatchewan showed that the nurses performed as well as, and sometimes better than their medical counterparts. Silburt, 'Nursing,' 4; Editorial, 'Courage Needed to Cure Ills of Medicare,' *Toronto Star*, 30 July 1983, D7. In a recent Alberta court case involving a nurse practitioner who had worked quite successfully for some time in a community medical clinic, one of the physicians at the clinic commented, 'She was doing exactly what I do everyday.' That is, she was apparently quite capable of either functioning as a GP, or knowing when to refer cases over to a GP/FP or other specialized medical practitioners. The trouble had come not from the quality of her work, but from the clinic's admission to the government billing agency that they were billing for the services of a nurse practitioner under the category of a physician. CBC Television, *Fifth Estate*, 'Canadian Nurse Practitioners,' 11 Jan. 1994.

283 The cost assumption was based mainly on the fact that the nurse practitioner would be paid a much lower salary than the medical doctor for the same work. In the Alberta case mentioned above, an economist referred to savings in the salary differential (the nurse practitioner earning approximately $44,000 per year to the MD's $148,000 per year), in the lower cost of training, and in the reduced levels of hospitalization and drug utilization found for nurse practitioner care compared with that of medical care. Some Ontario nurse practitioners argued for fee-for-service remuneration rather than salary. Carol Slauenwhite et al., 'Independent Nurse Practitioners: Is Society Ready for Us? Should they be?' 24. However, in 1994, the decision was made to place nurse practitioners on salary – estimated at $60,000 to $80,000 per year. 'Nurse Practitioner Program Coming to Queen's,' *Kingston Whig-Standard*, 14 Dec. 1994, 1. An RNAD offical commented in mid-1999 that the salary range for PNs is really $57,000 top $70,000 per year, without benefits. Interview of RNAO official, 7 July 1999. Research on NP cost-effectiveness is under way. Interview of NPAO official, 8 July 1999.

284 With regard to the nurse practitioners, the report has this to say: 'Careful studies in Burlington and Southern Ontario have demonstrated that the outcomes of employing nurse practitioners in primary care settings [health status, quality of care, acceptability by patients] were comparable to those of conventional practise [i.e., by doctors]. However, some of the barriers to the use of allied health personnel with expanded roles which require further study are the extent of

role conflicts with physicians, the desire of physicians to avoid extra supervisory responsibilities, and the decrease in net practise income experienced by physicians who employ nurse practitioners. [With the utilization of the nurse practitioners estimated] reductions in medical manpower requirements of 20 to 30 percent could be achieved by 2001.' Despite their research, they went on to recommend the training of more physicians. Ontario, Council of Health, *Medical Manpower for Ontario: A Report of the Ontario Council of Health, Senior Advisory Body to the Minister of Health* (Toronto: Queen's Printer, 1983), 38–9, 172.

Interestingly, there was little or no mention of the nurse practitioner by the nursing organizations who presented briefs to the HPLR team. Later discussions of expanded nurse categories by the nursing profession added a nursing position which would be at a higher level than the RN, but references to this independent nurse (level III) were left rather vague. CNO, *College Communiqué*, 12/15 (1987), 9–10.

285 Ontario, Council of Health, *Medical Manpower*, 39.
286 Rod Mickleburgh, 'Nurse Practitioner Plan Alarms Family doctors,' *Globe and Mail*, 12 Feb. 1994), A6. By Dec. 1994 plans were announced to start training nurse practitioners (an estimated seventy-five students per year) in ten Ontario universities. 'Nurse Practitioner,' *Kingston Whig-Standard*. The Ontario nursing leadership predicts that the role of the nurse practitioner will increase dramatically in the near future.
287 The president of the OCFP clearly saw the implications of this announcement. His reply, 'Frankly, it alarms me,' quoted in Mickleburgh, 'Nurse Practitioner.'
288 Silburt, 'Nursing,' 4; Mickelburgh, 'Nurse Practitioner.' When they refer to increased costs, they assume the nurse practitioners will be added into the system without any reduction in the number of physicians in the system – a debatable assumption.
289 HPRAC, 'Advice to the Minister: Nurse Practitioner Referral' (Mar. 1996).
290 'They can order lab tests and X-rays, communicate diagnosis, prescribe and treat medical conditions, and [engage in] health promotion ... within their scope-of-practise as defined by the Expanded Nursing Services for Patients Act, 1998. The scope-of-practise is generally based on the notion they are only treating common illnesses and conditions, stable conditions and episodic illness as defined by the Act.' Interview with nurse practitioner coordinator, 2 June 1998.
291 It was explained to me as follows: 'There are a lot of people who use the nurse practitioner title and do all kinds of things ... Why restrict others' use of [the term]? We do not want to have to prosecute others.' Interview with college official, 4 Mar. 1997.

Notes to pages 126–7 309

292 'The "RN NP(EC)" must be an RN who takes a Nurse Practitioner course test, then goes through a year-long quality assurance monitoring program where they are evaluated at the end of the year, or simply takes an NP course through the universities that offer NP education. It is actually many universities that all offer specific components of the course, and they all work together. This includes RN education, the college NP exam and the year of quality assurance review.' Interview with nurse practitioner coordinator, 2 June 1998.
293 Ibid.
294 In early 1999 the Ontario Conservative government was increasing funding for primary care nurses practitioners for, as the minister of health referred to it, 'under-serviced areas and long-term care.' Global Television, *Global News*, 15 Mar. 1999.
295 ODHA submission to HPLR (Dec. 1984), 2–3.
296 RCDSO, Appendix A, titled 'Dental Hygienists,' submission to HPLR (Dec. 1983), 1. Here the authors (all dentists) claim, 'It is neither necessary nor productive to promote self-regulation of dental hygiene as a profession. Dental hygienists have demonstrated the effectiveness of the present collaborative approach to the supervision and government of their members' (p. 1). The dental hygienists had apparently been promised by both the MOH and the RCDSO, that the failure to include them as a self-regulating profession in the 1974 HDA, was temporary. The minister of health had reiterated this promise in 1977. ODHA submission to HPLR (Dec. 1983), 2; repeated (May 1986), 10–11.
297 ODHA submission to HPLR (June 1984), 13, and (May 1986), 3. They also referred to their having waited patiently for their governing body, the RCDSO, to settle the issue of supervision, but after that body had 'tabled the issue three times in the last year' without resolution, the hygienists were beginning to get 'disillusioned and frustrated by the inflexibility of the dental profession.' Ibid. (Dec. 1983), 10.
298 RCDSO submission to HPLR (Jan. 1987), 57.
299 Interview with former RN, 10 Aug. 1992.
300 Dental hygienists were probably helped by the fact that their association (ODHA) became their voice. Not having had self-regulation, they did not have their own governing body. In addition the dental college had kept them so weak within that organization that there was no effective voice there either. As we saw earlier, the section on dental hygiene was written by the dentists who submitted the RCDSO submission.
301 This read, 'A member [dental hygienist] shall not perform a procedure under the authority of section 4 [their authorized acts] unless the procedure is ordered by a member of the Royal College of Dental Surgeons of Ontario.' Dental Hygiene Act, 1991, S.O. c.22 s.5(1). The HPLR recommendation had deliber-

ately used the word 'order' rather than 'supervision,' the latter of which would have assumedly necessitated the employee–employer relationship. HPLR Report, 154.
302 One practising Ontario hygienist I interviewed said she thought that many young women like herself would not want either the worries or the hassle that went with 'borrowing all that money for equipment' or 'trying to get malpractice insurance.' Interview with dental hygienist, 6 Aug. 1991; follow-up interview, 10 Aug. 1992. It was also pointed out to me in a later interview that the dental hygienist's services are much more portable than the dentist's for servicing off-site locations such as nursing homes and for running mobile dental hygiene clinics. In 1997 there was only one independent dental hygienist's office operating in Ontario (without the performance of any authorized acts and with a dentist next door). Interview with dental hygiene college official, 30 Jan. 1997.
303 The authorized acts referred to 'scaling teeth and root planning' as well as 'orthodontic and restorative procedures,' but it was the former the hygienists were concerned about regarding self-initiation, since it constituted an important portion of their work. Dental Hygiene Act, 1991, S.O. c.22 s.4(1)(2) and s.5(1).
304 Dental hygienists are allowed to practise in Quebec and British Columbia under the more lax interpretation of 'order' or 'supervision.' ODHA submission to HPLR (June 1984), 6–7. They also practise independently in the Netherlands and some U.S. states. Interview with dental college official, 16 Sept. 1992. The word 'supervision' has a history of committee scrutiny and varying interpretations, as well. (Does it mean direct supervision, under-the-same-roof supervision, occasionally-drop-by-and-spot-check supervision, and so on?) ODHA submission to HPLR (May 1986), 6.
305 ODHA submission to HPLR (May 1986) 3.
306 Ibid., (Dec. 1983), 1, 10. These service gaps and the cost-effective solution of freeing up dental hygienists to practise 'off-site' were again discussed in the June 1984 submission (p. 12) and the May 1986 submission (pp. 6–7). They continued to be discussed in 1997. Interview with dental hygiene college official, 30 Jan. 1997. The reference to the home refers to the home-bound or home-care programs. The dental college did initially agree to support this continuation of the dental hygienists' working without the direct supervision of a dentist in these institutions – as one MOH official said to me, this is work the dentists don't want to do anyway. Interview with civil servant, 21 Feb. 1990.
307 ODHA submission to HPLR (June 1984), 6–7.
308 Ibid., (Dec. 1983), 1, 10.
309 HPRAC, 'Advice to the Minister of Health: Dental Hygiene Referral' (May 1996).
310 Ibid., 28. This detailed study also provided alternative options to legislative amendment.

Notes to pages 127–9 311

311 Ibid., 27, 25.
312 Interview with dental hygiene college official, 30 Jan. 1997. The minister's decision was partly influenced by the difficulty of making any change to the legislation when his Conservative government was acting under a very full legislative agenda.
313 CDHO, letter to Minister of Health Jim Wilson, 29 Nov. 1997, 2.
314 Interview with dental hygiene college official, 3 June 1998 and 6 July 1999.
315 The new legislation has switched to usage of the term 'technologist' (rather than the old double nomenclature, technologist/technician) for all of the professional 'tech' groups. Previous legislation referred to them all as technicians, therefore reference here to the old governing bodies will retain that usage. I will also use the term 'technician' for non-professional technically educated or trained assistants. Note: The distinction 'registered technologist' was also used to indicate the former, and the new legislation does prohibit the use of 'dental technician' by a member of the profession of dental technology. Dental Technology Act, 1991, c.23 s.7(2).
316 You will remember from the earlier dental care discussions that the dentists were given the right to veto any proposed regulations that the dental technicians might wish to make to their own act – by the state officials who passed the relevant legislation in 1946.
317 This board was, at the time, comprising three registered dental technicians, one lay person, and one dentist.
318 ARDT, 'Response to the Submission by the Governing Board of Dental Technicians,' submission to HPLR (July 1984). It is interesting to note that the two submissions by the governing body and the association have exactly the same layout, format, and print type. It looks very much as if the same authors wrote both submissions.
319 GBDTc submission to HPLR (Dec. 1983), topic 1.
320 See Appendix 7 for their standing with regard to the '9 Criteria.'
321 Ibid., topic 5, p. 2.
322 Ibid., topic 5, p. 3.
323 GBDTc submission to HPLR (July 1984), section entitled 'Question #6.'
324 ARDT, 'ARDT News Update: The Newsletter of the Association of the Registered Dental Technicians,' *Newsletter* (June 1988), 1.
325 Interview with dental technician college official, 3 Mar. 1997. There is no separate laboratory governing legislation for dental technology labs such as exists for medical technology labs.
326 GBDTc submission to HPLR (Dec. 1983), topics 7 and 9.
327 Although dentists may hire technologists or technicians to work for them or their patients under direct supervision, there is some concern, e.g., about 'basement

312   Notes to pages 129–31

   labs' taking over the registered dental technologist / technician's (RDT) work. Interview with dental technician college official, 3 Mar. 1997.
328 ARDT submission to HPLR (Mar. 1989), 1–3. Here they make the comment, 'If audiologists have a license to prescribe hearing aids and optometrists have a license to prescribe ophthalmic appliances, there should be a license to prescribe dental appliances in the Dentistry Act.' Ibid., 3.
329 Dental Technology Act, 1991, S.O. c.23 s.3.
330 BRT submission to HPLR (Dec. 1983), 1; (July 1986), 8ff to (Jan. 1988), 1. OSRT (Dec. 1983), 2–3. (Like nursing, there are two associations for this group.) OAMRT submission to HPLR (July 1986), 1; RTSO submission to HPLR (Dec. 1983), 30, 32; (July 1986), 10; (Jan. 1988), 1; and (June 1988), 1. OSMT submission to HPLR (Dec. 1983), 8; (Sept. 1985), 8ff to (Jan. 1988), 1–2. There was, at the time, no governing body for either the respiratory or the medical laboratory group. For the scope-of-practise statements granted in the new legislation, see Appendix 8.
331 BRT submission to HPLR (Dec. 1983), 1; (July 1986), 8ff to (Aug. 1988), 1. OSRT submission to HPLR (Dec. 1983), 1–2; OAMRT submission to HPLR (July 1986), 2ff to (Jan. 1986), 1. RTSO submission to HPLR (Dec. 1983), 31–2; (July 1986), 13; (Jan. 1988), 1; and (June 1988), 1. OSMT submission to HPLR (Dec. 1983), 8; (Sept. 1985), 9ff to (Jan. 1988), 3–4. The medical radiation technologists were given licensed acts allowing them to perform the following: (1) Taking blood samples from veins; (2) administering substances by injection or inhalation; (3) administering contrast media through or into the rectum or an artificial opening of the body; (4) tattooing. Medical Radiation Technology Act, 1991, S.O. c.29 s.4. The respiratory therapists were licensed to do the following: (1) Performing a prescribed procedure below the dermis; (2) intubation beyond the point in nasal passages where they normally narrow or beyond the larynx; (3) suctioning beyond the point in the nasal passages where they normally narrow or beyond the larynx; (4) administering a substance by injection or inhalation. Respiratory Therapy Act, 1991, S.O. c.39 s.4. The medical laboratory technologists were licensed to take blood samples from veins or by skin pricking. Medical Laboratory Technology Act, 1991, S.O. c.28 s.4.
332 The suggestion was made that they might amalgamate with the respiratory therapists (who did get in), but they were not at all inclined in this direction.
333 HPLR, *Striking*, 220.
334 Medical Radiation Technology Act, 1991, S.O. c.29 s.3.
335 Ontario Regulation 107/96, 'Controlled Acts: Forms of Energy,' 28 Mar. 1996.
336 OSMT submission to HPLR (Dec. 1983), 30.
337 There are three specialties: radiography, nuclear medicine, and radiation therapy.
338 For this reason the MRTs have been arguing that they ought to be given authorized

acts for the use of electromagnetism and sound waves. They could then move to control their use by non-regulated practitioners. Interview with medical radiation technologist college official, 5 Mar. 1997; follow-up, 20 Mar. 1997.

339 Because of their cross-over with nursing, pharmacy, and medicine (with regard to, e.g., urinary catheterization, tracheal suction, barium enemas and swallows, plus other contrast 'drugs'), there is considerable confusion over necessary acts such as delegation, and administration and dispensing of drugs. Interview with medical radiation technologist college official, 5 Mar. 1997.

340 The RN(EC) can order (and therefore also read) x-rays, but cannot take an x-ray. The issue with the orders to the respiratory therapists has yet to be dealt with, since, as we saw earlier, the legislative changes do not apply to acute care practitioners.

341 OSMT had argued for this from the beginning. OSMT submission to HPLR (Dec. 1983), 15.

342 Conversation with laboratory-related MOH official, 15 Sept. 1989.

343 The educational hierarchy was not just one of amount of education required, but also the facility in which one had been educated, i.e., it was also related to the long-held university/college hierarchical in-fighting and prejudices – with the college graduates generally resentful of their inferior educational status, and the university graduates generally misinformed of the high level of training received by the college-trained technologists (i.e., three years of intense lecture and laboratory work using the same textbooks as the university courses tended to use).

344 OSMT submissions also referred to clinical microbiologists, but they are not on the HPLR list of practitioner groups who requested self-regulatory professional status.

345 They both failed on the grounds of membership size, alternative regulatory mechanisms, and sufficiency of supervision. The physicists also failed to meet the risk-of-harm criterion. See Appendix 7. The clinical chemists were, justifiably, upset that one of the reasons given for their exclusion from the new act was their ability to effectively govern themselves without regulation.

346 OSCC submission to HPLR (Dec. 1983), 4–6.

347 OSMT submission to HPLR (June 1984), 30. This position was then held by one person, often a medical director.

348 As of Sept. 1994 a few clinical chemists had registered with the CMLT, but many were still disaffected with their current status. Interview with medical laboratory technologist college official, 29 Sept. 1994.

349 OSMT submission to HPLR (Jan. 1988), 4.

350 Clinical chemists are scientists with a PhD and sometimes an MD as well.

351 As usual, the subordinates in the laboratory have tended to be women while their superiors are men.

352 OSMT submission to HPLR (Dec. 1983), 11, and (Jan. 1988), 3.
353 The association also argued that some of the more educated laboratory workers were inadequately trained, e.g., those with a university BSc rather than technology training and certification. Ibid., (Dec. 1983), 17.
354 Ibid., 29.
355 In the post-proclamation stage, e.g., of developing the regulations to the legislation, there was concern at the college over the exemption allowed other laboratory workers the controlled act of drawing blood. Interview with medical laboratory technologist college official, 19 Feb. 1997.
356 The ophthalmologists define orthoptics rather generously for an assistant group. 'Orthoptics [is] the science of *diagnosing* and treating anomalies of binocular vision which are associated with the malalignment of the eye's normal, straight, conjugate relationship ... The orthoptist, the most senior and well-established of the workers aiding the ophthalmologist, specializes in ocular motility. He or she assists in *diagnosis* and treatment of such conditions, when necessary, with occlusion, exercises or prisms.' OMA (Section on Ophthalmology) submission to HPLR (June 1984), Appendum 2, p. 1 (emphasis added).
357 It should be said here that the development of the assistants by the elite practitioners does not necessarily represent the same end-goal for medical specialists as it does for the dentists, as was illustrated in the dentists' bid to bypass the dental hygienists. The assistant is trained to assist and, therefore, may well be more appropriately trained to work in cooperation with the medical specialist. Where the problem comes in is with the use of that assistant to do more than assist, i.e., to work more as a distantly supervised para-professional which is what the dentists wanted with the new level of assistant. This person can then be used to do the work which is being billed to the state as the costly work of the professional.
358 COO submission to HPLR (June 1984), 12. OAO submission to HPLR (Dec. 1983), 5.
359 Boase commented on this disagreement. She refers to a letter to the HPLR from the Orthoptists Society (June 1984) in which they claim, 'We are *medical* orthoptists – we do not aid optometrists in any way.' Boase, 'Public Policy,' 207–8.
360 ODNAA requested 'official regulation,' which would be similar to the regulation of the dental hygienists and 'preventive dental assistants' prior to the review (R.S.O. 447 s.49 and s.50), i.e., regulation which would leave them under the control of the dental profession. ODNAA submission to HPLR (Dec. 1983), 1.
361 Ibid.
362 ODNAA did use this 'extension of the dentist's own hands' phrase in their June 1984 submission (p. 3). The minor intra-oral functions were, e.g., suture removal,

placement and removal of rubber dam, and matrix and wedge placement for fillings. ODHA submission to HPLR (June 1984), 4.
363 ODHA submission to HPLR (June 1984), 4, 12.
364 ODNAA submission to HPLR (June 1984), 5.
365 Interview with civil servant, 21 Feb. 1990.
366 Interview with dental college official, 8 Aug. 1998 and 9 July 1999.
367 The registered nurses' organizations argued against this name change. Both the RNAs' and the RNs' positions were summarized by an address in the nurses' journal *College Communiqué*: 'It is the OARNA's belief that the current title of RNA implies an assistant relationship to the RN when in reality the RNA, while working under the direction and general supervision of an RN, is accountable for his or her own practise. There is opposition to a name change from the RNAO and the ONA. These associations believe that the title RNA reflects the intent which prevailed when this worker was originally introduced (in 1941) and that the title remains appropriate.' CNO, 'President's Message,' *College Communiqué*, 2/3 (June 1986), 2.
368 The McRuer Report had commented unfavourably on the control of the assistants by the nurses on the grounds of fairness (or justice): 'We see no justification for the present situation, which is thoroughly undemocratic.' McRuer Report, 1205. This was quoted in the initial submission by the RNAs' association. OARNA submission to HPLR (Dec. 1983), 7. Krever, a CHA investigator, was also quoted in the next submission as saying, 'The College of Nurses should continue, but should only have jurisdiction over registered nurses.' OARNA submission to HPLR (June 1984), 3.
369 CNO submission to HPLR (Dec. 1983), 11, and (June 1984), 3–4. The main reason given for this opposition was that joint regulation would ensure 'open discussion' and conflict resolution between the two branches of nursing, as well as reducing costs, but the CNO also argued that the RNAs appeared to be confused as to the role a separate governing college would play. That is, they pointed to expectations on the part of the RNAs that a separate governing college would improve job security and working conditions – areas lying outside the jurisdiction of a governing college. Ibid. (June 1984), 5.
370 OARNA, 'Two Colleges Considered,' *Bedside Specialist: A Quarterly Newsmagazine for Ontario's RNAs*, 2/1 (1986), 11–12. For some time the RNAs believed this split college arrangement was going to be accepted. They were quite disillusioned when it fell through. Cheryl Cornacchia, 'Ministry Will Split Regulatory Body for Ontario Nurses, RNA Predicts,' *Globe and Mail*, 9 Feb. 1987, 1.
371 The 2:1 RN:RNA representation on the existing college council had been brought up at the beginning of the review process. OARNA submission to HPLR (Dec. 1983), 6–7. Also see, OARNA submission to HPLR (June 1984), 3–4.

372 The new act called for 14 RNs and 7 RPNs on the college council. Nursing Act, 1991, S.O. c.32 s.9(1a).
373 One of the criteria, e.g., which looked at the group's distinct body of knowledge (as had the HPLR) failed to show enough distinction between the RN's and the RPN's body of knowledge. HPRAC, 'Advice to the Minister of Health: Separate College for Registered Practical Nurses' (June 1996), 33; see also 49, 68.
374 They were (a) a separate scope-of-practise for RPNs, (b) proposed self-initiation of authorized acts, and (c) delegation, assigning, and initiating. RPNAO, 'A Separate College for Registered Practical Nurses: Response to the Submissions of Other Participants in the Minister's Referral' (Mar., 1996).
375 Interview with registered practical nurses association official, 5 June 1998 and 7 July 1999.
376 OHA submission to HPLR (June 1984), 42. In a report predating the HPLR, the OHA had argued that the RNAs had 'proven themselves capable of taking on additional responsibilities and tasks beyond those outlined in the (1976 Standards of Nursing) document.' OHA, 'Submission to the College of Nurses of Ontario on the Role of the Registered Nursing Assistant' (Dec. 1981), 6.
377 Interview with registered practical nurses association official, 5 Mar. 1997.
378 Ibid. This same official spoke of the problem the RPNs were having with regard to their public image. Citing a CBC, *Market Place*, television program which had portrayed the RPNs 'badly' with regard to their skills and education, she pointed out that the RPN is 'guided by the same standards of practise within the nurses' college [as are the RNs].'
379 One author quoted the executive director of OARNA, in 1988, as interpreting the current elevated-standards thrust of the RN organizations as no more than 'a professional ego trip.' Carol Thomas, 'Proposed Changes to Nursing Standards Mean Profession-Wide Debate,' *Toronto and Region Hospital News* (Jan. 1988), 4.
380 OARNA submission to HPLR (Dec. 1983), 2, and (June 1984), 5–9.
381 Interview with nursing assistant, 13 Jan. 1993. There are, of course, other workers in the hospital, e.g., health care aides, ward aides, orderlies, and in other health care institutions, e.g., personal care attendants, who also do many of the unpleasant tasks common to the institutionalized care of the ill. ONA submission to HPLR (Dec. 1984), 5.
382 OHA submission to HPLR (June 1984), 43.
383 The practical nurses are concerned about the increased usage of 'generic' unregulated workers. Interview with registered practical nurses association official, 5 Mar. 1997. See also, RPNAO, 'A Position Statement on Unregulated Health Care Workers' (Mar. 1995).
384 Interview with registered practical nurses association official, 5 June 1998.

Notes to pages 140–5   317

385 As we saw earlier, the HPRAC was set up to function as an ongoing means of communication and dispute resolution between the state and all health practitioners.

7 Continuity and Realignment of the Positions of Connection

1 See Table 3.2.
2 An OCFP official said there had been 'a lot of doctor bashing.' Interview with family physicians college official, 16 June 1998.
3 In the early 1900s, e.g., while nurses negotiated wage increases of 30–40 per cent, medical fees declined 5–10 per cent. Interview with former senior civil servant, 28 Apr. 1994. However, in Dec. 1996 the OMA negotiated a wage deal which outsiders were calling a government sell-out. 'Interim Agreement between the Ontario Medical Association and Her Majesty the Queen in Right of the Province of Ontario, represented by the MOH' (15 Dec. 1996).
4 See the scale referred to in Figure 4.1: autonomy – negotiation – consultation – audience – exclusion.
5 Interview with family physicians college official, 16 June 1998. This official mentioned a recent (1998) rejection letter in reply for a meeting request with the Minister of Health, as well as the fact that the OCFP had filed a court injunction against Minister Grier, when she was in office, for bypassing public hearings and medical input in her decision to institute nurse practitioners.
6 The ongoing relations between all self-professed health practitioner groups and the new HPRAC, the Professional Relations Branch of the MOH and the minister of health, at least potentially gives them that voice.
7 This showed up, e.g., in the case of the ophthalmologists' fight with the optometrists, the obstetricians' concerns about midwifery, the surgeons' and physiatrists' concerns about chiropractic and chiropody, and the psychiatrists' concerns about psychology or other counselling specialists.
8 Interview with family physicians college official, 16 June 1998. The interviewee referred to a study put out by the Health Council on Policy and Economics as well as an OMA study called, 'The Cost Effectiveness of the Family Physician,' which demonstrates the 'cost effectiveness of primary health care providers' (FPs) as gatekeepers for medicine per se, i.e., over medical specialists.
9 J.W. Grove, *Organized Medicine in Ontario: A Study for the Committee on the Healing Arts* (Toronto: Queen's Printer, 1969) 276–7.
10 From the beginning, one of the proclaimed goals of the early Canadian medical (local) societies was the suppression of health care practises by other practitioners. The CMA's 1868 Code of Ethics forbade consultation with 'irregulars,' and the CMA strictly enforced this. David C. Naylor, *Private Practice Public Payment:*

Canadian Medicine and the Politics of Health Insurance 1911–1966 (Montreal: McGill-Queen's University Press, 1986), 19–22. MacNab provides examples of the Ontario medical profession's attempts at 'openly opposing the new groups' developing in the early 1900s. Elizabeth MacNab, *A Legal History of Health Professions in Ontario: A Study for the Committee on Healing Arts* (Toronto: Queen's Printer, 1970), 38–9. Hamowy provides numerous examples throughout his text of the medical profession's attempts to exclude other practitioners from health care. Ronald Hamowy, *Canadian Medicine: A Study in Restricted Entry* (Vancouver: Fraser Institute, 1984). Also see Chapters 2 and 3 of this work.

11 'Some acts which are now delegated may, in the future, be transferred to the domain of other professions as the acts become more commonplace and as the education and training of other professions is expanded to include preparation for performing such acts.' CPSO submission to HPLR (Jan. 1984), 20. Note the implications of this statement with regard to old assumptions about expertise.

12 Ibid., 18–19. The suggestions included cross-profession referrals and a requirement 'that a report of encounters with practitioners of certain professions be made to a practitioner, designated by the patient, of another specified profession' (p. 19).

13 At least one comment implied that these independent practitioners might not be so independent. 'Members of a profession may provide services to patients quite independently of other professions in terms of supervision, yet that profession might not be permitted to receive patients directly but only on referral from members of another profession to ensure that an accurate diagnosis has been made and an appropriate treatment selected.' Ibid., 23. However, names were not named here, so it is not clear just who might need referral from whom. In addition, a later statement appears to soften this suggestion considerably. CPSO submission to HPLR (June 1984), 26.

14 Ibid., 14–15. Recognition would indicate to the public the ministry's approval of the activities of these groups while at the same time indicating the lack of necessity of their being regulated (an interesting idea, although it was never taken up by the review team or the policy makers who followed it).

15 The following positions and quotes are taken from CPSO submission to HPLR (June 1984), 16, 24, 16, and 62.

16 Interview with the OMA director of health policy who, as he informed me, had been the author of the OMA's HPLR submissions, 16 Sept. 1994.

17 Particular disputes are referred to in specific group discussions. Medical specialists such as the ophthalmologists, e.g., whose entrepreneurial territory was being tread upon, were not so friendly to the competition. Nor was the medical profession concerned with medical–chiropractic relations in its pursuit of a scope-of-practice statement or an authorized act for 'spinal manipulation.'

18 Ibid.
19 Interview with the OCFP president, 16 June 1998.
20 HPRAC, 'Transcript of Public Meeting: Naturopathy' (3–4 Nov. 1996), 25–33, 68–77.
21 As noted in Chapter 6, the naturopaths, e.g., continue to refer to themselves as 'naturopathic doctors.' Regarding medical policing of alternative practitioners, ironically, the few prosecutions the medical profession actually takes the time and expense to carry out may well serve the cause of quackery as a whole. These cases tend to give alternative practitioners a useful cry in the arena of public rhetoric – with the medical profession portrayed rather effectively as the bully.
22 Many alternative techniques, such as hypnosis, acupuncture, Eastern relaxation techniques, and so on, have been practised by licensed medical professionals. Interview with an MD practising in a multidisciplinary 'Wellness Centre' in Toronto, 28 Sept. 1994. The successful disciplinary procedures of Dr Jozef Krop, MD, by the CPSO have been viewed by many supporters of alternative health care as a witch hunt. See, e.g., literature of the Citizens for Choice in Health Care lobby group, for 1998–9.
23 It may well be countered that the burden of proof ought not to fall on the medical profession. I would argue, however, that since they have been given the judicial privilege of taking actions which might lead to the prosecution of other practitioners whom they deem to be crossing into their territory, there are legal grounds for a call to a burden of proof on the part of the prosecutors. Also, the act of directing public funds towards self-serving purposes, i.e., the encouragement of funding only questions of interest to one's own profession, at the same time as one criticizes the inadequate science of those one has helped exclude from that funding, is rather morally suspect. The scientific imperative itself would argue for the investigation of any claims to scientific fact or patient outcomes, and since the medical professionals have long portrayed themselves as being on the side of objective scientific inquiry it would remain incumbent on them to assist in the development of all such inquiry. Lastly, since there have always been cases of licensed medical practitioners making use of these alternative techniques, there is a professional reason for the instigation of further investigation.
24 BDO submission to HPLR (June 1984), 12.
25 OOA submission to HPLR (Dec. 1983), 4. This critique was reiterated in the BDO's second submission, 5–8.
26 U.S.-trained osteopaths were no longer allowed to register as physicians under the CPSO, and the Canadian-trained osteopaths had proven to be trained at standards considerably lower than those required by the CPSO. Interview with former osteopath board of directors member, 30 Jan. 1997.
27 Elaine Gort and David Coburn, 'Naturopathy in Canada: Changing Relationships

to Medicine, Chiropractic and the State,' *Social Science Medicine*, 26/10 (1988), 1065-7. The report being referred to is by the Canadian RCHS (1964).
28 Gort and Coburn give excerpts from these briefs and proceedings which make one wonder just what world the naturopaths were living in. They also comment that the submissions to the HPLR were 'vastly improved' over those to the RCHS and the CHA, but, in my opinion, they still fell far short of the sophistication of other 'outsider' groups, e.g., the midwives. Gort and Coburn, 'Naturopathy,' 1065-7.
29 These comments were passed on to me with regard to a statement overheard at a public rally in the early 1990s by a naturopath to the minister of health, no less.
30 RCHS (1964).
31 D.L. Mills, 'Study of Chiropractors, Osteopaths, and Naturopaths in Canada,' RCHS (1964). Referenced in Gort and Coburn, 'Naturopathy,' 1065.
32 RCHS (which asked which health providers ought to be included in the national health insurance scheme) did not recommend public insurance coverage for the naturopaths. (However, B.C. did partially include them in its plan in 1965.) Likewise, the CHA and the HPLR did not recommend naturopathy for self-regulatory professional status. Grove, however, disagreed with this recommendation in his CHA report on the medical profession. He felt the naturopaths ought not to be 'banned,' but rather, to be brought 'under a firmer measure of public control.' Grove, *Organized Medicine*, 283. I should note, not all naturopaths wanted to be included in the RCHS recommendations for health insurance coverage. Like other objectors, e.g., medicine and dentistry, some naturopaths thought their income might decline with inclusion in any such plan. Gort and Coburn, 'Naturopathy,' 1065.
33 This report had not made any recommendations towards naturopathy per se, but the sense at the time was that there would be follow-up recommendations, and these were not likely to bode well for the naturopaths.
34 These tactics included political party contributions, dinners, and club memberships. Gort and Coburn, 'Naturopathy,' 1065. This is the same sort of 'politicking' which Boase describes for the chiropractic campaigns and which were common for the elite health care practitioners. Joan Price Boase, 'Public Policy and Regulations of the Health Disciplines: An Historical and Comparative Perspective' (PhD dissertation, York University, 1986), 342.
35 This was partly for reasons mentioned above, especially the division within the group itself as to whether or not attainment of this goal would constitute a positive move.
36 The draft legislation for the HDA had accepted the CHA's recommendations to cease regulation of any more persons practising naturopathy, however, this restriction was deleted from the act itself. According to Gort and Coburn, 'The principle reason for the deletion ... appears to have been the political action campaign spear-

headed by Schnell, the head of the national [naturopathy] association ... [who] concentrated on ... a patient letter writing campaign.' Gort and Coburn, 'Naturopathy,' 1066. For the reasons given for the 1990s' RHPA decision, see Appendix 7.
37 In the 1995 HPRAC public meetings regarding naturopathy, the Toronto Women's Network's presentation strongly supported the naturopaths' bid for inclusion in the RHPA. HPRAC, 'Transcript of Public Meetings: Naturopathy' (1995), 39–44.
38 The Canadian chiropractic school had taught naturopathy courses for some time, and the DPA had allowed dual registration of the drugless practitioner groups. The numbers I came across for this dual registration varied, but appear to have been between 50 and 80 per cent.
39 This issue presented a problem for the HPLR group and the Professional Relations Branch officials because, although it was being fought vigorously, the decision had been made during this time not to regulate naturopathy, on the ground, among others, that its practise was not harmful enough to the public to require regulation, so it should be left in the public domain. But to prohibit chiropractors from practising care, which was in the public domain, would go against the principles on which the contested new scope-of-practice model rested. However, there was also a great deal of concern in the whole process for the problems the board had raised, especially for clarity for the consumer's sake and for effective self-regulation of professional members.
40 RHPA allowed double registry of nurses who were trained in midwifery (mostly British).
41 'Dual Registrants: College of Chiropractic of Ontario (CCO) Policy: P-018,' reaffirmed by the CCO council (1 Nov. 1997).
42 OCA submission to HPLR (Dec. 1986), 13; BDC submission to HPLR (Dec. 1986), 14.
43 In the 1995 HPRAC public meetings regarding naturopathy, the chiropractic college and association argued to restrict naturopathy's potential scope-of-practice and controlled acts. They both went as far as questioning the naturopaths' fulfilment of the requirements of RHPA regulation per se – although also at one point asserting that the naturopaths 'offer valuable services to many people.' HPRAC, 'Transcript: Naturopathy,' 88–91, 99–107.
44 They also had concerns about limitations on homeopathy should naturopathy be given its requested scope-of-practice. Ibid., 33–9, 56–61, 107–29.
45 BDDT submission to HPLR (Dec. 1983), 3.
46 ONaA submission to HPLR (June 1984), 12.
47 BDDT submission to HPLR (June 1984), 24.
48 ODA summarizes this as follows, 'The mix of different providers of care, with different levels of training who participate in the fulfilment of the overall objectives of a treatment plan initiated by one professional, indicates the need to have one person

responsible overall for the provision of such care and to have one regulatory body (the RCDSO) responsible for the enforcement of standards applicable to all members of the team.' ODA submission to HPLR (Dec. 1983), 18.

49 RCDSO started out (p. 1 of submission one) with a lecture which was paternalistic towards both the MOH and the other dental groups under consideration for 'the status of a profession.' RCDSO submission to HPLR (Dec. 1984), 1. They went on, soon after, to dispel any idea that dentistry might be considered under the new legislation to be 'one group of professionals among several professions.' Ibid., 2. According to them, dentistry's existing scope-of-practice was 'appropriate,' (p. 3), but those of all other dental care groups were in need of 'supervision' (p. 6). 'Taken to its extreme [they predicted], permitting non-professionals to effect procedures to an unlimited extent and without supervision in effect *destroys the profession at large*' (emphasis added; p. 6). ODA described its reaction as one of apprehension and shock to what it perceived as the HPLR's idea of 'increasing the number of professions (other dental care groups) and not professionals (dentists).' ODA submission to HPLR (Dec. 1984), 6. Some of ODA's statements were both arrogant and politically naive. For example, while others were carefully (and therefore respectfully) explaining what it was they believed their contribution (as experts in their field) to be, the dentists flippantly claimed, 'a dentist is what a dentist does.' Ibid., (Dec. 1983), 19.

50 Ron Bell (ODA president), 'Letter,' *Ontario Dentist*, 62/2 (Feb. 1985), 2 (emphasis added).

51 Interview with civil servant, 21 Feb. 1990.

52 DAO, 'Response to Clustering Proposals in the Workshop Document' (June 1986), 1. No clustering of dental groups occurred.

53 David J. Kenny, 'Dental Hygienists Are Dentists' Assistants,' *Ontario Dentist* (Sept. 1985), 4 (emphasis added).

54 Randy Lang (chairman of the legal and legislative committee of the council of the RCDS, also one of the authors of the RCDSO submissions to HPLR), 'MDs Advise Deregulating Hygienists/Assistants,' letter to the *Ontario Dentist* (Nov. 1985). He was also quoting the medical governing board's submissions to HPLR as having agreed in principle with Kenny's claim.

55 Interview with dental college official, 16 Sept. 1992.

56 ODHA submission to HPLR (Dec. 1983), 9. They did not answer the part of the question posed by the HPLR team which referred to their supervising anyone else (only the dentists' supervising them), nor did the HPLR team ask for the answer in the follow-up submission. Compare this also to the registered nurses' bid to control the assistant nurses.

57 ODHA submission to HPLR (May 1986), 9–10. They refer here to promises from the dentists, in 1982, coupled with an 'absence of any substantial documentation

Notes to pages 153–4   323

[which] compelled [them] to question' the good faith of the dentists (p. 9). Here the hygienists also add, 'This lack of representation has, e.g., resulted in arbitrary changes to the scope-of-practice and a total inability to come to grips with the supervision issue – two key issues in the dental hygiene profession' (p. 10). They also pointed out that the 'present regulatory system denies peer review for dental hygienists involved in complaints or disciplinary procedures' (p. 12). The hygienists end this whole discussion, very smoothly, with the comment, 'The ODHA does not believe that the RCDS has either the interest in, or the commitment to, the profession of dental hygiene that is appropriate for a governing body. This does not suggest ... that the relationship of individual dentists and dental hygienists ... has not generally been one of professional co-operation and mutual respect. It does, however, underline the reality that dental hygiene is an integral part of ... the system [and] cannot be dealt with as an afterthought by a profession which has its own and different priorities, and is burdened by the issue of inherent conflict of interest' (p. 15).

58 Interview with dental college official, 16 Sept. 1992.
59 Interview with civil servant, 21 Feb. 1990. This 'level II assistant' is discussed in the nurses and assistants' submission (see below).
60 *CHA Report*, vol. 2, 112.
61 The best example of this, to my mind, was the occasion when the HPLR team proposed that the rather pretentious title of 'Royal' be dropped from medicine's and dentistry's governing bodies, since it was not to be used by any of the other regulated colleges. The medical profession complied with the request, but the RCDSO said no. Not only did they show themselves to be out of sync with the egalitarian thrust of the day, but also they did not win any friends in the officialdom in the process. RCDSO submission to HPLR (Jan. 1987), 52. Interview with civil servant, 21 Feb. 1990.
62 While no one would come out and say this to me directly, or on the record, I was given the distinct impression that the dentists had not enamoured themselves to ministry officials during this process. There were more than a few pairs of eyes rolled during the interviews which discussed the behaviour of the dental profession. In their turn, the ODA president openly referred to the MOH's review process as 'the monster,' even before the final decisions had been made. Jim Brookfield, 'ODA Actions Draw Unexpected Reactions: Despite Criticism from Some Quarters, the ODA Will Continue to Get Involved in Issues that Concern Its Members.' President's Page, *Ontario Dentist*, 64/8 (1987), 7. Another influential co-drafter of the HPLR submissions wrote a sarcastic, inflammatory (ironically entitled) editorial, in 1987, which clearly indicated his opinion regarding the agency relationship of the dental profession and the state. He ended by saying, 'For the Government to suddenly destroy [the Health Disciplines Act] and attempt to take over the dental

324   Notes to page 154

governing body by using abusive power is a terrible and inexcusable abuse of their power.' Randy Lang, 'Power Corrupts: Absolute Power Corrupts Absolutely,' *Oral Health*, 77/9 (1987), 7-8. One assumes there must have been a few politically astute members of the profession arguing against such openly vitriolic reactions. One influential voice came from the dentist and historian whose work I have made use of in this work, James Shosenberg. In an editorial following soon after the association's presidential 'monster' reference above, Shosenberg called for some moderation. He said, 'Our attempts to cope [with the harsh reality of our decline] sometimes remind me of the old saying, "If you can't be right, at least be wrong in a loud voice."' He went on to suggest that 'the good old days' are gone and recommend that they move on and 'adapt to a new environment.' 'Above all, [he said] we have to stop looking through a rear view mirror and start looking ahead. It's time to get back to the future.' James Shosenberg, 'Back to the Future: Dentistry Cannot Afford to Live in the Past. We Can Prepare for the Future, or Await Our Demise.' Editorial, *Ontario Dentist*, 64/11 (1987), 5.

63 In its 'Vision 2000: Mission and Goals of the Ontario Dental Association,' ODA includes as one of its goals, 'to maintain self-regulation' Amazingly, it would appear they thought even this to be threatened. Reproduced in Appendix F of James W. Shosenberg, *The Rise of the Ontario Dental Association: 125 Years of Organized Dentistry* (Toronto: ODA, 1992), 275.

64 In the U.S. a report in 1992 noted that 'cosmetic work [had] tripled in the last five years, with over 80% of the dentists now offering such services.' The (Canadian) commentator adds, 'That's wonderful news for an industry that was on the verge of a crisis. A victim of its own success. Cavities have decreased by half over the last 20 years, and, with every indication they would eventually be eliminated completely, the drill 'n fill school of dentistry needed something for its practitioners to do.' Robert Hercz, 'Dental Plans: The Bright Side,' *Toronto Life Fashion* (Summer 1992), 40. But it should also be kept in mind that a lot of this work might also prove to be just as easily done by a technologist or hygienist. The technologists are capable of making the mould used in teeth whitening, and the hygienists are capable of executing the remaining portion of this lucrative task. However, as long as the technologists do not directly serve the public, and the dental hygienists' autonomy is curbed, this business will remain under the control of the dentists.

65 One gets the distinct impression that there were more than a few undocumented phone calls between the elite practitioners and the decision makers during this whole process.

66 OCPh submission to HPLR (June 1984), 3.

67 This was usually with reference to delegated acts. Even the assistant groups said they would have to go with their 'professional judgment' if they felt the patient was at risk.

Notes to pages 154–7   325

68 Interview with the president of the OCFP, 16 June 1998.
69 OCPh submission to HPLR (June 1984), 5.
70 'Under the new legislation there are no longer going to be General Product numbers which are used to indicate products that are not drugs by definition and can be sold in non-pharmacy outlets. If it is a drug, it would have a drug identification number and make a medicinal claim.' Interview with pharmacy college official, 23 June 1998 and 9 July 1999.
71 The chiropodists were given this function. Chiropody Act, 1991, S.O. c.20 s.5(3).
72 OCPh submission to HPLR (June 1984), 5–6.
73 Chiropody Act, 1991, S.O. c.20 s.4 and s.5(1).
74 See Chapter 6. Ironically, the chiropodists were given this controlled act in the new legislation.
75 I also went through the miles of files handed over by the HPLR to the MOH and found nothing on the reasoning behind these decisions. Nor did interviews turn up any of these details.
76 In a recent dispute over the placement of new physicians in state-designated areas of practice, e.g., the medical organizations composed of those not to be affected by any such new policy fought hard for the students' freedom of choice.
77 The medical specialists here are the ophthalmologists (sometimes referred to as occultists, eye physicians, or eye doctors). They define themselves as follows: 'An ophthalmologist ... is a medical doctor who is trained and qualified to diagnose and treat all eye and visual system problems as well as general diseases of the body.' OMA (Section on Ophthalmology) submission to HPLR (June 1984), 57.
78 Ibid., 'Comments on Initial Submission to HPLR by the Ontario Association of Optometry' (Dec. 1983). It might also be noted in regard to their claim to the cost-effectiveness of using an ophthalmology team that the ophthalmologists nowhere addressed the fact that while the actual wages of their assistants are lower than those of optometrists, it is the very expensive ophthalmologist who submits the OHIP bill according to services provided. So their claims about their cost-effectiveness are suspect; they would have to be demonstrated rather than merely asserted.
79 Perhaps, as was suggested earlier, the OMA (which represents all MDs, both general practitioners and specialists), having to balance the particular interests coming from the specialties of medicine with the general interests of the profession as a whole, ended up giving little backing to the demands made by the medical specialty groups, as did their other representative, the CPSO.
80 See the discussion on optometry in Chapter 6. The optometrists were granted a scope statement which makes reference to the 'diagnosis' of 'prescribed diseases' and a authorized act of 'applying a prescribed form of energy' (as in laser surgery). These areas both creep into what used to (legally) be clear medical territory. Optometry Act, 1991, S.O. c.35 s.3(c) and s.4(3). See also OMA (Section on Oph-

thalmology) submission to HPLR (June 1984), (Sept. 1984), and (Nov. 1986). Interestingly, the chiropractors tried to do the same to the medical practitioners who might wish to practise spinal manipulation, but failed (see chiropractic section below).

81 The request was for the use of therapeutic pharmaceutical agents. http://www.hprac.org/english/referrals

82 Interview with optician college official, 5 Mar. 1997. This relationship was described by an opticianry representative as 'good.'

83 Ibid.

84 See Chapter 2.

85 Interview with OMA official, 16 Sept. 1994.

86 J. Dvorak, 'Manual Medicine in the United States and Europe in the Year 1982,' *Manual Medicine*, vol. 1 (1983), 3–9.

87 A 1993 Ontario study which looked at international data found the evidence 'overwhelmingly' in favour of the use of chiropractic treatment for low-back pain, rather than medical treatment. Pran Manga, et al., 'A Study to Examine the Effectiveness and Cost-Effectiveness of Chiropractic Management of Low-Back Pain,' (Toronto: MOH, 1993). One U.S. study concluded, 'Chiropractors deliver a substantial amount of health care to the U.S. population.' Paul G. Shekelle and Robert H. Brook, 'A Community-Based Study of the use of Chiropractic Services,' *American Journal of Public Health* 81/4 (Apr. 1991), 439. There was also a commission of inquiry into the issue of chiropractic effectiveness and efficiency in New Zealand in 1978–9. OCA included a summary of this inquiry by D.A. Chapman-Smith, 'New Zealand Commission of Inquiry Into Chiropractics (1978–9): Its Constitution, Procedure, Findings and Significance' (May 1984). Attachment to the CCA submission to the Ontario HPLR (June 1984). After it had, in the words of the inquiry, 'read and heard all that could be said against chiropractic,' it reported, 'findings supporting all the central claims of the modern chiropractic profession, straight or otherwise.' Chapman-Smith, 'New Zealand Commission,' 12. A second report by Manga and Angus was released at the time of the publication process for this book. See http://www.chiropractic.on.ca/execsummary.html 4/28/98.

88 Citing international studies, particularly one done by a New Zealand Commission of Inquiry into Chiropractic, the OCA argued that the short training courses these other practitioners attend in order to learn spinal manipulation are 'inadequate.' OCA submission to HPLR (June 1984), 3–5; (Dec. 1986), 13. See also, BDC submission to HPLR (June 1984), 6, 10, and (July 1986), 9–12. This claim was also made with regard to the medical profession, by independent researchers in Saskatchewan, one a medical orthopedic specialist and one a chiropractor involved in clinical research, who claim that 'manipulation requires much practise to acquire the necessary skills and competence. It is a full time vocation, few medical practi-

tioners have the time or inclination to master it.' W.H. Kirkaldy-Willis and J.D. Cassidy, 'Spinal Manipulation in the Treatment of Low-Back Pain,' *Canadian Family Physician*, vol. 31 (Mar. 1985), 539.

89 Both medicine and physiotherapy were given specific authorized acts for 'moving the joints of the spine beyond a person's usual physiological range of motion using a fast, low amplitude thrust' (the latter being the hallmark of chiropractic). Medicine Act, 1991, S.O. c.30 s.4(4). Physiotherapy Act, 1991, S.O. c.37 s.4(1). Massage therapy was also given a wording in its scope-of-practise which the chiropractors interpreted as allowing them to engage in the practise of spinal manipulation. Although the chiropractors argued against the allowance of others to 'manipulate,' the HPLR recommended scope-of-practise for massage therapy did use the word 'manipulation' rather than the term suggested by the chiropractors, i.e., 'mobilization.' HPLR, *Striking a New Balance: A Blueprint for the Regulation of Ontario's Health Professions* (Toronto: Queen's Printer, 1989), 204. In the end, the new legislation has retained the term 'manipulation' in the massage therapists' scope of practice. Massage Therapy Act, 1991, S.O. c.27 s.3.

90 BDC submission to HPLR (Aug. 1988), 12–13.

91 They were a bit ambiguous on this point. Later they appeared to back off to some degree, allowing that physiotherapists would be competent enough for primary contact 'for certain things such as sports injury work [and] ... routine therapy in an institutional environment'; but they continued to argue for medical and chiropractic referral. BDC submission to HPLR (June 1984), 9. They did not, as we have seen, want any physiology control extended to spinal manipulation procedures.

92 BDC submission to HPLR (Dec. 1986), 16.

93 Physiotherapy Act, 1991, S.O. c.37 s.8(1).

94 Earlier mention was made of the increasing 'credentialism' of the physiotherapy profession – similar to that of nursing. A U.S. study shows their physiotherapy 'evaluators ... emphasizing ... [the] defining and validating of the body of knowledge [in the discipline].' G.M. Jensen, 'The Work of Accreditation On-site Evaluators. Enhancing the Development of a Profession,' *Physical Therapy*, 68/10 (1988), 1517. Our Canadian professions have tended to follow these U.S. trends.

95 Boase, 'Public Policy,' 219.

96 CPSO submission to HPLR (June 1984), 15, 43. Given the history of antagonism between the medical profession and chiropractic, one might suspect medicine's support of the chiropractors' territorial rivals, the physiotherapists, of being influenced by more than egalitarianism.

97 Boase, 'Public Policy,' 219. The physiotherapists' governing body also commented on the reluctance of the family practitioners to 'give up a historical referral relationship,' as expressed by that group in meetings with the governing body. BDP submission to HPLR (June 1983), 27.

328   Notes to pages 160–2

98   See, e.g., their section on the physiotherapists in a late submission to the review. It says little or nothing. OMA submission to HPLR (Jan. 1988), 13.
99   With regard to kinesiologists (who applied for, but failed to get, self-regulatory status) the physiotherapists' governing body said, 'This board has had several complaints regarding kinesiologists practising "physiotherapy" ... beyond the bounds of their expertise.' But the board does go on to argue for self-regulatory status for the kinesiologists, with cooperation, even a joint regulatory board, between the two professions. BDP submission to HPLR (June 1983), 27.
100 Their scope of practice and authorized acts lists, if granted, would have constituted invasion into the territory of the medical profession, medical laboratory technologists, chiropractors, dentists, anaesthesiologists, pharmacists, and midwives. They also made reference to their desire to practice in the territory of the acupuncturist, although they would first train at the Acupuncture Foundation of Canada. BDP submission to HPLR (June 1984), 24–5.
101 OPA submission to HPLR (June 1984), 32–7. BDP submission to HPLR (June 1984), 25–7.
102 Ibid., 37.
103 Ibid.
104 BDM submission to HPLR (June 1984), 9–10.
105 Both the BDM and the OMTA strongly supported shiatsu therapists, recommending that either they be given separate regulation, or inclusion, on a joint governing body, with the massage therapists. This issue had not been settled by the time RHPA legislation came out. There is no mention of shiatsu in that legislation, however, both the shiatsu and massage therapists continue to press the issue with the HPRAC. BDM submission to HPLR (June 1984), 5, 8, 16. OMTA submission to HPLR (Dec. 1983), 36.
106 BDM submission to HPLR (June 1984), 8–10.
107 Ibid., 8.
108 OMTA submission to HPLR (Dec. 1983), 15, 27. After reading hours and hours of vitriolic attacks among these groups, this was a surprising and refreshing change.
109 Ibid., 16.
110 Ibid., 24.
111 Michael Klein, 'Commentary: Midwifery – A Family Doctor's View from Quebec,' *Birth*, 18/2 (June 1991), 104.
112 MC submission to HPLR (June 1984), 59. CPSO concurred with this assertion.
113 Eleanor LeBourdais, 'Despite CMA Misgivings, Support for Midwifery Appears to be Growing,' *CMA Journal*, no. 139 (Oct. 1988), 770.
114 This issue was discussed in their internal newsletter, the CNO's, *College Communiqué*, 10/4 (Aug. 1985) 11/2, and 11/5 (Apr. and Oct. 1986).

115 There was a spate of them in the *Globe and Mail* in the spring of 1994. These letters are often written by medical professionals still opposed to midwifery. It is not clear, however, why there was so little overall opposition to the decision to include the midwives in the RHPA. Some of the general acceptance may have been influenced by the many positive articles which were then appearing in the popular press citing the impressive record of midwives in other countries, particularly the Netherlands.
116 Interview with midwifery program director, 9 June 1998.
117 Ibid. Interview with family physicians college official, 16 June 1998. Interview with CMO official, 7 July 1999. It was noted that there was some resentment that physicians are not paid for consultations with midwives.
118 Interview with midwifery program director, 9 June 1998.
119 David Coburn, 'The Development of Canadian Nursing: Professionalization and Proletarianization,' *International Journal of Health Services*, 18/3 (1988), 451.
120 CNO submission to HPLR (Jan. 1984), 4–5.
121 CMA, 'Perspectives on Health Occupation' (1986), partially reproduced in an article by Charlotte Gray, 'What Do Nurses Want?' *CMA Journal*, no. 136 (May 1983), 982.
122 This same wariness was displayed by the medical profession for any encroachment by other health care practitioners on their previously exclusive scope of practice. CPSO submission to HPLR entitled 'Commentary on Proposed Scopes of Practice and Licensed Acts' (Jan. 1987). See also OMA submission to HPLR entitled 'Response to the General Scope Statements Proposed by the HPLR Team,' 11, 16.
123 Such as, the Victorian Order of Nurses. Coburn, 'The Development,' 442–3.
124 Newsbriefs, 'British Physicians Back Nurses' Bid to Prescribe,' *Medical World News* (9 Mar. 1987), 37. Lillian Newbury, 'Doctors Versus Nurses: "Turf Tension,"' *Toronto Star*, 10 Sept. 1983, 12. Newbury takes the term 'pseudo-doctors' from an article in the *CMA Journal* by the CMA's director of publications.
125 In 1997, e.g., the nurses, like others such as the dental hygienists, were still arguing over the fine lines of a medical 'order,' 'delegation,' or 'supervision,' on issues such as venapuncture. Interview with nurses college official, 6 Feb. 1997.
126 Interview with family physicians college official, 16 June 1998.
127 'The RN(EC) can be the primary care giver, however, they must work collaboratively with all other (not just medical) health professionals. This means that the NP must diagnose the condition or assess the condition and then refer the patient to the physician or other professional if their assessment shows the condition does not fall within their legislated scope of practice ... The year-long quality assurance process enforces the concept that the NP is not supposed to be an island ... rather

the NP is expected to fill a specific piece missing from the health care system.' Interview with nurse practitioner RN(EC) coordinator, 2 June 1998.
128 Ibid. Interview with family physicians college official, 16 June 1998.
129 They referred to this as 'limiting flexibility in functional assignments.' OHA submission to HPLR (Jan. 1984), 3.
130 Interview with practising RN, 20 Jan. 1995.
131 Interview with registered nurses association official, 2 June 1998.
132 As the medical professionals are increasingly asked to trade off their desired benefits for guarantees of cost-containment, they are turning to more than their own work habits as a means of coming through.
133 RCDSO submission to HPLR (Jan. 1987), 57.
134 We have seen the specifics of these dynamics in the discussions of expertise turf in Chapter 6; I refer the reader back to that chapter to avoid repetition here.
135 Most of these relationships have already been discussed in Chapter 7 with regard to the issue of expertise.
136 Interview with dental technician college official, 3 Mar. 1997.
137 The large national laboratories, e.g., send out brochures to dentists enticing them with gifts such as air miles (rather than money), but while the CDT have questioned the ethics of this, they have no legal jurisdiction to oppose it. Nor would they have the resources to fight a large corporation over an issue such as this. Ibid.
138 The RDT may supervise a dental lab, but the denturist may not. Questions of actual roles (hampered by time constraints) rather than hypothetical roles have produced some tension between the two. Ibid.
139 Ibid. Pay differentials are not always realized, but as a general rule any type of technologist or technician (dental or medical) expects to be paid more than her or his less-educated counterpart.
140 Interview with medical laboratory technologist college official, 19 Feb. 1997. This cross-over legislation also presents a problem with confidentiality for the MLTs with regard to the OMA's Laboratory Proficiency Testing Program.
141 Interview with medical laboratory technologist college official, 20 Feb. 1997.
142 OSMT submission to HPLR (Dec. 1983), 11, and (Jan. 1988), 3.
143 RTSO submission to HPLR (Dec. 1983), 1. But all three professional technological groups refer to their work as needing only 'indirect supervision.' BRT submission to HPLR (Dec. 1983), Topic 7; RTSO submission to HPLR (Dec. 1983), 2; OSMT submission to HPLR (Dec. 1983), 11. They occasionally refer to the 'unsupervised' or 'independent' nature of their work. BRT submission to HPLR (Sept. 1985), 1; RTSO submission to HPLR (Dec. 1983), 2; OSMT submission to HPLR (Dec. 1983), 11. Some technologists or technicians also provide services for others like chiropractors, chiropodists, and podiatrists – although the new legislation does not allow for this. BRT submission to HPLR (Dec. 1983), Topic 6. The new

Notes to pages 166–72   331

legislation makes reference only to orders from the CPSO for the medical radiation technologists, respiratory therapists, and medical laboratory technologists – with the latter group's act allowing also for orders from the RCDSO. Medical Radiation Technology Act, 1991, S.O. c.29 s.5(1). Respiratory Therapy Act, 1991, S.O. c.39 s.5(1). Medical Laboratory Technology Act, 1991, S.O. c.28 s.5(1).
144 Interview with respiratory therapist college official, 19 Feb. 1997.
145 Ibid.
146 Interview with medical radiation technologist college official, 5 Mar. 1997.
147 Ibid.
148 OSRT submission to HPLR (Dec. 1983), 15.
149 Interview with two practising medical laboratory technologists, 27 Jan. 1992.
150 This was how the CHA referred to them. CHA Report, vol. 2, 404.
151 This nomenclature is misleading, because these 'technologists' are really assistants to the service group of dietetics, rather than technologists in the sense in which that term has been used throughout this study. I have, therefore, placed them in the assistant category.
152 It is likely that the real reason for their exclusion was the anti-monopoly orientation of the time which argued against unnecessary regulation.
153 The dieticians' association listed *thirty-six* 'closely related' designations in use by non-registered dieticians. ODtA submission to HPLR (July 1986), 5–6.
154 As one assistant group representative replied to the question of 'Expected disputes?' from the HPLR team. ODNAA submission to HPLR (Dec. 1983), 8.
155 Ibid., (June 1984), 6, and diagram p. 4.
156 The dentists' college claimed, 'This [regulatory control], however, does not result in a need for representation on Council or the committees of the College.' RCDSO submission to HPLR (June 1984), 22. This statement was made after the dental hygienists' arguments about the injustice of the same in their case. Arguments about procedural justice fell on deaf ears in the RCDSO.
157 I am referring here to agency as 'the empowerment of a person or persons to act for another.' The term is synonymous with delegated authority, proxy, or deputy. *New World Dictionary*, 2nd ed. (Cleveland: William Collins, 1979), 25. Also, I am using the term 'legal' here in the broad sense, as in the political–judicial rule of law.
158 I do not mean to imply a pure economic–legal distinction here. The political obligation, as we have seen, includes an economic concern for the utilization of the public purse.

8 The RHPA of 1991

1 This chapter is meant to provide an overview of the RHPA. Assessments of, or conclusions about, the changes it entails are presented in Chapter, 9.

2 During the regulation development stage of the process the decision was also made to designate more minor areas of the legislation, such as registration fees, as bylaw.
3 Hugh Heclo, *Modern Social Policies in Britain and Sweden: From Relief to Income Maintenance* (New Haven: Yale University Press, 1974), 304–22. Paul Sabatier, 'Knowledge, Policy-Oriented Learning, and Policy Change: An Advocacy Coalition Framework,' *Knowledge: Creation, Diffusion, Utilization*, 8/4 (1987), 654. HPLR noted, 'Professions that previously had little knowledge of each other and communicated infrequently have had an opportunity to learn about each other and to form lines of communication.' HPLR, *Striking a New Balance: A Blueprint for the Regulation of Ontario's Health Professions* (Toronto: Queen's Printer, 1989), 6.
4 A meeting is called if up to three colleges are interested in participating. Participation from all of the professional colleges, including medicine and dentistry, has been high, particularly with regard to difficult issues, such as sexual abuse and quality assurance. Interview with medical laboratory technologist college official, 19 Feb. 1997.
5 Interview with chiropody college official, 20 Feb. 1997.
6 Interview with medical college official, 29 June 1998.
7 Interview with psychology college official, 20 Feb. 1997. Interview with medical college official, 29 June 1998.
8 Interview with massage therapy college official, 19 Feb. 1997.
9 Interview with audiology and speech–language pathology college official, 19 Feb. 1997.
10 Interview with HPLR member, 21 Jan. 1992.
11 I was told this in an earlier interview (for another project) with one of the HPLR team that 'the Review's mandate is not economic. We don't even look at this. We [only] decide which groups should be regulated.' Interview with HPLR member, 11 July 1986.
12 HPLR, *Striking*, 4.
13 Interview with HPLR member, 21 Jan. 1992.
14 Carolyn J. Tuohy, 'Private Government, Property, and Professionalism,' *Canadian Journal of Political Science*, 9/4 (1976), 679–80.
15 The elite practitioners were quick to remind the HPLR team and ministry officials in their HPLR submissions of the inappropriateness of a single body making decisions on both regulatory and economic concerns. See, e.g., OMA submission to HPLR (June 1984), 3, 7.
16 As Boase pointed out in 1986, any MD could (and still can) practise physiotherapy, and she or he would be reimbursed 15–20 per cent more than a trained physiotherapist would be for the same treatment. Boase also noted that the director of physiotherapy programs was usually an MD who would have had a mere two days'

Notes to pages 176–7 333

training in physiotherapy techniques. Joan Price Boase, 'Public Policy and Regulation of the Health Disciplines: An Historical and Comparative Perspective' (PhD dissertation, York University, 1986), 115–16.
17 In some cases, e.g., the chiropractors, audiologists, speech–language pathologists, optometrists, psychologists, nurse practitioners, and denturists, scientifically based evidence was produced. See Chapters 6 and 7.
18 This is demonstrated by the case of chiropractic. As we saw in Chapters 6 and 7, the controlled-study literature argues overwhelmingly in favour of the efficiency of the use of chiropractors rather than medical practitioners for the costly treatment of a large portion of low-back pain, as Manga et al. found when they investigated it. Pran Manga, Douglas E. Angus, Costa Papadopoulos and William R. Swan, *A Study to Examine the Effectiveness and Cost-Effectiveness of Chiropractic Management of Low-Back Pain* (funded by the Ontario Ministry of Health) (Aug. 1993). But the new legislation allows any medical practitioner to engage in the 'fast, low-amplitude thrust,' or spinal manipulation which is the cornerstone of the chiropractic treatment. Given the lack of training the general medical practitioner is given in this field of practice, the quality-of-care arguments or knowledge criterion of the policy reviewers seems to have been overridden here by their anti-monopoly orientation.
19 Manitoba Deputy Minister of Health John D. Wade, 'Policy and Practice: Can They Live Together' (public lecture presented at Queen's University, Kingston, 28 Sept. 1995).
20 HPLR, *Striking*, 5.
21 RHPA c.18, Schedule 2 s.3(2). The college's 'objects' were defined as follows: (1) To regulate the practice of the profession and to govern the members in accordance with the health profession act, this code, and the RHPA, 1991, and the regulations and by-laws. (2) To develop, establish, and maintain standards of qualification for persons to be issued certificates of registration. (3) To develop, establish, and maintain programs and standards of practice to assure the quality of the practice of the profession. (4) To develop, establish, and maintain standards of knowledge and skill and programs to promote continuing competence among the members. (5) To develop, establish, and maintain standards of professional ethics for the members. (6) To develop, establish, and maintain programs to assist individuals to exercise their rights under this code and the RHPA, 1991. (7) To administer the health profession act, this code, and the RHPA, 1991, as it relates to the profession and to perform the other duties and exercise the other powers that are imposed or conferred on the college. (8) Any other objects relating to human health care that the council considers desirable. Ibid., c.18 Schedule 2 s.3(2).
22 Ibid., c.18 Schedule 2 s.18 s.85 (1–6), s.36–56 s.75–9 s.61, and s.79(1)-83. The HPLR team had recommended the establishment of two new college committees, a

fitness to practice committee and a continuing competence committee, in order to 'reflect the increasing emphasis being placed on identifying and preventing deficiencies in practitioners, as distinguished from primarily responding to individual complaints.' HPLR, *Striking*, sec. 7.01. The continuing competence committee recommended by the HPLR was renamed the quality assurance committee in the RHPA to better reflect the intentions of the MOH, since the latter encompassed a broader understanding of 'competence'; one which would include the obligation to assess the quality of one's work rather than just one's adherence to the general standards of medical practice. The committee was to administer the quality assurance program. RHPA, c.18 Schedule 2 s.80–1.

23 Suggestions from the medical profession for detailed changes to the proposed legislation, consisting mainly of legal details (what would 'hold up' if challenged in a court of law), were argued back and forth by the legal counsel of both sides, with the CPSO (or OMA) counsel occasionally winning. See, e.g., the eighty-eight objections made by the legal counsel for the CPSO, in July of 1988, to the HPLR team's legal and procedural proposals, as well as the thirteen objections to the details of the proposed separate act for medicine. CPSO, 'Commentary on Legal and Procedural Proposals and the Medicine Act: Submitted by the College of Physicians and Surgeons of Ontario,' submission to HPLR (July 1988). Some of these legal details were, of course, related to long-standing legal debates, such as the medical profession's policy on qualifications for foreign medical students, professional advertising, and professional incorporation – most of which would be settled in external court decisions or ministerial decisions beyond the reach of the policy designers.

24 It is hard to tell to what degree the submissions represent the views of the group's leaders rather than those of the rank and file. Although influential discussion with the lower levels of the group organization was held in some cases, e.g., the midwives, this may have had as much to do with the group's limited resources, i.e., their having no clearly discernable or available elite, as it did with any egalitarian ideology. The tight scheduling of responses demanded by the HPLR team served to limit the amount of democratic group input into the process. Non-leadership members of the groups making the submissions were sometimes given little more than updates after the fact. And in fairness to some of these leaders of the groups, many of their rank and file were not terribly excited or responsive to all the talk about legislation. I was met with the 'What legislation?' response more than a few times when I randomly asked health providers about their latest legislation debates – especially from those working for salary in a clinic or institution.

25 The tour was sponsored by commercial interests in the health food and vitamin retail business.

26 The Patients' Rights Association does not represent public *participation* per se,

since it consists of a small group of energetic volunteers who attempt to speak for 'the patient.'
27 HPLR, *Striking*, 16.
28 RHPA, c.18 Schedule 2 s.5(1) and (4).
29 Ibid. c.18 s.3 (emphasis added).
30 Ibid. c.18 s.6(1), and c.18 Schedule 2 s.10 and s.11.
31 HPLR, *Striking*, 29–32. The major changes were expansion of the number of board members (from 5–7 to 12–20) 'to accommodate the projected increase in the board's workload' (p. 29); expansion of the power of the board granted by the Health Disciplines Act 6(9) to hire employees, such that said employee might be an 'independent investigator to investigate complaints not dealt with by the colleges' (p. 30); clarification of the board's power to retain 'experts and professional (including legal) advisors' (p. 31) independent of the parties involved (4.13 of the draft legislation) 'as the board requires' (4.10); expansion of the 'obligation [of the board's tribunal] to disclose expert and professional advice obtained' (4.13); and, empowering the board 'to extend certain limitation periods' (p. 31).
32 That is, a non-college/council member or ex-college/council member, non-civil servant/crown agency appointed by the lieutenant governor in council on the recommendation of the minister. RHPA, c.18 s.18–19.
33 Ibid., c.18 s.18–26 refers to the board itself, and c.18 Schedule 2 s.21–2 and s.28–35 refer to the role of the board in review of the decisions of the registration and complaints committees respectively.
34 HPLR, *Striking*, 13; emphasis added.
35 RHPA, c.18 s.11. For the original HPLR recommendation, see HPLR, *Striking*, sec. 3, p. 25–8.
36 RHPA, c.18 s.14.
37 Ibid., c.18 s.6(2). Section 11, subsection 2 here had required that HPRAC 'monitor each college's patient relations program and ... advise the Minister about its effectiveness.'
38 Ibid., c.18 s.6(3).
39 This decision was made by Minister Gigantes. These dates were extended because of 'the regulatory burden that the RHPA had placed on the colleges and government.' Interview with civil servant, 10 June 1998.
40 H.U. Cummings, C. Lipski, and C. Wasteneys, 'A Framework for Evaluating the Quality Assurance Programs of the Colleges of Health Professions in Ontario,' submission to HPLR (July 1997). HPRAC, 'Advice to the MOH: The Regulation of Funding for Therapy and Counselling for Patients Sexually Abused by Health Professionals' (Feb. 1995). Bille Laskin and Paula Klein, 'Report to HPRAC: Sexual Abuse Prevention Plans of the Regulated Health Professions, Recommended Approaches and Evaluation Methods' (Dec. 1996). Andrée Côté, 'Recommended

Approach to Evaluating the Effectiveness of Complaints and Discipline Procedures with Respect to Professional Misconduct of a Sexual Nature,' submission to HPLR (Dec. 1994).
41 HPRAC, 'Discussion Paper #2: Five Year Review of the RHPA' (Dec. 1996). For early developments in 1999, see http://www.hprac.org.
42 The quote is taken from HPLR, *Striking*, 36.
43 Ibid., 12.
44 RCDSO, CPSO, CNO, COO, and the CPhO joint submission to HPLR (Feb. 1987), 2.
45 Ibid.
46 They argued: 'To subvert the authority of the governing body in favour of some outside authority would require demonstrable want of good faith.' RCDSO submission to HPLR (Dec. 1983), 13. It is interesting to note that they view the authority of the state as 'some outside authority.'
47 'The college does not see the need for the creation by statute of yet another level of bureaucracy with the functions suggested, nor does it believe such a Council to be desirable if its function is to assume a policy formulating responsibility that belongs to, and should remain at, the political level.' RCDSO submission to HPLR (Jan. 1987), 16.
48 RCDSO submission to HPLR (Dec. 1983), 14. Their opposition was subsequently softened in their June 1994 submission (p. 25) – probably in light of the distinct impression all of the provider groups soon started getting with regard to the seriousness of the policy designers about the importance of this quality/cost control mechanism.
49 Ibid., 21. This was reiterated throughout the entire process.
50 RCDSO submission to HPLR (Jan. 1987), 8.
51 See p. 18–55 of the RCDSO submission to HPLR (Jan. 1987). Some of these objections were also voiced in an earlier submission. Ibid., (Oct. 1985), 1–7.
52 Ibid. (June 1984), 24–6.
53 CPSO submission to HPLR (Nov. 1985), 3–4.
54 Ibid. (Feb. 1987); RCDSO, CPSO, CNO, COO, CPhO joint submission to HPLR (Feb. 1987), 3–4. By Apr. 1989 they began to hold such meetings despite internal opposition. The nurses had no 'opposition to public discipline hearings and making available transcripts of hearings' p. 3.
55 RHPA, c.18 Schedule 2 s.7(1) s.34(2) s.45.
56 Ibid., s.32(2) and (3).
57 Ibid., s.23(3), s.56.
58 HPLR, *Striking*, 7.
59 When asked about the origin of the 'nine criteria' Schwartz explained, 'Our group [the HPLR team] created the nine criteria.' When asked about the role of the practi-

Notes to pages 183–5   337

tioner groups with regard to these criteria, he replied, 'Yes, [the criteria] changed as we talked [with the practitioner groups], but they didn't change much.' Interview with Alan Schwartz, head of HPLR, 26 Sept. 1994.

60 Interview of health practitioner college representative, 19 Feb. 1997.
61 The female composition of the new groups was estimated for the HPLR team to be as follows: midwives, 100%; dieticians, 99.8%; occupational therapists, 96.8%; speech–language pathologists, 92.7%; medical laboratory technologists, 80%; and audiologists, 74.7%. It should be noted that there does remain a gender gap between the 'equal' and the 'more than equal' professional groups. These predominantly female groups were allowed into the new legislation, but none of them were given the diagnosis function or the title 'doctor.'
62 RHPA, c.18 s.35(1). This exemption relates to aboriginal healers and midwives 'providing traditional healing/midwifery services to aboriginal persons or members of an aboriginal community,' only. An aboriginal person who enters one of the regulated professions to practice within its scope of practice and authorized acts would be subject to the rules and obligations of that profession's statutes, regulations, and bylaws.
63 Interview with civil servant, 21 Jan. 1992.
64 Others, such as the naturopaths, who refused 'to play the game' had no such broader ideational climate to back them up, so their difference was not agreed to.
65 Those engaged in this process would probably argue it was not up to them to correct society's history of prejudicial treatment of particular groups of people. My purpose here is not to point the finger so much as point the problem.
66 A recent North American survey found that 'a little more than half [55 per cent] of respondents say their working relationships with female doctors are no better or no worse than those with male doctors ... [But] many respondents – women and men alike – identified the gender issue as a factor in all their [health care] relationships.' Editorial, 'A Special Survey Report: The Nurse Doctor Game,' *Nursing*, no. 91 (June 1991), 63.
67 Emily Friedman, 'Nursing: New Power, Old Problems,' *Journal of the American Medical Association*, 264/23 (1990), 2978. Calliste also points out that black immigrant nurses had to be more qualified than their white counterparts for nursing positions of equal status. Agnes Calliste, 'Women of Exceptional Merit: Immigration of Caribbean Nurses,' *Canadian Journal of Women and the Law*, 6/1 (1993).
68 Paul Carfagninir, 'Black Nurses Fight for Representation,' *Share*, no. 17 (May 1985), 17.
69 Marina Strauss, 'Court Allows Probe of Nursing Board's Disciplinary Methods,' *Globe and Mail*, 1 May 1985, M 2.

70 The commission found 'there was systemic [racial] discrimination' against nurses of colour at the Toronto Northwestern Hospital. The hospital agreed to a monetary settlement for the nurses, as well as a review of management practices and a program for anti-discrimination awareness. *Global News*, television, Canwest–Global Broadcasting System, 12 May 1994.
71 Tania Das Gupta, 'Anti-Black Racism in Nursing in Ontario,' *Studies in Political Economy*, 51 (Fall 1996) 100. A mid-1999 interview of an RNAD official indicated continued concern. 'It is a problem, but there are pockets of things happening to change it.' Interview with RNAO official, 7 July 1999.
72 Interview with midwifery program director, 9 June 1998.
73 With regard to the successes, 'in 1994 there were 68 midwives; in 1996 out of 92 midwives there were 4 women of colour; in 1998 we have 126 midwives, 13 of whom are women of colour or Aboriginal women, that is, we went from 1.5% to 4.3% to 10.3% (in 4 years).' Ibid.
74 Ibid.
75 This was commented on in both the college and the association interviews.
76 See definitions given in Chapter 4.
77 This comes from C.E.S. Franks, *The Parliament of Canada*, (Toronto: University of Toronto Press, 1987) 233.
78 Morone shows this dynamic at work in the U.S. He argues, 'The democratic wish offers a communitarian counter to individualism.' James Morone, *The Democratic Wish: Popular Participation and the Limits of American Government* (New York: Basic Books, 1990), 8.
79 See Appendix 3.
80 See earlier comment in Chapter 2. This comes from Tuohy, 'Private Government,' 678.
81 See, e.g., CPSO submission to HPLR (Dec. 1983), 5, 16; OMA submission to HPLR (Dec. 1983), 21.
82 P.H. Russell, 'Canadian Constraints on Judicialization from Without,' in Mark Charlton and Paul Baker, eds., *Crosscurrents: Contemporary Political Issues*, 3rd ed. (Toronto: ITP Nelson, 1998), 294.
83 Interview with J. Grove, 11 Oct. 1991. It should be added that the review report does give good, brief statements on the changes (and some of the reasoning) to the parts and pieces of the act, section by section.
84 I have, of course, argued in Chapter 6 that the wording of the Introduction to the HPLR Report as well as its recommendations gives us a good indication of the key ideas which informed its course, but this analysis has taken a considerable amount of historical contextualization and thought in order to be arrived at. Not many of my fellow citizens have the luxury of such an indulgence. Also, in the end, the weight of these ideas remains open to conjecture since the people responsible for

the HPLR nowhere explained their reasoning or the assumptions on which their claims were based.
85 Carolyn Tuohy, 'Public Accountability of Professional Groups: The Case of the Legal Profession in Ontario,' in R.G. Evans and M.J. Trebilcock, eds., *Lawyers and the Consumer Interest* (Toronto: Butterworths, 1982), 107. This concern for 'depoliticization' has also been expressed in relation to other policy areas and issues. See, e.g., P.H. Russell, 'The Political Purposes of the Canadian Charter of Rights and Freedoms,' *Canadian Bar Review*, no. 61 (1983), 30; or Michael Mandel, *The Charter of Rights and the Legalization of Politics in Canada* (Toronto: Wall and Thompson, 1989), ch. 2. Tuohy also counters this (in the same discussion as above) with the 'risk of overly "politicizing" a decision making system (via 'arrangements for political accountability'), allowing groups and individuals to overload it with demands.'
86 Interview with civil servant, 10 June 1998.
87 HPRAC, 'Discussion Paper #2: Five Year Review of the RHPA' (Dec. 1996).
88 They also say here that 'the definition of harm should not be unduly restricted and should be recognized to include psychological and emotional damage ... and health care practices that are not based on a Western medical model' (p. 2).
89 This comment was made by one of the more influential members of the advisory council. Interview, 5 Mar. 1997.
90 The statutory mandate here is being argued and may have to be more closely defined.
91 The practitioner groups under review foot the bill for their own expenses, which can be considerable given the legal nature of the issues.
92 The advisory council itself argued that their reports should be public 'in keeping with the spirit of HPRAC and RHPA.' It also pointed out that the limiting nature of the ministerial referral of issues prohibited HPRAC from addressing problems, even 'horrendous actions,' made apparent to them in the course of their investigations of other issues. In this sense, it was resulting in a waste of valuable information and resources. Interview with member of HPRAC, 5 Mar. 1997.
93 HPRAC, 'Discussion Paper #2,' 8.
94 Interview with member of (original) HPRAC, 4 Mar. 1997.
95 Ibid.
96 Interview with senior civil servant, 5 Feb. 1997.
97 Interview with HPRAC representative, 11 June 1998. Most surprisingly one of the council members, as of mid-1999 is a former associate director of the Ontario Dental College who worked in this latter capacity during the HPLR. Given the ongoing turf wars between dentistry and other dental groups, this seems more than a little inappropriate.
98 Interview with senior civil servant, 5 Feb. 1997.

340 Notes to pages 194–208

99 Cummings, Lipski, and Wasteneys, 'A Framework for Evaluating.'
100 These terms were used in one form or another by most of the college representatives interviewed.
101 Interview with dietician's college representative, 7 Mar. 1997.
102 Interview with nurse practitioner program coordinator, 2 June 1998.
103 Interview with RNAO representative, 2 June 1998.
104 Bill 100, 'An Act to amend the *RHPA, 1991*,' had been added to the professional bills, post-royal assent, in order to deal with the problem of sexual misconduct by the professionals – which had been investigated by the CPSO and found to be a much more serious problem than expected. Later, HPRAC provided 'Advice to the MOH: The Regulation of Funding for Therapy and Counselling for Patients Sexually Abused by Health Professionals' (Feb. 1995). And consultants were hired in 1996 to provide a 'sexual abuse prevention plan.' Laskin and Klein, 'Report to HPRAC.'
105 RHPA, c.18 Schedule 2 s.30(2)(3).

9 Conclusions from the Story

1 This analogy was used in Chapter 1 in the section entitled 'Methodological Introduction.'
2 See discussion on agency in Chapters 3, 7, and 8.
3 Tuohy quotes this from a member of a labour union commenting on a similar process in another province. Carolyn J. Tuohy, 'Institutions and Interests In the Occupational Health Arena: The Case of Quebec,' in William D. Coleman and Grace Skogstad, eds., *Policy Communities and Public Policy In Canada* (Mississauga: Copp Clark Pitman, 1990), 260.
4 See, e.g., Michael Gibbons's 'Hermeneutics of Recovery,' in Michael T. Gibbons, ed., *Interpreting Politics* (Oxford: Basil Blackwell, 1987), 3.
5 Paul Sabatier, 'Knowledge, Policy-Oriented Learning, and Policy Change: An Advocacy Coalition Framework,' Knowledge: Creation, Diffusion, Utilization, 8/4 (1987), 649–92.
6 I was given this sense in quite a number of my practitioner group interviews.
7 Here the institutional analysis would bring in the state as another key actor in terms of shifting power. And this is true; there was an institutional shift in power to the state, as discussed in Chapter 8.
8 It is interesting to see, e.g., the change which occurred in the chiropractors' proposed scope of practice for their profession. Their original version contained words which had long been argued by their professional spokespersons as fundamental to the practice of chiropractic. These words conveyed an alternative conception of health care in their emphasis on the 'promotion of health, and the

treatment and prevention of ill health, through a holistic approach, recognizing the inherent healing powers of the body and the importance of good habits of rest, exercise, diet and posture, and the importance of other aspects of life-style influencing psychological and physical well being ... treatment by conservative means, not using surgery or drugs ... The principle aim is to restore ... normal function.' OCA submission to HPLR (July 1986), 2. But by the time the HPLR was over the chiropractors had dropped all traces of the alternative talk of their earlier scope recommendations. The board's 'concerns' tabled in a 1988 submission made no mention of the deletions made to the original scope of practice as proposed by the profession. BCD submission to HPLR (Jan. 1988). Instead they were acting like 'wanna-be' medical doctors. For example, their insistence on winning the title 'doctor,' their determination to become attached to the establishment educational facilities (universities) which house the medical faculties, and even the adoption in their official flyers of all the medical profession's symbolic paraphernalia like stethoscopes, white laboratory coats, and grey-suited, grey-haired, elderly, Anglo-Saxon-looking men. CCA, 'Which of These Doctors Are Chiropractors?' Advertising Supplement (1988).

9 It is interesting to note how little weight the alternative practitioners' arguments about their preventive medicine function seemed to carry with the decision makers. See, e.g., OOA submission to HPLR (June 1984), 3. Despite all the official talk about prevention in health care and the environmental/biological holism this implies, the practitioners who have long fought for just such an approach to health care practices, like the osteopaths, the homeopaths, and the naturopaths, fared poorly when it came time for those same officials to hand out the benefits.

10 Paul Pross, *Group Politics and Public Policy* (Oxford: Oxford University Press, 1986), 18.

11 Diana Ralph, André Régimbald, and Nérée St-Amand, eds., *Open for Business / Closed to People* (Halifax: Fernwood, 1997).

12 Hugh Armstrong and Pat Armstrong, *Wasting Away: The Undermining of Canadian Health Care* (Toronto: Oxford University Press, 1996).

13 Armstrong and Armstrong also criticize this shift. Ibid., 129; http://www.cna-nurses.ca/english/publications/pubscat/pub_list/policystatem ents.html, Canadian Nurses Association, taken 15 Feb. 1998. See especially, 'Reduced Quality and Availability of Health Services Top Concerns for Registered Nurses' (28 Jan. 1998); Janet M. Lum 'Backward Steps in Equity: Health System Reform's Impact on Women and Racial Minorities,' *National Women's Studies Association Journal*, 10/3 (1998), 101–14.

14 John Shields and B. Mitchell Evans, *Shrinking the State: Globalization and Public Administration 'Reform'* (Halifax: Fernwood, 1998).

15 Carolyn Hughes Tuohy, *Accidental Logics: The Dynamics of Change in the Health*

Care Arena in Britain, the United States, and Canada (Toronto: Oxford University Press, 1999).

16 Recognition of problems in need of specialization may well be a fairly technical skill available to other less learned health practitioners who might train in this skill in the same manner as general practitioners or family physicians have done. Ironically, general medical practitioners in the U.S. are making this same sort of move up the ladder of specialization (in 'Procedures') which moves into the borders of the medical specialists' territory *above them*. Interview with former GP from Ontario who is upgrading 'procedures' in the U.S, 10 July 1998.

17 Interview with senior civil servant, 5 Feb. 1997.

18 We might want to keep in mind that during Japan's recent fiscal crisis, more specifically at the time of the collapse of a major Tokyo brokerage firm in the winter of 1997–8, leading Canadian economists, such as Sylvia Ostrey, were claiming this was largely the result of *too little* external regulation in the Japanese financial sector.

19 I was told, in mid-1998, that plans for the future include moving beyond protection from, and retribution for, sexual misconduct to 'other areas of vulnerable client abuse.' Interview with MOH official, 10 June 1998.

20 Ministers, of course, respond rather quickly to adverse media coverage.

21 They continue to set the standard for inclusion or exclusion in that they form the basis of the criteria now used by HPRAC in their decisions regarding access to the system.

22 The bioethics literature has long pointed out the importance of *informed* consent with regard to the relationship between the health practitioner and the health care patient. See, e.g., Tom L. Beauchamp and James F. Childress, *Principles of Biomedical Ethics*, 3rd ed. (Oxford: Oxford University Press, 1989). For a similar concern with regard to the participatory nature of professional organizations, see Carolyn J. Tuohy, 'Regulation and Scientific Complexity: Decision Rules and Processes in the Occupational Health Arena,' *Osgoode Hall Law Journal*, 20/3 (1982), 580.

23 An interesting in-depth look at this culture is provided by Diana Scully, *Men Who Control Women's Health: The Mis-Education of Obstetricians-Gynaecologists* (Boston: Houghton-Mifflin, 1980). This book may be dated, but embedded cultures die hard.

24 Raisa B. Deber, 'Physicians in Health Care Management: The Patient–Physician Partnership – Changing Roles and the Desire for Information,' *CMA Journal*, 151/2 (1994), 175.

25 It should be noted here, under the Red Tape Reduction Act, that the Harris government has allowed the professional colleges to determine the professional–public composition of any new committees it might design into its new (professionally controlled) bylaws.

Notes to pages 221–30   343

26 As Tuohy has pointed out, public participants in previous health care policy-making processes in Ontario have had difficulty gaining the information and access necessary for informed consent. Legislation, e.g., has not been provided in draft form to allow for scrutiny by the public or by those interest groups out of the loop of power. Likewise, access to annual reports and other sources of ongoing information has been limited. Tuohy, 'Public Accountability,' 134.

27 There was continual communication between the practitioner groups and the decision makers (the HPLR team, the Professional Relations Branch of the MOH and the office of the minister of health).

28 The talk in the MOH at the time of my research for this project included a suggestion for an assertiveness training course for public representatives.

29 See, e.g., the review in Cummings, Lipski, and Wasteneys, 'Framework for Evaluating.'

30 'Health Report,' *Maclean's*, 15 June 1998.

31 As we saw it do for the issue of illegal charging by the council members (governors) of the profession of pharmacy. See the section on pharmacy in Chapter 6.

32 Minister Witmer agreeing with Mr David McKinnon OHA president. Ontario, Health Minister Witmer (presentation to the OHA in Toronto, 5 Nov. 1997).

33 'Health Report,' *Maclean's*, 15 June 1998.

34 Tom L. Beauchamp and James F. Childress, *Principles of Biomedical Ethics, 3rd ed.* (Oxford: Oxford University Press, 1989). 278. CHA Report, vol. 1, 8. I saw this orientation often in reading through the HPLR submissions.

35 Bruce J. Fried, Raisa B. Deber, and Peggy Leatt, 'Corporation and Deprivatization of Health Services in Canada,' *International Journal of Health Services*, 17/4 (1987), 574.

36 Tuohy, 'Private Government,' 677.

37 Martin Rein and D. Schon, 'Reframing Policy Discourse,' in Frank Fischer and John Forester, eds., *The Argumentative Turn in Policy Analysis and Planning* (Durham, NC: Duke University Press 1993), 147.

38 For a review of the orientation of Ontario's (and Canada's) health policy reports up to 1993, see Sharmila Laxmi Mhatre, 'Future Developments of Canada's Health Care System: Stakeholders' Perceptions' (PhD dissertation, University of Toronto, 1993). For a flavour of the new Canadian health policy language, see the 'Report of the National Forum on Health' (1997); and the Provincial/Territorial Ministers of Health, 'A Renewed Vision for Canada's Health System' (29 Jan. 1997).

39 See Chapter 3.

40 See the discussions in Chapter 6 of, e.g., the denturists, the dental hygienists, and the massage therapists.

41 Nelson Goodman, *Ways of World-Making* (Indianapolis: Hackett, 1978), 7. Goodman uses the terms 'decomposition,' and 'composition,' but on reflection I prefer

the terms 'decomposition' and 'recomposition' since I am not composing here – that is what the actors involved are doing as they live this story – rather I am recomposing both their composition and my decomposition of that.

42 Sven Steinmo, Kathleen Thelen, and Frank Longstreth, eds., *Structuring Politics: Historical Institutionalism in Comparative Analysis* (Cambridge: University of Cambridge, 1992), 13.

43 Ibid., 13. Likewise, we saw the importance of the 'role of the state' and the 'relationships' which contemporary institutionalists have emphasized. In the Canadian context, authors such as Atkinson, Coleman, and Skogstad, and the contributors to their collected works have emphasized these factors. Michael M. Atkinson, ed., *Governing Canada: Institutions and Public Policy* (Toronto: Harcourt Brace Jovanovich, 1993); William D. Coleman and Grace Skogstad, eds., *Policy Communities and Public Policy in Canada: A Structural Approach* (Mississauga, Ont: Copp Clark Pitman, 1990).

44 Steinmo et al., *Structuring Politics*, 14.

45 See, e.g., Peter A. Hall, *The Political Power of Economic Ideas: Keynesianism across Nations* (Princeton, NJ: Princeton University Press, 1989).

46 H. Hugh Heclo, 'Issue Networks and the Executive Establishment,' in Anthony King, ed. *The New American Political System* (Washington: American Enterprise Institute for Public Policy, 1978). Pross, *Group Politics*.

47 In Chapter 5 we saw that there were over 120 groups and individuals (mostly groups) who responded to calls for input into the HPLR process. There were also many lawyers, civil servants, institutional actors, and (some) patients' groups giving voice to expertise over the course of the policy process.

48 Manzer has illustrated this in his discussion of the boundaries of the Canadian climate of principles. Ronald Manzer, *Public Policies and Political Development in Canada* (Toronto: University of Toronto Press, 1985).

49 See Appendix 3 for a list of the HPLR words which ought now to sound familiar.

50 Margaret S. Archer, *Culture and Agency: The Place of Culture in Social Theory* (Cambridge: Cambridge University Press, 1988).

Glossary

Aestheticians use things of beauty for therapeutic reasons.
Acupuncturists insert needles under the skin, e.g., to stimulate 'meridian pathways' in order to reduce pain.
Aromatherapists 'heal and balance' the body using aromatic, botanical essential oils.
Art therapists utilize the practice of making objects of art as therapy for their patients.
Athletic therapists use organized athletic activities for physical and psychological rehabilitation of patients.
Audiologists treat hearing (and related communication) dysfunctions.
Aura and colour healers apply colours (actual or through visualization) to the body's aura (the 'electromagnetic field which surrounds the body') to heal the body.
Bioenergetic analysts analyse and 'open blocked or tensed' areas of the body through specific exercises.
Biofeedback practitioners 'heal and restore balance to the body' via technological devices which 'monitor the unconscious processes and feed-back this information to the conscious mind.'
Biological photographers photograph medical conditions and procedures.
Botanic medicine practitioners use botanic substances (vegetable drugs prepared from bark, roots, herbs, and such) to treat a variety of diseases and disorders.
Chiropodists treat disorders of the foot.
Chiropractors treat spinal (and joint-related) disorders without the use of drugs or surgery, using mostly quick thrusts or spinal manipulation.

---

[1]The following definitions constitute a loose interpretation of the function of most of the health provider groups involved in the regulatory processes discussed in this work. For the formal definitions of those groups that now have legal definitions, see Appendix 8.

Christian Scientists practise a system of healing which interprets the Christian scripture as saying all diseases and death have no existence other than as a product of mental error and, therefore, can be overcome by faith.

Clinical biomedical engineers apply engineering principles to medicine.

Clinical hypnotists induce a sleep-like condition in their patients to gain a better understanding of their mental state.

Clinical chemists train in biochemistry and the pathophysiology (malfunction) of disease.

Colon therapists use colonic lavage (deep enemas) to cleanse the colon of impurities which have accumulated there.

Consultants, counsellors, psychometrists, and psychotherapists make up an organization of mental health workers self-described as 'an important but not-yet-legally-recognized faction in psychology.'

Dance movement therapists use dance for the physical and psychological rehabilitation of patients.

Dental assistants assist dentists in their work.

Dental hygienists clean teeth and give dental maintenance advice.

Dental nurses act in dentistry as medical nurses act in medical care.

Dental technicians is the old term for dental technologists (although a technician is not a technologist, the latter having more education than the former).

Dental technologists make dental devices (such as bridges and crowns) on order of a dentist.

Dentists mostly do the more difficult dental work and leave the easier work to their auxiliary workers (dental hygienists and dental assistants) whom they are supposed to supervise.

Denturists are independent merchants who design and sell dentures (partial and complete).

Diagnostic medical sonographers run the equipment which takes pictures of the body's interior, such as the computed tomography (CT) or magnetic resonance imaging (MRI) scan.

Dieticians give nutritional advice and treat nutrition-related disorders.

Eclectics faded away in the 1800s. They were a cross between the early natural healers called Thomsonians, the homeopaths, and the orthodox medical profession. Their eclecticism consisted in combining the seemingly most reliable treatment techniques of their day.

Electroencephalogram technologists operate electroencephalographic (EEG) equipment to record electrical charges of the brain.

Electrologists remove unwanted body hair by applying an electrical current to the root of the hair shaft.

Esthetics and cosmetology practitioners used to be referred to as 'beauticians.' They correct surface imperfections of the skin.

Health record administrators work in health care institutions keeping all medical records.

Hearing aid dispensers sell hearing aids on prescription.

Herbal therapists use herbal treatments both to treat bodily disorders and disease and to maintain good health.

Holistic medical doctors are medical doctors who attempt to incorporate into their treatments some of the knowledge gained by other (particularly Asian) health practitioners over the centuries. They tend to be relegated to the fringes of organized medicine.

Homeopaths use very minute doses of drugs or plant abstracts to treat human diseases and disorders. They believe the human body has the power to cure itself, once rid of foreign matter (by such treatments) and/or of tensions (by lifestyle counselling).

Iridologists assess present and past pathological and functional disturbances of the body by 'reading' the markings in the eye.

Kinesiologists use a variety of biochemical and biomechanical tests to assess body movement, particularly the muscular components of movement, and to assess body chemistry and nutrient levels. They also recommend health supplements and products.

Macrobioticists treat illness with chosen and combined natural foods rather than with medicines of any kind.

Marriage and family therapists are physicians, psychologists, social workers, nurses, and educators who practise marriage or separation counselling, and/or family therapy.

Massage therapists manually manipulate or stimulate the soft tissue and joints of the body to prevent or rehabilitate dysfunction or to relieve pain.

Medical doctors (MDs) claim to be the only health practitioners capable of understanding and treating the whole body. Their orientation is more pharmaceutical, interventionist, and technologically oriented than practitioners advocating alternative approaches to health care.

Medical physicists specialize in the application of their knowledge (the study of natural forces and phenomena) to medicine.

Medical laboratory technologists collect samples of body fluids or matter and run laboratory tests as ordered by authorized health professionals.

Medical radiological technologists run diagnostic or therapeutic tests and treatments using ionizing radiation (x-rays), or, more recently, other forms of energy.

Midwives advise and assist birth-mothers during prenatal care, pregnancy, normal (low-risk) vaginal delivery, and postnatal care.

Natural scientists or hygienists or healers regard nature as the ultimate healer. They believe the body may be helped in its own natural healing processes by products found in nature, but the use of synthetic drugs or treatments is not advocated.

Nurses' assistants is the old term for today's practical nurses (see below).

Nutritional consultants set themselves up as experts on nutrition. They are not necessarily formally trained. (Dieticians do nutritional consultation, but they do not refer to themselves as nutritional consultants.)

Obstetricians are physicians who specialize in pregnancy and the delivery of babies.

Occupational therapists assist people to function in, and adapt to, their personal, work, and leisure environments.

Ophthalmologists are physicians who specialize in eye care, particularly, optical pathologies.

Opticians are independent merchants who make, fit, adjust, and sell devices to correct subnormal vision, including eye glasses and contact lenses, to persons who have obtained a prescription from either an optometrist or a physician.

Ophthalmic dispensers is the old name for opticians.

Optometrists are (non-MD) eye doctors who diagnose, treat, and intervene to prevent disorders and dysfunctions of the eye, as well as prescribe and dispense devices for subnormal vision, such as eye glasses and contact lenses.

Oriental therapists practise illness prevention and treatment as it has evolved in the Orient.

Orderlies work in health care institutions, mostly hospitals, doing various non-professional chores.

Osteopaths started out as natural healers, but ended up as quasi-MDs. There are not many in Canada, but there are a fair number of them in the United States.

Orthopticians work as ophthalmologists' aides. They specialize in the motility of the eye, often teaching the patient eye exercises to correct deviations of the visual axis of the eye.

Pastoral counsellors are priests or ministers who counsel their congregation members on matters related to their mental well-being.

Pedorthists fit and sell corrective footwear.

Pharmacists guard, compound, and dispense prescribed drugs.

Physiatrists are physicians who specialize in physical rehabilitation.

Physicians are all medical doctors, except surgeons, are also designated as physicians. Prior to the mid-1990s, general medical practitioners were referred to as GPs. They are now being phased out for the more highly trained family physician or FP.

Physiotherapists prevent, treat, and rehabilitate physical dysfunction of the body.

Podiatrists are (non-MD) foot specialists. They are like chiropodists, only they have a broader scope of practice.

Prosthetists fit artificial human parts on people.

Psychiatrists are physicians who treat mental disorders.
Psychologists treat behavioural and mental disorders.
Psychometrists test the behavioural and mental capacities of people through psychological testing.
Public health inspectors attempt to prevent or stop the spread of disease (especially infectious) throughout the population.
Radionics therapists detect a patient's 'peculiar radiations or vibrational energies' to diagnose an illness or 'imbalance' of the body.
Reflexologists deeply massage the reflex areas of the feet and hands to improve circulation, reduce tension, and remove 'body toxins.'
Registered nurses provide nursing care and perform minor medical procedures as well as supervising other less educated nurses or hospital staff.
Registered practical nurses provide nursing care which is not provided by registered nurses.
Remedial gymnasts (also called recreational therapists) use physical fitness programs for the physical and psychological rehabilitation of their patients (including the elderly).
Respiratory technologists run oxygen therapy equipment for patients.
Rolfing therapists use deep massage to 'loosen and restore' the body's membranous connective tissue.
Self-healing therapists teach patients to heal themselves using various techniques such as meditation and mental imagery.
Sexologists treat sexual disorders.
Shiatsu therapists use a Japanese manual therapy technique, applying pressure and stimulation to the traditional acupuncture meridian points to relieve tightening or pain.
Social workers work with individuals, families, and groups to enable them to restore healthy social functioning.
Speech–language pathologists treat speech and language disorders.
Straight chiropractors maintain their founder was correct to believe that all bodily disorders can be cured by chiropractic manipulations. They do not mix treatments.
Surgeons are physicians who cut into the body to fix it.
Vascular technologists specialize in the equipment and techniques related to the functioning of blood vessels.
Yoga teachers teach students to prevent illness and heal the body through relaxation, proper postural alignment, and strengthening of the muscles and connective tissues of the body.

Appendix 1

Exposure, Documents, and Interviews

Exposure

I attempted to expose myself to as much of the life of the policy system as possible, or feasible. More specifically,

1. I deliberately chose the health care system as my case study area because of my history of exposure to its workings:
    i) as a life science student and member of the medical research community,
    ii) as a political studies and philosophy student interested in social science analyses of health care policies and bio-ethical issues,
    iii) as a member of seminar series and conferences on medical and ethical issues.
2. For this specific project I chose a policy issue or event which was deliberately inclusive of all health care practitioners in Ontario.
3. I 'went inside' the health care bureaucracy during the course of the drafting of the RHPA in order to acclimate myself to the ideational/institutional dynamics.
4. I read all of the practitioner submissions to the policy review group (see Documents below).
5. I conducted over 100 extensive interviews (see Interview Methodology below).

Documents

The practitioner groups' Health Professions Legislation Review submissions (which consisted of a small room full of documents) provide a rich source for any reader's sense of how the group's themselves interpreted their own roles and relationships in the sector at the time of the review from 1983 to 1989 (see Chapter 5 for details about the submission process). This interpretation by the practitioner groups was, however, as discussed in the Methodological Notes section of Chapter 9, a strategic presentation and therefore provides us with an interpretive *political* story. Despite this limitation, these submissions constitute the only source, to my knowledge, of such an extensive and highly detailed (both technical and legal) review of all of the major health practitioner groups common to Western society.

Interview Methodology

During the course of this project, I interviewed representatives from all of the colleges (and some of the associations) of the health practitioner groups governed under the Regulated Health Professions Act 1991 (in 1994, again in 1997, and again in 1998), as well as a sample of non-RHPA regulated and non-regulated health practitioner organizations and some individual health practitioners. Throughout the 1990s, I also interviewed the key policy advisers and bureaucratic and government officials involved in this policy process, as well as representatives of the bodies set up by the RHPA in 1991. In total this constituted over 100 interviews.

Most of the literature on interview techniques read prior to my interviews focused on a standardized format which is designed for collecting data to be statistically analysed. Interview questions were therefore designed to elicit responses which could be statistically categorized. The discussions on the non-standardized interview were found to be more appropriate. Neither method took into consideration the concerns specific to the hermeneutics of my approach. For this, I simply did what seemed obvious, given the intent of the hermeneutical method. Therefore, my approach to the gathering of information during the time in which I was 'on the inside' was as non-interfering as possible. I mostly just listened and read. However, since the opportunity often arose for informal conversation I sometimes introduced relevant subjects in an informal manner meant to get the person talking about the policy politics and their, or their group's, experiences. (This material was not used herein as an 'interview,' for that, the interviewee was always informed I was conducting an interview and was offered the choice of attributable quotes or non-attributable quotes.)

For the actual interviews conducted later in the course of this study (after I had developed a framework around which to organize my story and its politics, which came out of the hermeneutical stage coupled with historical investigation), the suggestions given in the literature for the non-standardized interview became more useful. I made use of some of the advice on the non-standardized interview in Babbie, Gorden, Lofland, Mishler, and Wolff.[1] For example,

[1] Earl R. Babbie *Survey Research Methods* (Belmont CA: Wadsworth, 1973). Raymond L. Gorden *Interviewing: Strategy, Techniques, and Tactics* (Georgetown, Ont: Irwin-Dorsey, 1980). John Lofland. *Analyzing Social Settings: A Guide to Qualitative Observation and Analysis* (Belmont, CA: Wadsworth, 1971). Elliot G. Mishler, *Research Interviewing* (Cambridge, MA: Harvard University Press, 1986). Kurt H. Wolff, 'The Collection and Organization of Field

Appendix 1: Exposure, Documents, and Interviews 353

- Choose the open-ended question as opposed to the close-ended question to allow for an expanded answer (close-ended usually elicits an either/or response to a question; that is, yes or no, true or false, and so on)
- Use short questions to avoid confusing the respondent as to the type of information sought
- Avoid biased comments being incorporated into interview questions so as to influence the response as little as possible
- Avoid the double-barrelled questions which can cause a respondent to give more than one answer to what is intended to be one question
- Consider the relevancy of the question to the respondent (that is, modifying questions to suit the respondent by not focusing on questions outside their area of knowledge, therefore not hindering their expression)
- Place questions into categories so as to not confuse the respondent as to the subject of inquiry at any given point (for example, making clear distinctions between topic areas)
- Pay attention to the format of questions (for example, the lead-in or warm-up questions and the topic area according to the individuals expertise)
- Use contingency questions (where questions are asked contingent upon other related questions or contingent upon certain comments coming from the respondent).

During this stage, along with reflective questions on the policy process and outcomes (which I continued to ask to the end), I also asked confirmatory questions (to continue the documentation of facts and positions given in the Health Professions Legislation Review submissions and to confirm later developments).

Material: A Research Paper,' in R.N. Adams and J.J. Preiss, eds., *Human Organization Research: Field Relations and Techniques.* (Homewood, IL: Dorsey Press, 1960).

Appendix 2

Funding

Ontario Health Insurance Plan (OHIP) Coverage

Medicine (limits on price and volume – set high)
Chiropractors (limits on price, volume, and insured tests – set low)
Osteopaths (limits on price, volume, and insured tests – set low)
Podiatry (limits on price, volume, and insured tests)
Optometrists (refraction and prescribing covered, but not dispensing)
Physiotherapists (in a few private clinics with limits on price and volume)

Insurance Coverage under Public Health Programs of Special State Programs (e.g., for the elderly, disabled, children)

Audiologists
Chiropodists
Dental hygienists
Dental technicians
Nurses
Occupational therapists
Pharmacists
Physiotherapists
Speech–language pathologists

Institutional Salary (rather than fee-for-service OHIP coverage)

Audiologists
Chiropodists
Clinical chemists

Dentists
Diagnostic medical sonographers
Dieticians
Medical laboratory technicians
Nurses
Occupational therapists
Physiotherapists
Psychologists
Radiological technicians
Respiratory technicians
Speech–language pathologists
Vascular technicians

Institutionally Excluded[1]

Athletic therapists
Biological photographers
Clinical hypnotists
Denturist/denture therapists
Hearing aid dispensers
Marriage and family therapists
Massage therapists
Midwives (included under OHIP in 1993)
Naturopaths
Ophthalmic dispensers (opticians)
Psychometrists
Shiatsu practitioners

[1] Practitioners taken from the HPLR 'list of 39,' i.e., those the review team thought might potentially meet the requirements of professional status.

Appendix 3

Health Professions Legislation Review Words

The words or 'context' of the Health Professions Legislation Review (HPLR) introduction give a sense of the ideational orientation that informed this process (see Chapter 5), that is,

Pressure for change
Demanding more open and responsive ... processes
Frustration with the rigidity
Most efficient and cost-effective mix
Crisis ... by ever-increasing costs
The public interest
Protected from the unqualified, incompetent, and unfit
Freedom of choice
High quality care
Evolution in the roles
Flexibility
Maximum efficiency
Efficient and rational
Unprecedented consultation
Community
Communication
The right to govern themselves
Fully consulted
The public
Safe, high quality care
Governing ... members ... contributing time and effort ... altruistic
Comply with the Canadian Charter of Rights and Freedoms

Appendix 3: HPLR Words   357

Striking the proper balance between professional independence and public accountability
An opportunity to state their views
Not to enhance ... status or ... earning power
Older statutes ... grossly inadequate
Accountability, public participation, and quality assurance
Rights
Open forum for balancing the competing claims
Giving controlled access
Legitimate interests
Coercion is ... likely ... ineffective and expensive
Fairness
Wide and ill-defined monopolies
Freedom to choose
Protects the public
Flexibility and ... innovation
Quackery ... with relative impunity
Public protection
Hierarchical and therefore unequal relationships
Produces tensions
Tends to inhibit cooperation
The best service at the lowest cost
An alternative that will better protect the public
Consulting widely with expert members
Considerable consensus
Greater public protection
The ultimate authority will reside with the government
Consumers ... informed choices

Reinforced Words (in the HPLR Report is concluding section, pp. 16–17 and executive summary pp. 2–4)

Public protection
Cost effective
Efficient
Quality
Consumer's right to choice
Undesired effects on status and economic power
Young ... traditional ... female ... male ... equal standing

Appendix 3: HPLR Words

Safe alternatives
Accountable
Open to public scrutiny
Health professionals treated fairly
Due process of the law
A forum in which to express their views
Change
The public interest
Public protection
Quality
Cost
More consumer choice
Flexible, rational, and cost efficient
Equal status for professionals
Powers ... to regulate ... and ... be more accountable

Appendix 4

The Nine Criteria for Self-Regulation

1 Relevance to Minister of Health

A substantial portion of the profession's members are not engaged in activities under the jurisdiction of another ministry, and the primary objective of the treatments they perform must be the promotion or restoration of health.

2 Risk of Harm

A substantial risk of physical or emotional harm to individual patients arises in the practice of the profession.

3 Sufficiency of Supervision

A significant number of the members of this profession do not have the quality of their performance monitored effectively either by supervisors in regulated institutions, by supervisors who are themselves regulated professionals, or by regulated professionals who prescribe this profession's services.

4 Alternative Regulatory Mechanism
The profession is not already regulated effectively or will not soon be regulated effectively under an alternative regulatory mechanism.

5 Body of Knowledge

The members of this profession must call upon a distinctive, systematic body of knowledge in assessing or treating their patients, and the core activities they perform must constitute a clear, integrated, and broadly accepted whole.

6 Education Requirements for Entry to Practice

To enter the practice of this profession, the practitioner must be required to obtain a diploma or degree from a recognized Canadian educational institution.

7 Leadership's Ability to Favour the Public Interest

The profession's leadership has shown that it is able to distinguish between the public interest and the profession's self-interest and, in self-regulating, will favour the former over the latter.

8 Likelihood of Compliance

There is enough willingness among the members of this profession to acquiesce, at least, to self-regulation that widespread compliance is likely.

9 Sufficiency of Membership Size and Willingness to Contribute

The practitioners of the profession are sufficiently numerous to staff all committees of a governing body with committed members and are willing to accept the full costs of self-regulation. At the same time, the profession must be able to maintain a separate professional association.

Appendix 5

Key Events in the Health Professions Legislation Review

November 1982 – Health Professions Legislation review announced by Minister of Health

September 1983 – first '22 Topics' paper sent out by review (120 submissions received)

April 1984 – follow-up questions sent to first submitters (plus 15 new entrants) (133 responses – 118 of the original 120, plus 15 new ones)

September 1984 – minister announces first elimination results – 39 groups in, and the rest out

Summer 1985 – further questioning of 'the 39' as to their ability to be self-regulating

October 1985 – submissions received from 'the 39,' arguing for inclusion

Fall 1985 – 'Legal and Procedural' paper sent to potential professional groups for comment

April 1986 – minister announces winners – 'the 24' provider groups who will be given self-regulatory professional status

Summer-Fall 1986 – two participant workshops to educate 'the 24' on requirements for self-regulation

August 1986 – topics paper 'Legal and Procedural Issues Associated with the Self-Regulation of Health Professionals' (which focused on general principles)

Appendix 5: Key HPLR Events

Summer 1986 – Scope-of-Practice Workshop with preliminary statements from participant professions plus circulation and comments from other participants

October 1986 – review's first set of Legal and Procedural Proposals (the 'green book') circulated for comment

Early 1987 – review recommended 'clustering' or pairing of some professional groups; minister agrees and makes announcement of such

December 1987 – review circulated the initial scope-of-practice statements and lists of licensed acts (procedures)

June 1988 – the review's revised Legal and Procedural Proposals (the 'red books'), which included their proposed individual professional acts were circulated for comment

July 1988 – review's initial proposals concerning professional title were circulated for comment

January 1989 – HPLR report released

Appendix 6

The 22 Topics

Topic 1 Question: What proof is there of a need to ensure the effective regulation of this profession through the Minister of Health?

Topic 2 Question: What evidence is there that this profession can regulate itself effectively?

Topic 3 Question: If the Health Disciplines Act is an unsuitable model for the profession, is there another form of self-regulation that is appropriate?

Topic 4 Questions: Should a statute define a scope of practice for this profession? If so, what should it be?

Topic 5 Questions: Should a provincial statute grant this profession a certification of competence or an exclusive licence to practise? If so, what titles should the statute protect? How will (should, does) actual experience differ from the statutory provisions?

Topic 6 Questions: Should provincial statutes recognize any overlaps in the scope of practice between this profession and another from which it is independent? If so, what should they be? How will (should, does) actual experience differ from the statutory provisions?

Topic 7 Questions: Should members of this profession supervise the work of others outside the profession, or vice versa? What is the rationale for such supervision? Should this profession as a whole have any authority over another profession, or vice versa? Within what health care setting(s)? How direct should the supervision be? (Be specific about the supervised and supervising professions.)

Topic 8 Questions: Is it appropriate for members of a profession to delegate acts (licensed to them) to other persons who are not licensed to perform them? If it is appropriate, what legislative mechanisms are necessary to validate current practice?

Topic 9 Questions: Should the statutes recognize a right of any professional to disobey the order of a supervisor who is a member of another profession? If yes, in what circumstances? How should the statutes assign accountability for misconduct or negligence that occurs when a member of a profession supervises the work of someone outside that profession? Which body or bodies should have or share the authority for conducting complaints or disciplinary proceedings in cases of these kinds?

Topic 10 Question: Should a member of this profession require referral (or prescription) by a member of another profession (or vice versa) before making contact with a patient?

Topic 11 Question: What standards should an individual have to meet to enter practice in this profession?

Topic 12 Questions: Who should have influence over the design of course work necessary for entry to practise? How should this influence be shared? When a profession disagrees with the province about entry-to-practice requirements, where should the authority lie to accept or reject candidates in dispute?

Topic 13 Questions: Is it difficult for Ontario practitioners in this profession to enter practice in other provinces, and vice versa? If it is difficult, should Ontario attempt to negotiate reciprocity with the other province(s) involved?

Topic 14 Question: What mechanisms, if any, should the governing body use to ensure the continuing competence of members of this profession?

Topic 15 Questions: What mechanisms, if any, should the governing body use to ensure the continuing competence of members re-entering this profession? In what circumstances should their use be necessary?

Topic 16 Question: Should it be mandatory for practitioners in this profession to hold malpractice liability insurance?

Topic 17 Questions: Should the governing body of this profession have the authority to prosecute members for reasons of personal misconduct? If yes, should there be

Appendix 6: 22 Topics   365

any limits to the types of conduct to be regulated? If no, should any other body have this authority?

Topic 18 Questions: Who should have the authority to investigate and discipline contraventions of the statutes or regulations by members of this profession? Who should have this authority if a member acts outside his scope of practice? Who should have this authority when those accused are non-members acting within this profession's scope?

Topic 19 Questions: Should there be changes in the due process provisions of the health professions legislation? Should these changes apply to all regulated professions?

Topic 20 Questions: What other kinds of disputes do you expect this profession will face before the next review and with whom? What forum and set of procedures, if any, should the regulations recognize to encourage the parties to negotiate settlements of their disputes in a timely manner?

Topic 21 Questions: What other recommendations do you have concerning the governing body of the profession? What name should it have?

Topic 22 Question: Are there any other matters this review should address?

Appendix 7
The Nine Criteria Not Met

Practitioner groups	1 Minister of Health	2 Risk	3 Supervision	4 Alternative	5 Knowledge	6 Education	7 Public	8 Compliance	9 Number
Athletic therapy	?	x			?	?		?	x
Audiology									x
Biological photography	?	x	?		?	x		?	x
Chiropody									x
Chiropractic									
Clinical hypnosis		?		x		x		x	x
Clinical chemistry			?	?					x
Dental hygiene		?	?						
Dental technicianry		?	?				x		?
Dentistry							?		
Denture therapy							?		
Dietetics		?							
Family therapy	?					?			x
Health records	?	x	x						
Hearing aids		?			?	x	?	x	x
Laboratory tech.			?						
Massage therapy		?			?		?		
Medical physics		?	?	?					x
Medicine									
Midwifery					x	x	?	?	x
Naturopathy		?			x	?	?	?	x

Appendix 7: The Nine Criteria Not Met (Concluded)

Practitioner groups	1 Minister of Health	2 Risk	3 Supervision	4 Alternative	5 Knowledge	6 Eucation	7 Public	8 Compliance	9 Number
Nursing assistantry	?	?							
Nursing									
Occupational therapy		?					?		
Opticianry		?					x		
Optometry									
Osteopathy						x			x
Pharmacy							?		
Physiotherapy									
Podiatry						x	?		x
Psychology									
Psychometry				x					
Pulm'y-cardio tech.		?	?			x			x
Radiological tech.									
Respiratory tech.							?		
Shiatsu therapy		?							x
Sonography		?							x
Speech–lng'ge path.		?							?
Vascular tech.		?			?	x			x

x = criteria definitely not met; ? = criteria not decisively met or still in question

Appendix 8

The New Professional Scopes of Practice

Audiology Act, 1991, S.O. c. 19, s. 3(1): 'The practice of audiology is the assessment of auditory function and the treatment and prevention of auditory dysfunction to develop, maintain, rehabilitate or augment auditory and communicative functions.'

Chiropody Act, 1991, S.O. c. 20, s. 4: 'The practice of chiropody is the assessment of the foot and the treatment and prevention of diseases, disorders or dysfunctions of the foot by therapeutic, orthotic or palliative means.' (Podiatry is the same.)

Chiropractic Act, 1991, S.O. c. 21, s. 3: 'The practice of chiropractic is the assessment of conditions related to the spine, nervous system and joints and the diagnosis, prevention and treatment, primarily by adjustment, of, (a) dysfunctions or disorders arising from the structures or functions of the spine and the effects of those dysfunctions or disorders on the nervous system; and (b) dysfunctions or disorders arising from the structures or functions of the joints.'

Dental Hygiene Act, 1991, S.O. c. 22, s. 3: 'The practice of dental hygiene is the assessment of teeth and adjacent tissues and treatment by preventive and therapeutic means and the provision of restorative and orthodontic procedures and services.'

Dental Technology Act, 1991, S.O. c. 23, s. 3: 'The practice of dental technology is the design, construction, repair or alteration of dental prosthetic, restorative and orthodontic devices.'

Dentistry Act, 1991, S.O. c. 24, s. 3: 'The practice of dentistry is the assessment of the physical conditions of the oral-facial complex and the diagnosis, treatment and prevention of any disease, disorder or dysfunction of the oral-facial complex.'

Denturism Act, 1991, S.O. c. 25., s. 3: 'The practice of denturism is the assessment of arches missing some or all teeth and the design, construction, repair, alteration, ordering and fitting of removable dentures.'

Dietetics Act, 1991, S.O. c. 26., s. 3: 'The practice of dietetics is the assessment of nutrition and nutritional conditions and the treatment and prevention of nutrition related disorders by nutritional means.'

Massage Therapy Act, 1991, S.O. c. 27, s. 3: 'The practice of massage therapy is the assessment of the soft tissue and joints of the body and the treatment and prevention of physical dysfunction and pain of the soft tissues and joints by manipulation to develop, maintain, rehabilitate or augment physical function, or relieve pain.'

Medical Laboratory Technology Act, 1991, S.O. c. 28, s. 3: 'The practice of medical laboratory technology is the performance of laboratory investigations on the human body or on specimens taken from the human body and the evaluation of the technical sufficiency of the investigations and their results.'

Medical Radiation Technology Act, 1991, S.O. c. 29, s. 3: 'The practice of medical radiation technology is the use of ionizing radiation and other forms of energy prescribed under subsection 12 (2) to produce diagnostic images and tests, the evaluation of the technical sufficiency of the images and tests, and the therapeutic application of ionizing radiation.'

Medicine Act, 1991, S.O. c. 30, s. 3: 'The practice of medicine is the assessment of the physical or mental condition of an individual and the diagnosis, treatment and prevention of any disease, disorder or dysfunction.'

Midwifery Act, 1991, S.O. c. 31, s. 3: 'The practice of midwifery is the assessment and monitoring of women during pregnancy, labour and the post-partum period and of their newborn babies, the provision of care during normal pregnancy, labour and post-partum period and the conducting of spontaneous normal vaginal deliveries.'

Nursing Act, 1991, S.O. c. 32, s. 3: 'The practice of nursing is the promotion of health and the assessment of, the provision of care for and the treatment of health conditions by supportive, preventive, therapeutic, palliative and rehabilitative means in order to attain or maintain optimal function.'

Occupational Therapy Act, 1991, S.O. c. 33, s. 3: 'The practice of occupational therapy is the assessment of function and adaptive behaviour and the treatment and prevention of disorders which affect function or adaptive behaviour to develop, maintain, rehabilitate or augment function or adaptive behaviour in the areas of self-care, productivity and leisure.'

Opticianry Act, 1991, S.O. c. 34, s. 3: 'The practice of opticianry is the provision, fitting and adjustment of subnormal vision devices, contact lenses or eye glasses.'

Optometry Act, 1991, S.O. c. 35, s. 3: 'The practice of optometry is the assessment of the eye and vision system and the diagnosis, treatment and prevention of a) disorders of refraction; b) sensory and oculomotor disorders and dysfunctions of the eye and vision system; and c) prescribed diseases.'

Pharmacy Act, 1991, S.O. c. 36, s. 3: 'The practice of pharmacy is the custody, compounding and dispensing of drugs, the provision of non-prescription drugs, health care aids and devices and the provision of information related to drug use.'

Physiotherapy Act, 1991, S.O. c. 37, s. 3: 'The practice of physiotherapy is the assessment of physical function and the treatment, rehabilitation and prevention of physical dysfunction, injury or pain, to develop, maintain, rehabilitate or augment function or to relieve pain.'

Psychology Act, 1991, S.O. c. 38, s. 3: 'The practice of psychology is the assessment of behavioral and mental conditions, the diagnosis of neuropsychological disorders and dysfunctions and psychotic, neurotic and personality disorders and dysfunctions and the prevention and treatment of behavioral and mental disorders and dysfunctions and the maintenance and enhancement of physical, intellectual, emotional, social and interpersonal functioning.'

Respiratory Therapy Act, 1991, S.O. c. 39, s. 3: 'The practice of respiratory therapy is the providing of oxygen therapy, cardio-respiratory equipment monitoring and the assessment and treatment of cardio-respiratory and associated disorders to maintain or restore ventilation.'

Speech-Language Pathology Act, 1991, S.O. c. 19, s. 3(2): 'The practice of speech-language pathology is the assessment of speech and language functions and the treatment and prevention of speech and language dysfunctions or disorders to develop, maintain, rehabilitate or augment oral motor or communicative functions.'

Appendix 9

Licensed, Controlled, and Authorized Acts

Regulated Health Professions Act, 1991, S.O., s. 27.

(1) No person shall perform a controlled act set out in subsection (2) in the course of providing health care services to an individual unless,
(a) the person is a member authorized by a health professions Act to perform the controlled act; or (b) the performance of the controlled act has been delegated in accordance with section 28 to the person by a member described in clause (a).

(2) A 'controlled act' is any one of the following done with respect to an individual:
1. Communicating to the individual or his or her personal representative a diagnosis identifying a disease or disorder as the cause of symptoms of the individual in circumstances in which it is reasonably foreseeable that the individual or his or her personal representative will rely on the diagnosis.
2. Performing a procedure on tissue below the dermis, below the surface of a mucous membrane, in or below the surface of the cornea, or in or below the surfaces of the teeth, including the scaling of teeth.
3. Setting or casting a fracture of a bone or a dislocation of a joint.
4. Moving the joints of the spine beyond the individual's usual physiological range of motion using a fast, low amplitude thrust.
5. Administering a substance by injection or inhalation.
6. Putting an instrument, hand, or finger,
    i   beyond the external ear canal,
    ii beyond the point in the nasal passages where they normally narrow,
    iii beyond the larynx,
    iv beyond the opening of the urethra,
    v   beyond the labia majora,
    vi beyond the anal verge, or

vii into an artificial opening into the body.
7 Applying or ordering the application of a form of energy prescribed by the regulations under this Act.
8 Prescribing, dispensing, selling or compounding a drug as defined in clause 113 (1) (d) of the Drug and Pharmacies Regulation Act, or supervising the part of a pharmacy where such drugs are kept.
9 Prescribing or dispensing, for vision or eye problems, subnormal vision devices, contact lenses or eye glasses other than simple magnifiers.
10 Prescribing a hearing aid for a hearing impaired person.
11 Fitting or dispensing a dental prosthesis orthodontic or periodontal appliance or a device used inside the mouth to protect teeth from abnormal functioning.
12 Managing labour or conducting the delivery of a baby.
13 Allergy challenge testing of a kind in which a positive result of the test is a significant allergic response.

(3) An act by a person is not a contravention of subsection (1) if the person is exempted by the regulations under this Act or if the act is done in the course of an activity exempted by the regulations under this Act.

Index

Aboriginal healers, 184
Aboriginal midwives, 184, 185
Aboriginal peoples, treatment of, 184, 215
accountability, 51, 223–4; administrative, 63, 65, 186, 223; in hospitals, 64; professional, 63–4; public, 38, 41, 49, 62–3, 66, 186. *See also* financial accountability; political accountability
acupuncturists, 23, 160, 161, 171
advertising, optometrists and, 157
aestheticians, 161
agency relationships, 40, 212; private or market, 168–9, 212; professionals and the patient, 51, 203; provincial government, 61; public or legal, 168–9, 212
alternative practitioners, 59, 207–10; HPLR/RHPA policy process and, 139; and the medical profession, 43–4, 50; nineteenth-century, 16–17, 29, 33; under DPA, 22–6
alternative whole body practitioners, 150; HPLR/RHPA policy process and, 147; lack of support for, 170; and medical practitioners, 213
Archer, Margaret S., 238

assessment: chiropodists, 104; and chiropractors, 107; non-elite practitioners, 86; and physiotherapists, 109
assistant groups, 21–2, 34, 50, 55, 202, 230; dependent group, 29, 171; and elite practitioners, 29; HPLR/RHPA policy process and, 134–8, 140, 176; and institutional administrators, 171; patterns of connection, 165–8, 171; restructuring arguments, 84
Association of Concerned Citizens for Preventive Medicine, 179
Association of Hearing Aid Dispensers, 102
Association of Registered Dental Technicians, 128–9
athletic therapists, 140
athletic trainers, 161
audience, implication of term, 56
audiologists, 27, 34, 56, 125; HPLR/RHPA policy process and, 92–3, 100–2, 139, 176
Audiology Act (1991), scope of practice, 368
authority: and connection, 51–2, 56, 82; and decision-making, 55, 56n; over the public, 50; positions of, 39–42,

50; and 'say,' 55, 56n; and self-governance, 41
authorized acts, 175; chiropractors, 107; psychologists, 13; regulated practitioners, 83–4; under RHPA (1991), 371–2
autonomy and exclusion, poles of, 40

Babbie, Earl R., 352
basket clause, 83; elite opposition to, 85
Bell, Ron, 151
biomedical engineering, 132
biomedical physics, 132
birth specialists. *See* midwifery; midwives
blueprints: cost control, 210; economic, 48, 174, 199, 203, 216, 237; of governance, 199–200; ideational, 12, 34; of market liberalism, 174; medicare, 203; nineteenth-century professional licensing, 16; political, 48, 199, 237; and principles, 12, 237–41; public participation, 37, 48; public–private, 217; public welfare, 53–4; restructuring, 215–16; state welfare, 53–4. *See also* judicial blueprint
Board of Directors of Chiropractic, 149–50
Board of Directors of Osteopathy, 91
Board of Ophthalmic Dispensers, 103
Boase, Joan Price, 103, 160
bodily harm. *See* harm clause
Bohnen, Linda, 79
botanic healers, 34, 106; HPLR/RHPA policy process and, 139, 170; and medical profession, 43, 50; nineteenth-century, 17, 21
Brown, E. Richard, 31
bureaucratic organization: of health care, 4, 67; power and control in, 53, 58

Burrows, Alan, 79
business: denturists, 28; drug companies, 43; healing arts, 47; pharmacy, 20; vision care, 28. *See also* merchant–service practitioners

Calliste, Agnes, 31
Canada Consulting Group, 70
Canada Health Act, public administration standards in, 64
Canadian College of Osteopathy (CCO), 91
Canadian Guild of Dispensing Opticians, 103
Canadian Jewish Congress, 179
Canadian Medical Association, 163
Canadian Memorial Chiropractic College (CMCC), 108
Canadian Society of Laboratory Technologists, certification examination, 132
Caplan, Elinor, 89, 122
cardiology technicians, 145
cardiovascular technologists, 130
Carnegie Foundation, 44
change, pressure for, 52
Chinese herbal retailers, 178
Chinese massage therapists, 161
chiropodists, 51, 56, 125, 145, 170; assessment of, 104; HPLR/RHPA policy process and, 104–6, 139, 155–6, 159, 176; under DPA, 23, 25–6
Chiropody Act (1944), 26, 104; (1991), scope of practice, 368
chiropractic, 209; American, 23–4; diagnostic privilege under RHPA, 86; and naturopathy connection, 150, 170
Chiropractic Act (1991), scope of practice, 368
chiropractors, 33–4, 44, 50–1, 145, 205,

208, 214; authorized acts, 107; connections, 171; and diagnostic function, 85, 107; HPLR/RHPA policy process and, 107–9, 138–40, 148, 158–9; medical profession and, 158–9; OHIP billing, 107; under DPA, 23–4, 45–6; university affiliation, 108
Christian Scientists, 21, 29–30
civil rights, McRuer Report (1968), 64
class prejudice: and health care, 31–2, 214–15; nursing, 122
clinical chemists, HPLR/RHPA policy process and, 55, 132–3, 140
clinical controls, tension over, 51–2
clinical hypnotists, 140
CNO. *See* College of Nurses of Ontario
Coalition of Major Christian Denominations, 179
Coburn, David, 148
collectivity, 226–7
College of Dental Hygienists, 128
College of Nurses of Ontario (CNO), 121, 123, 136; and midwives, 162; race and class relations, 185
College of Pharmacy, 155
College of Physicians and Surgeons of Ontario (CPSO), 45, 213; and consultation role for pharmacists, 94; HPLR/RHPA policy review and, 88, 145–6, 160; and midwives, 161–2; and other health practitioners, 169, 214; state connections, 142
Committee on the Healing Arts (CHA), 58–9, 60, 61–4, 67, 69, 71, 72; criticism of HPLA, 187; dental hygienists, 126; egalitarian rhetoric of, 87; pharmacy ownership, 93–4; registered practical nurses, 136; on x-rays, 108. *See also Report of the Committee on the Healing Arts*
communication, in HPLR/RHPA policy process, 206
communitarianism, 226
community, in policy community literature, 236
community care: nurse practitioners, 126; territorial disputes, 163–4. *See also* multi-disciplinary health clinics
competence: of practice, 38, 49; standards of, 177
complaints committee, 39, 198–9
complementary health care, 92, 209–10
connection: between institutional and excluded practitioners, 51; external group, 144; internal group, 142–3; non-elite, 45–7; patterns of, 141; positions of, 42–5; positions of the public, 47–8; of professionals, 48; for recipients of health care, 51
conservative empiric practitioners, 51; of homeopathy, 17; massage therapists, 24–5
Conservative government: and naturopaths, 90, 149; power over HPRAC, 128, 192–3
consultation, 56; interest-group, 62; pharmacists' role, 94
Consumers Association of Canada (Ontario branch), 179
contact lens dispensers, 34, 101; HPLR/RHPA policy process and, 139
control, and trust, 224
controlled acts: chiropodists, 104; and HPLR/RHPA, 138; medical radiation technologists (MRT), 130, 131; and naturopathy, 90; pharmacists, 95; of regulated practitioners, 83–4, 138, 175; under RHPA (1991), 371–2

cost: of free choice of practice, 176; interest group participation, 178; and lowest cost care providers 217; of quality assurance programs, 195; of training programs, 195–6

cost-benefit ratio, of drug utilization, 94–5

cost control, 64, 175, 187; blueprint, 210, 239; dental services, 128; and extended class nurse practitioners, 164; and medical practitioners, 87; performance measurements, 239; and technique specialists, 87

CPSO. *See* College of Physicians and Surgeons of Ontario

credentialism, 34, 51, 175; dental hygienists, 29; and economy of service delivery, 215; eye care, 102; and hearing, 102; and registered nurses, 34; technology field, 131–2

credentials: medical technologists, 131–3; nursing, 121–3; practical nurses, 137; in twentieth-century health care, 20–1

decision-making, relationships, 55, 56n

dental assistants, 153; HPLR/RHPA policy process and, 134–6; level II, 135

dental care, 26–9

Dental Hygiene Act (1991), 127; scope of practice, 368

dental hygienists, 29, 44, 50, 98, 125, 145, 205, 211; HPLR/RHPA policy process and, 119, 126–8, 135–6, 139, 176, 178; patterns of connection, 151–3, 164–5, 170–1

dental laboratory technicians, 129

dental nurses, 135

dental technicians, 152

dental technologists, 44, 50; HPLR/RHPA policy process, 128–9, 140; patterns of connection, 151, 166; supervision by dentists, 28

Dental Technology Act (1991), scope of practice, 368

dental therapists. *See* denturists

dentistry: diagnostic privilege under RHPA, 86; enemies of, 50; hegemony of, 87, 98; HPLR/RHPA policy process and, 98–100; merchant–service function of, 98–9; patterns of connection, 151–4; restructuring, 84; technology groups in, 28; under HDA (1974), 65

Dentistry Act (1991), scope of practice, 368

dentists, 21–2; and denturists, 43–4, 99, 170; HPLR/RHPA policy process and, 92–3, 139, 176; nineteenth-century, 18–19; opposition to legislation, 182–3; patterns of connection, 165–6; and technologist/entrepreneurs, 27

Denturism Act (1991), scope of practice, 369

Denturist Association of Canada, 99

Denturist Association of Ontario, 99, 152

denturists, 34, 50, 125, 214; and dentists, 43–4, 99, 170; on diagnostic function, 85–6; HPLR/RHPA policy process and, 92–3, 98–9, 135, 139, 176; independence from dentists, 28, 33; patterns of connection, 151–2, 165–6

dependent group, of practitioners, 29, 33, 44, 136, 139, 171, 205

diagnosis: and chiropractors, 107; debate over, 209–10; expertise issue of, 85–6; extended class nurse practitioners, 164; optometrists, 101–2

diagnostic medical sonographers, 131
diagnostic technologists, 56
Dickens, Bernard, 99
Dietetics Act (1991), scope of practice, 369
dietetic technologists, 167
dieticians, 44, 50, 168; and elite practitioners, 26; HPLR/RHLR policy process and, 119–20, 139
disciplinary committee, 38–9, 48, 198–9
discrimination: against French-speaking citizens, 31; in health care sector, 54, 67; in medical profession, 30–2, 34; in nursing, 122
doctor (title): chiropractic use of, 108; naturopaths use of, 90; optometrists, 101–2; psychologists use of, 113
DPA. *See* Drugless Practitioners Act
Druelle, Philippe, 91
Drugless Practitioners Act (DPA) (1925), 22–6, 45, 203; naturopaths under, 89; and osteopaths, 45, 91, 148; physiotherapists, 109; amendments (1944), 45
drugless therapists. *See* naturopaths
Drug and Pharmacies Regulation Act, 94
drug utilization, cost-benefit ratio of, 94–5
Dupré, Stefan, 72

ear–speech care, merchant–service practitioners, 100–4, 156–7
echocardiography, 131
eclecticism, 66
eclectics, 24, 169; as enemies of the medical profession, 43, 44–5, 50; nineteenth-century, 16–17
economic issues, 215–18
economic liberalism, and private enterprise, 15–16

economic monopoly. *See* monopoly
egalitarianism, 87–8; of dental hygienists, 170; political arguments for, 42, 68; principle of, 61, 227
electromagnetism, 131
electrotherapy, 23
elite professionals, 44, 48, 232–3; benefits of self-governance to, 37–9; and cost control, 88; and independent practitioners, 29, 33–4, 44; old embedded blueprints, 240–1; and the public, 64, 220
elite professions: entrepreneurial concerns of, 47; and licensed scope of practice, 47, 84–5; and power politics, 85
Elston, Murray, 89, 162
embedment, 4, 11, 15; alternative pressures on, 230; challenges to, 33; of elite privileges, 48, 51, 240–1; mode of public organization, 204; in old legislation, 202–4
empiricism: in health care, 209; ideational commitment to, 230; versus heroic health care, 17, 209
empirics, 169; exclusion of, 29, 56; naturopaths, 148
entrepreneurs, 216; competition, 173; medical practitioners, 47; public reimbursement of, 207
epidemiology studies, 211
ergonomic specialists, 22
European Hydrotherapy, Nature Cure health movement, 23
excluded practitioner groups, 4, 8, 29–32, 34, 49, 51, 144, 172
exclusion: and autonomy, 40; and Health Disciplines Act, 66
expertise, redefinition of, 209–10
extended class nurse practitioners, 126,

136, 210–11, 218; HPLR/RHPA policy process and, 124–6; OCFP and, 147; patterns of connection, 164; training programs, 195–6
eye care, 100–4; control of, 27–8; merchant–service practitioners, 156–7, 170

family physicians: coordinating role concerns, 154, 218; and disputes with specialists, 143; gatekeepers, 86, 218; and midwives, 162; and new professionals, 170; and restructuring, 217–18
Federation Exchange newsletter, 173
Federation of Health Regulatory Colleges, 173–4, 182, 197
financial accountability, 65, 68, 186–7, 223
fitness to practise issue, 173, 177
Flexner Report, 44, 45
Florida, Schedule C products in, 95
food service supervisors, 167
foot care, merchant–service practitioners, 104–6, 156
freedom–welfare dichotomy, 61–2, 66
free market: economic arguments, 42; for health care, 47, 60, 203

gatekeepers: diagnostic function and, 85; family physicians, 86, 218; medical practitioners, 54, 67, 147
gender equality, RHPA, 214–15, 222
general practitioners. *See* family physicians
generic workers (non-regulated workers), 138, 164, 217
'get a reading,' meaning of, 7, 228–9
Gibbons, Michael T., 8
Goodman, Nelson, 8

Gort, Elaine, 148
Governing Board of Dental Technicians, 128–9
Governing Board of Denture Therapists, 99
governing bodies, practitioner groups, 38, 41, 48, 50, 51, 142–3
Grahamian healers, 21, 29–30
Grier, Ruth, 125
Grossman, Larry, 70, 87
Grove, J.W., 58, 59, 144

Hall, Peter A., 236
Hamowy, Ronald, 47
harm clause, 85, 112, 147; blueprint 1980s, 83; support for, 179
Harris government, 128
Harry Cummings and Associates, 194
Heagerty, J., 30
Healing Arts Radiation Protection Act, 131
health care: alternative forms, 59, 69; definition of 'good,' 34–5; dehumanizing nature of institutionalized, 59; groups within organized institutions, 50; organization of, 81–2; patterns of, 21–2; state protected market, 37–8
health care aids, 138
Health Disciplines Act (HDA) (1974), 64, 65–6, 68, 71, 108, 183, 186, 204; complaints and discipline committees, 198
hygienists, 126; professional tribunals under, 65; and restructuring, 84
Health Disciplines Board, 65
health food retailers, 120, 178
health policy, social policy sector, 57
health practice utilization assessments, 211

Health Professions Board, 180, 198
Health Professions Legislation Review (HPLR), 3–5, 70–80, 204; and accountability, 186; advisory group, 72; consent to final product, 183–4; criticism, 187; ideational slant of, 87; key events, 361–2; legislation, 79–80; 'Nine Criteria for Self-Regulation,' 76–7; patterns of connection in, 168; policy process, 72–3, 76, 173, 206–7, 211, 220; public participation recommendations, 182; terms of reference, 71–2; '22 topics,' 73, 363–5, 366–7; words, 356–8
Health Professions Regulatory Advisory Council (HPRAC), 84, 175, 180–1, 207; colleges on, 192–3; comments of RHPA, 188, 190–1; dental hygienists, 127; future role of, 222; limited powers of, 191–4; naturopathy regulation, 89; politics around, 193–4
health records administrators, 140, 145
hearing aid dispensers, 34, 214; HPLR/RHPA policy process and, 101–14, 139, 170, 176; pharmacists, 94
Heclo, H. Hugh, 236
Heilbrun, Carolyn, 10
herbalists, 155, 170
hermeneutics, and story gathering, 7–9
heroic scientific health care, 17, 21–2, 35, 49, 51, 67; versus conservative empiricism, 17, 209
hierarchy, 227; clinical chemists and medical laboratory technologists, 132; in clinical specialization, 21; in health care systems, 31, 41, 42; and legislative reform, 71; medical, 221; of practitioners, 81–2; within new institutions, 54
holism, 226–7, 230

holistic health care, 124, 148, 160, 226
home care helpers, 145, 164
homeopaths: HPLR/RHPA policy process and, 91, 92, 138, 161; and the medical profession, 43, 50, 147; and naturopaths connection, 150
homeopathy, 23; early history, 16–18, 21–3; in Ontario, 92; training schools, 44
Hospital Act, physiotherapy under, 25
hospitals: hierarchical ordering in, 54; as institutional bureaucracies, 53–4; pharmacies, 93
HPLR/RHPA policy process. *See* Health Professions Legislation Review; Regulated Health Professions Act
Hubbard, Ruth, 6
hydrotherapy, 23
Hygienics, 29–30

ideas, 11–12; historical development of, 231–2; and institutional power, 201
ideational assumptions, 206
ideational and institutional interaction, 7–8, 10–14, 208, 231–4, 241; HPLR/RHPA policy process, 201, 232–3
ideational per se, importance of, 235–7
ideational shifts, 57–60, 68
ideology, of the sector, 208
Imperial Optical Company, 103
incompetence, 38, 177
independent group, of practitioners, 28, 33, 136, 140, 205
individualism, of judicial blueprint, 226
institutional administrators, and assistant group, 171
institutionalists, 12–13, 236
institutionalization, 39, 48, 53–9, 64, 66–7, 202, 231–3
institutions, role of, 11, 13

interest groups: and resources, 205–6; stories, 8, 234
interest group theory of power, 178
interests, 233–5
interpretation, politics of, 230–1
ionizing radiation, 130–1
iridologists, 102

Jeffries, Christie, 193
Johns Hopkins medical training school, 45
Joint Provincial Nursing Committee, 124
judicial blueprint, 48, 49, 176–88, 199, 225–7, 237

Kett, Joseph F., 31
kinesiologists, 120, 160, 171

laboratory employees, 55
laboratory legislation, 28
Laboratory and Specimen Collection Centre Licensing Act, 132, 166
laboratory technologists, 56
labour practices, and quality assurance programs, 196
labour relations. *See* unions
legal aspects, RHPA, 176–7, 187–8
'Legal and Procedural Issues Associated with the Self-Regulation of Health Professions,' 78
'Legal and Procedural Proposals' (Green Book), HPRL, 78
legislation: Aboriginal exemption from, 184; changes, 180–4; early Canadian, 15–18, 38; embedment in old, 202–4; laboratory, 28; practical assessment of, 188–99; profession-specific, 78; whole-body practitioners, 18. *See also* Health Professions Legislation Review

Lenoir, Timothy, 31
Liberal government, and naturopaths, 90
licensed acts, 216, 371–2; fight over, 83–4; HPLR, 78; scope of practice, 47; under RHPA (1991), 371–2
licensure: fight against change in, 88; marginalization through, 44; monopolies through, 174
lithotripsy, 131
Lockwood, David, 7
Lofland, John, 352

McRuer Commission, 60, 67; dental hygienists and, 126
McRuer Report (1968), 58, 61, 72, 87; civil rights, 64; public interest in self-regulation, 62–3; registered practical nurses and, 136
magnetic resonance imaging, 131
mail order dispensers, 97, 103–4
Manga, Pran, 109
marginalization: of nurses, 20; pharmacy, 20; practitioners, 20, 44, 66; specialists, 22–6; through licensure, 44
market system, 42, 48; critique of, 60; health care, 47, 174–5; and pharmacists, 96–7
marriage and family therapists, 113–14, 140, 145
massage therapists, 22, 25, 33, 51; connections, 171; and elite providers, 26; HPLR/RHPA policy process and, 110–11, 139, 158–61, 178; RHPA inclusion, 184; scope-of-practice statement, 161; under DPA, 24–5, 45, 46. *See also* masseurs
Massage Therapy Act (1991), scope of practice, 369
masseurs, 23, 25, 46, 50–1, *See also* massage therapists

Medical Act (1874), 17; (1875), midwifery under, 30
Medical Council, nineteenth-century, 17
medical education, assessment of, 44
medical-imaging energy forms, 130
Medical Insurance Act (1966), 61
medicalization, concern over, 114
medical laboratory assistants, 133
medical laboratory technologists (MLTs), 28, 34; HPLR/RHPA policy process and, 130–4; patterns of connection, 166
Medical Laboratory Technology Act (1991), scope of practice, 369
Medical Manpower for Ontario Task Force Report, 125
medical photographers, 140
medical physicists, HPLR/RHPA policy process and, 140
medical practitioners, 146, 169; and alternative practitioners, 43–5, 50, 59, 86, 147, 169, 205; and chiropractors, 158–9; discipline hearings, 183; entrepreneurial choice of, 217; gatekeeper role, 54, 67, 147; hostility to new specialists, 44–5; HPLR/RHPA policy process and, 176; nineteenth-century, 16–17; patterns of connection, 144–51; Saskatchewan strike, 55; societal power of, 30; state and, 41, 67; and technologist/entrepreneurs, 27; vested interests of, 36. *See also* heroic scientific health care
medical radiation technologists (MRT), 28, 130–1; HPLR/RHPA policy process and, 130–1; patterns of connection, 167
Medical Radiation Technology Act (1991), scope of practice, 369

medical technologists, 44, 50, 140; patterns of connection, 165–6
medicare blueprint, 55; public–private tension, 203
medicine: diagnostic privilege under RHPA, 86; embedment of, 21; and HDA (1974), 65; hegemony of, 86–8; heroic scientists, 17, 21–2, 33, 35, 49, 51, 67; and HPLR, 86–8; internal tension within, 143; restructuring, 84; technology groups in, 28
Medicine Act (1991), scope of practice, 369
mental health, 112–15
merchant–service practitioners, 21–2, 34, 92–100, 202, 205, 214, 230; ear–speech care, 100–4; entrepreneurial competition in, 2–7, 173; eye care, 100–104; foot care, 104–6; HPLR/RHPA policy process and, 139, 178; natural drugs, 33; patterns of connection, 151–8, 170; pharmacists, 19, 33, 170; restructuring arguments, 84; and self-regulation, 28; state connections, 142; and state support, 30; threat from medical profession, 157–8. *See also* business
methodology, 6–10, 227–41; interview method, 352–3
microbiologists, 133
midwifery, 178, 215; blueprint, 240; cost of process to, 179; home births, 117–18; and male practitioners, 185; nineteenth-century, 17, 21, 30; philosophy, 118–19; profession of, 185–6; public support for (1875), 30; women of colour in, 185
Midwifery Act (1991), scope of practice, 369
Midwifery Coalition, 115–16

Midwifery Task Force, 115, 117
midwives, 33–4, 125, 205, 208, 211, 214, 226; in 1960s and 1970s, 59; in hospitals, 56, 175; HPLR/RHLR policy process and, 115–19, 139–40, 148; and medical profession, 30, 32, 43–4, 50, 116, 176; mother and child mortality rates and, 115–16; -nurses connections, 149; OCFP and, 147; patterns of connection, 161–2, 171; public support for, 182; RHPA inclusion, 184
Ministry of Community and Social Services, 114
Ministry of Health, 69; chiropractic care, 108–9; connections with CPSO, 142; cost control concerns, 88; laboratory proficiency tests, 132; omnibus act proposals 1980, 83; secrecy of, 220
Ministry of Health Professional Relations Branch (PRB): changing nature of technology, 131; chiropractors, 108; complaints and discipline committees, 198–9; fight over areas of expertise, 84; and HPRAC, 194; recommendations, 79
Ministry of Health Women's Health Bureau, 179
minority groups, attitudes about, 60
misconduct, professional, 177, 198–9
Mishler, Elliot G., 352
monopoly, 214; and competition, 216; decrease, 216; of elite practitioners, 37–8, 48, 51, 60, 175; licensure and, 174, 203; nineteenth-century, 16, 33; and technology, 27
morticians, 106, 139
multi-disciplinary health clinics, 58–9, 69

muscular-skeletal manipulation, 23

native healers, 21, 29–30
natural healers, 43–4
'natural products' merchants, 33, 139
Natural Therapies and Products Coalition, 178
naturopaths, 33, 44, 50, 214; diagnostic claims, 86; exclusion from hospitals, 56; and homeopaths connection, 150; HPLR/RHPA policy process and, 88–91, 120, 138, 147–8, 178; patterns of connection, 145, 147–51; political acuity of, 149; under DPA, 23–4, 45–6
naturopathy: and chiropractic connection, 150, 170; deregulation of, 89; Grove on, 59; therapeutic claim of, 23
neuro-muscular-skeletal specialists, 107–11, 158–61, 171
New Democratic government: and HPRAC, 193; and midwifery profession, 185; and naturopaths, 90, 149
'Nine Criteria for Self-Regulation' (HPLR), 76–7, 183–4, 220, 359–60
non-practitioner groups, 179
non-prescription drugs, control of, 95
non-regulated practitioners, state connections, 142
nuclear magnetic resonance, 130
Nurse Midwives Association of Ontario, 115
Nurse Practitioner course test, 195–6
nurses, 44, 50, 56, 211, 214; credentials, 121–3; embedment of, 21; and holistic health care, 124; HPLR/RHLR policy process and, 119, 120–4, 136, 161, 163–4, 176; and institutionalized health care, 54; labour conditions, 120–1; marginalization of, 20; medical profession and, 163; and midwives

connections, 149; patterns of connection, 163–4, 171; and physicians connections, 149; restructuring, 84; split in, 55; title protection, 122; under HDA (1974), 65. *See also* extended class nurse practitioners; registered nurses
Nurses Registration Act (1951), 20
Nursing Act (1991), 122, 125, 136
nursing assistants, 121, 140, 145, 205
Nursing Effectiveness, Utilization, and Outcomes Research Unit, 124
nursing home care, as institutional bureaucracies, 53
Nursing Task Force, 124
nutritional specialists, 22, 120

occupational therapists, 34, 160; HPLR/RHPA policy process and, 112–13, 140
occupational therapy, 25
Occupational Therapy Act (1991), scope of practice, 369–70
Offe, Claus, 7
OHIP. *See* Ontario Health Insurance Plan
Ontario Association of Dispensing Opticians, 103
Ontario Association of Midwives, 115
Ontario Association of Naturopathic Doctors, 90
Ontario Association of Prosthetists and Orthotists, 94
Ontario Association of Registered Nurses' Assistants, 121
Ontario Chiropractic Association, 46
Ontario College of Family Physicians: attitudinal shift of, 146; coordinating role concerns, 154; reduced role of, 143; state connections, 141–2

Ontario College of Pharmacists, 93–4, 96
Ontario Contact Lens Association, 103
Ontario Dental Association (ODA), 151, 183
Ontario Dental Hygienists Association, 126, 153
Ontario Dental Nurses and Assistants Association (ODNAA), 168
Ontario Dentist newsletter, 151–2
Ontario Denturists Association, 28
Ontario Health Insurance Plan (OHIP), 67; chiropody under, 104; chiropractors, 24, 46, 54, 107; funding, 354–5; included and excluded, 54; physiotherapists, 109, 160; and podiatrists, 106; reimbursement of entrepreneurs, 207
Ontario Homeopathic Association, 92
Ontario Hospital Association, 179, 213; cost control concerns, 164; and RNAs, 137–8
Ontario Human Rights Commission, 185
Ontario Medical Association: on eye care, 157; and midwives, 161–2; and physiotherapists, 160; protest of legislation, 88;
state connections, 141–2; as unionlike, 143
Ontario Ministry of Health. *See* Ministry of Health
Ontario Naturopathic Association, 90
Ontario Nurses Association, 121
Ontario Pharmacists Association, 93, 96
Ontario Pharmacy Act (1871), 19
Ontario Pharmacy Association, 97–8
Ontario Physiotherapy Association, 160–1
Ontario Public Hospitals Act (amended 1989), 124, 126

Ontario Society of Medical Technologists (OSMT), 131–3
Ontario Teachers Federation, 179
ophthalmic dispensers. *See* opticians
ophthalmologists, 134–5, 169; HPLR/RHPA policy process and, 100, 102, 156–7; and optometry, 214
ophthalmology assistants, 134–5, 157
Opticianry Act (1991), scope of practice, 370
opticians, 27, 34, 170; HPLR/RHPA policy process and, 100–4, 139, 156–7
Opticians Act, 103
optometrists, 27, 33, 125, 145, 170; HPLR/RHPA policy process, 92–3, 100–4, 139, 156–7, 176
optometry, 22; diagnostic privilege under RHPA, 86; under HDA (1974), 65–6; and ophthalmologists, 214; restructuring, 84
Optometry Act (1991), scope of practice, 370
orderlies, 138
orthoptists, HPLR/RHPA policy process and, 134–5, 157
orthotic practitioners, 159, 170, 176
osteopaths, 33, 44–5; and HPLR/RHPA process and, 91–2, 138; and medicine, 147–8; under DPA, 23–4, 45; in U.S., 24, 91
osteopathy, American, 23–4
otolaryngologists, 100

Paris, D.C., 8
pastoral counsellors, 113, 114
paternalism, 42; between unequals in health care, 47; of dentists, 151; medical, 54, 214, 221
patient: agency relationship, 40, 203, 212; and health practitioners, 56, 170, 213; and patients-public, 47, 56–7, 179, 212–13, 237; as source of information, 211–12; state and medical practitioners, 41, 50, 213
patient relations, 196–8, 219–20
patients' rights, 39, 42
Patients' Rights Association, 179
patron–client relationships, 43
pedorthists, 106, 156
Peterson, David, 89
pharmacare program, 98
pharmaceuticals, overuse of, 95
pharmacists, 50, 214; authority to write prescriptions, 96; control of non-prescription drugs, 95; HPLR/RHPA policy process and, 92–8, 154–5, 176; marginalization of, 20; nineteenth century, 18–19; patron–client relationship with medical doctors, 43; and physicians connections, 149; professional status of, 97; scope of practice, 154–5; state connections, 142
pharmacy, 93–8; and corporate ownership, 93–4, 96–7; under HDA (1974), 65; patterns of connection, 154–8; restructuring, 84
Pharmacy Act (1991), 96; scope of practice, 370
physical therapist, 110, 159
physicians. *See* family physicians; medical practitioners
physiotherapists, 44, 50–1, 56, 145, 205, 214; connections, 171; under DPA, 23, 45–6; HPLR/RHPA policy process, 109–10, 136, 139, 158–61; OHIP billing, 160
physiotherapy, 25
Physiotherapy Act (1991), scope of practice, 370

podiatrists, 145, 170; HPLR/RHPA policy process and, 104–6, 155–6, 159, 176. *See also* chiropodists
policy analysis: contemporary, 236; ideational and institutional interaction, 233; interpretive, 228–31; positivism in, 6–7
policy making, health care sector, 53
policy methodology, 6–10
political accountability, 64, 65, 68, 186–7
political-governance issues, 218–25
political-judicial blueprints, 176–88
political story, 8–9, 201; interpretive, 229; public organization of health care, 4
politics: around HPRAC, 193–4; in institutions, 13; of interpretations, 230–1
positivism, in policy analysis, 6–7
post-positivism, approach to health care, 7
potion business, 21, 106, 139
power: ideational interpretation of, 8; interest group theory of, 178; political, 9–10; transfer of to Minister of Health, 182
power politics, elite professions, 85
power relations, and regulated groups, 42–3
power struggles, 81, 232
practical nurses. *See* registered practical nurses
practitioner groups: cooperation within, 173; expertise, 83–6, 205–12; history of positions, 22, 35, 82; patterns of connection, 169–70; positions after RHPA, 105, 202; stories, 8, 82; substitution, 211; turf wars, 211. *See also* excluded practitioner groups
prejudice, embedded, 34

private enterprise, economic liberalism and, 15–16
private or market agency, 168–9
private practice–public payment system, 60
professionalism, critiques of, 63–4
Professional Organizations Committee (POC), 60, 61–4, 67, 72–3; egalitarian rhetoric of, 87; market liberalism of, 174. *See also Report of the Professional Organizations Committee*
Professional Relations Branch (PRB). *See* Ministry of Health Professional Relations Branch
professional self-regulation. *See* self-governance
Pross, Paul, 210
prosthetic practitioners, 170, 176
protection: and prosecution, 39; role of state, 15
provider groups, submissions for self-regulatory status, 73–8
psychiatrists, 113
psychological associate, use of term, 114
psychologist, use of term, 114
psychologists, 50, 56, 145; HPLR/RHPA policy process, 112–14, 140, 176; recognition of, 26
Psychologists Registration Act (1960), 26
psychology, diagnostic privilege under RHPA, 86
Psychology Act (1991), 114; scope of practice, 370
psychometrists, 114, 140
psychopharmacology, 113–14
psychotherapists, 114
public: patron–client control of practitioners, 47; positions of connection for, 47–8; and private tension of medicare

blueprint, 203; and regulatory system, 42; response to HPLR/RHPA policy process, 178
public accountability. *See* accountability, public
public administration, standards, 64
public funding, 54–5, 67; and patient–public shift, 57; and private decision-making, 53, 66–7
public goods, stewardship of, 61
public interest, 219, 223, 237; and health professions, 180; and public policy, 62–3; and responsible governance, 186
public organization, of health care, 4, 201–2
public participation, 62, 222; blueprint of, 37, 48; and self-governance, 220–1; under RHPA (1991), 179–84
public regulation, agents of the patient, 40–1
public welfare: arguments, 61, 68; blueprint on health care, 53–4; and freedom dichotomy, 60–2

quality assurance, 173, 177, 181, 223; programs, 194–6
Quality Assurance review, 196
quality control, 64–5

race and class relations, 214–15, 222; complaints of, 185; in medical profession, 30–2, 34; tensions during review process, 184–5
radiation technologists. *See* medical radiation technologists
radiological technologists, 145
rationalism, 18, 33, 35–6, 81
recreational therapists, 160
Red Tape Reduction Act, 173

reflexologists, 156, 161, 171
registered dental technologists (RDTs), 166
registered nurses, 21, 164, 205, 214–15; and credentialism, 34; HPLR/RHPA policy process and, 139; and nurses' assistants, 46; scope of practice, 163
Registered Nurses Association of Ontario, 121–2; on quality assurance programs, 196
Registered Practical Nurses Association of Ontario (RPNAO), 138, 185
registered practical nurses (RNAs), 21, 121, 164, 214; HPLR/RHPA policy process and, 136–8
Regulated Health Professions Act (1991), 3–5, 63, 65, 70–1, 78, 177, 207; accomplishments, 84; and accountability, 186; diagnostic privilege under, 86; gender equality, 214–15; and institutionalization, 231–2; pharmacists' arguments, 155; practical assessments of, 188–91; practitioner group positions after, 105; public participation, 179–84; public–private relationship, 218–19; reviews of, 188–91
Rein, Martin, 225
relationships, 212–15; clinical and entrepreneurial, 216; decision-making, 55, 56n; insider–outsider, 50; medical practitioner and state, 55; pharmacists and medical doctors, 43; state–public–practitioner, 42, 66. *See also* agency relationships; connection
religious healers, 29–30
Report of the Committee on the Healing Arts (1970), 58, 61
Report of the Professional Organizations Committee (1980), 58, 64, 72

representation, through public participants, 222
research information, access to, 221
respiratory technologists, 166
respiratory therapists, 130–1, 166
Respiratory Therapy Act (1991), scope of practice, 370
responsible governance, and public interest, 186
restructuring: blueprints, 215–17; of health professions legislation, 3–4, 70–1, 81, 83, 139, 201, 203
Reynolds, J.F., 8
Royal College of Dental Surgeons of Ontario (RCDSO), 126, 128; HPLR/RHPA policy process and, 151, 153, 168; opposition to legislation, 182–3
Royal Commission on Health Services (1964), 149
Russell, P.H., 187

safety-net clause, 83
Saskatchewan, strike by medical profession, 55
Schedule C products, classification of, 95–6
Schedule Two products, 96
Schon, D., 225
Schwartz, Alan, 70
science: and alternative forms of care, 30; ideational commitment to, 230; and the state, 15
scientific bureaucratic rationalism, 33, 53–4, 59, 67; embedded in the health sector, 202. See also bureaucratic organization; rationalism
scientific paradigm, of health care, 21, 208
scope of practice, 138, 174; blueprint 1980s, 83; challenges to, 176; chiropodists, 104; chiropractors, 158; CPSO, 146; elite practitioners, 47; and HPLR/RHPA, 138; massage therapists, 111, 161; medical radiation technologists, 130, 131; model, 88; new professional, 368–70; nurses, 122, 163; optometrists, 157; pharmacy, 20, 95; psychologists, 113; registered practical nurses, 137; statements, 78, 84
'Scope of Practice Workshop,' 78
self-governance, 219, 223–4; benefits and burdens of, 37–9, 48, 172; critiques, 60–4; dentists, 19; and dynamics of authority, 41; of health professions, 16, 38; and merchant function, 28; and nurses, 20; optometry, 66; pharmacy, 19–20; provider groups and submissions to HPLR, 74–8; public interest in, 62, 72–3; realignment of rules, 174; whole-body practitioners, 18
self-regulation. See self-governance
sexism, in medical profession, 30–2, 34
sexual misconduct, 173, 177, 181; and patient relations program, 196–8, 219–20
shiatsu therapists, 140, 160–1, 171
Shoppers Drug Mart, 97
'Snakes and Ladders,' ideational and structural in, 11
social contract, Western society, 177
social discrimination, 184–6
social health, 112–15
social policy, health sector, 57
social service workers, 114
social tensions, 34
social workers, 34, 113–14, 140, 145
society, state in 1960s and 1970s, 57, 67
sound waves, 131

specialists, 18–26
specialization, 54, 67, 81, 227; source of tension, 34; within nursing, 54; within specialization, 26–9
Speech–Language Pathology Act (1991), scope of practice, 370
speech–language specialists, 27, 34; HPLR/RHPA policy process and, 100–1, 111–12, 140, 176. *See also* ear–speech care
spinal manipulation, 22, 158–9, 171
state: and agency relationship, 40, 168–9; and control, 56; and health care organization, 4; patterns of connection, 141–2; and practitioner groups, 41, 55; protectionist role of, 15; and public-practitioner relationships, 41–2, 66; role of in 1960s and 1970s, 57; in welfare–freedom dichotomy, 61
state intervention, arguments against, 60
state payment, included and excluded, 54
state stewardship, versus ownership, 61, 175
surgery, origins of, 19

Task Force on Midwifery in Ontario, 115
technicians, 55
technique specialists, 202, 205, 214, 230; and cost-containment argument, 87; dependent group, 29, 44, 214; HPLR/RHPA policy process and, 106–28, 139; patterns of connection, 158–62; restructuring arguments, 84; state connections, 142; twentieth-century, 22, 33
technology specialists, 55, 202, 205, 214, 230; and cost-containment argument, 87; dependent group, 27, 44, 171, 214; as entrepreneurs, 27; HPLR/RHPA policy process and, 128–38, 140; patterns of connection, 165–8; restructuring arguments, 84; state connections, 142; twentieth-century, 22
teeth. *See* dental care; dental hygienists; dentists; denturists
tension: over clinical controls, 51–2; over expertise turf, 131–2; health care sector, 204; within medicine, 143; nursing categories, 164; between professional image and union concerns, 55; public–private, 203; specialization as source of, 34, 55
Thomsonian healers, 21–2, 29–30
title protection: legislation, 173; nurses, 122
Toronto school of medicine for women, 30
'Transitional Council for the College of Osteopathic Manual Practitioners of Ontario,' 91
Trebilcock, Michael J., 64, 72
trust: and control, 224; definition of, 224–5; reinterpretation of, 239
Tuohy, Carolyn J., 40, 61, 64, 65, 72, 175, 187, 207, 225
turf wars, 51; HPLR/RHPA policy process and, 84, 85, 138–40, 205–12
'22 topics' HPLR, 73, 356–8, 363–5; criteria not met, 366–7

ultrasound (MRI), 130–1
unions: health care practitioners, 55, 67; OMA as unionlike, 143; Ontario Nurses Association, 121; voluntary associations as unionlike, 143, 202
United States, alternative health care in, 59

universality, and federal government, 61
University of Florida, 96
unregulated practitioners: naturopathy, 89; support for, 171

Vision Care Council of Canada, 102–3
vision care. *See* eye care
voluntary associations: as lobby groups, 41, 50; unionlike functions of, 143, 202
vulnerable client abuse, 219

Weber, Max, 4
welfare state, health care, 53
Western society: judicial issues, 225; social contract, 177
whole-body practitioners, 21–2, 86–92, 202, 230; and diagnostic claims, 86; licensed procedures, 84; medicine, 205; patterns of connection, 144–51; self-regulatory legislation, 18
Wolff, Kurt H., 352
Wolfson, Alan D., 40, 64
Wolin, Sheldon, 58
women: attitudes about, 60; in management hierarchies, 184; medical colleges, 31; in newly included groups, 184; and nursing, 122; patterns of inequality, 31–2
women of colour: in midwifery, 185; in nursing, 31–2
Women's Health Bureau. *See* Ministry of Health Women's Health Bureau
Workplace Safety and Insurance Board, 109

x-rays and laboratory tests, chiropractors, 107–8